Adventures in
Social Research

To our students:
past, present, and future.
We challenge each other and profit from it.

Adventures in Social Research

Data Analysis Using SPSS™ 11.0/11.5 for Windows®

5TH EDITION

Earl Babbie
Chapman University

Fred Halley
SUNY, Brockport

Jeanne Zaino
Iona College

PINE FORGE PRESS
An Imprint of Sage Publications, Inc.
Thousand Oaks • London • New Delhi

For information:

Sage Publications, Inc.
2455 Teller Road
Thousand Oaks, California 91320
E-mail: order@sagepub.com

Sage Publications Ltd.
6 Bonhill Street
London EC2A 4PU
United Kingdom

Sage Publications India Pvt. Ltd.
B-42, Panchsheel Enclave
Post Box 4109
New Delhi 110 017

Printed in the United States of America

Library of Congress Cataloging-in-Publication Data

Babbie, Earl R.
Adventures in social research : data analysis using SPSS (11.0/11.5) for Windows/
by Earl Babbie, Fred Halley, Jeanne Zaino. — 5th ed.
    p. cm.
Includes bibliographical references and index.
ISBN 0-7619-8790-8 © — ISBN 0-7619-8758-4 (P)
  1. Social sciences-Statistical methods-Computer programs. 2. SPSS for Windows.
I. Halley, Fred. II. Zaino, Jeanne. III. Title.
HA32 .B285 2003
300'.285'5369—dc21
Rev.   2002015793

03   04   05   06   07   08   10   9   8   7   6   5   4   3   2   1

Acquiring Editor:	Jerry Westby
Editorial Assistant:	Vonessa Vondera
Production Editor:	Claudia A. Hoffman
Typesetter:	C&M Digitals (P) Ltd.
Indexer:	Molly Hall
Cover Designer:	Michelle Lee

ABOUT THE AUTHORS

Earl Babbie was born in Detroit, Michigan, in 1938, although he chose to return to Vermont three months later, growing up there and in New Hampshire. In 1956, he set off for Harvard Yard, where he spent the next four years learning more than he initially planned. After three years with the U.S. Marine Corps, mostly in Asia, he began graduate studies at the University of California, Berkeley. He received his Ph.D. from Berkeley in 1969. He taught sociology at the University of Hawaii from 1968 through 1979, took time off from teaching and research to write full-time for eight years, and then joined the faculty at Chapman University in southern California in 1987. Although an author of research articles and monographs, he is best known for the many texts he has written, which have been widely adopted in colleges throughout the United States and the world. He also has been active in the American Sociological Association for 25 years and currently serves on the ASA's executive committee. He has been married to his wife, Sheila, for more than 30 years, and they have a son, Aaron, who would make any parent proud.

Fred Halley, Associate Professor of Sociology, the State University of New York College at Brockport, has been developing computer-based tools for teaching sociology since 1970. His major projects have included the design of a computer-managed social statistics course and an introduction to sociology course with computer labs. Halley has served as a collegewide social science computing consultant, directed Brockport's Institute for Social Research, and now directs the college's Data Analysis Laboratory. He is the author of GENSTAT, an IBM PC-based program that generates individualized data sets for statistics students and correct answers for their instructors. He recently codirected a three-year evaluation project concerning a Head Start Family Service Center in Rochester, New York, and an evaluation of a community action program in two rural upstate New York counties.

Jeanne Zaino earned a bachelor's degree in political science at the University of Connecticut, Storrs. Upon graduation, she remained in Storrs to get a master's degree in survey research and work as a research assistant at the Roper Center for Public Opinion Research. She went on to earn a master's degree in political science from the University of Massachusetts, Amherst, where she is currently ABD and completing work on her Ph.D. In addition to her teaching responsibilities, while at UMass she worked as a research assistant at the Massachusetts Institute of Social and Economic Research (MISER). Upon completing her course work at UMass, she relocated to Westchester County, New York, where she taught a variety of courses at several area colleges, including research methods, computer-based data analysis, statistics, and American politics and government. She recently joined the faculty at Iona College, New Rochelle, where she is serving as an Assistant Professor in the History and Political Science Department. She and her husband Jeff are the proud parents of two sons, Maxim and Logan.

BRIEF CONTENTS

DETAILED CONTENTS

Part II   Getting Started / 29

Part III   Univariate Analysis / 59

Part IV   Bivariate Analysis / 185

> *A Theory of Involvement*
> Charles Y. Glock, Benjamin R. Ringer, and Earl R. Babbie
>
> *The Social Bases of Abortion Attitudes*
> Elizabeth Adell Cook, Ted G. Jelen, and Clyde Wilcox
>
> *Ideal Family Size as an Intervening Variable Between*
> *Religion and Attitudes Towards Abortion*
> Mario Renzi
>
> *Religion, Ideal Family Size, and Abortion: Extending Renzi's Hypothesis*
> William V. D'Antonio and Steven Stack

PREFACE

This workbook is offered to you with a number of aims in mind. To begin, we want to provide students with a practical and hands-on introduction to the logic of social science research, particularly survey research. Moreover, we want to give the students an accessible book that guides them step-by-step through the process of data analysis using current GSS data and the latest versions of SPSS. Most importantly, we want to involve students directly in the practice of social research, allow them to experience the excitement and wonder of this enterprise, and to inspire them to pursue their own adventure in social research.

As we pursue these goals, however, there are a number of agendas in the background of this book. For example, students who complete the book will have learned a very useful, employable skill. Increasingly, job applicants are asked about their facility with various computer programs: word processing, spreadsheets, and data analysis. As of this writing, SPSS is still clearly the most popular professional program available for social science data analysis, hence our choice of it as a vehicle for teaching social research.

A Focus on Developing
Professional and Intellectual Skills

What sets this book apart from others that teach SPSS or similar programs is that we cast that particular skill within the context of social research as a logical enterprise. Thus, in addition to learning the use of SPSS, students are learning the intellectual "skills" of conceptualization, measurement, and association. Whereas those who know only SPSS can assist in data analysis, our intention is that our students will also be able to think for themselves, mapping out analytic paths into the understanding of social data. As they polish these intellectual skills, they should be able to progress to higher levels of research and to the administration of research enterprises.

More generally, we aim to train students who will use computers rather than be used by them. It is our experience that when students first confront computers in school, they tend to fall into two groups: those who recognize computers as powerful instruments for pursuing their goals in life, or at least as the grandest of toys; and those who are intimidated by computers and seek the earliest possible refuge from them. Our intention is to reveal the former possibility to students and to coax them into that relationship with computers.

Educators are being challenged increasingly to demonstrate the practical value of instruction, in the social sciences no less than in other fields. Too often, the overreaction to this demand results in superficial vocational courses that offer no intellectual meaning or courses hastily contrived as a home for current buzzwords, whose popularity is often short-lived. We are excited to be able to offer an educational experience that is genuinely practical for students and that also represents an intellectual adventure.

Those who have taught methods or statistics courses typically find themselves with a daunting task: to ignite their often involuntary students with the fire of enthusiasm they themselves feel for the detective work of social research at its best. In this book, we seek to engage students' curiosity by setting them about the task of understanding issues that are already points of interest for them: topics such as abortion, religion, politics, poverty, gender roles, environment, sexual attitudes, mass media, gun control, child-rearing, and others. For many of our readers, we imagine that mathematical analysis still smacks of trains leaving Point A and Point B at different speeds, and so on. Now, they are going to learn that some facility with the logic and mathematics of social research can let them focus the light of understanding on some of the dark turbulence of opinion and hysteria. We do not tell students about opinions on abortion as much as we show them how to find out for themselves. We think that will get students to Point C ahead of either of the trains.

A Focus on Active and Collaborative Learning

As we are teaching students to learn for themselves, this book offers a good example of what educators have taken to calling "active learning." We have set up all of our demonstrations so that students should be executing the same SPSS operations we are discussing at any given point. Although we may give them the "answers" to assure them that they are on the right track, we leave them on their own often enough to require that they do the work rather than simply read about it.

Finally, the culture of personal computers has been one of "collaborative learning" from its very beginning. More than people in any other field of activity, perhaps, computer users have always delighted in sharing what they know with others. There is probably no better context within which to ask for help: Those who know the answer are quick to respond, and those who do not often turn their attention to finding an answer, delighting in the challenge.

Because this book is self-contained, even introductory students can walk through the chapters and exercises on their own, without outside assistance. However, we imagine that students will often want to work together as they progress through this book. That has been our experience in student testing and in earlier courses we have taught involving computers. We suggest that you encourage cooperation among students; we are certain they will learn more that way and will enjoy the course more. In fact, those who are initially intimidated by computers should especially be encouraged to find buddies with whom to work.

Intended For Students in Various Social Science Disciplines

This book is intended for use in any social science course that either introduces or focuses exclusively on social research methods, social statistics, data analysis, or survey research. It can be easily combined with or used as a supplement to most standard social science textbooks, including, but not limited to those in fields as varied as communication science, criminal justice, health studies, political science, public policy, social work, and sociology.

As far as possible we have designed this book to be "self-writing" and "open-ended" to ensure that it is relevant to students with varying interests across numerous disciplines. Throughout the text we encourage students to focus on issues and questions that are relevant to their particular area of interest. After walking through the demonstrations that introduce the fundamentals of the data analysis process, students are given a chance to apply what they have learned. In many of the lab exercises, students are encouraged to design their own hypotheses, choose their own variables, and interpret the results. Moreover, we encourage instructors to apply the principles, techniques, and methods discussed to other data sets that are relevant to their field.

Intended For Both Beginning and More Advanced Students

We have designed and structured this book to support students at a variety of levels. This includes both those students who are taking their first course in social research, as well as more advanced students (including graduate students) who either want to hone their social research, statistical, and data analysis skills, or those who merely want to become acquainted or reacquainted with the latest versions of SPSS for Windows. More advanced students who come at this book full speed may choose to either work through the text from beginning to end, or skip around and focus on particular chapters and sections.

However, it is important to note that because this book is "self-contained" and guides the student-analyst step-by-step through the demonstrations and exercises, no previous experience with social research, statistics, computers, Windows, or SPSS is required. Those who have never taken a research methods, statistics, or computer-based course will find that they can easily make it through this book.

The Book and the CD-ROM: What Is Included?

The book and CD-ROM provide the instructions and data needed to introduce students to social science data analysis. Most college and university computing services make SPSS available to students. A student version of SPSS may be purchased through most college and university bookstores.[1] The CD includes two data sets containing a total of more than 80 variables from the 2000 General Social Survey, which can be analyzed by most versions of SPSS, including the Student Version. As you will see, the variables cover a fairly broad terrain, although we have provided for analysis in some depth in a few instances. In addition to working their way through the demonstrations and exercises presented in the book, students will be able to find original lines of inquiry that grow out of their own interests and insights.

This book will illustrate the use of SPSS, using Versions 11.0 and 11.5 for Windows 95 and 98. While the text focuses specifically on the latest version of SPSS, it can also be easily used with earlier versions including SPSS 10.0. Regardless of the version you are using, throughout the text we will refer to the program simply as "SPSS for Windows."

Using the General Social Survey data on your CD-ROM is easy. After starting SPSS for Windows, insert your CD and click the following sequence:

File → Open → Data

---

1. *Adventures in Social Research* is available with or without the student version of SPSS. For more information, go to http://www.pineforge.com or call 1-800-818-7243.

Next, click on the **Look in** field and select the drive that contains your CD (the name of the CD is **Social Research,** and it is usually found on the **[D:]** drive). Next, make sure SPSS-format data files (.sav extension) are displayed in the **Files of type:** drop down list. If not, simply click on the down arrow and select the suffix for SPSS for Windows data files, **SPSS(*.sav)**. Now open the **Documents** folder either by **double-clicking** on it or highlighting it and clicking **Open**. Three SPSS.sav files should be visible. To select **DEMO.SAV,** highlight it and double click or click the **Open** button in the lower right corner of the dialog box. In a few seconds, SPSS will display the GSS data in the Data View portion of the Data Editor.

SPSS for Windows comes with extensive help screens. They are almost like having a coach built in to your computer! Begin with the menu farthest to the right. You can click **Help** or hit **ALT-H** to see the options available to you. "Topics" will usually be your most useful choice. This will give you three options. "Contents" and "Index" present you with two ways of zeroing in on the topic of interest to you. "Find" will search for the specific terms or keywords you indicate. You should experiment with these several options to discover what works best for you.

Organization and Content

The chapters are arranged in an order that roughly parallels the organization of most introductory social science research methods texts. Parts I and II (Chapters 1-5) include an overview of the essentials of social research, an introduction to SPSS for Windows, and a description of the 2000 GSS. Parts III-V (Chapters 6-20) introduce data analysis, beginning with univariate analysis, bivariate and finally multivariate analysis respectively. Part VI (Chapters 21-22) focuses on primary research and additional avenues for secondary research.

Part I includes three chapters that help prepare students for social research. Our goal in these chapters is to give students an introduction to some of the fundamental elements of social scientific research, particularly those they will encounter later in the text. Chapter 1 discusses the main purposes of the text and introduces students to some of the historical background that lies behind computerized social research, data analysis, and statistical software packages. In Chapters 2 and 3 we introduce students to the logic of social research by focusing on theory, research, and measurement.

Part II is designed to help students "get started" using the GSS data and SPSS. Chapter 4 describes the GSS and the data sets included with this book. While Chapter 5 introduces students to SPSS by guiding them through the steps involved in launching the program, opening their data sets, and exploring the variables contained on the disk that accompanies this book.

Data analysis begins in Part III with univariate analysis. In Chapter 6 we introduce frequency distributions, descriptive statistics, recoding, and saving and printing data. Chapter 7 focuses on the graphic presentation of univariate data by covering the commands for creating bar and pie charts, line graphs, and histograms. While the bulk of the discussion of bivariate analyses is reserved for Part IV, in Chapter 8 we give students a preview by showing them how they can use crosstabs to examine the structure of attitudes in more depth. Chapter 9 introduces several techniques for creating composite measures. In Chapter 10, students are given a chance to strike out on their own and apply the methods and techniques discussed in Part III to other topics.

Part IV focuses primarily on bivariate analyses. In Chapters 11-13 we limit our discussion to the analysis of percentage tables. In Chapters 14 and 15 we introduce other methods for examining the extent to which two variables are related to one another. Chapter 14 focuses on some common measures of association, including lambda, gamma, Pearson's r, and simple regression. Chapter 15 introduces tests of statistical significance, such as chi-square, t tests, and ANOVA. Once again in Chapter 16, students are given a chance to apply the bivariate techniques and methods discussed in Part IV to other topics and issues.

Our discussion of data analysis concludes in Part V with a discussion of multivariate analyses. Chapter 17 focuses primarily on multiple causation. Chapter 18 picks up on some of the loose threads of our bivariate analyses and pursues them further, while Chapter 19 guides students through the steps involved in creating composite measures to predict opinions. Finally, in Chapter 20 students are given a chance to apply the methods and techniques discussed in Part V to other topics and issues.

The final section is composed of two chapters that explore some further opportunities for social research. Because students often express an interest in collecting their own data, Chapter 21 focuses on primary research. We introduce students to the steps involved in designing and administering a survey, defining and entering data in SPSS, and writing a research report. This Chapter is supplemented by Appendix C, as well as CD-Appendixes D, E, and F, all of which give students additional information regarding preparing a research proposal, designing and administering a survey, constructing a sample questionnaire, and writing a research report. Chapter 22 suggests other avenues for pursuing secondary social research by focusing on the unabridged GSS, additional data sources, and other statistical software packages that students may find useful.

In addition to Appendix C and CD Appendixes D-F, which primarily supplement Chapter 21, we have also included four other Appendices, two in the back of the book and two on the CD-ROM. Appendix A, for instance, contains a Codebook that describes all the variables contained on the data files. Appendix B contains answers to selected SPSS Lab Exercises. CD-Appendix G includes a comprehensive list of all the SPSS Commands introduced in the text. CD-Appendix H includes five recommended readings that relate to topics and issues covered in the text. Finally, we have updated and expanded the reference, Index, and Glossary sections.

Structure of Each Chapter

Each chapter includes explanations of basic research principles, techniques, and specific instructions regarding how to use SPSS, demonstrations, "Writing Boxes," a brief "Conclusion," a list of "Main Points," "Key Terms," "SPSS Commands Introduced in the Chapter," "Review Questions," and "SPSS Lab Exercises." Students are expected to follow along with the demonstrations in the body of each chapter. They are aided in this process by both the text, which walks them step-by-step through the process of data analysis, and screens, which help them understand what they should be seeing on their own monitor. In an effort to stress the importance of describing research findings in prose, most chapters include "Writing Boxes," which give readers an example of how a professional social scientist might describe the findings being discussed. The

"Review Questions" at the end of each chapter are designed to test the students' knowledge of the material presented in the text. Because they do not require SPSS, they can be assigned as either class work or homework assignments. In the "SPSS Lab Exercises" students are given a chance to apply what they learned in the explanatory sections and demonstrations. These exercises generally follow a fill-in-the-blank format for presenting, analyzing, and summarizing results. Instructors may wish to assign these exercises as lab assignments to be completed either in lab or as homework, provided students have access to SPSS.

Although, the book is designed to guide students through the process of computerized data analysis from beginning to end, we encourage instructors, and particularly more advanced students, to skip around and focus on chapters and sections of interest to them. We designed the book with the understanding that students at various levels may find different demonstrations, techniques, discussions, and methods of varying interest. Consequently, all of the chapters are self-contained and both students and instructors should feel comfortable picking and choosing among topics, issues, and material of particular interest to them. Instructors and students who choose to take this approach may want to refer to the Detailed Table of Contents, Introductions to each Part, Chapter conclusions, and summaries of main points to get a better sense of what sections and chapters they want to focus on.

Software Support and Service

If you or your students should run into any problems using this package, there are several sources of support that should serve your needs. Frequently, college and university computing centers have student assistants who are very helpful to new computer users. In fact, most academic computing centers employ a user services coordinator who can help faculty plan student use of the school's computers and provide aid when problems arise.

One source of SPSS assistance available via the Internet is a home page (www.spss.com) maintained by SPSS, Inc. In addition to providing answers to frequently asked questions, it provides a variety of tips and white papers on important issues in data analysis. Specific questions may be submitted to consultants via e-mail from the homepage. SPSS requests that a legitimate license or serial number be submitted with questions for questions to receive a response.

You can also call SPSS, Inc., in Chicago for technical support at (312) 329-2400. Be forewarned that SPSS cannot give assistance with pedagogical or substantive problems and that you may have a long wait in a telephone queue for your turn to talk to a technical support person. It has been our experience that our best help comes from local resources.

Acknowledgments

In conclusion, we would like to acknowledge a number of people who have been instrumental in making this book a reality. First, Jerry Westby, of Sage Publications/ Pine Forge Press. Our thanks also go to former Pine Forge Press editor Steve Rutter, and the many others at Pine Forge Press/Sage Publications who aided us along the way, particularly Claudia Hoffman, Kristin Snow, and Vonessa Vondera.

We would also like to thank the many reviewers who helped us along the way: Dhruba J. Bora, Wheeling Jesuit University; Xiaogang Deng, University of Massachusetts, Boston; Stephen J. Farnsworth, Mary Washington College; John R. Hagen, Health Strategies, Inc.; Mary Jane Kuffner Hirt, Indiana University of Pennsylvania; Steven L. Jones, University of Virginia; Quentin Kidd, Christopher Newport University; Wanda Kosinski, Ramapo College of New Jersey; Peter Allen Lee, San Jose State University; William H. Lockhart, University of Virginia; Karyn D. McKinney, Penn State University, Altoona College; Maureen McLeod, The Sage Colleges; Philip Meyer, University of North Carolina; David B. Miller, Case Western Reserve University; Melanie Moore, University of Northern Colorado; Thomas O'Rourke, University of Illinois at Urbana-Champaign; Linda Owens, University of Illinois; Sue Strickler, Eastern New Mexico University; Jennifer L. S. Teller, Kent State University; Lanny Thomson, University of Puerto Rico; Madine VanderPlaat, Saint Mary's University; Roland Wagner, San Jose State University; Assata Zerai, Syracuse University; Thomas G. Zullo, University of Pittsburgh.

We reserve our final acknowledgment for our students, to whom this book is dedicated. We recognize that we have often asked them to think and do things they sometimes felt were beyond their abilities. We have admired their courage for trying anyway, and we have shared their growth.

Part I Preparing for Social Research

In the opening chapters, we introduce you to computerized data analysis and the logic of social science research. Chapter 1 discusses the book's two main purposes and gives you some of the historical background that lies behind computerized social research.

In Chapter 2, you will discover that social research (like other forms of scientific inquiry) is based on two pillars: logic and observation. You will see how theory (the logic component) informs our investigations, making sense out of our observations, and sometimes offers predictions about what we will find. The other aspect of research, on which we will focus in this book, is the collection and analysis of data, such as those collected in a survey.

Chapter 3 delves more deeply into one central component of scientific inquiry: measurement. We look at some of the criteria for measurement quality and start examining the kinds of measurements represented by the data at hand.

Chapter 1 **Introduction**

Social research is the detective work of big questions. Whereas a conventional detective tries to find out who committed a specific crime, the social researcher looks for the causes of crime in general. The logic of social scientific investigation extends beyond crime to include all aspects of social life, such as careers, marriage and family, voting, health, prejudice, environment, and poverty. In fact, anything that is likely to concern you as an individual is the subject of social science research.

Overview

The purpose of this book is to lead you through a series of investigative adventures in social research. We can't predict exactly where these adventures will lead, because you are going to be the detective. Our purpose is to show you some simple tools (and some that are truly amazing) that you can use in social investigations. We'll also provide you with a body of data, collected in a national survey, that is so rich you will have the opportunity to undertake investigations that no one else has ever pursued.

If you have access to a computer that uses Windows 95/98, 2000, ME, or XP and SPSS for Windows (Version 10.0 or higher), this book and the CD-ROM that comes with it contain everything you need for a wide range of social investigations.[1] This tool is designed specifically for exploring data. If you are already comfortable with computers, you can jump right in, and very quickly you will find yourself in the midst of a fascinating computer game. Instead of fighting off alien attacks or escaping from dank dungeons, you'll be pitting your abilities and imagination against real life, but you'll be looking at a side of life that you may not now be aware of.

This tool is also well-designed for the creation of college term papers. Throughout the book, we suggest ways to present the data you discover in the context of a typical term paper in the social sciences. Whereas most students are limited in their term papers to reporting what other investigators have learned about society, you will be able to offer your own insights and discoveries.

---

[1] Earlier versions of SPSS for Windows (7.0 or higher) may be used, but a few of the instructions, procedures, and screens may be slightly different than those in the book.

Finally, the data sets included here are being analyzed by professional social scientists today. Moreover, the analytical tools that we've provided for you are as powerful as those used by many professional researchers. Frankly, there's no reason you can't use these materials for original research worthy of publication in a research journal. All it takes is curiosity, imagination, practice, and a healthy obsession with knowing the answers to things. In our experience, what sets professional researchers apart from others is that they have much greater curiosity about the world around them, are able to bring powerful imagination to bear on understanding it, are willing to put in the time required of effective investigation, and are passionately driven to understand it.

Why Use a Computer?

Social and behavioral scientists' use of data-processing machinery has evolved to its present state over a period of more than 50 years. In the late 1800s, as the various disciplines which now make up the "social sciences" were developing, becoming more professional and arguably "scientific," many students of the budding social and behavioral sciences found that there was a greater need to record, organize, and analyze observations of social phenomena. Data analysis needs quickly became so great that it was too time-consuming, if not impossible, to keep track of data in ledgers or on index cards.

In 1885, Herman Hollerith, an employee of the U.S. Census Bureau, developed the punch card, a prototype of the now obsolete IBM card, to help meet the data analysis needs of the Census Bureau at a time when the U.S. population was growing and changing rapidly. By the 1930s, social scientists had adapted the new technology for more sophisticated research purposes. (In 1896, by the way, Herman Hollerith established the Tabulating Machine Company, later renamed International Business Machines: IBM.)

In the early 1960s, the electromechanical data tabulation machinery was replaced by electronic computers. Although by today's standards the early computers had small capacity and were expensive and very prone to breakdowns, they greatly enhanced social scientists' ability to organize and analyze data. Tasks that took days or weeks using data tabulation equipment took only a few hours on computers.

In addition to the development of electronic computers, or hardware, social scientists' use of computing was also advanced by the development of computer programs, or software. In 1962, the computer programming language FORTRAN (an acronym for formula translation) was developed. FORTRAN made it possible for social scientists to write programs for data analysis that could be used on different kinds of computers. Prior to FORTRAN, programming could be accomplished only by manually rewiring accounting machinery or by using machine languages limited to specific computers.

In the 1960s, social scientists used programs written by themselves and by colleagues, graduate students, and programmers in university computing centers. Most information about programs was gained informally through professional grapevines. These programs greatly expanded the research capabilities of social scientists, but there was no standardization of programs or of the format of the data to be analyzed by them. Searching for and using a statistical program could be a harrowing and time-consuming experience. Most of the programs were transported on punch cards, and if one card got out of order, the program might not run; worse yet, it might run and produce inaccurate results.

By 1970, the data analysis problems of social and behavioral scientists were well recognized. To answer these needs, social scientist-programmers (most notably at the University of Chicago and the University of Michigan) developed the concept of a program package. In addition to statistical calculations, these program packages allowed researchers to modify or recode data, to create indexes and scales, and to employ many other techniques you will learn in this workbook.

Today, the two statistical packages most widely used by social scientists are *SPSS* (the Statistical Package for the Social Sciences) and *SAS* (the Statistical Analysis System).[2] Until the mid-1980s, these large, generalized statistical packages were available only for large mainframe computers. The advent of personal computers created a revolution in the way social science data analysis was done. By the mid-1980s, personal computers became powerful enough to run statistical packages and cheap enough for individuals to purchase them. This made it feasible for statistical package producers to rewrite their packages for personal computers. Although some older personal computers do not have the storage capacity to work with large amounts of data, many newer ones are capable of handling data sets previously only analyzable on large mainframe computers.

We have selected SPSS for your use in these exercises for three reasons. First, early versions of SPSS date back to 1968. The package is well-known, and there is hardly a social scientist who has earned a graduate degree in the past 25 years who has not had some contact with SPSS. Second, SPSS takes you through all the basic issues of using a statistical package. This knowledge will give you a head start if you learn some other package later.

Finally, SPSS for Windows is suitable for IBM-compatible computers with Microsoft Windows 95/98, 2000, ME, or XP. The *SPSS Base* package, like a car, is sold as a basic package. Then, if the buyer wishes, it can be "souped up" with powerful statistical accessories, all of which are beyond the scope of this book.

SPSS also offers two packages specifically designed for students: *SPSS Student Version* and the *SPSS Graduate Pack*. While both versions are available for use with Windows, they differ in terms of their capabilities. Unlike the SPSS Base system or the SPSS Graduate Pack, the Student Version is limited to 50 variables and 1,500 cases, and it can't be upgraded. The SPSS Student Version has fewer statistical procedures, but it has most of the procedures that will ever be needed by an undergraduate social science major or a master's-level graduate student. The SPSS Graduate Pack contains the SPSS Base system plus two advanced statistical modules. Both the Student Version and Graduate Pack are commonly available at college bookstores. You can also learn more about SPSS and the various versions available by visiting the "store" on their web site at www.spss.com.

A Word of Caution: Throughout the book we suggest various web sites that you may find useful. Keep in mind, however, that the World Wide Web is constantly changing. For this reason some web sites referred to may no longer be available; things can change overnight. If particular web sites are no longer available, you can use one of the many search engines that are available and use key words to locate the information you are looking for. Your instructor should be able to help you if necessary.

---

[2] While "SPSS" originally stood for the "Statistical Package for the Social Sciences" (and the package is still most commonly referred to in this way), SPSS, Inc. recently "updated the meaning of the letters to more accurately reflect the company and its products. Today, SPSS stands for 'Statistical Product and Service Solutions.'" See the SPSS Inc. web site at www.spss.com/corpinfo/faqs.htm.

Conclusion

This book has two educational aims. First, we want to share with you the excitement of social scientific research. You are going to learn that a table of numerical data, which may seem pretty boring on the face of it, can hold within it the answers to many questions about why people think and act the way they do. Finding those answers requires that you learn some skills of logical inquiry.

Second, we will show you how to use a computer program that is very popular among social scientists. SPSS is the tool you will use to unlock the mysteries of society, just as a biologist might use a microscope or an astronomer a telescope.

You may have seen prepared foods with the instruction: Just add water and heat. Well, the package in your hands is something like that, but the instructions read: Just add you, and let's get cooking.

Main Points

- The main purpose of this text is to introduce you to the logic and practice of social scientific research by showing you some simple tools you can use to analyze real-life data.
- Social and behavioral scientists' use of data-processing machinery has evolved over many years, from the early punch cards and IBM cards to the statistical packages used today.
- SPSS is a widely used state-of-the-art statistical software program that will take you through all the basics of using any sophisticated statistical package.
- SPSS comes in different packages. While this textbook is designed specifically for use with both the SPSS Base and SPSS Student Versions of SPSS 11.0 and 11.5 for Windows, it may be used with versions 7.0 and higher with the understanding that a few of the instructions are incongruous with the earlier versions and some of the screens will be slightly different than those in the book.

Key Terms

SPSS   SPSS Graduate Pack
SPSS Student Version   SPSS Base
SAS

Review Questions

1. Describe the historical development of social scientists' use of data-processing machinery beginning with the development of tabulating machines that used punch (IBM) cards.

2. What are the two most widely used statistical packages today?

3. What revolutionized the way social scientific data analysis was done in the mid-1980s?

4. Which of the versions of SPSS described is the least powerful in terms of the number of cases and variables it can handle?

5. Which version of SPSS is the most powerful in this regard?

6. What version (or versions) of SPSS are you using?

7. Name two tasks a statistical package such as SPSS can be used for.

Chapter 2 **The Theory and Process of Social Research**

This book addresses the techniques of social science data analysis. Thus, we're going to be spending most of our time analyzing data and reaching conclusions about the people who answered questions in the General Social Survey, which is described in more detail in Chapter 4.

Data analysis, however, doesn't occur in a vacuum. Scientific inquiry is a matter of both observing and reasoning. Consequently, before getting into the techniques of data analysis, let's take a minute to consider some of the central components of social science research. We will start this chapter by looking at the role of theory in conjunction with the social research process. Then, in the next chapter, we will turn our attention to another fundamental aspect of scientific inquiry—measurement. While these chapters are not designed to give you an in-depth understanding of the social research process, they will give you the background necessary to master the techniques of data analysis presented in this book.[1]

Theories and Concepts: Deprivation Theory

Given the variety of topics examined in social science research, there is no single, established set of procedures that is always followed in social scientific inquiry. Nevertheless, data analysis almost always has a bigger purpose than the simple manipulation of numbers. Our larger aim is to learn something of general value about human social behavior. This commitment lies in the realm of theory. A primary goal of social scientific research is to develop theories that help us explain, understand, and make sense of the social world.

A *theory* is a statement or set of statements describing the relationships among concepts. Theories provide explanations about the patterns we find in human social life. For example, American social research has consistently shown

---

[1] If you are thinking about designing a research study or you just want to learn more about the process and practice of scientific inquiry, you may find the discussion in Chapter 21, Appendix C, and CD-Appendixes D, E, and F a useful starting point. You may also want to browse through the Reference section for citations to texts that focus on the nature of social scientific inquiry, designing a research project, and other aspects of the research process.

that women are more religious than men. The key concepts in that observed pattern are religiosity and gender. We'll examine a theory that explains the pattern in a moment. Because concepts are the building blocks of theories, it is important that we focus briefly on what they are.

Concepts are general ideas or understandings that form the basis of social scientific research. Some of the social scientific concepts with which you are familiar might include social class, deviance, political orientations, prejudice, and alienation. The most useful concepts describe variations among people or groups. When thinking about social class, for example, we might distinguish upper class, middle class, and working class, while the concept of prejudice leads us to consider those who are more prejudiced and those who are less prejudiced.

Developing social theories is a matter of discovering concepts that are causally related to one another. We may ask questions like "Does education reduce prejudice?" "Does gender affect how much people are paid?" Or, "Are minority group members more liberal than majority group members?"

Because one of the subjects we are going to examine in this textbook is religiosity, we will begin with an example of a theory deriving from the sociology of religion. The sociologists Glock, Ringer, and Babbie developed what they call the "deprivation theory of church involvement." Having asked why some church members participated more in their churches than others, the researchers' analyses led them to conclude that those who were deprived of gratification (e.g., money, prestige, power, opportunities, freedom) in the secular society would be more likely to be active in church life than were those who enjoyed the rewards of secular society.

In this case, the concepts under examination are deprivation, gratification, and church involvement. Some people are more deprived of gratification than others; some people are more religiously involved than others. The research question is to find out if the degree to which people are deprived is somehow related to their degree of religious involvement.

Deprivation theory offers a plausible explanation as to how the concepts of deprivation and religious involvement are related. It gives us a possible explanation—a theory—to help us make sense of why some people are more religious or more active in church than others. In this form, however, the concepts are too general to test the theory empirically. Before a theory can be tested, another step has to be taken, namely, we need to create hypotheses. Unlike theories, well-developed hypotheses pose relationships between variables that are specific enough to permit testing.

In short, while theory is an important starting point in social science research, the empirical relationships predicted by the theory must be tested. To do that, we shift our focus from relationships between concepts to relationships between variables, from theories to hypotheses.

Hypotheses and Variables: Religiosity

A *hypothesis* is a statement of expectation derived from a theory that proposes a relationship between two or more variables. Specifically, a hypothesis is a tentative statement which proposes that variation in one variable causes or leads to variation in the other variable.

Table 2.1 illustrates the differences between theories and hypotheses. Theories specify relationships between concepts in the world of ideas, while hypotheses specify expected relationships between variables in the world of

Table 2.1   Theories, Concepts, Hypotheses, and Variables

World of Ideas	Concepts:	1. Secular Deprivation
		2. Religious Involvement
	Theory:	The more people experience secular deprivation, the more likely they will be religiously involved.

Variables representing dimensions of secular deprivation:
   a. Age
   b. Gender
   c. Socioeconomic Status

World of Experiences

Hypotheses:
a. As people get older, their religious participation increases.
   Independent variable: Age
   Dependent variable: Religiosity
b. Women will have greater religious participation than men.
   Independent variable: Gender/Sex
   Dependent variable: Religiosity
c. The lower your income, the more likely you are to participate in religious activities
   Independent variable: Income
   Dependent variable: Religiosity

empirical experiences. *Variables* are empirical indicators of the concepts we are researching. Variables, as their name implies, have the ability to take on two or more values. For instance, people can be classified in terms of their gender (male or female) or religious involvement (involved or not involved). By identifying empirical indicators for our concepts, they become variables.

As Table 2.2 demonstrates, each variable contains at least two or more *categories*. The categories of the variable gender, for instance, are male and female, while the categories of the variable social class may be: upper class, middle class and working class.

The categories of each variable must meet two requirements: They should be both exhaustive and mutually exclusive. By *exhaustive* we mean that the categories of each variable must be comprehensive enough that it is possible to categorize every observation. Imagine, for instance, that you are conducting a survey and one of your variables is "religious affiliation." In order to measure respondents' religion you devise a question that asks respondents simply: "What is your religion?" Let's say you give respondents only three choices: Protestant, Catholic, and Jewish. While most Americans would identify with one of these religious traditions, the categories certainly are not exhaustive. Muslims and Hindus, among others would not find categories descriptive of their traditions. To correct this problem, we would have to add traditions, add an "Other" category, or both so that all respondents could fit themselves into at least one category. Moreover, we'd want a "None" category for those with no religious affiliation.

Table 2.2   Variables and Categories

Variable	Category
Gender	Female
	Male
Religious Involvement	Involved
	Not involved
Party Identification	Democrat
	Independent
	Republican
Social Class	Upper class
	Middle class
	Working class

The requirement of *exclusiveness* refers to the fact that every observation should fit into only one category. For instance, if we asked people for their religious affiliation and gave them the choices of "Christian," "Protestant," "Catholic," and "Jewish," the categories would not be mutually exclusive. Both Protestants and Catholics would see themselves as also being in the "Christian" category.

Looking back at the deprivation theory then, you may recall that it was expected that poor people would be more active in the church than rich people, given that the former would be denied many secular gratifications enjoyed by the latter. Or, in a male-dominated society, it was suggested that because women are denied gratifications enjoyed by men, women would be more likely to participate actively in the church. Similarly, in a youth-oriented society, the theory would suggest that older people would be more active in church than the young.

As Table 2.1 illustrates, one hypothesis that can be derived from the deprivation theory is that women will be more involved in church than will men. This hypothesis proposes a relationship between two variables: a dependent and an independent variable. A *dependent variable* is the variable you are trying to explain (i.e. in this case, church involvement/religiosity), while the *independent variable* is the variable that is hypothesized to "cause," lead to, or explain variation in another variable (i.e., in this case, gender).

It is important to recognize that relationships such as the one predicted in the hypotheses in Table 2.1 are *probabilistic*. The hypothesis says that women, as a group, will have a higher average level of church involvement than men will as a group. This does not mean that all women are more involved than any men. It does mean, for example, that if we asked men and women whether they attend church every week, a higher percentage of women than of men would say yes, even though some men would say yes and some women would say no. That is the nature of probabilistic relationships.

Social Research Strategies: Inductive and Deductive

After developing a hypothesis, a researcher may decide to design and conduct a scientific study to test whether there is a relationship such as the one proposed between gender and church involvement. Social scientists generally approach research in one of two ways: inductively or deductively.

In the study mentioned previously by Glock, Ringer, and Babbie, the researchers employed an *inductive research* strategy. First they collected data regarding people's religious involvement and gender. After their observations were completed, the data were examined, and a theory was then constructed to explain the relationships found among the variables.

An alternative and somewhat more common approach is *deductive research*. Unlike inductive research, which begins with data collection, deductive research begins with social theory. A specific hypothesis is then deduced from the theory and tested to discover whether there is evidence to support it. Most generally, the deprivation theory suggests people who lack secular gratification will be more involved in religious activities. From that, we could derive the hypothesis that persons of lower socioeconomic status will attend church more often than those of higher socioeconomic status. We could then collect data about people's socio-economic status and church attendance. The data could then be examined to see if lower status people really did attend more than high status people. This would be considered deductive research because we began with the theory and tested a hypothesis with data.

Perhaps the simplest way to distinguish between inductive and deductive research approaches is by where they "begin." While inductive research begin with data analysis and then moves to theory, deductive research begins with theory, then proceeds to data analysis and back to theory again. More simply, deduction can be seen as reasoning from general understandings to specific expectations, whereas induction can be seen as reasoning from specific observations to general explanations.

You can see, then, that there are many steps or stages in the social research process. When conducting deductive research, social scientists proceed from the general (theory) to the specific (data collection), and back to theory again:

1. Theory

2. *Deduce* hypotheses to test theory

3. Collect data

4. Analyze data

5. Evaluate hypotheses

In the case of inductive research, researchers move from the specific (data collection) to the general (theory):

1. Collect data

2. Analyze data

3. *Induce* a theory to account for data

While in practice the process of social research is not nearly as linear as these steps suggest, you can see that whether a researcher employs a deductive or inductive strategy, the goal is always the same: to develop theories that help us explain, make sense of, and understand human social behavior.

The possible topics for exploration are, as you can imagine, endless. Whereas some social researchers are interested in understanding religiosity, others are interested in issues such as spousal abuse, child abuse, violence in schools, unemployment, political party identification, poverty, alcoholism, drug addiction, health care, crime, starvation, overpopulation, governmental corruption, and so on. The problems and issues of concern to social scientists are as manifold and complicated as human beings themselves. Despite the diversity in questions and concerns, what connects social scientists is the belief that if used properly, the techniques and process of social science research can help us examine and begin to understand these complicated issues. Only when we understand what causes these problems, how they come about, and why they persist, will we be able to solve them.

While the primary focus of this book is on one stage in the social research process, data analysis, we hope you take some time to reflect on which of the many problems in contemporary life interest you. What issues or questions are you passionate about? What social problems or issues would you like to examine, understand, and potentially address?

Political Orientations

Now that we have focused a little on the relationship between theory and the social research process, let's examine some of the theoretical work that informs two of the many subjects we are going to analyze together in this book: political orientations and attitudes toward abortion.

One of the more familiar variables in social science is political orientation, which typically ranges from liberal to conservative. It lies at the heart of much voting behavior, and it relates to a number of nonpolitical variables as well, which you are going to discover for yourself shortly.

There are several *dimensions* of political orientations, and it will be useful to distinguish them here. Three commonly examined dimensions are (1) social attitudes, (2) economic attitudes, and (3) foreign policy attitudes. Let's examine each dimension briefly.

Some specific social attitudes and related behaviors might include abortion, premarital sex, and capital punishment. Let's see where liberals and conservatives would generally stand on these issues:

Issue	Liberals	Conservatives
abortion	permissive	restrictive
premarital sex	permissive	restrictive
capital punishment	opposed	in favor

In terms of economic issues, liberals are generally more supportive than are conservatives of government programs such as unemployment insurance, welfare, and Medicare, and of government economic regulation, such as progressive taxation (the rich taxed at higher rates), minimum wage laws, and regulation of industry. By the same token, liberals are likely to be more supportive of labor unions than are conservatives.

Attitudes Toward Abortion

Abortion is a social issue that has figured importantly in religious and political debates for years. The General Social Survey contains several variables dealing with attitudes toward abortion. Each asks whether a woman should be allowed to get an abortion for a variety of reasons. The following list shows these reasons, along with the *abbreviated variable names* you'll be using for them in your analyses later on.

Abbreviated Variable Name	
ABDEFECT	because there is a strong chance of a serious defect
ABNOMORE	because a family wants no more children
ABHLTH	because the woman's health would be seriously endangered
ABPOOR	because a family is too poor to afford more children
ABRAPE	because the pregnancy resulted from rape
ABSINGLE	because the woman is unmarried
ABANY	because the woman wants it, for any reason

Before we begin examining answers to the abortion attitude questions, it is worth taking a moment to reflect on their logical implications. Which of these items do you suppose would receive the least support? That is, which will have the smallest percentage of respondents agreeing with it? Think about that before continuing.

Logically, we should expect the smallest percentage to support ABANY, because it contains all the others. For example, those who would support abortion in the case of rape might not support it for other reasons, such as the family's poverty. Those who support ABANY, however, would have to agree with both of those more specific items.

Three of the items tap into reasons that would seem to excuse the pregnant woman from responsibility:

Abbreviated Variable Name	
ABDEFECT	because there is a strong chance of a serious defect
ABHLTH	because the woman's health would be seriously endangered
ABRAPE	because the pregnancy resulted from rape

We might expect the highest percentages to agree with these items. We'll come back to this issue later to find out whether our expectations are correct.

When we analyze this topic with data, we will discover useful ways of measuring overall attitudes toward abortion. Once we've done that, we'll be in a position to find out why some people are generally supportive and others generally opposed.

Conclusion

By now, you should have gained an initial appreciation of the relationship between theory and the social research process. This examination will continue throughout the book. While most of our attention will focus on the skills of analyzing data, we will always want to make logical sense out of what we learn from our manipulations of the numbers.

Measurement is a fundamental topic that bridges theory and research. We turn our attention to that topic next.

Main Points

- The primary goal of all social scientific research is to develop theories that help us explain, make sense of, and understand human social behavior.
- A theory is a general statement or set of statements that describes and explains how concepts are related to one another.
- A hypothesis is a tentative statement of expectation derived from a theory.
- A hypothesis proposes a relationship between two or more variables (the independent and dependent) that can be tested by researchers employing scientific methods.
- The categories of variables must be both exhaustive and mutually exclusive.
- When a social scientist proceeds from theory to hypotheses development, data collection, and data analysis, the process is called deduction.
- When a social scientist moves from data collection to data analysis and then induces a general theory based on those observations, the process is called induction.
- Theoretical work informs all of the subjects we are going to analyze in this book and, indeed, all questions and issues of relevance to social scientists.

Key Terms

Theory	Dependent variable
Exhaustive	Dimensions
Inductive research	Variables
Concepts	Independent variable
Exclusive	Abbreviated variable name
Deductive research	Categories
Hypothesis	Probabilistic

Review Questions

1. What is the primary goal of social scientific research?
2. Name two social scientific concepts.
3. What is the relationship between theory and hypotheses?
4. Theories are to concepts as hypotheses are to _____.
5. Does a hypothesis propose a relationship between dimensions or variables?
6. The categories of each variable should meet what two requirements?
7. What, if anything, is the problem with the categories of the variable "Political Views": Liberal, moderate. If there is a problem, how might you correct it?
8. What, if anything, is the problem with the categories of the variable "Political Perspective": Liberal, Democrat, Republican, or Conservative. If there is a problem, how might you correct it?

9. Construct a hypothesis based on the deprivation theory of church involvement using level of education as your independent variable.

10. List the categories of the variables you used to construct your hypothesis in response to Question 9.

11. Construct potential hypotheses to relate the following concepts and identify the independent and dependent variable in each hypothesis. In addition, list the categories of each variable.
    a. Age and Health
    b. Race and Attitude toward affirmative action
    c. Gender and Income

12. Which of the following is not be a dependent variable: grade point average, church attendance, age, number of children.

13. Which of the following is not a variable: occupation, amount of television viewing, female, education level.

14. Consider the following hypothesis: People who earn more than $50,000 a year are more likely to vote Republican than people who earn less than $50,000 a year. Does this mean that all people who earn more than $50,000 a year vote Republican? Why or why not?

15. Is the following statement T (True) or F (False): A researcher who begins by collecting data and then develops a theory to explain her findings is engaged in deductive research.

16. A researcher formulates a hypothesis based on the 'magic bullet theory' and then selects independent and dependent variables to test this hypothesis. What process is the researcher engaged in?

17. A researcher collects data on the spread of AIDS in the United States and then, based on his or her findings, develops a theory to explain why the rate of exposure and infection to the disease is higher among certain racial and ethnic groups than among others. What process is the researcher engaged in?

Chapter 3 **The Logic of Measurement**

Measurement is one of the most fundamental elements of science. In the case of social research, the task typically is one of characterizing individuals in terms of the issues under study. Thus, a study of voting will characterize respondents in terms of the candidate for whom they plan to vote. A study of abortion attitudes will describe people in terms of their attitudes on that topic.

Validity Problems

Validity is a term used casually in everyday language, but it has a precise meaning in social research. It describes an indicator of a concept. Most simply, an indicator is said to be valid if it really measures the concept it is intended to measure, and it is invalid if it doesn't.

As a simple example, let's consider political orientations, ranging from very liberal to very conservative. For an example of a clearly valid measure of this concept, here's the way the General Social Survey asked about it.

POLVIEWS: We hear a lot of talk these days about liberals and conservatives. I'm going to show you a seven-point scale on which political views that people might hold are arranged from extremely liberal to extremely conservative. Where would you place yourself on this scale?
1. Extremely liberal
2. Liberal
3. Slightly liberal
4. Moderate, middle-of-the-road
5. Slightly conservative
6. Conservative
7. Extremely conservative

At the opposite extreme, a simple question about respondent gender would not be a valid measure of political orientations. Political orientations and gender are different concepts. But now let's consider another questionnaire item that does not come from the General Social Survey. This item lies somewhere in between these two extremes of validity with regard to measuring political orientations.

Which of these two political parties do you most identify with?

1. Democratic Party
2. Republican Party
3. Neither

This second item is another reasonable measure of political orientation. Moreover, it is related to the first, because Democrats are, on the whole, more liberal than Republicans. On the other hand, there are conservative Democrats and liberal Republicans. If our purpose is to tap into the liberal-conservative dimension, the initial item that asks directly about political orientations is obviously a more valid indicator of the concept than is the item about political party.

This particular example offers us a clear choice as to the most valid indicator of the concept at hand, but matters are not always that clear-cut. If we were measuring levels of prejudice, for example, we could not simply ask, How prejudiced are you? because no one is likely to admit to being prejudiced. As we search for workable indicators of a concept such as prejudice, the matter of validity becomes something to which we must pay careful attention.

Validity is a concern, not only when you collect and analyze your own data (what is known as *primary research*), but also when you reanalyze data previously collected by someone else, as we do in this book. The process of reanalyzing someone else's data is referred to as *secondary analysis*. Even if you can think of a survey question that would have captured your concept perfectly, the original researchers might not have asked it. Hence, you often need to use ingenuity in constructing measures that nevertheless tap the quality in which you are interested. In the case of political orientations, for example, you might combine the responses to several questions: asking for attitudes about civil liberties, past voting behavior, political party identification, and so forth. We'll return to the use of multiple indicators shortly.

In large part, the question of validity is settled on *prima facie* grounds: We judge an indicator to be relatively valid or invalid on the face of it. It was on this basis that you had no trouble seeing that asking directly about political orientations was a valid indicator of that concept, whereas asking a person's gender was definitely not a valid measure of political orientations. Later in the book, we'll explore some simple methodological techniques that are also used to test the validity of measures.

Reliability Problems

Reliability is a different but equally important quality of measurements. *Reliability* refers to the quality of a measuring instrument that would cause it to report the same value in successive observations of a given case (provided the phenomenon being measured has not changed). For instance, if you step on a bathroom scale five times in a row, and each time it gives you a different weight, the scale has a reliability problem. Conversely, if you step on a bathroom scale five times in a row and the scale gives you the same weight each time (even if the weight is wrong), the scale is reliable.

Similarly, if your statistics instructor administered the same test to you three times, and each time you got a different score even though your knowledge of statistics had not changed in the interim, the test has a reliability problem. Conversely, if your instructor administered the same test three times and your score was the same each time, the test is reliable.

In the context of survey research, reliability also refers to the question of whether we can trust the answers that people give us even when their misstatements are honest ones.

For instance, in medical research, some patients report a particular organ had been removed in one survey, only to indicate they have those organs in subsequent surveys.[1] Similarly, students of voting behavior regularly encounter individuals who claim they did vote in the last presidential election. However, in subsequent surveys these same individuals often claim they either did not vote or that they do not remember if they voted. As noted previously, these statements are often honest ones. It is difficult enough for most of us to recall what we did a few months ago, let alone several years earlier.

Conceptually, the test of reliability is whether respondents would give the same answers repeatedly if the measurement could be made in such a way that (a) their situations had not changed (they hadn't had additional surgery to remove organs . . .), and (b) they couldn't remember the answer they gave before.

As we suggested, testing the reliability of an item empirically, requires multiple measures (i.e., your instructor must administer the statistics test at least two or more times in order to determine its reliability). However, we can sometimes assess the reliability of a single item on its practicality. Years ago, one of us was asked to assist on a survey of teenage drivers in California. Over researcher objections, the client insisted on asking the question, "How many miles have you driven?" and providing a space for the teenager to write in his or her response. Perhaps you can recognize the problem in this question by attempting to answer it yourself. Unless you have never driven an automobile, we doubt that you can report how many miles you have driven with any accuracy. In the survey mentioned, some teenagers reported driving hundreds of thousands of miles. By the way, if we administered the same survey to these respondents again, we would most likely have gotten widely different answers to this question, even if they had not driven a significant number of miles in the interim.

A better technique in that situation, by the way, would be to provide respondents with a set of categories reflecting realistically the number of miles respondents are likely to have driven: fewer than 1,000 miles; 1,000 to 4,999 miles; 5,000 to 9,999 miles; and so on. Such a set of categories gives respondents a framework within which to place their own situations. Even though they still may not know exactly how much they had driven, there would be fair likelihood that the categories they chose would actually contain their correct answers. The success of this technique, of course, would depend on our having a good idea in advance of what constitutes reasonable categories, determined by previous research, perhaps. As an alternative, we might ask respondents to volunteer the number of miles they have driven, but limit the time period to something they are likely to remember. Thus, we might ask how many miles they drove the preceding week or month, for example.

Validity and Reliability

Perhaps the difference between validity and reliability can be seen most clearly in reference to a simple bathroom scale. As we noted earlier, if you step on a scale repeatedly (scales don't remember) and it gives you a different weight each time,

---

[1] The authors are grateful to Professor Randall MacIntosh, California State University, Sacramento for this suggestion.

then the scale has a reliability problem. On the other hand, if the scale tells you that you weigh 125 pounds every time you step on it, it's pretty reliable, but if you actually weigh 225, the scale has a problem in the validity department; it doesn't indicate your weight accurately.

Both validity and reliability are important in the analysis of data. If you are interested in learning why some people have deeply held religious beliefs and others do not, then asking people how often they attend church would be problematic. This question doesn't really provide a valid measure of the concept that interests you, and anything you learn will explain the causes of church attendance, not religious belief. And suppose you asked people how many times they had attended church in the past year; any answers you received would probably not be reliable, so anything you might think you learned about the causes of church attendance might be only a function of the errors people made in answering the question. (It would be better to give them categories from which to choose.) You would have no assurance that another study would yield the same result.

Multiple Indicators

Often, the solution to the problems discussed above lies in the creation of *composite measures* using *multiple indicators*. As a simple example, to measure the degree to which a sample of Christian church members held the beliefs associated with Christianity, you might ask them questions about several issues, each dealing with a particular belief, such as the following:

- belief in God
- belief that Jesus was divine
- belief in the existence of the devil
- belief in an afterlife: heaven and hell
- belief in the literal truth of the Bible

The several answers given to these questions could be used to create an overall measure of religious belief among the respondents. In the simplest procedure, you could give respondents 1 point for each belief to which they agreed, allowing you to score them from 0 to 5 on the index. Notice that this is the same logic by which you may earn 1 point for each correct answer on an exam, with the total score being taken as an indication of how well you know the material.

Some social science concepts are implicitly multidimensional. Consider the concept of social class, for example. Typically, this term is used in reference to a combination of education, income, occupation, and sometimes dimensions such as social class identification and prestige. This would be measured for data analysis through the use of multiple indicators.

When it becomes appropriate in the analyses we are going to undertake together below, we'll show you how to create and use some simple composite measures.

Levels of Measurement

As we convert the concepts in our minds into empirical measurements in the form of variables, we sometimes have options as to their level of statistical sophistication. Specifically, there are a number of different possibilities regarding the relationships among the categories comprising a variable. In social research we commonly speak of four *levels of measurement*: nominal, ordinal, ratio, and interval.

Nominal Variables

Some variables simply distinguish different kinds of people. Gender is a good example of this; it simply distinguishes men from women. Political party distinguishes Democrats from Republicans and from other parties. Religious affiliation distinguishes Protestants, Catholics, Jews, and so forth. We refer to these measurements as nominal, in that term's sense of naming. *Nominal variables* simply name the different attributes constituting them.

The attributes comprising a nominal variable (e.g., gender, composed of male and female) are simply different. Republicans and Democrats are simply different from each other, as are Protestants and Catholics. In other cases, however, we can say more about the attributes making up variables.

Ordinal Variables

Many social scientific variables go a step beyond simply naming the different attributes comprising a variable. *Ordinal variables* arrange those attributes in some order: from low to high, from more to less, and so on. Whereas the nominal variable religious affiliation classifies people into different religious groups, religiosity might order them in groups, such as very religious, somewhat religious, and not at all religious. And where the nominal variable political party identification simply distinguishes different groups (e.g., Democrats and Republicans), an ordinal measure of political philosophy might rank order the very liberal, the somewhat liberal, the middle-of-the-road, the somewhat conservative, and the very conservative. Ordinal variables share the nominal variable quality of distinguishing differences among people, and they add the quality of *rank ordering* those differences.

At the same time, it is not meaningful to talk about the distances separating the attributes that make up an ordinal variable. For example, we have no basis for talking about the amount of liberalism separating the very liberal from the somewhat liberal or the somewhat liberal from the middle-of-the-road. We can say that the first group in each comparison is more liberal than the second, but we can't say how much.

Ratio Variables

Some variables allow us to speak more precisely about the distances between the attributes comprising a variable. Consider age for a moment. The distance between 10 years old and 20 years old is exactly the same as that between 60 years old and 70 years old. Thus, it makes sense to talk about the distance between two ages (i.e., they are 10 years apart).

Moreover, *ratio variables* such as age have the additional quality of containing a genuine zero point, in this case no years old. This quality is what allows us to examine ratios among the categories constituting such variables. Thus, we can say that a 20-year-old is twice as old as a 10-year-old. By comparison, notice that we would have no grounds for saying one person is twice as religious as another.

Ratio variables, then, share all the qualities associated with nominal and ordinal variables, but they have additional qualities not applicable to the lower-level measures. Other examples of ratio measures include income, years of schooling, and hours worked per week.

Interval Variables

Rarer in social research are variables that have the quality of standard intervals of measurement but lack a genuine zero point, or *interval variables*. One example is intelligence quotient (IQ). Although IQ is calculated in such a way as to allow for a score of zero, that would not indicate a complete lack of intelligence, because the person would at least have been able to take the test.

Moving outside the social sciences, consider temperature. The Celsius and Fahrenheit measures of temperature both have 0° marks, but neither represents a total lack of heat, given that it is possible to have temperatures below zero. The Kelvin scale, by contrast, is based on an absolute zero, which does represent a total lack of heat (measured in terms of molecular motion).

For most statistics used by social scientists, interval and ratio scales may be considered the same. When we start using SPSS, we'll see that its creators have lumped interval and ratio variables into a single category called *scale*. Although these variables may be combined for practical purposes, the distinction between them helps us understand why a negative income might be interpreted as debt and a negative age is impossible!

Measurement and Information

Knowing a variable's level of measurement is important for selecting an appropriate statistic. Variables of different levels of measurement contain different amounts of information. The only information we have about nominal variables is the number of cases that share a common attribute. With ordinal variables, in addition to knowing how many cases fall in a category, we know a greater than/less than relationship between the cases. Variables measured at the interval level have their points equidistant from one another. With equidistant points, we know how much greater than or less than cases are from each other. Finally, with ratio variables, we have all the characteristics of nominal, ordinal, and interval variables, plus the knowledge that zero is not arbitrary but means an absence of the phenomena.

The statistics that SPSS has been programmed to compute are designed to make maximum use of the information preserved in a level of measurement. Using the mode on a sample of GPAs ignores information used by the mean. Conversely, using the mean for a sample of religious preferences assumes information (equidistant points) not contained in a nominal measure. Responsible use of statistics requires selecting a statistic that matches the data's level of measurement. We'll talk about this more later. Right now, we want you to know that being able to identify a variable's level of measurement is essential for selecting the right statistical tool. We don't want to see you using a screwdriver when you need a hammer.

Table 3.1 displays the three primary levels of measurement that we discuss in this book: nominal, ordinal, and interval/ratio (scale). We purposefully designed the table as a series of steps, in order to remind you that there is a hierarchy implied in the levels of measurement idea. Variables at the nominal level ("bottom step") contain the least amount of information, followed by variables at the ordinal level ("middle step"), and finally variables at the interval/ratio level ("highest step"), which contain the most information. You should also note that as you move

Table 3.1   Levels of Measurement

INTERVAL/RATIO
Distance between categories is
   meaningful
*Income (measured in thousands
   of dollars)*
Age (measured in years)

ORDINAL
Categories can be rank ordered
*Social class (lower, working,
   middle, upper)*
*Attitudes toward gun control
   (strongly oppose, oppose,
   favor, strongly favor)*

NOMINAL
Categories differ in name
Gender (male, female)
*Party identification
   (Democrat, Republican)*

"up" from the nominal to the ordinal and finally interval/ratio level, each has the qualities of the level(s) below it, plus a new trait.

Measurement Options

Sometimes you will have options regarding the levels of measurement to be created in variables. For instance, although age can qualify as a ratio variable, it can be measured as ordinal (e.g., young, middle-aged, old) or even as nominal (baby-boomer, not baby-boomer).

The significance of these levels of measurement will become more apparent when we begin to analyze the variables in our data set. As you'll discover, some analytic techniques are appropriate to nominal variables, some to ordinal variables, and some to ratio variables. On one hand, you will need to know a variable's level of measurement in order to determine which analytic techniques are appropriate. On the other hand, where you have options for measurement, your choice of measurement level may be determined by the techniques you want to employ.

Classifying Variables as Discrete or Continuous

In addition to distinguishing variables by their level of measurement, researchers often classify variables as discrete or continuous. Just as distinguishing between levels of measurement helps us choose appropriate statistics, so too does knowing whether variables are discrete or continuous.

However, unlike levels of measurement which tell us the amount of information provided by a measure, the discrete versus continuous distinction gives us

Table 3.2   Tips for Distinguishing Between Discrete and Continuous Variables

Discrete Variable	*Example: Number of siblings* • Unit CANNOT be reduced to even smaller units. • Is NOT an infinite number of other possible categories between any two categories of this variable (i.e., 1 and 2 siblings, or 2 and 3 siblings, etc. . . .) • Can be nominal, ordinal, or I/R (scale) variables.
Continuous Variable	*Example: Age measured in years* • Unit CAN be further reduced to smaller units (i.e., months, weeks, days, hours, minutes, seconds, etc. . . .) • IS an infinite number of other possible categories between any two categories of this variable (i.e. 19 and 20 years old, 20 and 21 years old, etc. . . .) • Can be ordinal or I/R (scale) variables.

information about the underlying characteristics of a variable. In particular, it refers to the phenomena's divisibility, or whether the values of a variable can be subdivided into ever smaller units.

Discrete variables are variables whose values are completely separate from one another, such as RACE or SEX. These are variables with a limited number of distinct (i.e. discrete) values or categories, which cannot be reduced or subdivided into smaller units or numbers.

Discrete variables can be nominal (sex), ordinal (class rank), or I/R (number of siblings). All these variables are discrete because the values of these variables cannot be subdivided or reduced. A respondent may, for instance, have 1 sibling, but she cannot have .5 or .25 siblings. People come in discrete units of 1; they cannot be subdivided into smaller units.

Continuous variables, on the other hand, are variables whose values can be infinitely subdivided, such as AGE or EDUC (education measured in years). These variables are continuous because they both have a time dimension and time can be infinitely subdivided (i.e., years, months, weeks, days, hours, minutes, seconds, etc. . .).

The level of measurement for continuous variables can be either I/R (age measured in years) or ordinal (age measured as infant, toddler, adolescent, pre-teen, teenager, etc. . .).

Conclusion

Measurement is a fundamental aspect of social science research. It may be seen as the transition from concepts to variables—from sometimes ambiguous mental images to precise, empirical measures. Whereas we often speak casually about such concepts as prejudice, social class, and liberalism in everyday conversation, social scientists must be more precise in their uses of these terms.

Chapters 2 and 3 have given you a brief overview of two important issues in social scientific inquiry that are directly relevant to our primary focus—computerized statistical analysis. The chapters that follow will build on this discussion of theory and measurement and show you the concrete techniques you need to engage in data analysis. Those of you who are interested in designing and conducting your own research, or who just want to learn more about the process and practice of social research, may want to consult Chapter 21, Appendix C, CD-Appendixes D, E, F, or some of the books listed in the Reference section that discuss these and other issues relevant to social scientific research in greater detail.

Main Points

- Measurement is a vital component of social scientific research.
- In designing and evaluating measurements, social scientists must pay particular attention to the problems of validity and reliability.
- A common remedy for problems of validity and reliability is the construction of composite measures using multiple indicators.
- Level of measurement signifies the different amount and type of information obtained about a variable and is essential for selecting appropriate statistical tools.
- The four levels of measurement are nominal, ordinal, ratio, and interval.
- Variables of different levels of measurement contain different amounts of information.
- There is an implied hierarchy in the levels of measurement idea.
- In addition to classifying variables by their level of measurement, researchers also distinguish between discrete or continuous variables.
- Discrete variables cannot be infinitely subdivided into ever smaller units, whereas continuous variables can.

Key Terms

Validity   Composite measures
Ordinal variables   Discrete variables
Primary research   Multiple indicators
Ratio variables   Continuous variables
Secondary analysis   Level of measurement
Interval variables   Nominal variables
Reliability scale

Review Questions

1. A researcher sets out to measure drug use on U.S. college campuses by asking a representative sample of undergraduates whether they are currently receiving federal grants or loans. What is the problem with this measure?

2. A researcher asks a representative sample of baby-boomers how much alcohol they consumed during their college years and leaves a space for them to write in their response in terms of the actual number of drinks. Four weeks later, the researcher administers the same questionnaire to the same respondents. However, this time more than half of the respondents report consuming much

less alcohol during their college years than they did just a month earlier. What is the problem with this measure?

3. Multiple indicators are useful in dealing with what types of problems?

4. Name one reason why it is important to know or to be able to identify a variable's level of measurement.

5. Ordinal variables have all the qualities of variables at which other level of measurement?

6. Ratio variables have all the qualities of variables at which other levels of measurement?

7. The creators of SPSS have combined ratio and interval variables into one category which they refer to as _____.

8. How do social scientists often classify variables whose values can be infinitely subdivided?

Identify the level of measurement of each of the following variables (Questions 9-11):

9. A researcher measures respondents' attitudes toward premarital sex by asking the following question: "If a man and woman have sexual relations before marriage, do you think it is always wrong, almost always wrong, wrong only sometimes, or not wrong at all?"

10. A researcher measures the amount of television viewing by asking the following question: "On the average day, how many hours do you personally watch television?" Respondents are then asked to fill in the actual number of hours in the space provided.

11. A researcher measures marital status by asking respondents whether they are currently married, widowed, divorced, separated, or never married.

12. Classify the variables in Questions 9-11 as either discrete or continuous.

Indicate whether the following statements (Questions 13-18) are T (true) or F (false):

13. Certain variables can be measured at both the nominal and ordinal levels.

14. You are invited to screen a new movie and then asked to rate it as either: excellent, good, fair, poor. The level of measurement is nominal because the ratings differ in name.

15. A researcher asks respondents to indicate the last four digits of their social security number. The level of measurement for this variable is interval/ratio because the distance between categories is meaningful.

16. A researcher asks respondents how many siblings they have. This variable can be categorized as continuous.

17. A researcher asks respondents how long they have lived at their current residence. This variable can be categorized as continuous.

18. Discrete variables can be either nominal or ordinal, but not interval/ratio.

19. Construct measures of "annual income" at two levels of measurement.

20. Classify the variables you constructed in response to Question 19 as either discrete or continuous.

21. Construct measures of "individual age" at two levels of measurement.

22. Classify the variables you constructed in response to Question 21 as either discrete or continuous.

Part II Getting Started

In the following two chapters we introduce you to the data you will be using throughout the text and show you how to use SPSS to load and access the data. Chapter 4 describes the real-life data that accompany this textbook. The data come from the 2000 General Social Survey (GSS), which was conducted among a national sample of American adults.

The computer program we will be using, Statistical Package for the Social Sciences (SPSS), is introduced in Chapter 5. This chapter provides you with some initial familiarization with the version of the program you will be using, and you will see how it differs from the others that are available.

Starting with Chapter 5, each chapter contains a series of "Demonstrations" you can follow along with on your computer. When the images on your computer screen match ours in the book, you will know you successfully used SPSS's commands. In Chapter 5, for instance, we begin with Demonstration 5.1 "Starting an SPSS Session" and end with Demonstration 5.14 "Ending Your SPSS Session." By the time you work your way through these demonstrations, you should be fairly comfortable accessing SPSS, moving through the Data Editor, opening a data file, and ending your SPSS session. You can further check your abilities by completing the Lab Exercise at the end of the chapter.

Chapter 4 Description of Your Data Sets

The data we provide for your use here are real. They come from the responses of 2,817 adult Americans selected as a representative sample of the nation in 2000. These data are a major resource for professional social scientists and are the basis of many published books and articles.

The *General Social Survey (GSS)* is conducted regularly by the *National Opinion Research Center (NORC)* in Chicago, with financial support from the National Science Foundation (NSF) and private sources. The purpose of the GSS program is to provide the nation's social scientists with accurate data for analysis. This activity was the brainchild of Jim Davis, one of the most visionary social scientists alive during your lifetime. The GSS, which began in 1972, was conducted annually until 1994 when it became biennial.[1]

During the last thirty years, the GSS has asked more than 38,000 respondents over 3,260 questions on topics ranging from their attitudes toward abortion to their star sign in the zodiac. In 2000 alone, the GSS asked questions on issues ranging from freedom, internet use, muliculturalism, and national security, to health status, religion, environment, and social inequality.

While this chapter will provide you with a brief overview of some of the central components of the GSS, you can access further information by visiting one of the following web cites:

A. The National Opinion Research Center (NORC) is a nonprofit corporation affiliated with the University of Chicago that conducts the GSS.
   NORC home page: **www.norc.uchicago.edu**
   Once there, click on **Projects General Social Survey**
   OR
   www.norc.uchicago.edu/projects/gensoc.asp
B. The Inter-University Consortium for Political and Social Research (ICPSR) is associated with the University of Michigan. Part of its mission is to maintain and provide access to a vast archive of social science data for research and instruction.
   ICPSR home page: **www.icpsr.umich.edu**

---

[1] Funding shortages precluded GSS studies in the following years: 1979, 1981, and 1992.

OR
www.icpsr.umich.edu/GSS/
C. The Roper Center for Public Opinion Research is a nonprofit corporation for public opinion research affiliated with the University of Connecticut that provides access to the GSS.
Roper Center home page: **www.ropercenter.uconn.edu**
Click on **Quick Links GSS 2000**
OR
www.ropercenter.uconn.edu/GSS.html/
D. You can also access this information on the World Wide Web by using one of your favorite search engines. Simply log on and search for one of the following: General Social Survey (GSS); GSS 2000; National Opinion Research Center (NORC); Inter-University Consortium for Political and Social Research (ICPSR); Roper Center for Public Opinion Research.

Sampling

The data provided by the GSS are representative of American adults. This means that anything we learn about the 2,817 people sampled can be taken as an accurate reflection of what all (non-institutionalized, English-speaking) American adults (18 years of age or older) would have said if we could have interviewed them all. This is the case because of a technique known as *multistage probability sampling*.

The researchers began by selecting a random sample of cities and counties across the country, having grouped them in such a way as to ensure that those selected would reflect all the variations in cities and counties in the nation. At the second stage of sampling, the researchers selected a random sample of city blocks or equivalent units in rural areas within each of the selected cities and counties.

The researchers then visited each of the selected blocks and chose specific households at random on each block. Finally, when interviewers visited each of the selected households, they determined the number of adults living in the household and selected one of them at random as the respondent.

This complex and sophisticated sampling process makes it possible for the responses of 2,817 individuals to provide an accurate reflection of the feelings of all adult Americans. Similar techniques are used by the U.S. Census Bureau for the purpose of government planning and by polling firms that predict voting behavior with relative accuracy.

For a detailed description of the sample design used by the GSS, visit www. icpsr.umich.edu/GSS/ and then click on Appendix → A – Sampling Design and Weighting.

We have reduced the size of the samples on your CD-ROM to 1,500 cases each, so that the data provided with this book can be analyzed using either the Student, Graduate, or Professional Versions of SPSS for Windows. As we noted in Chapter 1, whereas the professional and graduate versions of SPSS for Windows are for all practical purposes limited only by the size of the computer on which they are installed, the student version is limited to 1,500 cases and 50 variables.

The CD-ROM included with this book contains two files named *DEMO.SAV* (for DEMOnstration) and *EXER.SAV* (for EXERcise), respectively. Each file contains a subsample of 1,500 cases from the 2000 General Social Survey's 2,817 cases. DEMO.SAV contains 41 variables, while EXER.SAV contains 47 variables.

Consequently, both files may be used with the Student, Graduate, or Professional Versions of SPSS for Windows. Because both files come from the same sample and the identification numbers have been preserved, anyone using the Professional or Graduate Versions of SPSS can merge the files.

The data you have at hand, then, can be taken as an accurate reflection of the characteristics, attitudes, and behaviors of Americans 18 and older in 2000. This statement needs to be qualified slightly, however. When you analyze the data and learn that 42 percent of the sample said that they supported a woman's unrestricted right to have an abortion for any reason, you are safe in assuming that about 42 percent of the entire U.S. adult population feels that way. Because the data are based on a sample rather than on asking everyone, however, we need to anticipate some degree of sampling error. You can think of **sampling error** as the extent to which the responses of those sampled, in this case using multistage probability sampling, differ from the responses of the larger population (English-speaking persons 18 years of age or older living in non-institutionalized arrangements within the United States in 2000). As a general rule, the greater the sampling error, the less representative the sample. It would not be strange, based on the example given, to discover that 40 percent or 44 percent of the total adult population (rather than exactly 42 percent) support a woman's unrestricted right to have an abortion for any reason. It is inconceivable, however, that as few as 10 percent or as many as 90 percent held the opinion in question.

As a rough guideline, you can assume that the sampling error in this data set is plus or minus only a few percentage points. In Chapter 15, we'll see how to calculate the actual sampling error for specific pieces of data.

Even granting the possibility of sampling error, however, our best estimate of what's true among the total U.S. population is what we learned from the probability sample. Thus, if you were to bet on the percentage of the total U.S. population who supported a woman's unrestricted right to an abortion, you should put your money on 42 percent. You would be better off, however, to bet that it was, say, between 40 percent and 44 percent.

Data Collection

The GSS data were collected in face-to-face household interviews. Once the sample households were selected, professional interviewers were dispatched to call on each one. The interviewers asked each of the questions and wrote down the respondents' answers. Each interview took approximately 90 minutes.

To maximize the amount of information that can be collected in this massive interviewing project, NORC asked some questions in only a random subsample of the households, asking other questions in the other households. Some questions were asked of all respondents. When we begin analyzing the GSS data, you will notice that some data items have a substantial number of respondents marked **missing data**. For the most part, this refers to respondents who were not asked that particular question.

Although only a subsample was asked some of the questions, you can still take the responses as representative of the U.S. adult population except that the degree of sampling error, mentioned above, is larger.

For more information about how the GSS data were collected, visit www.icpsr. umich.edu/GSS and then click on Appendix → B- Field Work and Interviewer Specifications → C- General Coding Instructions.

The Codebook: Appendix A

The questionnaire items included in the files you will be using throughout this text (DEMO.SAV and EXER.SAV) are listed in Appendix A. We attempted to choose variables that are not only interesting, but relevant to students from a variety of social science disciplines, including communications, criminal justice, health studies, political science, public administration, social work, and sociology.

Before proceeding to Chapter 5, you may want to take a few minutes to review the variables in Appendix A. Before long, you'll be getting much more familiar with them. As you analyze survey data, it is important to know exactly how questions were asked if you are to understand the meaning of the answers given in response. Appendix A includes the following information for each of the variables contained in your DEMO.SAV and EXER.SAV files:

- Abbreviated Variable Names (used by SPSS to access variables)
- Question Wording (how the interviewer asked the question)
- Values (sometimes called numeric values or numeric codes used to code responses)
- Value Labels (used to identify categories represented by Values. Please note that in Appendix A we have excluded the following value labels: "NA," "DK" and "NAP." These labels refer to cases when the respondent offered "no answer," said he/she "did not know" or the question was not asked and thus "not applicable")
- Level of Measurement for each variable

Subsample 1: DEMO.SAV

DEMO.SAV will be used and referred to primarily in the demonstrations in the body of the chapters. These examples are basically demonstrations that you can "follow along with" on your own computer. This subsample contains 1,500 cases and 41 variables drawn from the 2000 GSS. The items are arranged according to the following subject categories: Abortion, Children, Family, Politics, Religion, Social-Political Opinions, and Sexual Attitudes.

Subsample 2: EXER.SAV

EXER.SAV will be used primarily in the exercises at the end of the chapters. This file contains 1,500 cases and 47 variables drawn from the 2000 GSS. The 35 items below are arranged according to the following subject categories: Sex Roles, Police, Environment, Mass Media, National Government Spending Priorities, Teen Sex, Affirmative Action, and Equalization.

Conclusion

After reading this chapter and Appendix A, you should be familiar with the GSS and the two subsamples you will be working with. The data you will be using are real and can be taken as an accurate reflection of the attitudes, opinions, beliefs, characteristics, and behaviors of adult Americans in 2000.

In the next chapter we are going to get started using SPSS. Once you have learned how to launch an SPSS session and access the files contained on your CD-ROM, you will be ready to begin exploring your data. With the help of SPSS and some simple tools, we think you will find that the possibilities for discovery can be both rich and rewarding.

Main Points

- The GSS is a national survey of adult Americans that has been conducted more or less annually since 1972.
- The 2000 data are based on a sample of 2,817 adult Americans and can be taken as an accurate reflection of the opinions, attitudes, behaviors, and characteristics of all adult Americans (18 years of age or older, non-institutionalized, English-speaking) in 2000.
- The data were collected in face-to-face household interviews averaging approximately 90 minutes each.
- The CD-ROM included with this book contains two subsamples of data from the 2000 GSS named DEMO.SAV and EXER.SAV, respectively.
- DEMO.SAV is the file you will be using as you work your way through the chapters. EXER.SAV is referred to primarily in the exercises at the end of each chapter.
- To ensure that the files can be used with the Student, Graduate, and Professional versions of SPSS for Windows, we reduced the size of the subsamples; DEMO.SAV contains 1,500 cases and 41 variables, whereas EXER.SAV contains 1,500 cases and 47 variables.

Key Terms

General Social Survey (GSS)	DEMO.SAV
Abbreviated variable name	NA
National Opinion Research Center (NORC)	EXER.SAV
	NAP
Values (numeric values, numeric codes)	Sampling error
	DK
Multistage probability sampling	Missing data
Labels	

Review Questions

1. What is the GSS?

2. When was the data discussed in this chapter collected?

3. How were the 2,817 respondents were selected?

4. What is this method of sampling called?

5. If the data show that 55 percent of respondents favor capital punishment, what would be your best estimate in terms of the percentage(s) of adult Americans who feel this way as well?

6. Is it possible, based on this example, that as few as 10 to 15 percent of adult Americans favor capital punishment? Why or why not?

7. When social scientists refer to "sampling error," what are they referring to?

8. Would you agree that as a general rule, the smaller the sampling error, the less likely it is that the data are representative of the population?

Indicate whether the following statement is T (True) or F (False) (Questions 9-13):

9. Respondents to the 2000 GSS were interviewed on the telephone.

10. Each interview takes approximately one and a half hours.

11. When an interviewer forgets to ask a respondent a particular question, this is called "missing data."

12. The label "DK" is used when a respondent refuses to answer a question.

13. The label "NAP" is used when a respondent is not asked a particular question.

In order to answer Questions 14-17 you may want to consult Appendix A:

14. List three items from the DEMO.SAV file that deal with sexual attitudes.

15. List three items from the EXER.SAV file that deal with the environment.

16. Name one issue from your DEMO.SAV file that you are interested in exploring further.

17. Name one issue from your EXER.SAV file that you are interested in exploring further.

Chapter 5 Using SPSS

Like most data analysis programs, SPSS is capable of computing many different statistical procedures with different kinds of data. This makes SPSS a very powerful and useful tool, but because of its generalization, we need to specify what we want it to do for us.

In many ways, SPSS is a vehicle for discovering differences and relationships in data, the same way a car is a vehicle for discovering places we have not yet visited. The car does not know where we want to go or what we wish to see. We, rather than the car, plan the trip and set the direction. Similarly, when we use SPSS, we choose the data we wish to explore and select the statistical procedures we wish to use. Sitting at our computer keyboards, we are in SPSS's driver's seat.

We tell SPSS where to go and what to do in our social research adventure with SPSS commands. These commands instruct SPSS where to find our data, ways in which we want to modify the data, and the statistical procedures we want to use. While there are several ways to issue commands to SPSS, you usually rely on the mouse connected to your computer. By **moving your cursor** and **clicking** or **double-clicking** the **button on the left side of your mouse**, you will be able to tell SPSS what you want it to do.

Demonstration 5.1: Starting an SPSS Session

SPSS for Windows has probably already been installed for you by computer center personnel, lab assistants, or your instructor. You need to learn which of the machines available to you are equipped with the system. Your instructor will probably help you get started, but we think you will find it pretty simple.

Once you have run Windows, you will see a "desktop" with several small graphics (called icons) representing programs. At this point you have several options.

Option 1

If, for instance, you see an *SPSS icon* similar to Screen 5.1 below, simply double-click on it. It will take SPSS a little while to respond, with the length of time depending on the kind of computer you are using. Don't become impatient and double click again, as that will launch a second instance of SPSS. Unlike earlier versions, multiple instances of SPSS 11.0 can run simultaneously. For now, we'll do better dealing with one SPSS session at a time.

Option 2

If you do not find the SPSS icon on the desktop, as shown in the screen above, don't panic. There are other ways of launching SPSS. A second option is to click the **Start** button in the lower left corner of your screen. Move the cursor up the list to **Programs**, and look for SPSS among the programs resident on your computer.

Programs ▶	QuickTime for Windows ▶	
Favorites ▶	Real ▶	
Documents ▶	Seagate ▶	
Settings ▶	SPSS for Windows ▶	SPSS Map Geodictionary Manager
Find ▶	StartUp ▶	SPSS Map Geoset Manager
	TextBridge Pro 9.0 ▶	SPSS 11.0 for Windows
	U.S. Geological Survey ▶	SPSS 11.0 Production Facility
	WordPerfect Office 2000 ▶	

When you find **SPSS For Windows**, highlight it and then click.[1]

If neither of these alternatives works, you can panic if you like. Better yet, try using one of the additional options outlined in Footnote 1 or ask your instructor for assistance.

After launching SPSS, you may see an SPSS for Windows *dialog box* asking "What would you like to do?"[2] For now, click on the **Cancel** button or the "**X**" (Close button) in the upper right hand corner, and this box will disappear. SPSS will finish loading and you should see something like what is shown in the following screen.

---

[1] A *third option* is to click the **Start** button and move your cursor up the list of **Documents**. At this point you should be able to see if DEMO.SAV, EXER.SAV, or a similar data set is listed as a recently used document. If so, **highlight** it and **click**. This will load both SPSS and the data file. A *fourth option* is to use the **My Computer** icon on your desktop to locate either SPSS or a recently used SPSS file such as DEMO.SAV or EXER.SAV. Once you have located either SPSS or a recently used file, **highlight** and **click** to load the file and/or program.

[2] If you do not see this dialog box, don't worry. It just means that someone using SPSS before you requested that this box NOT be displayed every time the program is opened.

After each new SPSS command is introduced, you will see a summary of the command in a box like the one below (SPSS Command 5.1). The box contains a brief description of the command, as well as a summary of how to accomplish the procedure. You will also find a list of new SPSS commands at the end of the chapter. In addition, CD-Appendix G contains a comprehensive list of all the SPSS commands introduced in the text.

SPSS Command 5.1: Starting an SPSS Session

Once you are in Windows you have two major options:

Option 1:

Double-click **SPSS icon**

Option 2:

Click **Start → Programs → SPSS for Windows**

Demonstration 5.2: Becoming Acquainted with the SPSS Data Editor

Once SPSS opens, you will notice that most of the screen is taken up by the SPSS *Data Editor*. You can find that name in the *title bar* on the top left-hand side of your screen.

The Data Editor displays the contents of the active file. However, because we haven't loaded any data yet, the screen is currently empty (thus the name "Untitled – SPSS Data Editor").

If you look to the bottom left-hand corner of the screen you will notice that there are two "tabs" representing the two primary components of the Data Editor: *Data View* and *Variable View*. Both screens contain important information about the data you are working with. The Data View screen is designed to hold raw data for analysis, while the Variable View screen contains information about that data.

We are going to examine each aspect of the Data Editor in turn, beginning with the Data View screen (Demonstrations 5.3-5.11).

Demonstration 5.3: Data View
Portion of the Data Editor – Menu Bar

The Data View screen is designed to hold data for analysis. If you wished, you could enter data directly into the screen now and analyze it. Instead, however, we are going to load the GSS data set into the screen in a moment.

Directly beneath the title bar is a set of menus called a *menu bar*, running from File on the left to Help on the right. You are going to become very familiar with these menus, because they are the control system or the primary means through which you will operate SPSS.

As a preview, click on the word **File** on the menu bar and a *drop down menu* will appear. Notice how some commands in the drop down menu appear black, whereas others are faint gray. Whenever you see a list like this, you can execute the black commands (by clicking on them), but the gray ones are not currently available to you. Right now, for example, you could Open a data set, but you can't Save it because there's nothing to be saved at this time.

You will also notice that some of the options in the drop down menu (i.e New, Open, Open Database, Recently Used Data, and Recently Used Files) are followed by a right pointing arrow. These are several additional commands which will appear on a sub-menu when the category is picked. If you hold your cursor over **Open** for a moment, you will notice that a sub-menu of options appears on the screen.

Now click on the word **File** again, and the list disappears. Do that to get rid of the File menu now, and we'll come back to it shortly.

Demonstration 5.4: Getting Help

At the far right-hand side of the menu bar you will see the SPSS Help menu, something that you may want to take note of in case you need to use it later. As you are now aware, SPSS is a powerful state-of-the-art statistical package that allows users to accomplish numerous tasks and procedures. While this textbook will introduce you to a variety of SPSS commands, options, and procedures, we cannot hope to cover all of the program's capabilities. If you find that you want to use SPSS to perform a procedure that is not covered in the text or if you have a question or problem that hasn't been addressed in the book, you may want to consult the Help feature. All you have to do is click on the word **Help** and a drop down menu containing several options will appear.

The first option available in the Help menu is Topics. Click on **Topics** to open the Help Topics: SPSS for Windows dialog box. This box gives you several options for getting assistance. The "**Contents**" tab, for example, is useful if you are looking for general information or are unsure of what index term to use to find what you're looking for. Now click on the "**Index**" tab found in the upper left-hand side of the dialog box. The index tab is organized in alphabetical order and provides a searchable index that makes it easy to find specific topics. To close The Help Topics dialog box, simply click on **Cancel** or the "**X**" (close button) in the upper right-hand corner.

Another Help feature that you may find useful is the online tutorial that gives a comprehensive overview of SPSS basics. You can access the tutorial by clicking **Help** and then selecting **Tutorial** in the drop down menu. You will have an opportunity to explore the tutorial in the exercises at the end of this chapter.

SPSS Command 5.2: Accessing the Help Menu

> Click **Help** → select the Help option you wish to access
> (i.e., Topics, Tutorial, etc. . . .)

These are just some of the Help features available. In addition to the Help menu, assistance is also available in other ways. We will mention some of these as we go on.

Demonstration 5.5: Tool Bar

In addition to the menu bar, a second common way to communicate with SPSS is through the use of the *tool bar*. The tool bar is the line of buttons or "tools" running from left to right directly below the menu bar. While you can use the menu bar and drop down menus to perform most tasks, sometimes it is easier to just click a button on the tool bar.

You can find out what tasks each button on the tool bar performs by placing your cursor on the button and waiting a moment until a brief description of the tool pops up on the screen. For instance, if you place your cursor on the button toward the left end of the toolbar that contains a picture of a disk, you will soon see the words "Save File" pop up on the screen. This, of course, lets us know that we can use this tool to save a file.

If you want to take a moment to explore what other tools are available on the tool bar, you can do that now. Otherwise we will move ahead.

Demonstration 5.6: Dialog Boxes

Often when you click on one of the tool bars or choose an option from the menu bar, SPSS responds by opening a dialog box. Recall a few moments ago when you clicked on Help and chose Topics from the drop down menu, SPSS responded by opening the Help Topics: SPSS for Windows dialog box. Similarly, if you **click** on the **Open File** tool on the far left-hand side of your tool bar (the tool depicting a partially opened file), SPSS responds by displaying the Open File dialog box.

Dialog boxes, such as Open File and Help Topics, are important because they tell you what else SPSS needs to know in order to fulfill your command. In short, they serve as a collection of prompts or hints indicating what other information is necessary in order for SPSS to comply with your command.

Recall earlier when we said that there are other ways to get assistance beyond using the Help option on the menu bar. One of the primary ways in which to access assistance on SPSS is through dialog boxes. There are three primary ways to get help once you have opened a dialog box.

The first option is to **right click** on **any control** in the dialog box to display a description of the option and directions for its use. The second option is to click on the **Help** push button. Most dialog boxes contain a Help button that takes you directly to the Help Topic for that particular dialog box. This Help Topic will provide you with general information and links to related issues. A third option is to click on the small **question mark** in the upper right-hand corner of the dialog box, then **move your cursor** to the **command or control you need help with** and click.

After a moment, information regarding that command and directions for its use will be displayed on your screen.

SPSS Command 5.3: Getting Help in a Dialog Box

> *Option 1*:
>
> **Right click** on any control/command
>
> *Option 2*:
>
> Click on **Help** push button
>
> *Option 3*:
>
> Click on **question mark** (**?**) in upper right hand corner -> click on **command/control need help with**

Demonstration 5.7: Scroll Bars – Moving Through the Data Editor

So far we have introduced you to three important bars, the title, menu, and tool bars. Before we move ahead we want to mention one last set of bars which will make it easier for you to move through the Data Editor: the scroll bars.

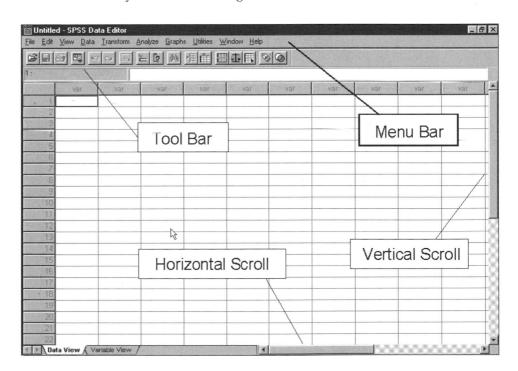

The horizontal scroll bar situated across the bottom right side of your screen allows you to move from left to right, while the vertical bar located on the far right side of your screen allows you to move up and down.

In addition to using the scroll bars, you can also use your cursor or the arrow keys on the keyboard to move through the data screen. If you take a moment to experiment with these options, you may notice that you can move the *active cell* (the cell in the screen with the thick black lines around it). Once a cell has been designated as the active cell you can go ahead and enter data in it (or if data already exists, modify it), something which we are going to focus on in the next demonstration.

SPSS Command 5.4: Moving Through the Data Screen

Option 1:

Use horizontal and/or vertical scroll bars

Option 2:

Use cursor → click

Option 3:

Use arrow keys on key pad

Demonstration 5.8: Entering Data—A Preview

Take a moment now to designate the cell in the far upper left-hand corner as the active cell. Once you have done that, you are ready to begin entering data for analysis. In fact, if you decide to conduct your own survey later on, this is how you would enter those data. As a quick preview of this feature, type a **1** and press the **Enter** key on your keyboard.

You have now created the world's smallest data set: with one piece of information about one person. The 1 on the left of the screen represents Person 1. If you entered another number as you did just above, you would have brought Person 2 into existence with one piece of information. Why don't you do that now—enter a **2** for that person.

The var00001 at the head of the column in the screen represents the specific information we are storing about each person. It might represent his or her gender, for example. Moreover, a value of 1.00 might mean male and a value of 2.00 might mean female. Therefore, we would have indicated that Person 1 is a man, Person 2 a woman.

This is the basic structure of the data sets analyzed by SPSS. The good news for you is that we've already prepared large data sets for your use, so you won't have to keep entering data like this. However, if you are interested in using SPSS to create your own data file, you may want to consult Chapter 21, which takes you through this process step-by-step.

Before loading our GSS data, we want to close the small data set that we just created. To do that, click **File**, followed by **New** and then **Data**. At this point SPSS will ask you if you want to "save the contents of data editor to Untitled?" which is just a fancy way of asking if you want to save the "world's smallest data set" which we just created. Because we are not interested in saving this data set, click **No**. If we wanted to save the data, we would click **Yes** and follow the instructions in the dialog box.

Demonstration 5.9: Loading a Data Set

At this point you should once again be looking at an empty screen. But not for long, because we are finally ready to load one of the GSS data sets provided with this book. This is easily done in SPSS for Windows. Once you insert the CD that came with this book in the CD-ROM drive, you have two options. If you wish to use the menu bar, simply click **File,** and then from the drop down menu choose **Open**, and **Data**. If you want to use the tool bar, all you have to do is click on the **Open File** tool. Either way, SPSS will respond by displaying the Open File dialog box as shown below. This box will assist us in selecting the data set we want.

In order to access the DEMO.SAV file on your CD simply follow these instructions. Click on the **Look in** field and select the drive that contains your CD (usually it will be the **[D:]** drive). Next, double click on the **Documents** folder. Then make sure SPSS-format data files (.sav extension) are displayed in the **Files of type:** drop down list. If not, simply click on the down arrow and select the suffix for SPSS for Windows data files, **SPSS (*.sav)**. Now you should see names of the files on your CD. To select **DEMO.SAV** highlight it and double click or click the **Open** button in the lower right corner of the dialog box. In a few seconds, SPSS will display the GSS data in the Data View portion of the Data Editor.

SPSS Command 5.5: Opening a Data File

Option 1: Menu Bar

Click on **File → Open → Data →**

Option 2: Tool Bar

Click on **Open File tool →**

Once the Open File dialog box is displayed:

Click on the **Look in field:** → Select the **drive** that contains your CD → Double click on **Documents** folder → Click **down arrow** to choose **SPSS (*.sav)** from **Files of type:** drop down list → highlight the **name of the data file** → **double click** OR click **Open**

Demonstration 5.10: Raw Data in Data View – Respondents and Columns

Now you should be looking at the data in the DEMO.SAV file. This is the GSS data we will be using for the demonstrations in the body of each chapter. The information in the Data View portion of the Data Editor consists of variables and respondents or cases.

Each row (horizontal) represents a person or *respondent* to the survey (what is sometimes referred to as a *case*). Based on our discussion in Chapter 4, we already know the DEMO.SAV file has 1,500 rows representing each of the 1,500 respondents or cases. You may want to take a few minutes to scroll from the first case or respondent (row 1) to the last respondent (row 1500).

Each column (vertical) represents a variable, indicated by the abbreviated variable name in the column heading. This data set contains 41 variables or columns. If you scroll from left to right across the screen, you can see this file contains variables ranging from ID and ABANY to WORKHARD and XMOVIE.

You can get a brief description of each abbreviated variable name by placing your cursor on the variable name at the top of the columns and waiting for a moment until the description pops up on the screen. For instance, if you place the cursor on the variable name ATTEND, a brief description of the variable that reads "How often R [respondent] attends religious services" will magically appear on your screen.

Demonstration 5.11: Finding Variable Information – Values and Labels

Now turn your attention to respondent record number 1 and the variable MARITAL. Be careful not to confuse the *record numbers,* which run down the far left side of the screen, with the "ID" numbers (an actual variable, listed in the first column).

You will notice that respondent record number 1 has a 5 in the column for MARITAL. This variable reflects respondents' marital statuses (if you forgot that, simply place your cursor on the variable name at the head of the column and a brief description of the variable will appear on your screen). As you may recall from the list of variables in Appendix A, a 5 (the *numeric value* or *code*) on MARITAL means the respondent has never been married (the *value label*). If you didn't recall this, don't worry. There are several ways you can use SPSS to access the information.

Option 1: Variables Dialog Box

One option is to click on the **Utilities** menu and select **Variables**. Alternatively, you can click on the **Variables icon** on the tool bar (the one with the question mark on it). Either way, SPSS will respond by opening the Variables dialog box as shown below.

As you can see, the Variables box has two main parts. On the left is a list of the variables contained in our data set. On the right side is some information about the highlighted variable ID.

Now click on the variable **ABANY** in the list on the left side of the box. Notice how information about the highlighted variable ABANY is displayed on the right side of the dialog box, including the information we are looking for: numeric values and value labels. This box tells us that for the variable ABANY, a "1" (value) means "yes" (label), a "2" (value) means "no" (label), and so on.

Consequently, if you didn't recall what a value of "5" on MARITAL means, you can easily access the information by scrolling down through the list of variables until you see MARITAL.[3] Now click on **MARITAL**, and this is what you should see.

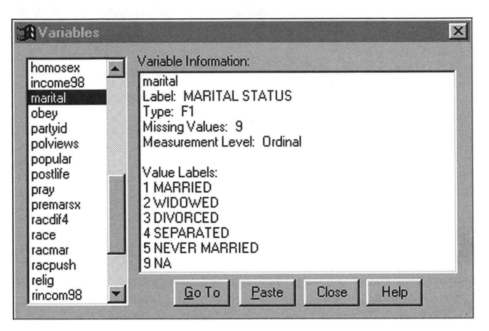

The box on the right side tells us that anyone with a code of 1 is married, anyone with a 2 is widowed, and so forth. You might want to take a minute to explore some of the other variables in the data set, because it will be useful for you to be familiar with them later on.

SPSS Command 5.6 (1): Finding Information on Variables

Option 1: Variables Box

Click **Utilities** → **Variables** → OR click on the **Variables icon** on the tool bar
highlight variable name in list on left side

---

[3] In addition to scrolling, there are several other ways to move through the list of variables on the left side. You can, for instance, click on the up and down arrows on the right-hand side of the variable list. You can also use the arrow keys on your keyboard or type the first letter of the variable's name. The highlight will then move to the first variable that begins with that letter in your data set.

When you get bored with the Variables box, there are a couple of ways to leave it. You can either click the **Close** button or the **"X."** Either will produce the same result.

Option 2: Toggling Between Numeric Values and Value Labels

Another way to find out what a numeric value (such as a "5" on MARITAL) means is to click on **View** in the menu bar. Then click on **Value Labels** in the drop down menu. This command tells SPSS to change the numeric values in the data screen into descriptive value labels. You will see, for instance, that the numeric value "5" under MARITAL for respondent 1 has been replaced by a descriptive value label indicating that the respondent has never been married.

	id	abany	abdefect	abhlth	abnomore	abpoor	abrape	absingle	age	attend
1	1	NO	YES	YES	NO	NO	YES	NO	26	ONCE A
2	2	NO	YES	NO	NO	NO	NO	NO	48	NRLY E
3	4	NAP	NAP	NAP	NAP	NAP	NAP	NAP	39	2-3X A
4	5	NAP	NAP	NAP	NAP	NAP	NAP	NAP	25	ONCE A
5	7	NO	YES	YES	NO	NO	YES	NO	36	SEVRL
6	8	NO	YES	YES	NO	NO	YES	NO	44	2-3X A
7	9	NAP	NAP	NAP	NAP	NAP	NAP	NAP	44	NRLY E
8	10	NAP	NAP	NAP	NAP	NAP	NAP	NAP	47	MORE T
9	11	NAP	NAP	NAP	NAP	NAP	NAP	NAP	53	EVERY
10	12	YES	YES	YES	YES	YES	YES	YES	52	NEVER
11	14	NO	YES	YES	DK	DK	YES	DK	51	NRLY E
12	18	NAP	NAP	NAP	NAP	NAP	NAP	NAP	44	NEVER
13	20	NO	YES	YES	NO	NO	YES	NO	45	DK,NA
14	21	NAP	NAP	NAP	NAP	NAP	NAP	NAP	48	2-3X A
15	23	NO	NO	NO	NO	NO	DK	NO	19	ONCE A
16	24	YES	YES	YES	YES	YES	YES	YES	54	EVERY
17	27	DK	NO	DK	DK	DK	DK	DK	89	LT ONC
18	28	NAP	NAP	NAP	NAP	NAP	NAP	NAP	88	EVERY
19	29	NAP	NAP	NAP	NAP	NAP	NAP	NAP	72	EVERY
20	31	NAP	NAP	NAP	NAP	NAP	NAP	NAP	89	NEVER
21	32	DK	YES	YES	DK	DK	NO	DK	34	NRLY E
22	33	NO	NO	YES	NO	NO	NO	NO	55	MORE T

To display numeric values in the data screen once again, all you have to do is click on **View**. You will now see a check mark next to Value Labels in the drop down menu. Click on **Value Labels** and the check mark will disappear. You should now see the numeric values in the data screen once again. This process of switching back and forth between numeric values and value labels is known as *toggling*.

SPSS Command 5.6 (2): Finding Information on Variables

Option 2: Toggling

Click **View** → **Value Labels**

Option 3: "Value Labels" Tool

A third way to discover what a numeric value refers to is to click on the button in the tool bar which looks like a price tag, the **Value Labels** tool (second from the right side of the tool bar). You will notice that the numeric values in the data screen have now magically changed into value labels. To change the value labels back into numeric values, all you have to do is click on the **Value Labels** tool once again.

SPSS Command 5.6 (3): Finding Information on Variables

> *Option 3:* Value Labels Tool
>
> Click **Value Labels** tool

Demonstration 5.12: Variable View Tab

A fourth way to determine value labels is through the Variable View portion of the Data Editor. So far we have focused primarily on the Data View screen, which contains the raw data for analysis. However, the Variable View tab also contains important information about the data in your file. In particular, Variable View contains descriptions of the attributes of each variable in your data file.

Click on the **Variable View** tab at the bottom left side of the screen. You will notice that in Variable View, rows represent variables. Take a moment and scroll from the first variable ID (row 1) to XMOVIE (row 41).

Unlike Data View, here each column is an attribute associated with the variables. The ten columns or attributes are listed below, followed by a brief description of their contents:

Name   Abbreviated variable name (i.e., ID, ABANY, ABDEFECT)

Type   Data type (numeric)

Width   Number of digits or characters

Decimals Number of decimal places

Labels   Variable labels or description of variable (i.e., respondent Identification; Abortion if woman wants it for any reason; strong chance of serious defect)

Values   Values and labels (i.e., ABANY – 0 = NAP, 1 = Yes, 2 = No, 8 = DK, 9 = NA)

Missing   Missing values (values designated as missing)

Columns   Column width (width of column in Data View)

Align   Alignment (alignment of data in Data View, either to right, left, or center)

Measure   Level of measurement (i.e., Nominal, Ordinal, Scale)

When in Variable View you can add or delete variables and modify the attributes of each variable. We will focus more specifically on how to modify attributes in Variable View later in the text.

For now it is enough that you are aware the Values column in the Variable View window is another way to find information about values and labels. Earlier, for instance, we were focusing on the variable MARITAL. In Variable View identify the cell corresponding with the variable MARITAL (row) and the column Values. Now **double-click** in the **far right side of that cell** (intersection between MARITAL and Values) and the Value Labels dialog box will open. Once the dialog box opens you can see that the values and labels for the variable MARITAL are listed. To close the box, click **Close** or the "**X**" in the upper right hand corner.

SPSS Command 5.6 (4): Finding Information on Variables

Option 4: Variable View

In the Variable View portion of the Data Editor. . .

Click on **cell corresponding with the variable at question** (row) and **Value** (column)

Demonstration 5.13:
Windows Options – Minimizing and Reducing

Before concluding our introduction to SPSS, it is important to mention a couple of Windows options that you may find useful. Notice that there are three small buttons in the upper right corner of the screen. Click the **leftmost button**, the one with heavy underscore on it.

Notice that the window has disappeared! Not to worry. Look now at the task bar at the bottom of the screen and locate the button titled **DEMO.SAV**. Click it.

Aha! The window didn't exactly disappear; Windows says it was minimized. That's certainly not an overstatement. This feature will be very useful to you once you have several documents on the screen at once. The minimize option lets you move windows out of the way without actually closing them.

Now click the **middle button** and notice how the window shrinks. If you click on the **window's title bar and hold your mouse button down**, you can drag the window around the screen. Sometimes this is a useful alternative to minimizing a window. Click the **middle button** again, and the window once more fills the screen.

Demonstration 5.14: Ending Your SPSS Session

When you've finished for this session, you have a few options. First, you can use the last of the three windows options we just mentioned. To do so, simply click on the **"X" in the upper right hand corner**. If you click it now, SPSS will ask if you want to save the contents of the data editor. Because the data set is already saved, we can safely click the **No** button now. If you had entered your own data or changed the existing data set, you definitely would have wanted to save the data and the computer would have asked you to name the new data set.

You can also end your session by clicking **File** and then **Exit**. Before terminating your session, SPSS will ask if you want to save the file. Once again we can click **No** because we have not altered the data file.

SPSS Command 5.7: Ending Your SPSS Session

Option 1: Close Button

Click on "**X**" (Close button)

Option 2: File Menu

Click **File → Exit**

Conclusion

In this first encounter, you've learned how to launch SPSS for Windows, load a data set, and explore it. In the next chapter, we'll revisit some of the variables in the data set and see how SPSS lets us explore more deeply than we've done in this first incursion.

Main Points

- Because SPSS is generalized, we use SPSS commands to tell it what to specifically do.
- To issue commands to SPSS, you usually click or double-click on the button on the left side of your mouse.
- There are two main options for starting an SPSS session.
- The SPSS Data Editor is a screen designed to enter, display, and hold data for analysis.
- The two major components of the Data Editor are Data View and Variable View screens.
- The Data View screen contains the raw data on your file.
- Variable View contains descriptions of the attributes of each of the variables on your data file.
- The menu bar, drop down menus, tool bars, and dialog boxes are the primary means by which you operate SPSS for Windows.
- You can use SPSS to either enter data or load an existing data set, such as the data provided on the CD that came with this book.
- In Data View, rows represent respondents or cases, and columns represent variables.

- Once you have loaded your data set, you can explore the data and find out what values refer to by looking in the Variables box, toggling, using the Value Labels tool, or accessing the Values column in Variable View.
- In Variable View, each row is a variable and each column is an attribute associated with the variables.
- If you are using several documents at once, you may want to take advantage of Windows minimizing and reducing options.
- Once you finish your SPSS session, you can easily exit by selecting **File** and **Exit**. If you entered data or changed an existing data set, do not forget to save it.

Key Terms

SPSS icon
Tool bar
Respondent
Dialog box
Command push button
Case
Data Editor
Push button with ellipsis
Record Number
Title bar
Text box
Numeric value (value)

Data View
Check box
Code
Variable View
Radio button
Value label (label)
Menu bar
Scroll bars
Toggling
Drop down menu
Active cell

SPSS Commands Introduced in This Chapter

5.1   Starting an SPSS Session
5.2   Accessing the Help Menu
5.3   Getting Help in a Dialog Box
5.4   Moving Through the Data Screen
5.5   Opening a Data File
5.6   Finding Information on Variables
5.7   Ending Your SPSS Session

Review Questions

1. What are the two main sections (tabs) in the SPSS Data Editor?

2. What type of information does the Data View screen contain?

3. What type of information does Variable View screen contain?

4. In Data View, Rows represent _____ and Columns represent _____.

5. In Variable View, Rows represent _____ and Columns represent _____.

6. If a researcher has conducted a survey and wants to enter the raw data into SPSS, would she enter it into the Data View, Variable View, or Utilities View portion of the Data Editor?

7. If you have a question or problem, what is one of the features SPSS provides to offer you assistance?

8. If you don't recall what a value of a particular variable in your data set means, what three SPSS commands can you use to find this information?

9. What does "toggling" refer to?

10. If you are using several documents at once, what Windows features might you want to take advantage of?

11. If you use SPSS to enter your own data or change an existing data set, what one thing should you do before ending your SPSS session?

NAME _____

CLASS _____

INSTRUCTOR _____

DATE _____

To complete the following exercises, load the data file EXER.SAV (found on the CD that came with this book). You can find answers to selected Questions (1-8) in Appendix B.

1. What does the variable GRWTHARM measure (hint: in Data View, place cursor on column heading to determine descriptive variable label OR in Variable View, double click on cell corresponding with GRWTHARM and Label)?

2. Using the variable GRWTHARM, note the numeric value for each of the following respondents (listed by record number, the column on the far left side of the screen). Then open the Variables dialog box to determine the value label:

	Numeric Value	*Value Label*
Record #89		
Record #837		
Record #1243		

3. What does the variable GRNPRICE measure?

4. Using the variable GRNPRICE, note the numeric value for each of the following respondents (listed by record number). Then use the toggle command to determine the appropriate value label:

	Numeric Value	*Value Label*
Record #1		
Record #500		
Record #1500		

5. What does the variable GRNTAXES measure?

6. Using the variable GRNTAXES, note the numeric value for each of the following respondents (listed by record number). Then use the value labels tool to determine the appropriate value label:

	Numeric Value	Value Label
Record #11		
Record #902		
Record #1236		

7. What does the variable GRNSOL measure?

8. Using the variable GRNSOL, note the numeric value for each of the following respondents (listed by record number). Then access the Variable View tab, identify the cell which corresponds with GRNSOL and the Values column, and double-click to access the Value Labels dialog box. Use the Value Labels box to determine the appropriate value label.

	Numeric Value	Value Label
Record #7		
Record #389		
Record #495		

9. Select any variable from the EXER.SAV file that interests you (other than those we have worked with previously in this exercise). Then use SPSS to find the following variable information:
   a. What is the abbreviated variable name?_____
   b. What does the variable measure (i.e., variable label)?

   c. List the numeric values and value labels for the variable.
      Numeric Value   *Value Label*

   d. Choose three respondents and list how they responded to the variable/question item you chose (list case number, numeric value, and value label).

	Numeric Value	Value Label
Case #		
Case #		
Case #		

10. Access the SPSS Help feature Tutorial.
    Hint: Click **Help** → **Tutorial** → Click on the **Table of Contents** button/icon on bottom right side of the screen (icon that looks like a house).
    Once you have opened the Table of Contents, work your way through the following aspects → of the tutorial: **Introduction**; **Using the Help System**; and **Reading Data**.
    To exit or close the Tutorial, click on the "**X**" (Close button) OR **File** → **Close** OR
    To return to the Data Editor, click on the **EXER.SAV** button at the bottom of your screen.

Part III Univariate Analysis

We are going to begin our data analyses with some basic measurements of variables. In the body of the chapters, we are going to pay special attention to three concepts: religiosity, political orientations, and attitudes toward abortion. In the exercises at the end of each chapter, you will have a chance to explore other issues, such as sex roles, law enforcement, health, mass media, national government spending priorities, teen sex, affirmative action, and the environment. We've chosen these topics on the basis of general interest and the possibilities they hold for analysis.

In Part III, we are going to begin with univariate analysis, the analysis of one variable at a time. This is a basic act of measurement. In Chapter 6, for example, we are going to examine the different ways we might measure the religiosity of the respondents to the GSS, distinguishing the religious from the nonreligious and noting variations in between. In so doing, we are going to learn how to instruct SPSS to create frequency distributions, produce descriptive statistics, modify variables with recodes, and save and print our output.

In Chapter 7 we look at differences in political orientations and show you how to present your data in graphic form by reviewing commands for creating bar charts, pie charts, line graphs, and histograms.

In Chapter 8 we turn our attention from univariate to bivariate analysis, or the analysis of two variables at a time. Whereas the bulk of our discussion of bivariate analysis is reserved for Part IV, in Chapter 8 we give you a preview of sorts by showing you how you can use crosstabs to examine the structure of attitudes toward abortion.

In Chapter 9 we build on our discussion in the previous chapter by focusing on the way social researchers combine several responses into more sophisticated measures of the concepts under study. You'll learn a basic technique for doing that.

Finally, Chapter 10 suggests a number of other topics you might be interested in exploring: desired family size, child training attitudes, sexual behavior, and prejudice. We'll give you some guidance in applying the techniques we've focused on in the previous chapters to examine these topics. The major goals of this chapter are not only to review the SPSS techniques discussed in Chapters 6-9, but more importantly, to give you the opportunity to strike out on your own and experience some of the open-endedness of social research. The exercises at the end of this chapter are designed to assist you in the process of writing up your research results.

Chapter 6 Describing Your Data

Religiosity

In this chapter we are going to analyze data. Before we begin, we want to give you a shortcut for opening a frequently used data file and show you how to set SPSS's display options so what you see on your screen matches the screens in the text.

In order to begin, you'll need to launch SPSS as described earlier. If you have trouble recalling how to open the program, simply refer back to the discussion at the beginning of Chapter 5.

Demonstration 6.1: Opening a Frequently Used Data File

One shortcut when opening a frequently used file is to select **File** on the menu bar and then click **Recently Used Data** in the drop down menu. Since SPSS keeps track of files that have been used recently, you may see the **DEMO.SAV** file listed in the box. To access the file, click **DEMO.SAV**.[1]

If the DEMO.SAV file is not listed, don't worry. You can also open the file by following the instructions for opening a data file given in Chapter 5.

---

[1] If the "What would you like to do?" dialog box is displayed when you open SPSS, you can also access a recently used data file by clicking the **button** next to the SPSS icon labeled **Open an existing data file** (the last option displayed). If the **DEMO.SAV** file is listed, highlight it and click **OK**. If you prefer that this dialog box not be displayed every time you open SPSS, click the **Don't show this dialog in the future** option in the bottom left corner.

SPSS Command 6.1: Shortcut for Opening a Frequently Used Data File

Click **File** → Select **Recently Used Data** → Click on **File name**

Demonstration 6.2: Setting Options: Variable Lists and Output Labels

Before we begin analyzing data, we want to make a few changes in the way SPSS displays information. This will make it easier for us to tell SPSS what we want it to do when we start running frequencies.

To set options, simply click on **Edit** (located on the menu bar). Now choose **Options** and the Options window will open. You will see a series of tabs along the top of the box. Select **General** (if it is not already visible).

Toward the top of the box you will now see the Variable Lists option. In that box choose **Display names** and **Alphabetical**. Now click **OK** at the bottom of the window. You may get a warning telling you that "Changing any option in this group will reset all dialog box settings and all open dialog boxes will be closed." If so, click **OK** once again. This option tells SPSS to display abbreviated variable names alphabetically whenever it is listing variables.

SPSS Command 6.2: Setting Options - Displaying Abbreviated Variable Names Alphabetically

Click **Edit** → **Options** → **General** tab → **Display names**
→ **Alphabetical** → **OK** → **OK**

A second change we want to make deals with the way SPSS displays output (such as frequency distribution tables, charts, graphs, and so on). By following the commands listed below, you can ensure that SPSS will display both the value and label for each variable you select for analysis, as well as abbreviated variable names and variable labels. Simply choose **Edit** and **Options** once again. This time click on the **Output Labels** tab located along the top of the Options window.

At the bottom left-hand corner of this tab, under where it says Pivot Table Labeling, you will see two rectangles labeled "Variables in labels shown as:" and "Variable values in labels shown as:." Click on the **down arrow** next to the first rectangle ("Variables in labels shown as:") and choose the third option, **Names and Labels**. Now click on the **down arrow** next to the second rectangle ("Variable values in labels shown as:") and select **Values and Labels**, then click **OK**.

This ensures that when displaying output, both variable names and labels and value names and labels are shown. When we begin producing frequency distributions in the next section, you will see why access to all this information is helpful.

SPSS Command 6.3: Setting Options — Output Labels

Click **Edit** → **Options** → **Output Labels** tab → Click **down arrow** next to "Variables in labels shown as:" → **Names and Labels** → Click **down arrow** next to "Variable values in labels shown as:" → **Values and Labels** → **OK**

Demonstration 6.3: Frequency Distributions

Now that you have loaded the DEMO.SAV file and set SPSS's options, we are ready to begin looking at some aspects of religious behavior. We will do this by first asking SPSS to construct a *frequency distribution*. A frequency distribution is a numeric display of the number of times (frequency) and the relative percentage of times each value of a variable occurred in a given sample.

We instruct SPSS to run a frequency distribution by selecting **Analyze** from the menu bar and then choosing **Descriptive Statistics** and **Frequencies . . .** in the drop-down menus.

Once you've completed these steps, you should be looking at the following screen:

Four of the variables in this data set have to do with religiosity:

RELIG   respondent's religious preference

ATTEND   how often the respondent attends religious services

POSTLIFE   belief in life after death

PRAY   how often the respondent prays

Let's start by looking first at the distribution of religious preferences among the sample. This is easily accomplished as follows. First, use the **scroll bar** on the right-hand side of the list of variable names to move down until RELIG is visible. You may notice that it is fairly easy to find RELIG because the abbreviated variable names are being displayed in alphabetical order (as opposed to the variable labels which can be cumbersome to sift through). This is a result of our first task in this chapter, setting the options so SPSS shows abbreviated variables names alphabetically. Once you locate **RELIG**, highlight it, and click on the **arrow** to the right of the list. This will transfer the variable name to the field labeled "Variable(s):." Alternatively, you can also transfer a variable to the Variable(s): field by **double-clicking** on it.

If you transfer the wrong variable, don't worry. You can move the variable from the Variable(s): field back to the variable list, by **highlighting** it and clicking on the **left** pointing **arrow** or simply **double-clicking** on the **abbreviated variable name**.

Once **RELIG** has been successfully transferred to the Variable(s): field, you can display its values and labels by highlighting it and then clicking the **right button on your mouse**. From the drop down menu select **Variable Information** and then click on the **down arrow** on the right hand side of the box. You should now see a complete list of all the values and labels for this variable.

Once you have moved RELIG to the Variable(s): field, click **OK**. This will set SPSS off on its assigned task. Depending on the kind of computer you are using, this operation may take a few seconds to complete. Eventually, a new window called the *SPSS Viewer* will be brought to the front of the screen, and you should see the following:

If you don't see the entire table as shown above, don't worry. It's probably because of differences on our monitors. To see all the information, simply use the vertical scroll bar.

SPSS Command 6.4: Running Frequency Distributions

Click **Analyze** → **Descriptive Statistics** → **Frequencies**. . . . → Highlight the **abbreviated variable name** → Click on **arrow pointing right** (toward Variable field) OR **double-click variable name** → **OK**

The SPSS Viewer — Output

You should now be looking at the SPSS Viewer. After you run a procedure, such as a table, graph, or chart, the results are displayed in the Viewer. This window is divided into two main parts or "panes": the *Outline pane* (on the left) and the *Contents pane* (on the right). As its name suggests, the Outline pane contains an outline of all the information stored in the Viewer. This outline gives us a complete list of everything we have instructed SPSS to do in this session. This is useful because if you use SPSS for several hours to run a large amount of analysis, you can use this feature to navigate through your output. If, for instance, you want to find a specific table, all you have to do is select the name of the table in the Outline and wait a moment. The table will then appear in the Contents pane, that part of the Viewer where charts, tables, and other text output are displayed.

Navigating Through the Viewer

There are several ways to navigate through the SPSS Viewer. You can use your **vertical** and **horizontal scroll bars**, or you can use the **arrow keys** or **Page Up** and **Page Down keys** on your keyboard.

For easier navigation, simply click on an **item** in the Outline and your results will be displayed in the Contents pane.

SPSS Command 6.5: Navigating Through the SPSS Viewer

Option 1:

Use the **vertical** or **horizontal scroll bars**

Option 2:

Use the **arrow** or **page up** and **page down keys** on your keyboard

Option 3:

Click on **item** in the **Outline pane**

You can also change the width of the Outline, by **clicking** and **dragging** the **border** to the right of the pane (the border which separates the Outline and Contents panes). You may want to take a few moments to experiment with each of these options before we move ahead.

SPSS Command 6.6: Changing the Width of the Outline Pane

Click and **drag border** to right of Outline pane

Hiding and Displaying Results in the Viewer

There are several ways to hide a particular table or chart. You can simply **double-click** on its **book icon** in the Outline pane. Alternatively, you can **highlight the item** in the Outline pane, then from the menu bar choose **View** and **Hide**. To display it again, simply **highlight the item** in the Outline pane, and select **View** and then **Show** from the drop-down menu. Easier yet, you can **highlight the item** in the Outline, then click on the **closed book (Hide) icon** on the Outlining tool bar. To display it again, simply **highlight the item** and then click on the **open book (Show) icon** on the Outlining toolbar.

SPSS Command 6.7: Hiding and Displaying Results in the Viewer

Option 1:

Double-click on **book icon** in Outline pane

To display again – **Double-click** on **book icon**

Option 2:

Highlight item in Outline pane → Click **View** → **Hide**

To display again - **Highlight item** in Outline pane → Click **View** → **Show**

Option 3:

Highlight item → Click **closed book (Hide) icon**

To display again – **Highlight item** in Outline pane
→ Click **open book(Show) icon**

In addition, you can also hide all the results from a procedure by clicking on the **box with minus sign (–)** to the left of the procedure name in the Outline. Once you do this you will notice that the minus sign turns into a plus (+) sign. This not only hides the results in your Contents pane, but compresses the Outline itself. To display the results again, simply click on the **box** to the left of the procedure name with the **plus (+) sign**.

SPSS Command 6.8: Hiding and Displaying All Results From a Procedure

Click on **box** to left of procedure name in Outline with **minus sign** (–)

To display again – click on **box** with **plus (+) sign**

Don't forget, you can also hide the SPSS Viewer itself, by using the minimizing and reducing options discussed in Chapter 5. If you minimize the Viewer and then want to restore it, all you have to do is click on the **SPSS Output icon** in the task bar toward the bottom of your screen.

There are several more advanced ways of working with SPSS Output and using the SPSS Viewer.[2] You can, for instance, change the order in which output is displayed, delete results, change the formatting of text within a table, and so on. We are going to mention some of these more advanced options as we go along. In addition, SPSS Lab Exercise 6.1 gives you an opportunity to work through a part

---

[2] You may, for instance, want to experiment with SPSS's Zoom feature. Simply click on the **Print Preview icon** (the **magnifying glass**) on the left side of the Outline tool bar. Now you can choose to **Zoom In** or **Zoom Out**. Once you have activated the Zoom feature, your cursor will change into a magnifying glass, and you can click directly on the output you want to zoom in (or out) on. When you are done experimenting, select **Close** and you will be back in the Viewer. Although we do not recommend deleting at this point, you can also delete results in the Viewer by **clicking on an item** in the Outline or Contents pane and then pressing **delete**. Alternatively, you can **select an item** and then choose **Edit** and **delete** from the drop-down menu. To delete multiple items that are not adjacent to one another, press and hold down the **Control** key on your keyboard and then **click on each item**.

of the SPSS Tutorial that provides an overview of some of these more advanced options.

Reading Frequency Distributions[3]

Now that we are more familiar with the SPSS Viewer, let's take a few minutes to analyze the output for the variable RELIG, which is located in the Contents pane.

The small box titled Statistics tells us that of the 1,500 respondents in our subsample of the 2000 GSS, 1,499 gave valid answers to this question, whereas 1 respondent has been labeled as Missing. The larger box below marked RELIG RS RELIGIOUS PREFERENCE contains the data we were really looking for.

Let's go through this table piece by piece. As we requested when we changed the options earlier, the first line identifies the variable, presenting both its abbreviated variable name and label. Variable names are limited to eight characters and are the key to identifying variables in SPSS commands. Sometimes, it is possible to express the name of a variable clearly in eight or fewer characters (e.g., SEX, RACE), and sometimes the task requires some ingenuity (e.g., RINCOM98 for the respondent's annual income).[4]

The leftmost column in the table lists the numeric values and value labels (recall that we asked SPSS to display both when we changed the options, SPSS Command 6.3) of the several categories constituting the variable RELIG. These include (1) Protestant, (2) Catholic, (3) Jewish, (4) None, (5) Other, and so on. As we discussed in Chapter 5, the *numeric values* (sometimes called *numeric codes* or simply *values*) are the actual numbers used to code the data when they were entered. The *value labels* (*labels*) are short descriptions of the response categories; they remind us of the meaning of the numeric values or codes. As you'll see later on, you can change both kinds of labels if you want.

The column headed *Frequency* simply tells how many of the 1,500 respondents said they identified with the various religious groups. We see, for example, that the majority of 815 said they were Protestant, 365 said they were Catholic, and so forth. Note that in this context, None means that some respondents said they had no religious identification; it does not mean that they didn't answer. Near the bottom of the table, we see that only 1 person failed to answer the question.

The next column tells us what percentage of the whole sample each of the religious groups represents. Thus, 54.3 percent are Protestant, for example, calculated by dividing the 815 Protestants by the total sample, 1,500.

Usually, you will want to work with the *valid percentage*, presented in the next column. As you can see, this percentage is based on the elimination of those who gave no answer, so the first number here means that 54.4 percent of those giving an answer said they were Protestant.

The final column presents the *cumulative percentage*, adding the individual percentages of the previous column as you move down the list. Sometimes this will be useful to you. In this case, for example, you might note that 78.7 percent of those giving an answer were Christians, combining the Protestants and Catholics.

---

[3] If your frequency table looks different from the one shown in the book, it may be a result of the "Missing" values for the variable ATTEND. We ran this frequency distribution with the value 9 "missing." The procedures for defining missing values are outlined in SPSS Command 6.12.

[4] For a brief overview of the "Rules" regarding abbreviated variable names on SPSS, access SPSS's Help feature.

Demonstration 6.4: Frequency Distributions: Running Two or More Variables at One Time

Now that we've examined the method and logic of this procedure, let's use it more extensively. As you may have already figured out, SPSS doesn't limit us to one variable at a time. (If you tried that out on your own before we said you could, you get two points for being adventurous. Hey, this is supposed to be fun as well as useful.)

So, return to the Frequencies window with:

Analyze → Descriptive Statistics → Frequencies . . .

If you are doing this all in one session, you may find that **RELIG** is still in the Variable(s): field. If so, you have a few options. You can **double-click** on **RELIG** to move it back to the variable list. Alternatively, you can **highlight** it. Once you do that you will notice that the arrow between the two fields changes direction. By clicking on the **arrow** (which should now be pointing left), you can return RELIG to its original location. A third option is to simply click the **Reset** button. Choose whichever option appeals to you, and then take a moment to move the RELIG variable back to its original position.

Now, let's get the other religious variables. One at a time, highlight and transfer **ATTEND**, **POSTLIFE**, and **PRAY**.[5] When all three are in the Variables(s): field, click **OK**.

After a few seconds of cogitation, SPSS will present you with the Viewer window again. You should now be looking at the results of our latest analysis. Bear in mind that if you are doing this all in one session, the results of the last procedure we ran (a frequency distribution for RELIG) may still be listed in the Outline and displayed in the Contents pane directly above the current procedure. If so, just scroll down, until your screen looks like this:

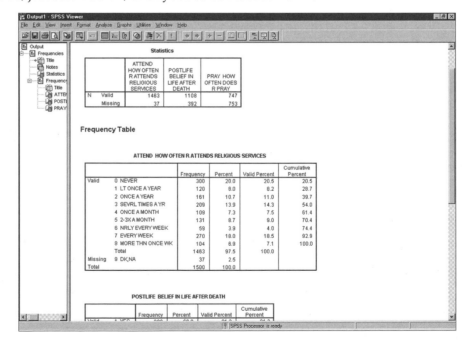

---

[5] For the variable ATTEND the value 9 should be labeled as "missing." For the variables PRAY and POSTLIFE the values 0, 8, and 9 should be labeled as "missing." The procedures for defining values as "missing" are outlined in SPSS Command 6.12.

SPSS Command 6.9: Running Frequency Distributions with Two or More Variables

Analyze → Descriptive Statistics → Frequencies . . . → Double-click on variable name OR **Highlight variable name →** click on **right pointing arrow → Repeat this step** until all variables have been transferred to the Variable(s): field **→ OK**

Take a few minutes to study the new table. The structure of the table is the same as the one we saw earlier for religious preference. This one presents the distribution of answers to the question concerning the frequency of attendance at religious services. Notice that the respondents were given several categories to choose from, ranging from *Never* to *More than once a week*. The final category combines those who answered ***Don't know*** (**DK**) with those who gave *No answer* (*NA*).

Notice that church attendance is an ordinal variable. The different frequencies of church attendance can be arranged in order, but the distances between categories vary. Had the questionnaire asked, How many times did you attend church last year? the resulting data would have constituted a ratio variable. The problem with that measurement strategy, however, is one of reliability: We couldn't bank on all the respondents recalling exactly how many times they had attended church.

The most common response in the distribution is Never. Just over one-fifth or 20.5 percent of respondents gave that answer. The most common answer is referred to as the ***mode***. This is followed very closely by 18.5 percent of the respondents who reported attending church every week.

If we combine the respondents who report attending religious services weekly with the category immediately below them, more than once a week, we might report that 25.6 percent of our sample reports attending religious services at least once a week. If we added those who report attending nearly every week, we see that approximately 29.6 percent attend church about weekly.

Combining adjacent values of a variable in this fashion is called ***collapsing categories***. It is commonly done when the number of categories is large and/or some of the values have relatively few cases. In this instance, we might collapse categories further, for example:

About weekly 30%

1-3 times a month 16%

Seldom 34%

Never 21%

Compare this abbreviated table with the original, and be sure you understand how this one was created. Notice that we have rounded off the percentages here, dropping the decimal points. As a result, you can see that the combined percentages are slightly more than 100 percent. Typically, data such as these do not warrant the precision implied in the use of decimal points, because the answers given are themselves approximations for many of the respondents. Later in this chapter, we'll show you how to tell SPSS to combine categories in this fashion. That will be especially important when we want to use those variables in more complex analyses.

Now let's look at the other two religious variables, beginning with POSTLIFE as shown below.

POSTLIFE BELIEF IN LIFE AFTER DEATH

		Frequency	Percent	Valid Percent	Cumulative Percent
Valid	1 YES	900	60.0	81.2	81.2
	2 NO	208	13.9	18.8	100.0
	Total	1108	73.9	100.0	
Missing	0 NAP	246	16.4		
	8 DK	134	8.9		
	9 NA	12	.8		
	Total	392	26.1		
Total		1500	100.0		

As you can see, there are significantly fewer categories making up this variable: Yes or No. Notice that 246 respondents are coded **NAP** (**not applicable**). This means that 246 people were not asked this question.

To collect data on a large number of topics, the GSS asks only subsets of the sample for some of the questions. Thus, you might be asked whether you believed in an afterlife but not asked your opinions on abortion. Someone else might be asked about abortion but not about the afterlife. Still other respondents would be asked about both.

Notice more than three out of four American adults believe in an afterlife. Is that higher or lower than you would have predicted? Part of the fun of analyses like these is the discovery of aspects of our society that you might not have known about. We'll have numerous opportunities for that throughout the remainder of the book.

Let's look at the final religious variable, PRAY, now.

PRAY HOW OFTEN DOES R PRAY

		Frequency	Percent	Valid Percent	Cumulative Percent
Valid	1 SEVERAL TIMES A DAY	211	14.1	28.2	28.2
	2 ONCE A DAY	216	14.4	28.9	57.2
	3 SEVERAL TIMES A WEEK	97	6.5	13.0	70.1
	4 ONCE A WEEK	53	3.5	7.1	77.2
	5 LT ONCE A WEEK	163	10.9	21.8	99.1
	6 NEVER	7	.5	.9	100.0
	Total	747	49.8	100.0	
Missing	0 NAP	746	49.7		
	8 DK	1	.1		
	9 NA	6	.4		
	Total	753	50.2		
Total		1500	100.0		

Writing Box 6.1

Once you've made an interesting discovery, you will undoubtedly want to share it with others. Often the people who read our research have difficulty interpreting tables, so it becomes necessary for us to present our findings in prose. A rule of thumb for writing research is to write it so it can be understood by reading either the tables or the prose alone. To aid you in this process, throughout the text we have incorporated "Writing Boxes" using a style appropriate for professional reports or journal articles. In this "Box," for instance, we present findings from the variables we just examined in prose.

Half the respondents in our study (54%) identify themselves as Protestants, while a quarter (24%) are Roman Catholics. Jews make up only 2 percent of the sample, and one in seven (14%) say they have no religious identification. The rest, as you can see, are spread thinly across a wide variety of other religious persuasions.

Religious identification is not the same as religious practice. For example, while 14 percent claimed no religious affiliation, half again as many (21%) say they never attend religious services. A third of the respondents (34%) attend several times a year or less, and 17 percent attend a few times a month. On the other hand, 30% attend about weekly.

Religious belief is another dimension of religiosity. In the study, respondents were asked whether they believed in a life after death. The vast majority—four out of five (81%)—said they did.

Finally, respondents were asked how often they prayed, if at all. Responses to this question are in striking contrast to earlier answers. Recall that 14 percent said they had no religious affiliation: 99 percent of the respondents say they pray at least now and then. Clearly, some respondents separate their spirituality from formal religious organizations. Over half of all respondents (57%) say they pray at least once every day.

This just about completes our introduction to frequency distributions. Now that you understand the logic of variables and the values that constitute them, and know how to examine them with SPSS, you may want to spend some time looking at other variables in the data set. You can see them by using the steps we've just gone through.

If you create a frequency distribution for AGE, you may notice the following. You will discover, for instance, that 0.2 percent of the sample is 18 years of age, 1.3 percent is 19, 1.4 percent is 20, and so forth. You may also notice that the table is not very useful for analysis. It is not only long (over 80 values) and cumbersome, but difficult to interpret. This is due primarily to the fact that AGE is presented here as a continuous, Interval/Ratio variable.

The Frequencies procedure we just reviewed is generally preferred when you are dealing with discrete variables. If you want to describe the distribution of a continuous variable, such as AGE, you will probably want to do one of two things.

One option is to use the descriptives procedure to display some basic summary statistics, such as common measures of central tendency and dispersion (we also use descriptive statistics when working with discrete variables as well). Alternatively, you might consider combining adjacent values of the variable (as we did with ATTEND previously) to decrease the number of categories and make the variable more manageable and conducive to a frequency distribution. When we collapse categories on SPSS it is called recoding.

We are going to consider each of these options in turn, beginning with basic measures of central tendency and dispersion.

Descriptive Statistics — Basic Measures of Central Tendency and Dispersion

While it is fairly easy to learn how to request basic statistics on SPSS, it is more difficult to learn which statistics are appropriate for variables of different types and at different levels of measurement. At your command SPSS will calculate statistics for variables even when the measure is inappropriate. If, for instance, you ask SPSS to calculate the mean of the variable SEX, it will dutifully comply and give you an answer of 1.57. Of course in this instance, the answer is meaningless because it would make no sense to report the "average" gender for the 2000 GSS as 1.57. What after all, does that mean? When it comes to a discrete, nominal variable, such as SEX, the mode not the mean, is the appropriate measure of central tendency.

Consequently, before running measures of central tendency and dispersion, we want to provide a brief overview of which measures are appropriate for variables of different types (Table 6.1) and at different levels of measurement (Table 6.2).[6]

Table 6.1   Basic Descriptive Statistics Appropriate for Different Types of Variables

	Measures of Central Tendency				Measures of Dispersion	
	Mode	Median	Mean	Range	Inter-quartile Range	Variance & Standard Deviation
Type of Variable						
Discrete	√	√				
Continuous		√	√	√	√	√

Table 6.2   Basic Descriptive Statistics Appropriate for Different Levels of Measurement

	Measures of Central Tendency				Measures of Dispersion	
	Mode	Median	Mean	Range	Inter-quartile Range	Variance & Standard Deviation
Level of Measurement						
Nominal	√					
Ordinal		√		√	√	
I/R	—	—	√	√	√	√

A check mark [√] indicates that the measure is generally considered both appropriate and useful, whereas a dash [—] indicates that the measure is permissible but

---

[6] In addition to the variables type and level of measurement, other issues may enter into the choice of particular statistics. Additional considerations which are beyond the scope of this text include (but are not limited to) your research objective and the shape of the distribution (i.e., symmetrical or skewed).

not generally considered very useful. For example, Table 6.2 shows that the mode is appropriate for variables at the nominal level, whereas the median, range, and perhaps the mode are appropriate for variables at the ordinal level, and every measure listed is generally appropriate for ratio and interval level data.

You are probably already familiar with the three *measures of central tendency* listed above. As we noted in the previous section, the *mode* refers to the most common value (answer or response) in a given distribution. The *median* is the middle category in a distribution, and the *mean* (which is sometimes imprecisely called the average) is the sum of the values of all the cases divided by the total number of cases.

You may already be familiar with some of the *measures of dispersion* as well. In this section we are going to focus on three: the range, interquartile range, and standard deviation. While variance is also listed in the tables, we'll save it for later in the text. The *range* indicates the distance separating the lowest and highest values in a distribution, whereas the *interquartile range* (*IQR*) is the difference between the upper quartile (Q3, 75%) and lower quartile (Q1, 25%) or the range of the middle 50% of the distribution. The *standard deviation* indicates the extent to which the values are clustered around the mean or spread away from it.

Demonstration 6.5:
The Frequencies Procedures

Several of SPSS's procedures produce descriptive statistics. To start, we are going to examine descriptive statistics options in the Frequencies procedure.

Open the Frequencies dialog box by choosing **Analyze → Descriptive Statistics → Frequencies . . .** Then select **Statistics . . .** in the lower portion of the dialog box. The Statistics box that appears allows us to instruct SPSS to calculate all the measures of central tendency and dispersion listed in Tables 6.1 and 6.2.[7]

The Frequencies procedure is generally preferred for discrete variables because in addition to calculating most basic statistics, it also presents you with a frequency distribution table (something which is not particularly useful for continuous variables).

To produce descriptive statistics using the Frequencies command, open the Frequencies dialog box. You know how to do this now. You've done it before. If there are any variables listed in the Variable window, click **Reset** to clear them. We will use a simple example to show you the commands and then you can practice on your own with other variables. Enter the variable **SEX**, then choose **Statistics** at the bottom of the window.

When the Statistics window opens you will see the measures of central tendency listed in the box in the upper right-hand corner and the measures of dispersion listed in the box in the lower left-hand corner. To select an option, simply click on the button next to the appropriate measure. For our simple example, all we have to do is click on the button next to **Mode** (upper right-hand corner). After you have made your selection(s), click **Continue**. You will now be back in the Frequencies box and you can select **OK**.

---

[7] To determine the Interquartile range, simply select **Quartiles**, then use your output to subtract Q1 from Q3 [**Q3-Q1** or Quartile 3- Quartile 1].

You should now see your output displayed in the Viewer. Remember, the output should include both the mode and frequencies for the variable SEX. By just looking at the frequencies you should be able to say quite easily what the mode (the most frequent response or value given) is for this variable. You can check to make sure you are right by comparing your answer with the one given by SPSS. By glancing through our output, we find that the mode in this instance is "2" because there are more females (numeric value 2) than males (numeric value 1) in our data set.

SPSS Command 6.10: The Frequencies Procedure—
Descriptive Statistics (Discrete Variables)

Click **Analyze → Descriptive Statistics → Frequencies . . . →** Highlight the **variable name** and click on the **right pointing arrow** OR **double-click** on the **variable name →** Select **Statistics . . . →** Choose statistics by clicking on the **button(s)** next to the appropriate measures → click **Continue → OK**

You may want to practice this command by choosing another discrete variable from the DEMO.SAV file, determining the appropriate measure(s) for the variable, and following the procedure listed above.

Demonstration 6.6: The Descriptives Procedure—
Calculating Descriptive Statistics for Continuous Variables

We can also instruct SPSS to calculate basic statistics using the descriptives procedure. This option is generally preferred when you are working with continuous, interval/ratio variables or when you do not want to run a frequency table. Bear in mind, the descriptives procedure allows you to run all the measures outlined in Tables 6.1 and 6.2 except mode, median, and interquartile range.

If you wanted to use SPSS to determine descriptive statistics for AGE, we could do that by clicking **Analyze** in the menu bar. Next, select **Descriptive Statistics** and then **Descriptives . . .** from the drop-down menus. You should now be looking at the Descriptives dialog box, as shown below:

To move **AGE** from the variable list on the left side to the Variable(s): box, either **double-click** on it or **highlight** it and click on the **arrow** between the two fields. Once you have done that, AGE will appear in the Variable(s): field. Now select **Options . . .** at the bottom of the window. This opens the Options window, which lets you specify what statistics you want SPSS to calculate.

The **Mean, Standard Deviation, Minimum**, and **Maximum** options may already be selected. If not, select those by pointing and clicking in the small box next to those options. You can also request **Range**, although in this case it is not necessary because it is just as easy to calculate the measure by hand. Now that you have specified which statistics you want SPSS to run, click **Continue** and then **OK** in the Descriptives box.

Descriptive Statistics

	N	Minimum	Maximum	Mean	Std. Deviation
AGE AGE OF RESPONDENT	1493	18	89	45.99	17.482
Valid N (listwise)	1493				

We can see that the mean age of respondents in this study is 45.99. As we already know, this was calculated by adding the individual ages and dividing that total by 1,493, the number of people who gave their ages.

Skipping a column, we see that the minimum age reported was 18 and the maximum was 89. The distance between these two values is the Range, in this case 71 years (89 - 18).[8]

The standard deviation tells us the extent to which the individual ages are clustered around the mean or spread out away from it. It also tells us how far we would need to go above and below the mean to include approximately two-thirds of all of the cases. In this instance, two-thirds of the 1,493 respondents have ages between 28.51 and 63.47: (45.99 − 17.48) and (45.99 + 17.48). Later, we'll discover other uses for the standard deviation.

SPSS Command 6.11: The Descriptives Procedure - Descriptive Statistics (Continuous Variables)

Click **Analyze → Descriptive Statistics → Descriptives** . . .

Highlight variable name and **double click** OR **click** on the **right pointing arrow** → Click **Options** . . . → Choose **statistic(s)** by clicking on the button next to the appropriate measure(s) → Click **Continue → OK**

You may want to practice using the Descriptives command by choosing other continuous variables and running appropriate statistics. If you run into any problems, simply review the steps outlined above.

Demonstration 6.7: Modifying Variables with Recode

At the end of our discussion of frequency distributions, we mentioned that frequency tables are not particularly useful when you are working with continuous

---

[8] For the variable AGE, the values 98 and 99 should be labeled as "missing." The procedures for defining values as missing are outlined in SPSS Command 6.12.

variables. As an alternative, we suggested you may want to use basic measures of central tendency and dispersion to describe a distribution.

A second option is to recode or collapse the categories of the variable. Those of you who have worked with frequency distributions may recognize that what we are doing is similar to the creation of a grouped frequency distribution. Only in this case, it is much easier because we have SPSS to assist in the process.

SPSS can be instructed to combine adjacent categories using the *Recode* command. *Recoding* is a technique that allows us to combine or group two or more categories of a variable together in order to simplify the process of analysis. When we recode, we can take a variable like ATTEND with nine valid categories and combine them to create four categories (or fewer). Recoding is a useful technique to master for several reasons. In addition to helping us create tables that are easier to read and identify patterns in responses, it also enables us to group continuous data into categories so we don't present our readers with an excessively long table.

Recoding takes several steps (outlined later in the chapter). While it may take a little time to get used to the process of recoding, if you follow along with the demonstrations below and then practice using the Lab Exercises, you should get the hang of it quickly. If you have trouble recalling the steps at first, don't worry, you will have plenty of other opportunities to practice recoding in later chapters and exercises.

To do a recode, you must be in the Data Editor. If you are still in the SPSS Viewer, you can switch back to the Data Editor by pointing and clicking on the button at the bottom of the screen which has your file name (**DEMO.SAV**).[9]

From the Data Editor, select **Transform,** and then from the drop down menu, click **Recode**. SPSS now asks if you want to replace the existing values of the variables with the new, recoded ones. Select **Into Different Variables . . .**, because we are going to assign a new name to the recoded variable.[10] SPSS now presents you with the following screen, in which to describe the recoding you want.

---

[9] Alternatively, you can select **Window** on the menu bar and then choose **DEMO.SAV** from the drop down menu.

[10] Because the Student Version of SPSS limits the number of variables that can be used to 50, you might want to save the recode under the same name. It's okay to do this if you save the modified data set later under a different name (e.g., DEMO1.SAV). That way, you can reopen one of the modified data sets or you can retrieve the original data in its unrecoded form.

In the variable list at left, find and select **ATTEND**. To transfer ATTEND to the Input Variable → Output Variable: field, either **double-click** on **ATTEND** or click on the **arrow** to the right of the variable list.

Notice that you need to tell SPSS what you would like to name the new, recoded variable. You can accomplish this easily in the section of the window called Output Variable.

Let's name the recoded variable CHATT (for CHurch ATTendance). Type **CHATT** into the space provided for the Output Variable Name and then label the variable (perhaps *Recoded Church Attendance*). When you are done, click the **Change** button. As you can see in the middle field, SPSS will now modify the entry to read ATTEND → CHATT.

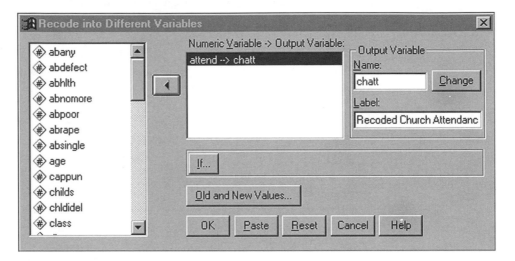

Thus far, we have created a new variable, but we haven't entered any data into it. We initiate this final step by clicking the **Old and New Values** button. Now SPSS presents you with the following window:

The left side of this window provides us with several options for specifying the old values we want to recode. The first, which SPSS has selected as a default, lets us specify a single value on the old variable such as 8 (More than once a week). A more efficient option, for our present purposes, is found farther down the list, letting us specify a range of values. (Remember, to find the numerical codes assigned to ATTEND, you can use one of the several options discussed in Chapter 5).

In our manual collapsing of categories on this variable earlier, you'll recall that we combined the values 6 (Nearly every week), 7 (Every week), and 8 (More than once a week). We can accomplish the same thing now by clicking the first **Range:** button and entering **6** and **8** in the two boxes.

At the top of the right side of the window, notice there is a space for you to enter the new value for this combination of responses. Let's recode it **1**. Enter that number in the box provided, as shown below:

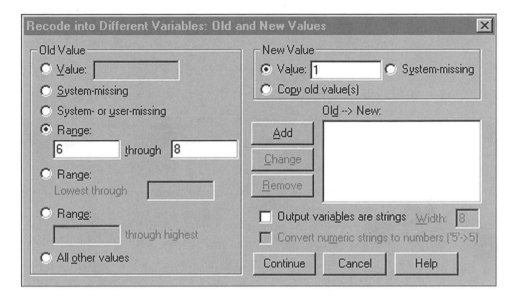

Once you've added the recode value, notice that the **Add** button just below it is activated. Where it was previously grayed out, it is now a clear black and available for use. Click it.

This action causes the expression 6 through 8 → 1 to appear in the field. We've given SPSS part of its instructions. Now let's continue.

Click **Range** again, and now, let's combine values **4** (Once a month) and **5** (Two to three times a month). Give this new combined category the value of **2**. Click **Add** to add it to the list of recodes.

Now combine categories **1** (Less than once a year), **2** (Once a year), and **3** (Several times a year). Recode the new category as **3** and **Add** it to the list.

Finally, let's recode 0 (Never) as **4**. On the left side of the window, use the **Value** button to accomplish this. Enter **0** there, and enter **4** as the new value. Click on **Add**.

To tidy up our recoding, we could have SPSS maintain the missing data values of the original variable. We would accomplish this by clicking **System-or user-missing** as an **old value** (on the left side) and **system-missing** as the **new value** (on the right side), and then clicking on **Add**.[11] Although it is a good practice to consciously recode every category, in this case it is not necessary. Any

---

[11] For a brief overview of the difference between "**System-or-user missing**" and "**System missing**," **right-click** on either **term** and after a moment a brief explanation will be displayed on your screen.

cases that were not covered by the range of the old values would be undefined and treated as missing values.

Your Recode window should now look like this:

As we wrap up, we should repeat that there are no hard-and-fast rules for choosing which categories to combine in a recoding process like this. There are, however, two rules-of-thumb to guide you: one logical, the other empirical.

First, there is sometimes a logical basis for choosing cutting points at which to divide the resulting categories. In recoding AGE, for example, it is often smart to make one break at 21 years (the traditional definition of adulthood) and another at 65 (the traditional age of retirement). In the case of church attendance, our first combined category observes the Christian norm of weekly church attendance.

The second guideline is based on the advantage of having sufficient numbers of cases in each of the combined categories, because a very small category will hamper subsequent analyses. Ideally, each of the combined categories would have roughly the same number of cases.

How do you suppose we'd continue the recoding process? Click **Continue**, you say? Hey, you may be a natural at this. Do that.

This takes you back to the Recode into Different Variables window. Now that you've completed your specification of the recoding of this variable, all that remains is to click **OK** at the bottom of the window. SPSS may take a few seconds now to accomplish the recoding you've specified.

Go to the Data View portion of the Data Editor window now. To see your new variable, scroll across the columns of the window until you discover CHATT in the last column used thus far.[12] Notice the values listed in the column. Case number 1 has a value of 2.00 on the new variable, Case number 2 has a value of 1.00, Case number 3 has a value of 2.00, and so on.

Now find ATTEND. Notice that Case number 1 has a 4 in ATTEND. That's correct because everyone with a 4 or 5 in the original variable was recoded as 2 in

---

[12] If you used the same variable name, look at ATTEND.

the new one. Similarly, notice that Case number 2 has a 6 in ATTEND. That too is correct because everyone with a 6, 7, or 8 in the original variable was recoded as a 1. You can check a few more people if you want to verify that the coding was accomplished as we instructed. This is a good idea, by the way, to ensure that you haven't made a mistake. (Presumably SPSS doesn't make mistakes.)

The next step in recoding is to define your new, recoded variable CHATT. We can do this by accessing the **Variable View** tab. Once you are in Variable View, scroll to the bottom of your screen until you see CHATT listed in the last row as shown below.

DEMO.SAV - SPSS Data Editor

File Edit View Data Transform Analyze Graphs Utilities Window Help

	Name	Type	Width	Decimals	Label	Values	Missing	Columns	Align	Measure
38	sibs	Numeric	2	0	NUMBER OF	{98, DK}...	98, 99	8	Right	Scale
39	thnkself	Numeric	1	0	TO THINK FO	{0, NAP}...	0, 8, 9	8	Right	Ordinal
40	workhard	Numeric	1	0	TO WORK HA	{0, NAP}...	0, 8, 9	8	Right	Ordinal
41	xmovie	Numeric	1	0	SEEN X-RATE	{0, NAP}...	0, 8, 9	8	Right	Ordinal
42	chatt	Numeric	8	2	Recoded Chur	None	None	8	Right	Scale

Remember that the Variable View tab stores important information about each of our variables. Since we just created the variable CHATT, we need to specify its characteristics.

Let's begin with the column labeled "Decimals." Simply **point** and **click** on the **cell** that corresponds with the column **Decimals** and the variable **CHATT**. Notice up and down arrows appear on the right side of the cell. Because decimal points are of no use to us in this situation, let's get rid of them by using the **down arrow** to change the number of decimal places to "**0**" as shown below.

	Name	Type	Width	Decimals	Label	Values	Missing	Columns	Align	Measure
40	workhard	Numeric	1	0	TO WORK HA	{0, NAP}...	0, 8, 9	8	Right	Ordinal
41	xmovie	Numeric	1	0	SEEN X-RATE	{0, NAP}...	0, 8, 9	8	Right	Ordinal
42	chatt	Numeric	8	0	Recoded Chur	None	None	8	Right	Scale

Now move to the column labeled "Width" directly to the left. To do that, click on the **cell** that corresponds with the column **"Width"** and the row **"CHATT."** Because our recoded variable contains codes that range from 1 to 4, the Width need only be set at 1. Again, use the **down arrow** to change the width to **1**.

Recall that when we began the process of recoding, we not only named our new variable CHATT, but we labeled it "Recoded Church Attendance" (in the "Recode Into Different Variables" dialog box). Consequently, you do not have to change any of the information in the "Label" column for the variable CHATT. However, if you want to view the entire label or if you want to change the label, simply double-click on the cell that corresponds with the column "Label" and the row "CHATT." You will notice that the width of the cell increases so you can better view the entire label and, if you desire, modify the variable label.

The next column "Values" is important because it allows us to store labels for the values of our new variable. To do this, simply click on the right side of the **cell** that corresponds with the column "**Values**" and the variable "**CHATT**." You will notice that the "Value Labels" box appears on the screen as shown below.

To add in the values and labels for our new variable, simply type **1** in the Value: box. Recall that this value represents people who originally scored 6 (Nearly every week), 7 (Every week), and 8 (More than once a week). Let's call this new, combined category "**About Weekly.**" Type that description in the Value Label: box and click **Add.** You can see that the information now appears in the field below telling us that "1 = About Weekly."

Now enter the remaining value labels as indicated below. Once you have entered all the value and label information (and your screen looks like ours below), click **OK**.

If you accidentally add the wrong information, don't worry. You can delete the information by **highlighting** it and clicking **Remove** as shown below.

The last bit of information of concern to us at this point is the variable's level of measurement. We can easily select the appropriate level of measurement by clicking on the **cell** that corresponds with the column "**Measure**" (the last column on the far right side of your Variable View tab) and the row "**CHATT**." Notice that once you point and click on that cell, three options appear representing each of the levels of measurement: Nominal, Ordinal, and Scale (Interval/Ratio). Use the down arrow and your mouse to select the appropriate level of measurement (in this case "Ordinal").

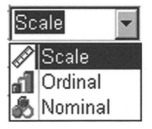

Now that we have used the Variable View tab to define our variable, let's review the results of our recoding process. We can do this most easily through the use of the now familiar Frequencies command. If you need help recalling how to run a Frequency Distribution, simply refer back to SPSS Command 6.4.

Once you have accessed the Frequencies dialog box, scroll down the variable list. You'll see that CHATT is now included in the list (in alphabetical order).

Once you have found CHATT, go ahead and run a frequency distribution for the variable CHATT. Your table should be similar to the one shown in the screen below.

Statistics

CHATT Recoded Church Attendance

N	Valid	1463
	Missing	37

CHATT Recoded Church Attendance

		Frequency	Percent	Valid Percent	Cumulative Percent
Valid	1 About weekly	433	28.9	29.6	29.6
	2 About monthly	240	16.0	16.4	46.0
	3 Seldom	490	32.7	33.5	79.5
	4 Never	300	20.0	20.5	100.0
	Total	1463	97.5	100.0	
Missing	System	37	2.5		
Total		1500	100.0		

Notice how much more manageable the recoded variable is. Now we can use the recoded variable in our later analyses.

Summary of Steps Involved in Recoding

Step 1: Preparing to Recode a Variable

■ Identify which variable you want to recode [i.e., ATTEND]
■ Run a frequency distribution for the variable you want to recode to see its current coding [as we did with ATTEND, Demonstration 6.4]
■ Figure out which values you want to combine to create the new variable [as we did with ATTEND, Demonstration 6.4] Keep in mind the loose guidelines for recoding discussed earlier. You should also consider the level of measurement for your new recoded variable because it will impact the type of statistical analyses you can perform.

Many of us find it helpful to make a list of the old values and new values with their labels before we start the recoding process. Here's what we did for ATTEND.

OLD VARIABLE ATTEND		NEW VARIABLE CHATT	
Value	Label	Value	Label
0	Never	4	Never
1	Less Than Once a Year		
2	Once a Year	3	Seldom
3	Several Times a Year		
4	Once a Month		
5	2-3 Times a Month	2	About Monthly
6	Nearly Every Week		
7	Every Week	1	About Weekly
8	More Than Once a Week		

■ Decide on a name and label for your new (recoded) variable [i.e, CHATT for CHurch ATTendance, Recoded Church Attendance]

Step 2: Recoding

■ Use the SPSS Recode Command to create your new variable [i.e. Transform Recode → Into Different Variables . . . → . . .]

Step 3: Checking Your Recode in the Data Editor

■ Check your new variable in the Data View portion of the Data Editor to make sure your recoding was correct.

Step 4: Defining Your Variable

■ Define your new variable using the Variable View tab [i.e., Decimals, Width, Label, Values, Measure . . .]

Step 5: Running a Frequency Distribution

■ Run a frequency distribution for your new variable to ensure the recoding was done correctly

Demonstration 6.8: Recoding AGE

The value of recoding is especially evident in the case of continuous interval/ratio variables such as age and education. Because these types of variables have so many categories, they are totally unmanageable in some forms of analysis. Fortunately, we can recode scale variables as easily as we just recoded ATTEND.

Why don't we go ahead and recode the variable AGE because in addition to giving us more practice with recoding, it will also allow us to take advantage of an additional feature in the recoding process.

If you follow the steps listed above, you will note that in accordance with Step 1, we have already identified the variable we want to recode (AGE).

Now take a moment to run a frequency distribution for this variable so you can see the categories we want to combine. Feel free to look back at the instructions given earlier in the chapter if you have any problem recalling how to run a Frequency Distribution.

In this case, we want to collapse this multitude of categories into four more manageable categories as follows:

OLD VARIABLE AGE	NEW VARIABLE	
Values	VALUES	LABELS
18-20	1	Under 21
21-39	2	21-39
40-64	3	40-64
65-89	4	65 and older

Note in this instance, the oldest respondent to the 2000 GSS was 89 years old. A value of "99" in this case refers to "NA" or people who did not answer the question, rather than the age of respondents.

In this case, the value of "99" for the variable AGE should be labeled as "Missing." If 99 is not labeled as "Missing" this is easily accomplished by accessing the **Variable View tab** and the clicking on the **cell** that corresponds with the column **"Missing"** and the variable **"AGE."** Once you have done that, the "Missing Values" box will open and you can select the "**Discrete missing values**" option, type "**99**" in the box below, and then click **OK**.

SPSS Command 6.12: Setting Values and Labels as Missing

Access **Variable View** tab → Click on **cell** that corresponds with column **Missing** and row containing appropriate **Variable** → In "Missing Values" box use one of several options available (i.e., **Discrete missing values . . .**) to insert appropriate missing values → **OK**

We will call our new, recoded variable AGECAT (to represent AGE CATegories) and label the variable "Recoded AGE."

Now we are ready to use the Recode command to create our new variable. To do that, simply select **Transform** → **Recode** → **Into Different Variables ...** again. Notice that the Recode into Different Variables ... window still has our recoding of ATTEND. Clear the boards by clicking **Reset** at the bottom of the window.

Then, select **AGE** and move it to the Input Variable window. Name the new variable **AGECAT,** add the **variable label,** and click **Change**. Now you can select **Old and New Values ...** to tell SPSS how to recode.

In recoding AGE, we want to make use of Range again, but for our first recode, check the second range option: the one that specifies **Range: lowest through** _____. This will ensure that our youngest category will include the youngest respondents. Enter 20 in the box, specify the new value as **1**, and click on **Add**.

You may also want to take advantage of the other Range option, **Range:** _____ **through highest**. When you do this, however, beware! Although the Range: lowest and highest specifications are handy, they must be used with care. If we hadn't run a frequency distribution for AGE and checked on our missing values, we could easily specify "65 through highest" as the range and not notice that in this case 99 refers to NA. As a result we may run the risk of including 7 people who didn't specify their ages as 60 years and older.

Now do what you have to do to create the remaining recode instructions indicated below.

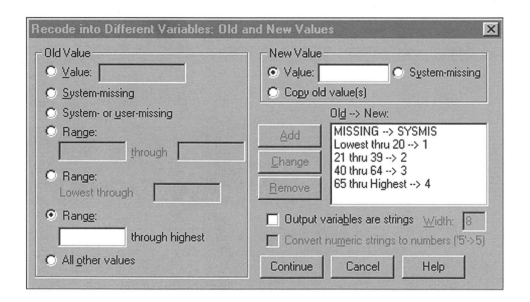

Click **Continue** to return to the main Recode window and then **OK** to make the recoding changes.

Now go to the Data View portion of the Data Editor and you should see your new, recoded variable, AGECAT, in the rightmost column. Check it out.

To complete the recode process, follow Steps 3 and 4. Check your new variable AGECAT against the old variable AGE in Data View and then define AGECAT in Variable View.

When defining your variable, remember to set your **Decimals** to "**0**," and your **Width** to "**1**." Then list the **values and labels** for your recoded variable AGECAT and select the appropriate **level of measurement** (in this case **Ordinal**) as shown below.

Once you've completed the recoding and labeling, check the results of your labors by following Step 5 and running a frequency distribution for your new variable AGECAT. Notice that CHATT may still be in the list of variables to be analyzed. You can place CHATT back in the list of abbreviated variable names by using one of the methods we discussed previously (clicking **Reset, double-clicking CHATT,** or highlighting **CHATT** and selecting the **left-pointing arrow**). If you fail to do this, SPSS will simply calculate and report the frequencies on CHATT again.

Statistics

AGECAT Recoded Age

N	Valid	1493
	Missing	7

AGECAT Recoded Age

		Frequency	Percent	Valid Percent	Cumulative Percent
Valid	1 Under 21	44	2.9	2.9	2.9
	2 21 to 39	573	38.2	38.4	41.3
	3 40 to 64	619	41.3	41.5	82.8
	4 65 and older	257	17.1	17.2	100.0
	Total	1493	99.5	100.0	
Missing	System	7	.5		
Total		1500	100.0		

SPSS Command 6.13: Recoding a Variable

Click **Transform** → **Compute** → **Into Different Variables** . . . →

Highlight **name of variable** to be recoded → Click on **right pointing arrow** OR **double-click on variable name** →

In Output Variable field **name** and **label new variable** → Click **Change** →

Click **Old and New Values** . . . →

Choose option for specifying old values you want to recode (i.e. **Range**, etc . . .) → Enter **old value codes** → enter **new value recodes** → click **Add** → [Repeat this step until all old values are recoded] → Click **Continue** → **OK** →

To Define New, Recoded Variable:

Select **Variable View** tab → identify new, **recoded variable** in last row →

Click on **cells** corresponding with new, recoded variable and the following columns to change **Width, Decimals, Values,** and **Measure**

Demonstration 6.9: Printing Your Output – Viewer

If you would like to print the frequency table for your new, recoded variable AGECAT, you have several options.

First, make sure that the **SPSS Viewer** is the *active window* (i.e., it is the window displayed on your screen). From the menu choose **File** and then **Print**. You can control the items that are printed by selecting either **All visible output** (allows you to print only the items currently displayed in the Contents pane, as opposed to hidden items, for instance) or **Selection** (prints only items currently selected in the outline or contents panes). Then click **OK**.

If, for instance, you want to print only a selected item (such as the frequency distribution for AGECAT as opposed to the other frequencies we have run in this Chapter), you click **directly on the Table** or the **name of the table in the Outline**. Once you have done this, you can access the Print Preview option to preview what will be printed on each page.

To access Print Preview, simply select **File** and then **Print Preview** from the drop down menu. When you are ready to return to the SPSS Viewer, select **Close**. You can then click **File**, **Print**, **Selection,** and **OK** to print your output.

SPSS Command 6.14: Printing Your Output (Viewer)

Make sure **SPSS Viewer** is active window

To select only certain items to print:

Highlight item in Contents or Outline pane → Click **File** → **Print** → **Selection** → **OK**

To print all visible output:

File → **Print** → **All visible Output** → **OK**

SPSS Command 6.15: Print Preview

File → Print → Preview →

Demonstration 6.10:
Adding Header/Footer and Titles/Text

Headers and footers are the information printed at the top and bottom of the page. When you are in the SPSS Viewer and ready to print output, you may want to enter text as headers and footers. This is particularly useful for those of you working in a classroom or laboratory setting and using shared printers.

You can add headers and footers by selecting **File** and then **Page Setup** from the drop down menu. Now click on **Options . . .** and **add any information** you want in the Header and/or Footer fields (such as your name, the date, title for the table, etc . . .). Then click **OK** and **OK** once again to return to the SPSS Viewer.

You may want to use the Print Preview option discussed earlier to see how your headers and/or footers will look on the printed page.

SPSS Command 6.16: Adding Headers and Footers

Click **File** → **Page Setup** → **Options** . . . → Add information in
Header and/or Footer fields → **OK** → **OK**

In addition to adding headers and footers, you can also add text and titles to your output by clicking on the place in either the Outline or Contents pane where you wish to add the title/text. Now simply click on the "**Insert Title**" or "**Insert Text**" tools on the tool bar and SPSS will display an area for you to add your title or text.

After inserting your text or title, you may want to use the Print Preview option to see how your text/title will appear on the printed page.

SPSS Command 6.17: Adding Title/Text

Click on area in Contents or Outline pane where you wish
to add Title or Text → Click on **Insert Title** OR **Insert Text**
tools on the tool bar → Add text or titles

Demonstration 6.11: Saving Your Output (Viewer)

That's enough work for now. But before we stop, let's save the work we've done in this session so we won't have to repeat it all when we start up again.

The recoding you've done so far is being held only in the computer's volatile memory. That means that if you leave SPSS right now, all the recoding changes will disappear. Because we will want to use the recoded variables CHATT and AGECAT, there's a simple procedure that will save us time at our next session.

Before we save our recoded variables, however, we will go through the instructions for saving the output that you've been accumulating in the Viewer window during this session. If you are writing a term paper that will use these results, you can probably copy portions of the output and paste it into your word-processing document. To save the Output window, first make sure it is the window front most on your screen, then select **Save As** under the **File** menu or alternatively, choose the **Save File tool** on the tool bar. Either way, SPSS will present you with the following window:

In this example, we've decided to save our output on the Drive A diskette under the name Output1 (which SPSS thoughtfully provided as a default name). As an alternative, you might like to use a name like Out1022 to indicate it was the output saved on October 22, or use some similar naming convention. Either way, insert your disk and change the file name if necessary, choose the appropriate drive in the "Save In" field, and then click **Save**.

SPSS Command 6.18: Saving Your Output (Viewer)

> Make sure the SPSS Viewer/Output is the active window → Click
> **File Save As** → OR click on **Save File** tool → choose appropriate
> **drive** → **name your file** → click **Save**

Demonstration 6.12: Saving Changes to Your Data Set

Because we will want to refer back to the recoded variables we just created, let's go ahead and save the data file. DEMO.SAV (or any other file) cannot be saved on the CD-ROM that came with the text because it is "read only." If you are sharing a computer with other users, you should save DEMO.SAV on a removable diskette for safe keeping. If you are using your own personal computer, you can save your work on your computer's hard drive.

Keep in mind that whenever you save a file in SPSS (whether you are saving output or your data set), you are saving only what is visible in the active window. To save your data set you need to make sure the Data Editor is the active window. You can do that by either clicking on **DEMO.SAV** in the task bar or choosing **Window** in the menu bar and then selecting **DEMO.SAV** in the drop-down menu. Then, go to the **File** menu and select **Save As**. From the "Save in:" drop down menu at the top of the Save As window, select a **location** for your data to be saved, either the diskette drive (usually **A:**) or the hard drive (usually **C:**). Type the **name** for your file in the File Name window. Although you can choose any name you wish, in this case we will use **DEMOPLUS** to refer to the file that contains both our basic DEMO variables, PLUS our new, recoded variables. Then click on **Save**. Now all the variables, including your recodes CHATT and AGE-CAT, have been saved, and you can leave SPSS with the **File → Exit** command. If you open this file the next time you start an SPSS session, it will have all the new, recoded variables.

SPSS Command 6.19: Saving Changes Made to an Existing Data Set

> Make sure the Data Editor is the active window → Click **File → Save As →**
> Select **appropriate drive → name** your **file → Save**

Conclusion

We've now completed your first interaction with data. Even though this is barely the tip of the iceberg, you should have begun to get some sense of the possibilities that exist in a data set such as this. Many of the concepts with which social scientists deal are the subjects of opinions in everyday conversations. A data set such as the one you are using in this book is powerfully different from opinion. From time to time, you probably hear people make statements like these:

Almost no one goes to church anymore.

Americans are pretty conservative by and large.

Most people are opposed to abortion.

Sometimes, opinions like these are an accurate reflection of the state of affairs; sometimes, they are far from the truth. In ordinary conversation, the apparent validity of such assertions typically hinges on the force with which they are expressed and/or the purported wisdom of the speaker. Already in this book, you have discovered a better way of evaluating such assertions. In this chapter, you've learned some of the facts about religion in the United States today. The next few chapters take you into the realms of politics and attitudes toward abortion.

Main Points

- In this chapter we began our discussion of univariate analysis by focusing on three ways of examining the religiosity of respondents to the 2000 GSS: running frequency distributions, producing basic descriptive statistics, and recoding variables.
- Before embarking on our analysis, we reviewed a shortcut for opening a frequently used data file and learned to change the way SPSS displays information and output.
- The Frequencies command can be used to produce frequencies for one or more variables at a time.
- When we request tables, charts, or graphs on SPSS the results appear in the SPSS Viewer.
- There are two main parts or "panes" in the Viewer: Outline (on the left) and Contents (on the right).
- The Outline pane lists the results of our output for the entire session
- The Contents pane presents the results of our analyses.
- Frequency distributions are more appropriate for discrete, rather than continuous variables.
- When working with continuous variables, a better option for describing your distribution is to either produce descriptive statistics or to reduce the number of categories by recoding.
- Certain measures of central tendency and dispersion are appropriate for variables of different types and at different levels of measurement.
- There are several ways to run measures of central tendency and dispersion on SPSS. We reviewed two: the frequencies procedure and the descriptives procedure.
- Modifying variables on SPSS by combining adjacent categories is called recoding.
- Recoding is particularly useful when you are dealing with continuous variables or variables with many response categories.
- There are no "rules" for deciding which categories to combine when you are recoding. There are, however, two guidelines — one logical and the other empirical.
- When you are ready to end your SPSS session, you may want to save and/or print your output so you can use it later on.
- Before exiting SPSS, don't forget to save any changes you made to the existing data set.

Key Terms

Frequency distribution	Frequency column
Median	Measures of central tendency
SPSS Viewer	Valid percentage column
Mean	Measures of dispersion
Outline pane	Cumulative percentage column
Range	Collapsing categories
Contents pane	Don't Know (DK)
Interquartile Range (IQR)	recode
Numeric value, numeric code, value	No Answer (NA)
Standard deviation	active window
Value label, label	Not Applicable (NAP)
Variance	Mode

SPSS Commands Introduced in This Chapter

6.1   Shortcut for Opening a Frequently Used Data File

6.2   Setting Options—Displaying Abbreviated Variable Names Alphabetically

6.3   Setting Options—Output Labels

6.4   Running Frequency Distributions

6.5   Navigating Through the SPSS Viewer

6.6   Changing the Width of the Outline Pane

6.7   Hiding and Displaying Results in the Viewer

6.8   Hiding and Displaying All Results From a Procedure

6.9   Running Frequency Distributions with Two or More Variables

6.10 The Frequencies Procedure – Descriptive Statistics (Discrete Variables)

6.11 The Descriptives Procedure – Descriptive Statistics (Continuous Variables)

6.12 Setting Values and Labels as Missing

6.13 Recoding a Variable

6.14 Printing Output (Viewer)

6.15 Print Preview

6.16 Adding Headers and Footers

6.17 Adding Title/Text

6.18 Saving Your Output (Viewer)

6.19 Saving Changes Made to an Existing Data Set

Review Questions

1. Analysis of one variable at a time is often referred to as what type of analysis?

2. What are the two parts of the SPSS Viewer called?

3. What is a frequency distribution?

4. In a frequency distribution, what information does the column labeled "frequency" contain?

5. In a frequency distribution, what information does the column labeled "valid percent" contain?

6. Is a frequency distribution generally preferred for continuous or discrete variables? Why?

7. List the measures of central tendency and dispersion that are appropriate for variables at each of the following levels of measurement:
    A. Ordinal —
    B. Nominal —
    C. Interval/Ratio —

8. List the measures of central tendency and dispersion that are appropriate for each of the following types of variables:
   A. Discrete —
   B. Continuous —

9. Calculate the mode, median, mean, and range for the following distribution: 7, 5, 2, 4, 4, 0, 1, 9, 6

10. If Q1 (Quartile 1) = 25 and Q3 (Quartile 3) = 40, what is the Interquartile range (IQR) for the distribution?

11. Is the standard deviation a measure of central tendency or dispersion?

12. In general terms, what information does the standard deviation tell us?

13. Describe the two general guidelines you might want to keep in mind when you are deciding how to combine adjacent categories for recoding.

14. If you were going to recode the variable POLVIEWS, which measures political orientations ranging from very liberal to very conservative, how might you collapse (or combine) the following categories?
    1. Extremely liberal
    2. Liberal
    3. Slightly liberal
    4. Moderate, middle-of-the-road
    5. Slightly conservative
    6. Conservative
    7. Extremely conservative

15. After recoding a variable and going back to the Data Editor window, we recommend that you access the Variable View tab because it allows you to accomplish what specific task(s)?

16. After recoding, which SPSS procedure gives you the best way to check your new recoded variable?

17. Explain why, for certain GSS variables, half or more of the responses may be labeled "missing."

18. In order to save or print Output, which SPSS window should be the "active window"?

19. In order to save your data file, which SPSS window should be the "active window"?

NAME _____

CLASS _____

INSTRUCTOR _____

DATE _____

To complete the following exercises, you need to open the EXER.SAV file. You can find answers to selected SPSS Lab 6.1 Exercises (#1-9, 13, 15, 17-18, 21-22) in Appendix B.

Produce and analyze frequency distributions and appropriate measures of central tendency for the variables RACE, HEALTH, and TEENSEX. Then use your output to answer Questions 1-6.

1. (RACE) The largest racial grouping of respondents to the 2000 GSS was _____, with _____%. The second largest grouping was _____, with _____%.

2. Which measure of central tendency is most appropriate to summarize the distribution of RACE and why? List the value of that measure in the space provided.

3. (HEALTH) _____% of respondents to the 2000 GSS reported that they are in good health. This was followed by _____% of respondents who reported being in excellent health. While approximately _____% of respondents reported being in either fair or poor health.[13]

4. Which measure of central tendency is most appropriate to summarize the distribution of HEALTH and why? List the value of that measure in the space provided.

_____
[13] For the variable HEALTH, values 0, 8, and 9 should be labeled as "missing."

5. (TEENSEX) Nearly _____% of respondents to the 2000 GSS believe that sex before marriage, particularly when it comes to teens 14-16 years of age, is either always wrong or almost always wrong. Only _____% think it is not wrong at all, whereas _____% think it is sometimes wrong.[14]

6. Which measure of central tendency is most appropriate to summarize the distribution of TEENSEX and why? List the value of that measure in the space provided.

Use the Descriptives procedure to examine the variables EDUC and TVHOURS. Then use your output to answer Questions 7 and 8.

7. (EDUC) The mean number of years of education of respondents to the 2000 GSS is _____, and two-thirds of respondents report having between _____ and _____ years of education.[15]

8. (TVHOURS) Respondents to the 2000 GSS report watching an "average" of _____ hours of television a day, with two-thirds of them watching between _____ and _____ hours of television per day.[16]

9. Are respondents to the 2000 GSS generally satisfied that the government is doing enough to halt the rising crime rate (NATCRIME) and deal with drug addiction (NATDRUG)?[17] (Hint: consider the type and level of measurement for each variable, before using either the Frequencies or Descriptives command to produce frequency tables and/or descriptive statistics.)

---

[14] For the variable TEENSEX, values 0, 8, and 9 should be defined as "missing."

[15] For the variable EDUC, values 97, 98, and 99 should be labeled as "missing."

[16] For the variable TVHOURS, values –1, 98, and 99 should be labeled as "missing."

[17] For the variables NATCRIME and NATDRUG, values 0, 8, and 9 should be labeled as "missing."

NAME _____

CLASS _____

INSTRUCTOR _____

DATE _____

Choose three variables from the EXER.SAV file you are interested in. Then based on the variable's type and level of measurement, use either the decriptives or frequencies command to produce a frequency table and/or appropriate descriptive statistics. Describe your findings in the space provided (Questions 10-12).

10. Abbreviated Variable Name _____

Written Analysis:

11. Abbreviated Variable Name _____

Written Analysis:

12. Abbreviated Variable Name _____

Written Analysis:

13. What does the variable GRNTAXES measure (hint: check the variable label)?

14. Produce and write an analysis of the frequency distribution for the variable GRNTAXES.[18]

15. Now follow these steps to recode the variable GRNTAXES.

*Recode the variable GRNTAXES to create a new variable RECGRNT (recoded GRNTAXES) as follows:

OLD VARIABLE GRNTAXES		NEW VARIABLE RECGRNT	
Values	Labels	Values	Labels
1	Very Willing	1	Willing
2	Fairly Willing		
3	Neither Willing/ Unwilling	2	Neither
4	Not Very Willing	3	Unwilling
5	Not at All Willing		

*Use the Recode command to create your new, recoded variable RECGRNT.

*Define your new variable.

*Run a frequency distribution for the variable RECGRNT, then list the valid percentages for each category below.

Valid Percent

1 Willing _____

2 Neither _____

3 Unwilling _____

[18] For the variable GRNTAXES, the values 0, 8, and 9 should be labeled as "missing."

NAME _____

CLASS _____

INSTRUCTOR _____

DATE _____

16. Now write a brief analysis of your table below:

17. What does the variable NEWS measure (hint: check the variable label)?

18. Now follow these steps to recode the variable NEWS. [19]

*Recode the variable NEWS to create a new variable RECNEWS (recoded NEWS) as follows:

OLD VARIABLE NEWS Values	Labels	NEW VARIABLE RECNEWS Values	Labels
1	Everyday	1	Once a Week or More
2	Few Times a Week		
3	Once a Week		
4	Less Than Once a Week	2	Less Than Once a Week
5	Never	3	Never

---

[19] For the variable NEWS, values 0, 8, and 9 should be labeled as "missing."

*Use the Recode command to create your new, recoded variable RECNEWS.

*Define your new variable.

*Run a frequency distribution for the variable RECNEWS, then list the valid percentages for each category below.

Valid Percent

1 Once a Week or More

2 Less Than Once a Week

3 Never

19. Now write a brief analysis of your table below:

20. Print the frequency distribution for your recoded variable RECNEWS and attach it to this sheet.

21. What does the variable EDUC measure (hint: check the variable label)?

22. Now follow these steps to recode the variable EDUC.

*Recode the variable EDUC to create a new variable EDCAT (recoded EDUC) as follws:

OLD VARIABLE EDUC Values	NEW VARIABLE EDCAT Values	Labels
0-11	1	Less than high school education
12	2	High school graduate
13-15	3	Some college
16	4	College graduate
17-20	5	Graduate studies and beyondmj

*Use the Recode command to create your new, recoded variable EDCAT.

*Define your new variable.

*Run a frequency distribution for the variable EDCAT, then list the labels and valid percentages for each category below.

NAME _____

CLASS _____

INSTRUCTOR _____

DATE _____

Valid Percent

1 _____

2 _____

3 _____

4 _____

5 _____

23. Now write a brief analysis of your table below:

24. Print the frequency distribution for your recoded variable EDCAT and attach it to this sheet.

25. Save your recoded variables RECGRNT, RECNEWS, and EDCAT so we can refer back to them later. Save the changes using the file name **EXERPLUS**.

26. Access the SPSS Help feature Tutorial.

    Hint: Click **Help** → **Tutorial** → Click on the **Table of Contents** icon on bottom right side of the screen (icon that looks like a **house**) →
    Once you have opened the Table of Contents, work your way through the following sections: **Using the Data Editor; Working With Output; Modifying Data Values**.
    To exit or close the Tutorial, click on the "**X**" (Close button). Alternatively, you can select **File** → **Close** OR the **EXER.SAV** button at the bottom of your screen to return to the Data Editor.

27. Now that you are comfortable using the Variable View tab to set variables to the appropriate level of measurement (SPSS Command 6.13), you may want to take a few moments to check the level of measurement for each of the variables on your DEMO.SAV and EXER.SAV files. Once you have selected the appropriate level of measurement for each variable, simply save the changes by following the instructions in SPSS Command 6.19.

Chapter 7 **Presenting Your Data in Graphic Form**

Political Orientations

Now let's turn our attention from religion to politics. Some people feel so strongly about politics that they joke about it being a "religion." The GSS data set has several items that reflect political issues. Two are key political items: POLVIEWS and PARTYID. These items will be the primary focus in this chapter. In the process of examining these variables, we are going to learn not only more about the political orientations of respondents to the 2000 GSS, but also how to use SPSS to produce and interpret data in graphic form.

You will recall that in the last chapter we focused on a variety of ways of displaying univariate distributions (frequency tables) and summarizing them (measures of central tendency and dispersion). In this chapter we are going to build on that discussion by focusing on several ways of presenting your data graphically.

We will begin by focusing on two charts that are useful for variables at the nominal and ordinal level: bar and pie. We will then consider two graphs that are appropriate for Interval/Ratio variables: histograms and line charts.

You may recall that at the end of the last chapter we asked you to save your new recoded variables on a file named DEMOPLUS. If you did so, go ahead and open that file now.[1] If not, don't worry, you can work through all the chapters using the DEMO.SAV file on the CD that came with the book.

Demonstration 7.1:
Frequency Table — POLVIEWS

We'll start our examination of political orientations with POLVIEWS.[2] Let's see what that variable measures. Use the **Frequencies** command to find out.

---

[1] If you are using the Student Version of SPSS, you may want to access the original file DEMO.SAV on the CD that came with the book. Then at the end of the chapter save the file with the new recoded variables from this chapter to disk or, if you are working on your own PC, to your hard drive so you can access the recoded variables later on.

[2] For the variable POLVIEWS, values 0, 8, and 9 should be defined as missing.

Take a few minutes to examine this table.

POLVIEWS THINK OF SELF AS LIBERAL OR CONSERVATIVE

		Frequency	Percent	Valid Percent	Cumulative Percent
Valid	1 EXTREMELY LIBERAL	53	3.5	3.8	3.8
	2 LIBERAL	149	9.9	10.6	14.3
	3 SLIGHTLY LIBERAL	153	10.2	10.9	25.2
	4 MODERATE	598	39.9	42.4	67.6
	5 SLGHTLY CONSERVATIVE	199	13.3	14.1	81.8
	6 CONSERVATIVE	217	14.5	15.4	97.2
	7 EXTRMLY CONSERVATIVE	40	2.7	2.8	100.0
	Total	1409	93.9	100.0	
Missing	8 DK	79	5.3		
	9 NA	12	.8		
	Total	91	6.1		
Total		1500	100.0		

As you can see, POLVIEWS taps into basic political philosophy, ranging from *Extremely liberal* to *Extremely conservative.* As you might expect, most people are clustered near the center, with fewer numbers on either extreme.

Demonstration 7.2: Bar Chart — POLVIEWS

Sometimes the information in a univariate analysis can be grasped more quickly if it is presented in graphic form rather than in a table of numbers. Without looking back at the table you just created, take a moment to think about the distribution of political orientations for respondents to the 2000 GSS. You may recall that most respondents were clustered near the center, but do you remember the relative sizes of the different groups? Was the "moderate" group a little bigger than the others or a lot bigger?

Sometimes a graphic presentation of such data sticks in your mind more than a table of numbers. SPSS gives us a variety of ways to present data graphically. In this section we are going to focus on one basic procedure to construct a simple *bar chart* for POLVIEWS. Bar charts display the same type of information as frequency tables (the number or percentage of cases in a category). The difference is that bar charts display this information graphically rather than in a table.

SPSS offers an easy method for producing a simple bar chart. Under the **Graphs** menu select **Bar . . .** and the Bar Charts dialog box will open. This box will give you an opportunity to select the kind of graph you would like: Simple, Clustered, or Stacked. Because we have only one variable, we want to choose the **Simple** type. Probably that's the one already selected, but you can click it again to be sure. Then, click the **Define** button.

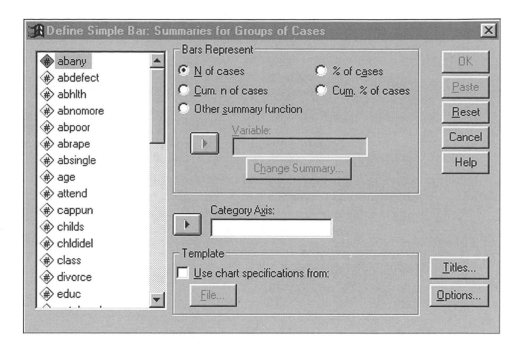

The next window allows you to further specify the kind of bar chart you would like, including a specification of the variable(s) to be graphed. As a start, let's find **POLVIEWS** in the variable list and highlight it. Now click the right-pointing **arrow** next to the Category Axis: box. This lets SPSS know that you want to construct the bar chart with the categories of POLVIEWS (Extremely liberal, Liberal, Slightly liberal, and so on) on the *horizontal* (or "*x*") *axis*.

The Bars Represent box at the top of the window allows you to specify a format for the *vertical* (or "*y*") *axis* of the bar chart. In other words, you can choose to display "N of cases" (frequencies), "% of cases" (percentages), "Cum. n of cases" (cumulative frequencies) or "Cum. % of cases" (cumulative percentages). For now let's click on **% of cases**.

Next, click on the **Options . . .** button in the lower right-hand corner. After you do this, you will be presented with a screen that allows you to select how missing values will be treated. Because we are not interested in cases coded as "missing," make sure that the check mark next to the line that says "Display groups defined by missing values" is NOT showing. If the box has a check in it, simply click on the box to make the mark disappear and then select **Continue**. If the box is already blank, click **Continue**.

You should now be back in the Define Simple Bar: dialog box. Before we tell SPSS to produce the chart, we want to draw your attention to one option that you may find useful. The **Titles . . .** button, located in the lower right-hand corner, opens a dialog box that allows you to specify titles, subtitles, and/or footnotes to further define your chart. While we are not going to do that now, you may want to keep this option in mind, particularly if you are planning to prepare charts for a presentation or inclusion in a paper, report, or publication.

Now that you are ready to instruct SPSS to produce the chart, click **OK**. It may take SPSS a few seconds to construct the bar graph to your specifications, but in a short time your chart will appear in the SPSS Viewer.

If you take a moment now to compare your bar chart to the frequency table you ran for POLVIEWS, it should become clear why graphic presentations are sometimes preferred to tables and why they can be more powerful. Viewing the data in graphic form makes it easy to see that most people are "Middle-of-the-road," and very few people are extreme in their political views. Graphic presentations are useful because they often do a better job of communicating the relative sizes of the different groups than a table of numbers. Chances are, for instance, that after analyzing this chart, you will have a more vivid memory of the distribution of political views in the United States.

Moreover, it should also be clear that bar charts are essentially just the graphic or visual equivalent of a frequency distribution—equivalent in the sense that they convey essentially the same information in a different format. Each category of the variable is represented by a bar whose height is proportional to the percentage of the category.

SPSS COMMAND 7.1: Simple Bar Chart

Click **Graphs** → **Bar . . .** → **Simple** → **Define** →

Highlight the variable name → Click **arrow** pointing to the "Category Axis:" box →

Select option for **vertical ("y") axis** in "Bars Represent" box →

Click **Options . . .** → Make sure there is NOT a check mark next to the "Display groups defined by missing values" option → Click **Continue** → **OK**

Demonstration 7.3: SPSS Chart Editor

After studying your chart, you may decide that you would like to change the appearance (i.e., color, style, etc. . . .) of this graphic. The good news is SPSS allows you to do this quite easily in the its' Chart Editor.

To start the Chart Editor, simply **double-click directly on your bar chart**. You should now see the Chart Editor, which provides you with a variety of options. The Chart Editor can be very useful, particularly if you are planning to present, publish, or otherwise share your analysis. While we can't cover all of the possibilities available in the Chart Editor, we will introduce you to a few fun and useful options. Remember, once you are familiar with how to access the Chart Editor, you can experiment on your own.

Once the Chart Editor is open, you can change the color of your chart. Single click on any bar in the chart to select all the bars. Then select the "**Color icon**" on the Chart Editor tool bar (the icon that looks like a crayon). Once the Color dialog box opens, you can change the color of the bars and/or borders by selecting either "**fill**" or "**border**," your choice of **color**, and "**apply**." To exit the Colors dialog box, click **Close** or "**X**."

You can also change the bar style clicking on the "**Bar Style**" option in the Chart Editor tool bar (the icon that looks like a simple black bar chart). From the Bar Styles box, choose one of three main bar types: Normal, Drop shadow, or 3-D effect. Then click "**Apply All**" to change the style of your bar chart. Click **Close** or **X** to return to the Chart Editor.

The last option we will mention also happens to be the most useful. The SPSS Chart Editor allows us to change the bar label style and add percentages to each bar on our chart by clicking the **Bar Label Style icon** (the icon that looks like a yellow bar chart). Once you have opened the Bar Label Style dialog box, you can experiment with three basic bar label styles. For now, click on **Framed**, **Apply All**, and then close the Bar Label Style box by selecting **Close** or **X**. You will see a preview of your newly redesigned bar chart, equipped with percentages for each bar, at the bottom of the Chart Editor. To close the Chart Editor, select **X** or **File** and **Close** from the drop down menu.

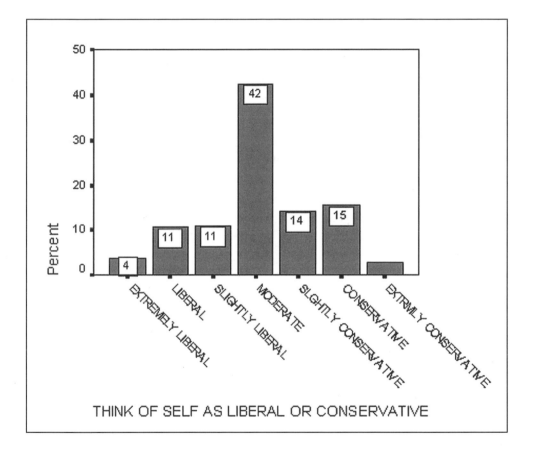

SPSS Command 7.2: SPSS Chart Editor

Double-click on chart you wish to edit → click on appropriate **icon** in SPSS Chart Editor to make necessary changes . . . →

These are only a few of the Chart Editor's capabilities. You should experiment with the Chart Editor features on your own. Familiarity with the Chart Editor makes it easy to modify SPSS's charts for use in black and white publications, color overhead transparencies, and computer presentations. We will try to do our part by mentioning some other options as we go along. In addition, in Lab Exercise 7.1, you will be given an opportunity to work with an aspect of the SPSS Tutorial that focuses on creating and editing charts.

Demonstration 7.4:
Recoding POLVIEWS → POLREC

After studying the frequency table and bar graph for POLVIEWS, you may decide that you want to work with fewer categories. Let's do that now by recoding the variable to just three categories: Liberal, Moderate, and Conservative.

Before we begin recoding, make sure values 0, 8, and 9 for the variable POLVIEWS are declared missing. And remember, if you have trouble recalling the steps involved in recoding, refer back on the discussion in Chapter 6.

Now let's go ahead and create a new variable called **POLREC** by recoding POLVIEWS as follows:

1 through 3 → 1

4 → 2

5 through 7 → 3

Once you have successfully recoded POLVIEWS, remember to access the Variable View tab and set the decimals, width, values, and appropriate level of measurement for your new, recoded variable POLREC. In this case, assign new labels to the values of POLREC as follows:

1 = **Liberal**

2 = **Moderate**

3 = **Conservative**

To see the results of our recoding, we repeat the Frequencies command with the new variable POLREC:

POLREC Recoded Political Views

		Frequency	Percent	Valid Percent	Cumulative Percent
Valid	1 Liberal	355	23.7	25.2	25.2
	2 Moderate	598	39.9	42.4	67.6
	3 Conservative	456	30.4	32.4	100.0
	Total	1409	93.9	100.0	
Missing	System	91	6.1		
Total		1500	100.0		

If your screen looks like the one shown above, congratulations! You have mastered the art of recoding and are ready to move ahead. If not, don't worry, you may just need to go back and review the steps involved in recoding outlined in Chapter 6.

If you think you did the recoding properly and your results still don't match ours, here's a small hint: before we recoded, we defined values 8 and 9 for POLVIEWS as "missing." If you forgot to do this, go ahead and do that now, then try recoding POLVIEWS again. Don't worry, we'll wait right here for you.

Demonstration 7.5: Bar Chart — POLREC

Before we turn to another basic chart that is useful for nominal and ordinal variables, let's take a few minutes to practice creating a simple bar chart for **POLREC**. This time, construct your chart so the bars represent the number of cases as opposed to the percentage of cases (hint: select "**N of cases**" in the Bars Represent box). By following the instructions listed in SPSS Command 7.1 you should get the following chart:

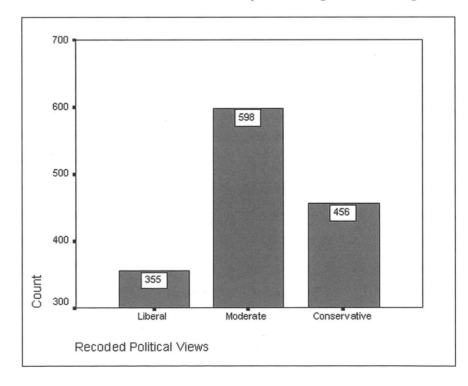

A quick look at both bar charts shows us that while collapsing categories produces groups of more nearly equal size, the amount of variation in POLVIEWS becomes obscured in the larger categories.

Demonstration 7.6:
Frequency Table — PARTYID

Another basic indicator of a person's political orientation is found in the party with which he or she tends to identify. Let's turn now to the variable PARTYID.[3] Get the **Frequencies** for that variable.

You should get the following result from SPSS.

PARTYID POLITICAL PARTY AFFILIATION

		Frequency	Percent	Valid Percent	Cumulative Percent
Valid	0 STRONG DEMOCRAT	209	13.9	14.0	14.0
	1 NOT STR DEMOCRAT	282	18.8	18.9	32.9
	2 IND,NEAR DEM	174	11.6	11.7	44.6
	3 INDEPENDENT	304	20.3	20.4	64.9
	4 IND,NEAR REP	142	9.5	9.5	74.5
	5 NOT STR REPUBLICAN	207	13.8	13.9	88.3
	6 STRONG REPUBLICAN	149	9.9	10.0	98.3
	7 OTHER PARTY	25	1.7	1.7	100.0
	Total	1492	99.5	100.0	
Missing	9 NA	8	.5		
Total		1500	100.0		

Demonstration 7.7:
Pie Chart — PARTYID

Pie charts are another common way of presenting nominal and ordinal data graphically. Like bar charts, pie charts depict the same type of information found in a frequency table graphically: the differences in frequencies or percentages among categories of a given variable. However, in this case, the information is not displayed on the "x" and "y" axis, but as segments of a circle or, as the name suggests, slices of a pie.

A *pie chart* is simply a graphic display of data that depicts the differences in frequencies or percentages among categories of a nominal or ordinal variable. The categories are represented as pieces of pie whose segments add up to 100 percent.

To create a pie chart, simply select **Graphs** and then **Pie** from the drop down menu. Once the Pie Charts dialog box opens, you will see that by default SPSS has selected the option that is appropriate for our purposes: "Summaries for groups of cases." To accept this and open the Define Pie dialog box, click **Define**.

---

[3] For the variable PARTYID, values 8 and 9 should be defined as missing.

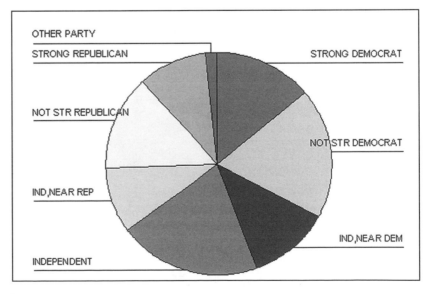

The Define Pie: dialog box may look somewhat familiar to you. That is because it is similar to the Define Simple Bar dialog box we used previously. In this case, the main difference is that after highlighting the variable **PARYID** on the left you need to click on the **arrow** pointing to the Define Slices by: window.

The rest of the steps are probably so familiar that you will not need much instruction, but just in case, follow the steps below:

- In the Slices Represent box at the top, select "**% of cases**."
- Choose **Options . . .** and turn off the "Display groups defined by missing values" by **clicking in the box to the left** and removing the check mark.
- Click **Continue** to return to the Define Pie box.
- Notice that similar to the Define Bar box, you can use the **Titles . . .** option to insert titles, subtitles, and/or text.
- When you are ready to run your pie chart, click **OK.**

You will see that by default SPSS does not display the percentages for each slice. Nevertheless, it appears that the largest "slices" are "Independent" and "Not Strong Democrat," followed closely by "Strong Democrat" and "Not Strong Republican."

SPSS Command 7.3: Pie Chart

> Click **Graphs → Pie . . . → Define**
>
> Highlight **variable name** → Click **arrow** pointing to Define Slices by: →
>
> Select desired **option** in Slices Represent box →
>
> Click **Options . . .** → Click on **check mark** next to Display Groups Defined by Missing Values to remove it → Click **Continue → OK**

We can request percentages for each slice by accessing the SPSS Chart Editor. To do that, simply **double-click** directly on your **pie chart**. Then in the Chart Editor tool bar click on the "**Chart options**" icon (the icon on the right side of the tool bar that looks a little like the Eiffel tower). When you do that the Pie Options dialog box will open. Simply click on **Percents** in the Labels box on the bottom, then select **OK**. You will now see a preview of your edited pie chart in the bottom of the Chart Editor. To close the Chart Editor select **File** and then **close** or click "**X**."

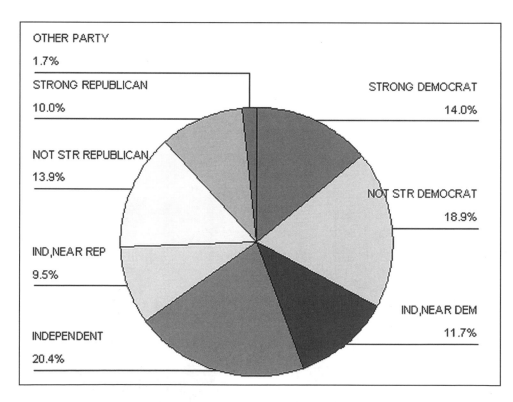

OTHER PARTY
1.7%

STRONG REPUBLICAN
10.0%

STRONG DEMOCRAT
14.0%

NOT STR REPUBLICAN
13.9%

NOT STR DEMOCRAT
18.9%

IND,NEAR REP
9.5%

IND,NEAR DEM
11.7%

INDEPENDENT
20.4%

SPSS Command 7.4: Accessing Pie Options (SPSS Chart Editor)

> **Double-click** on **pie chart** in SPSS Viewer → select **Chart Options icon** →
> Click **Percents** → **OK** → Click **X** *OR* **File** → **Close**

Remember that, in addition to adding (or deleting) percents and values for your pie chart, you can also change the color, text, and so on. One additional option that we did not discuss previously is the "fill pattern." The ability to vary fill patterns is especially useful when preparing charts for reproduction in black and white. To experiment with this, access the **SPSSS Chart Editor** once again. This time click one time on your **pie chart** displayed at the **bottom of the Chart Editor**. Now select the "**Fill Pattern**" icon (the picture that looks like a rectangle with dots in it). Once you have accessed the "Fill Patterns" dialog box, you can experiment with several different fill patterns. To apply the patterns to a particular slice click **Apply** and then **close** the dialog box to see a preview of your edited chart at the bottom of the Chart Editor. Once you are done experimenting, close the Chart Editor.

Demonstration 7.8:
Recoding PARTYID → PARTY

With the addition of the percentage for each slice or category of PARTYID, we now know that the largest grouping of respondents identified themselves as "Independent" (20%), followed closely by 19% who consider themselves "Not Strong Democrats," and 14% who consider themselves "Strong Democrats" and "Not Strong Republicans" respectively.

What becomes clear is that three-quarters (75%) of respondents to the 2000 GSS either consider themselves Independents or weak partisans on either side (calculated by adding Independent, Independent-Near Rep, Independent-Near Dem, Not Strong Republican, and Not Strong Democrat or 20+10+12+ 19+14).

What is also clear is that there are probably more answer categories here than we will be able to manage easily in our subsequent analyses (and perhaps more response categories than are useful for a simple pie chart). Consequently, we should recode PARTYID to create a new, less cumbersome measure of party identification called **PARTY**.

It makes sense to combine the first two categories: the "Strong" and "Not Strong" Democrats (0 and 1). Similarly, we will want to combine the corresponding Republican categories (5 and 6). Two of the categories, however, need a little more discussion: the two Independent groups, who said, when pressed by interviewers, that they were "near" one of the two parties.

Should we combine those near the Democrats with that party, for example, or should we combine them with the other Independents? There are a number of methods for resolving this question. For now, however, we are going to choose the simplest method. As we continue our analyses, it will be useful if we have ample numbers of respondents in each category, so we will recode with an eye to creating roughly equal-sized groups. In this instance, that means combining the three Independent categories into one group (2, 3, and 4). So, let's recode as follows:

> 0 through 1 → 1
>
> 2 through 4 → 2
>
> 5 through 6 → 3
>
> 7 → 4
>
> Then, label **PARTY** as follows:
>
> 1 = **Democrat**
>
> 2 = **Independent**
>
> 3 = **Republican**
>
> 4 = **Other**

Enter and execute these commands now. Once you've done so, we'll be ready to create a frequency table and pie chart for the new variable.

Demonstration 7.9: Pie Chart — PARTY

After running Frequencies and creating a pie chart, you should get the following results.

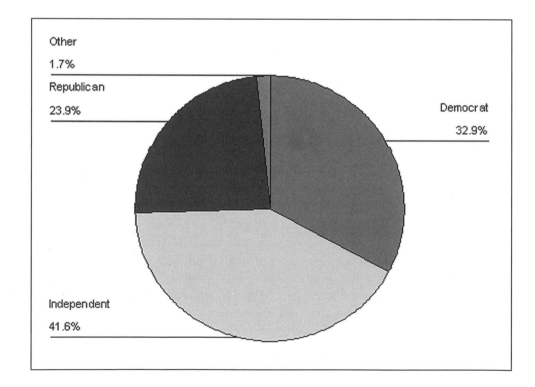

If you had trouble with the recoding, refer back to the discussion in Chapter 6. Did you forget to set values 8 and 9 for the original variable (PARTYID) to missing? If so, do that now and then try recoding again.

Now we have two basic measures of political orientations, both of which have been recoded and displayed graphically using two common charts that are appropriate for nominal and ordinal variables: bar and pie charts.

There are other possibilities, however.

Political Attitudes

The GSS data set contains other variables that also tap into people's political orientations. For instance, GUNLAW measures how people feel about the registration of firearms. This has been a controversial issue in the United States for a number of years, involving, on one hand, Second Amendment guarantees of the right to bear arms, and on the other, high rates of violent crime, often involving firearms. CAPPUN measures whether respondents favor or oppose capital punishment, another topic that is associated with political attitudes.

As you can see, there is no lack of ways to explore people's political outlooks in the data set. We're going to focus on some of these items in later sections of the book. You should take some time now to explore some of them on your own. Take capital punishment, for example. How do you think the American people feel about this issue? Do you think most are in favor of it or most are opposed? This is your chance to find out for yourself.

If you have any interest in political matters, you should enjoy this exercise. You may have your own personal opinion about extramarital sex or homosexuality, but do you have any idea how the general population feels about such things? How about the death penalty and permits to purchase firearms? Take a moment to think about how the general public feels about these issues. You can check to see if you are correct by running charts and graphs for HOMOSEX, PREMARSX, XMOVIE, CAPPUN, and GUNLAW. Once you have done that, compare your findings to those in Writing Box 7.1.

Writing Box 7.1

Here's where the sample stood a number of controversial issues. There is overwhelming support (82%) for requiring people to obtain police permits in order to buy a gun. Two-thirds (70%) support the death penalty for persons convicted of murder.

Three questions had to do with sexual matters, and levels of support differed widely among the three items. Asked whether premarital sex was "always wrong," "almost always wrong," "sometimes wrong," or "not wrong at all," 41 percent chose the last of these, saying it is always alright. Interestingly, 28 percent—the next most popular response—said it was always wrong, pointing to a polarization of opinions on this topic.

The same question was asked with regard to homosexuality: "sexual relations between two adults of the same sex." Again, opinions were polarized, but the skew was toward disapproval. Fifty-nine percent said it was always wrong, while 29 percent said it was not wrong at all.

Finally, respondents were asked whether they had attended an X-rated movie during the past year. One in four (23%) said they had.

Demonstration 7.10: Histogram — AGE

In the next few sections we will examine two other types of graphs that are appropriate for Interval/Ratio variables: histograms and line charts.

Like bar charts, histograms have two axes, the vertical (y axis) and the horizontal (x axis). The categories of the variable are displayed along the horizontal axis, while frequencies or percentages are displayed along the vertical axis.

Unlike bar charts, the categories of a histogram are displayed as contiguous bars (bars that touch each other). Both the height and width of each bar is proportional to the frequency or percentage of cases in each category. On a histogram, the sum of the areas covered by all the contiguous bars is 1 or 100% if proportions or percentages have been graphed. If frequencies were graphed, the sum of the areas is the number of cases.

Here's how SPSS can be instructed to produce a histogram for an interval/ratio variable. Because the political items that we have been focusing on in this chapter are nominal and/or ordinal, we need to turn our attention to another issue. For now, let's focus on AGE (respondents' ages at the time of the interview); a measure that you may suspect is at least peripherally related to political orientations and party identification.[4]

Now select **Graphs** and then **Histogram . . .** from the drop down menu. Highlight the variable **AGE** and then either **double-click** or click the **arrow** pointing toward the Variable: field. For this chart we don't have to worry about missing values because SPSS automatically removes them from display.

You will notice that once again, you have the option of adding titles, subtitles, and/or footnotes. We won't do that now, however; instead, we will go ahead and run the histogram by clicking **OK**.

---

[4] For the variable AGE, values 98 and 99 should be defined as missing.

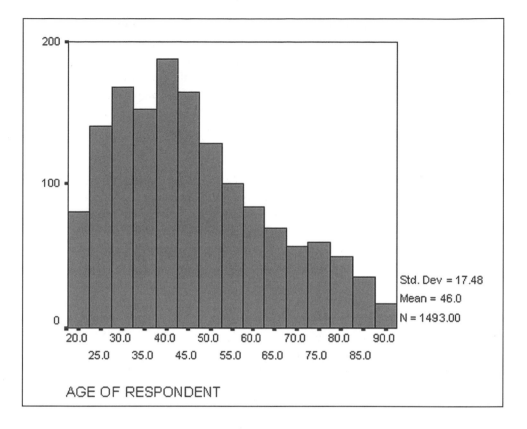

As with bar charts, the horizontal (x) axis shows categories of AGE that have been automatically created by SPSS. Depending upon the range of the variable, SPSS computes an interval width for each category. For AGE, SPSS calculated 15 intervals each with a width of 5 years. The numbers under the bars of the histogram are the midpoints of the intervals. As with the bars on a bar chart, the bars on the histogram are proportional to the numbers of cases the intervals. If you think it will improve the presentation of your data, you may replace the interval widths chosen by SPSS with the Chart Editor.

SPSS Command 7.5: Histogram

Click **Graphs Histogram . . .** → **double-click** on **variable name**
OR highlight **variable** and click on **arrow** pointing toward the
variable field → Click **OK**

The Chart Editor can be used to customize your histogram. Take a few moments to experiment with this option and see if you can improve on the way SPSS made your chart.

Demonstration 7.11: Line Chart – INCOME98

Total family income (INCOME98) is another interval/ratio variable that is some-what related to political orientations and party identification. While it is possible to represent this distribution using a histogram, we are going to consider another type of graph that you are probably already familiar with, a *line chart* (sometimes also called a *frequency polygon*).

A line chart is similar to a histogram and bar chart in that the categories for the variable are displayed on the horizontal (x) axis and the frequency or percentage is situated on the vertical (y) axis. Unlike the bar chart or histogram, however, the line chart has a single line running from the far left to the far right of the graph which connects points representing the frequency or percentage of cases for each category of the variable.

Line charts are particularly useful in showing the overall shape or distribution of variables with a large number of values or categories.

Consequently, while bar and pie charts are generally used to display discrete variables, histograms and line charts are most often used to display the distribution of continuous, interval-ratio variables.

Before we produce our line chart, we need to make sure the values 0, 24, 98, and 99 for INCOME98 are defined as "missing." This requires that we use an additional option available in the "Missing Values" dialog box.

Access the **Variable View** tab, then **double-click** on the far **right side** of the **cell** that corresponds with the variable INCOME98 and the column Missing.

Once you have opened the Missing Values box, you will notice that we cannot use the Discrete missing values option in this case because there is only room for three values and we want to include four (0, 24, 98, and 99). As an alternative, select the **Range plus one optional discrete missing value** by clicking on the **circle** to the left of that option.

Then insert **24** as the Low:, **99** as the High:, and **0** as the Discrete value: as shown below:

This tells SPSS to label all values ranging from 24-99 and 0 as "missing." This is appropriate in this case because 24 = Refused, 98 = Don't Know, 99 = No Answer, and 0 = Not Applicable.

Once you have done that, click **OK** and we are finally ready to produce our chart.

SPSS Command 7.6: Setting Values/
Labels as Missing Using Range Plus One Option

> Access **Variable View** tab → **double-click** on **right side of cell** that corresponds with appropriate variable and column "Missing" →
>
> Click on **circle** next to Range plus one optional discrete missing value Insert appropriate Low:, High:, and Discrete: **values** → Click **OK**

To begin, click **Graphs** once again. This time, however, select **Line . . .** and the Line Charts dialog box will open, as shown below:

On the left side of the box you see three types of graphs listed: Simple, Multiple, and Drop-line. Because we are charting only one variable, we want to choose **Simple**, which is probably already highlighted, but you can click on it once again just to be sure. Now click on the **Define** button and the Define Simple Line: dialog box will open:

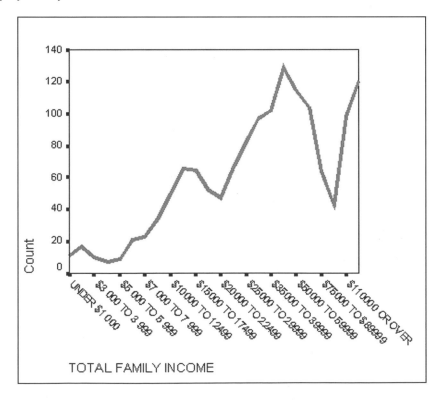

On the left side of the box you can see the list of variables. Scroll down the list until you find **INCOME98** and highlight it. Now click on the **arrow** next to the Category Axis: box to transfer the variable name. This time choose **N of cases** as opposed to % of cases (it may already be selected) and then click on the **Options . . .** button to make sure that there is not a check mark next to the Display groups defined by missing values. After you have done that, click **Continue** and you will be back in the Define Simple Line: box. As in the previous chart dialog boxes, the Titles . . . option can be used to add titles, subtitles, and/or footnotes to the chart. You can explore that option now or just click on **OK** if you are ready to produce your line chart. Once you do that, you should see the following line chart displayed in your Viewer:

Take some time to review your line chart. You can see how respondents' reported annual income ranged from those who received under $1,000 to those who received more than $110,000 in 2000. You may want to take note of the shape of the distribution and whether the sample is concentrated in a specific area or fairly evenly spread out.

SPSS Command 7.7: Simple Line Chart

Click **Graphs** → **Line** . . . → **Simple** → **Define** →

Highlight the **variable name** → Click **arrow** pointing toward the "Category Axis:" box →

Click **Options** . . . → Click on the **check mark** next to the Display groups defined by missing values option to make sure it is NOT showing →

Click **Continue** → **OK**

As before, you can use the Chart Editor to change the appearance of your line graph. You can, for instance, change the style of the line by accessing the **Chart Editor** and then clicking on the small **line graph** at the bottom of the Chart Editor. Once you have done that, click on the "**line style**" icon (the picture that looks like a horizontal line) to access the Line Styles dialog box. You can experiment with the various styles available and get a preview of your edited chart at the bottom of the Chart Editor box.

Some Guidelines for Choosing a Chart or Graph

In this chapter we have focused on four common and useful charts. The following tables present a summary of the discussion regarding which charts are appropriate for variables of different types (Table 7.1) and at different levels of measurement (Table 7.2).

It is important to bear in mind that you can also use SPSS to produce several additional types of charts and graphs. To get a sense of the options available, click **Graphs** on the tool bar. You can see that in addition to the four options discussed, you have the opportunity to work with several other types of charts.

While it is fairly easy to learn how to produce charts on SPSS or any other statistical package, it is more difficult to learn which types of graphs are appropriate for variables of different types and at different levels of measurement. Remember at your command SPSS will produce any chart or graph you request, regardless of whether it is appropriate.

Saving and Printing Your Charts

That is enough work for now. If you are interested in saving or printing any of your charts, you can do so easily by following the commands for saving and printing output discussed at the end of Chapter 6.

Table 7.1   Charts Appropriate for Variables of Different Types

	Type of Variable	
	Discrete	Continuous
Bar Chart	√	
Pie Chart	√	
Histogram		√
Line Chart		√

Table 7.2   Charts Appropriate for Variables at Different Levels of Measurement

	Level of Measurement		
	Nominal	Ordinal	I/R
Bar Chart	√	√	
Pie Chart	√	√	
Histograms			√
Line Chart			√

Saving Your Recoded Variables

Before ending your session, be sure to **Save** your new recoded variables. If you followed the suggestion at the beginning of the chapter and accessed the DEMO-PLUS file, we recommend you save your new variables on that file so all your recoded variables are in one place.

If you are using the Student Version of SPSS, please keep in mind the 50-variable limit and refer to the discussion in Chapter 6 regarding saving your work.

Conclusion

Politics is a favorite topic for many Americans, and it is a realm often marked by the expression of unsubstantiated opinions. Now you are able to begin examining the facts of political views. In later chapters, we'll move beyond describing political orientations and start examining why people have the political views they have.

Main Points

- In this chapter we focused on two key political items: POLVIEWS and PARTYID.
- POLVIEWS taps into basic political philosophy, whereas PARTYID measures political party affiliation.
- We recoded both items to reduce the number of categories and ensure that the distributions are easy to interpret in graphic form.
- We named the new recoded variables POLREC and PARTY.

- A graph or chart can sometimes communicate the relative sizes of different groups or the shape of the distribution of a variable more powerfully than can a table of numbers.
- You can use SPSS to produce two charts that are appropriate for discrete, nominal or ordinal variables: simple bar and pie charts.
- Bar and pie charts are the graphic equivalent of frequency tables, best used for variables with a limited number of categories.
- You can also use SPSS to produce two charts that are appropriate for continuous, interval/ratio variables: histograms and line charts.
- Line charts and histograms are most useful for variables with numerous response categories.

Key Terms

Bar chart
Histogram
Horizontal ("x") axis

Line chart (frequency polygon)
Vertical ("y") axis
Pie chart

SPSS Commands Introduced in This Chapter

7.1   Simple Bar Chart

7.2   SPSS Chart Editor

7.3   Pie Chart

7.4   Accessing Pie Options (SPSS Chart Editor)

7.5   Histogram

7.6   Setting Values/Labels as Missing Using Range Plus One Option

7.7   Simple Line Chart

Review Questions

1. What does the variable POLVIEWS measure?

2. What does the variable PARTYID measure?

3. Name one reason we chose to recode POLVIEWS and PARTYID.

4. Does PARTY (recoded PARTYID) show that most respondents to the 2000 GSS are Liberal, Moderate, or Conservative?

5. If you wanted to produce a chart for a discrete variable, which type of chart would be your best option: bar chart, line chart, or histogram?

6. If you wanted to produce a chart for a variable with many categories or values, which type of chart would be your best option: bar chart, pie chart, or line graph?

7. Why are graphic presentations of data useful?

8. Name one reason why you might make a pie chart for the variable POLREC (recoded POLVIEWS), as opposed to a line chart.

9. Name two measures of political attitudes (other than POLVIEWS and PARTYID) contained on either DEMO.SAV or EXER.SAV.

10. List the types of chart(s)/graph(s) that are generally recommended for variables at the following levels of measurement:
    a. nominal
    b. ordinal
    c. I/R

11. List the types of chart(s)/graph(s) that are generally recommended for variables of the following types:
    a. discrete
    b. continuous

12. A researcher creates a problematic, overcategorized bar chart for the variable AGE (measured in years). Which of the following is NOT a solution to this problem:
    a. recode the variable AGE and produce an appropriate chart for the new, recoded variable
    b. produce a pie chart for the variable AGE
    c. produce a line chart for the variable AGE

NAME _____

CLASS _____

INSTRUCTOR _____

DATE _____

To complete the following exercises, access the EXER.SAV file. You can find answers to selected questions (1-5A, 5D) in Appendix B.

1. (NEWS) Values 0, 8 and 9 should be defined as missing.
   A. What does this variable NEWS measure (hint: variable label)?

   B. What is the variable's level of measurement?_____
   C. List one type of chart that is appropriate for this variable

   _____

   D. Produce the chart listed in response to question 1C above and then based on your output, fill in the blanks below.
      About _____% of respondents read the newspaper once a week or more, whereas approximately _____% read the newspaper less than once a week. Only _____% of the sample said they never read the newspaper.

2. (TVHOURS) Values –1, 98, and 99 should be defined as missing.
   A. What does the variable TVHOURS measure?

   B. Would you describe the variable as discrete or continuous?

   _____

   C. List two charts that are appropriate for this variable:

   _____

   _____

   D. Produce one of the charts listed in response to question 2C above which will allow you to answer the question below. (hint: when you run a histogram, SPSS automatically calculates two statistics which are useful for answering this question – mean and standard deviation.)

Using the standard deviation, we would expect two-thirds of respondents to watch between _____ hours and _____ hours of television per day.

Questions 3 and 4: After you have produced and analyzed the charts for CONPRESS and CONTV, briefly describe the distribution in the spaces provided below. You may want to note the largest and smallest categories for the items as well as any other interesting or pertinent information.

3. (CONPRESS) Values 0, 8, and 9 should be defined as missing.

   A. List one type of chart that is appropriate for this variable

   _____

   B. Description of chart:

4. (CONTV) Values 0, 8, and 9 should be defined as missing.

   A. List one type of chart that is appropriate for this variable:

   _____

   B. Description of chart:

5. (RINCOM98) Values 0, 24, 98, and 99 should be defined as "missing."

   A. List one type of chart that is appropriate for this variable:

   _____

   B. Produce the chart listed in response to question 5A above, and then describe the distribution below.

NAME _____

CLASS _____

INSTRUCTOR _____

DATE _____

    C. Recode the variable RINCOM98 into five categories as listed below:
       $19,999 or less → 1
       $20,000-$39,999 → 2
       $40,000-$59,999 → 3
       $60,000-$89,999 → 4
       $90,000 or more → 5

    D. List one type of chart that is appropriate for your new, recoded variable:

       _____

    E. Now produce a chart for your new recoded variable and describe your findings below. When you are done, print and attach the chart for your recoded variable to this sheet.

6. How do American adults feel about sex education in public school? Produce and analyze a chart for the variable SEXEDUC, then describe your findings below.

7. Do Americans tend to think sex before marriage for teens 14-16 is appropriate or inappropriate? Produce and analyze a chart for the variable TEENSEX, then describe your findings below.

8a. Choose three "environmental" variables in your EXER.SAV file and list the abbreviated variable names and variable labels below:

Abbreviated Variable Name   *Variable Label*

Environmental variable 1 _____

Environmental variable 2 _____

Environmental variable 3 _____

8b. Produce and analyze charts for the three environmental variables listed in response to question 8a above. Based on your findings, how would you describe American attitudes toward the environment?

9. Access the SPSS Help feature Tutorial.

Hint: Click **Help** → **Tutorial** → Click on the **Table of Contents** icon on the bottom right side of the screen (icon that looks like a house) → Once you have opened the Table of Contents, work through the section of the Tutorial labeled "**Creating and Editing Charts**"
To exit or close the Tutorial, click on the "**X**" (Close button).
Alternatively, you can select **File** → **Close** OR the **EXER.SAV** button at the bottom of your screen to return to the Data Editor.

Chapter 8 **Exploring Attitudes Toward Abortion With Frequencies and Crosstabs**

Now that you have used *univariate analysis* to examine responses to a single item, we are ready to introduce you to *bivariate analysis*. While we will reserve the bulk of our discussion of bivariate analysis for Part IV, you can think of this as a preview of sorts. As the name suggests, bivariate analysis allows us to examine the relationship between two variables. Although there are several types of bivariate analysis, in this chapter we will explore just one, *crosstabulations* or *crosstabs.*

Some texts and statistical packages refer to crosstabulations as *bivariate distributions, contingency tables*, or *two-way frequency distributions*, but SPSS just refers to them as crosstabs.

When we examined the topic of abortion in Chapter 2, we discussed the different degrees of approval represented by the several questions and made some educated guesses as to which ones would receive the most (and least) support. Now that we have gained some proficiency in the use of SPSS to analyze data, we are going to check on how well we did in our predictions.

We will extend our analysis of this controversial issue using SPSS's crosstabs procedure. Crosstabs will allow us to gain a more in-depth understanding of the structure of abortion attitudes by cross-classifying respondents in terms of their answers to more than one question. This procedure is also the first step on the road toward one of the most exciting aspects of social scientific research — answering questions empirically and testing hypotheses. But before we begin running Crosstabs, we must familiarize ourselves with the variables we intend to include in our analysis.

Demonstration 8.1: Identifying the Seven Abortion Variables – File Info

To start the process, we will instruct SPSS to produce frequency tables for the abortion variables contained in the file DEMO.SAV. If you do not recall the names of the seven variables that measure abortion in this data set, there are several ways you can use SPSS to find this information.

One option is to select **Utilities** and then click on **File Info**. In a moment, information about the variables on your DEMO.SAV file should appear in the Output Navigator, as shown below:

```
Name                                                              Position

ID          RESPONDNT ID NUMBER                                        1
            Measurement Level: Scale
            Column Width: 8  Alignment: Right
            Print Format: F4
            Write Format: F4

ABANY       ABORTION IF WOMAN WANTS FOR ANY REASON                     2
            Measurement Level: Ordinal
            Column Width: 8  Alignment: Right
            Print Format: F1
            Write Format: F1
            Missing Values: 0, 8, 9

            Value     Label

                0 M   NAP
                1     YES
                2     NO
                8 M   DK
                9 M   NA

ABDEFECT    STRONG CHANCE OF SERIOUS DEFECT                            3
            Measurement Level: Ordinal
            Column Width: 8  Alignment: Right
            Print Format: F1
            Write Format: F1
            Missing Values: 0, 8, 9

            Value     Label

                0 M   NAP
                1     YES
                2     NO
                8 M   DK
                9 M   NA
```

Just **double click** in the Viewer window and you should be able to move through the viewer and access information for all the variables by using the **Page Up** and **Page Down** keys or the **arrow keys** on your keyboard.

SPSS Command 8.1: Identifying Variables – File Info

Click **Utilities → File Info . . .**

Demonstration 8.2: Running Frequencies for Several Variables at Once[1]

Once you have identified the names of the seven abortion variables, you can easily instruct SPSS to run **Frequencies** for all the items at once. As noted earlier, if the variables are clustered together (as the abortion items in our DEMO.SAV file are), you can simply scroll down the list of variables until all the names are highlighted and then click the right-pointing **arrow** to transfer them to the Variable(s): field.

---

[1] For each of the seven abortion variables, the values 0, 8, and 9 should be defined as missing.

If the variables are not clustered together, you can transfer them all at once by holding down the **Ctrl (Control) key** on your keyboard as you click on the **name of the item**. After all the items have been highlighted, click on the right-pointing **arrow** to transfer them to the Variable(s): field.

You may want to experiment with both of these options. Ultimately, however, you want to transfer all seven abortion items to the Variable(s): field as shown below.

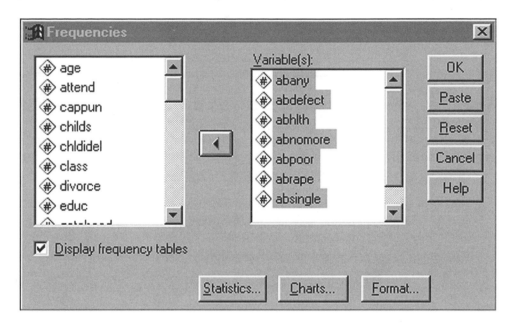

SPSS Command 8.2: Running Frequencies for Several Variables (Not Clustered)[2]

> **Analyze → Descriptive Statistics → Frequencies . . . →**
>
> **Press and hold Ctrl** (Control) key on keyboard as you **click** on the **names of the variables →**
>
> Click **right pointing arrow** to transfer selected variables to Variable(s):
>
> field → **OK**

Once you have given SPSS the command that will result in the frequency distributions for the various abortion items, you should get the results in your Output window. The two tables discussed below indicate the different levels of support for abortion under various circumstances.

---

[2] To run frequencies for several variables at once when the variables are clustered, see SPSS Command 6.9 (Chapter 6).

Items with the Highest Levels of Support

Although we don't have any basis for comparison yet, it would seem at first glance that very high percentages of the general public support a woman's right to an abortion if the woman's health is at risk (88%), if the pregnancy is a result of rape (81%) and if there is a strong chance of serious birth defects (79%).[3] Now, let's see how these compare with other reasons.

ABHLTH WOMANS HEALTH SERIOUSLY ENDANGERED

		Frequency	Percent	Valid Percent	Cumulative Percent
Valid	1 YES	825	55.0	87.8	87.8
	2 NO	115	7.7	12.2	100.0
	Total	940	62.7	100.0	
Missing	0 NAP	519	34.6		
	8 DK	38	2.5		
	9 NA	3	.2		
	Total	560	37.3		
Total		1500	100.0		

ABRAPE PREGNANT AS RESULT OF RAPE

		Frequency	Percent	Valid Percent	Cumulative Percent
Valid	1 YES	744	49.6	80.6	80.6
	2 NO	179	11.9	19.4	100.0
	Total	923	61.5	100.0	
Missing	0 NAP	519	34.6		
	8 DK	54	3.6		
	9 NA	4	.3		
	Total	577	38.5		
Total		1500	100.0		

---

[3] In each instance, the percentages have been rounded.

ABDEFECT STRONG CHANCE OF SERIOUS DEFECT

		Frequency	Percent	Valid Percent	Cumulative Percent
Valid	1 YES	735	49.0	78.9	78.9
	2 NO	197	13.1	21.1	100.0
	Total	932	62.1	100.0	
Missing	0 NAP	519	34.6		
	8 DK	46	3.1		
	9 NA	3	.2		
	Total	568	37.9		
Total		1500	100.0		

Items with Less Support

Let's look at the three items we identified as probably enjoying less support. Here's what you should get in return.

ABNOMORE MARRIED--WANTS NO MORE CHILDREN

		Frequency	Percent	Valid Percent	Cumulative Percent
Valid	1 YES	408	27.2	43.9	43.9
	2 NO	522	34.8	56.1	100.0
	Total	930	62.0	100.0	
Missing	0 NAP	519	34.6		
	8 DK	47	3.1		
	9 NA	4	.3		
	Total	570	38.0		
Total		1500	100.0		

ABPOOR LOW INCOME--CANT AFFORD MORE CHILDREN

		Frequency	Percent	Valid Percent	Cumulative Percent
Valid	1 YES	409	27.3	43.9	43.9
	2 NO	523	34.9	56.1	100.0
	Total	932	62.1	100.0	
Missing	0 NAP	519	34.6		
	8 DK	46	3.1		
	9 NA	3	.2		
	Total	568	37.9		
Total		1500	100.0		

ABSINGLE NOT MARRIED

		Frequency	Percent	Valid Percent	Cumulative Percent
Valid	1 YES	384	25.6	41.6	41.6
	2 NO	538	35.9	58.4	100.0
	Total	922	61.5	100.0	
Missing	0 NAP	519	34.6		
	8 DK	55	3.7		
	9 NA	4	.3		
	Total	578	38.5		
Total		1500	100.0		

The assumption that these reasons would garner less support proves accurate. It is also interesting that virtually the same proportions of respondents – 42 to 44%—support this second set of reasons.[4]

Unconditional Support for Abortion

Finally, let's see what proportion of the population would support a woman having unrestricted freedom to choose an abortion for any reason.

ABANY ABORTION IF WOMAN WANTS FOR ANY REASON

		Frequency	Percent	Valid Percent	Cumulative Percent
Valid	1 YES	389	25.9	42.0	42.0
	2 NO	538	35.9	58.0	100.0
	Total	927	61.8	100.0	
Missing	0 NAP	519	34.6		
	8 DK	50	3.3		
	9 NA	4	.3		
	Total	573	38.2		
Total		1500	100.0		

Notice that about the same proportion (42%) supports a woman's unrestricted freedom to choose abortion as supported by the specific situations described in ABNOMORE, ABPOOR, and ABSINGLE.

Support for Abortion—An Overview

Let's construct a table that summarizes those tables we've just examined.

---

[4] In each instance, the percentages have been rounded.

It is often useful to bring related tables such as these together in an abbreviated format.

Table 8.1 Variations in Levels of Support

Percentage Who Support a Woman's Right to Choose Abortion Because:

the woman's health would be seriously endangered	88%
the pregnancy resulted from rape	81%
there is a strong chance of a serious defect	79%
a family is too poor to afford more children	44%
a family wants no more children	44%
the woman is unmarried	42%
the woman wants it, for any reason	42%

The tables we've just examined suggest that attitudes toward abortion fall into three basic groups. There is a small minority of no more than 12% who are opposed to abortion under any circumstances. We conclude this because 88% would support abortion if the woman's life were seriously endangered.

Another group, approximately 44% of the population, would support a woman's free choice of abortion for any reason. The remainder of the population would support abortion in only a few circumstances involving medical danger and/or rape.

Demonstration 8.3: Producing Crosstabs

Now that we have had a chance to produce and analyze frequency tables for the seven abortion items in your sub-sample, we want to add a little more sophistication to the process. In this section we are going to continue our focus on abortion attitudes by showing you how to use the crosstabs procedure to examine the structure of attitudes toward this issue in more depth.

The crosstabs procedure is used to create a *crosstabulation*, a matrix that shows the distribution of one variable for each category of a second variable. While we begin in this chapter by focusing on how you can use this procedure to learn more about the structure of abortion attitudes, in Part IV we will broaden this discussion to focus on how you can use this procedure to answer questions empirically and to test hypotheses. For example, we can use crosstab tables to begin to address questions such as whether liberals are more likely to support abortion than conservatives; whether those who attend church regularly are less likely to support abortion than those who do not attend church regularly; or whether women are more likely to support abortion under any circumstances than men. For now, however, we will concentrate on using this procedure to examine the structure of abortion attitudes in-depth.

To begin, let's try a simple example. The command pathway to this technique is

Analyze → Descriptive Statistics → Crosstabs . . .

Work your way through these menu selections and you should reach a window that looks like the following:

Because the logic of a crosstab will be clearer when we have an example to look at, just follow these steps on faith and we'll justify your faith in a moment.

Let's analyze the relationship between the answers people gave to the question about whether a woman should be able to have an abortion if her health was seriously endangered (ABHLTH) and if she was too poor to have more children (ABPOOR).

In the Crosstabs window, click **ABHLTH** and then click the **arrow** pointing toward the Row(s): field. Next, click on **ABPOOR** and transfer it to the Column(s): field, producing the result shown below.[5]

_____

[5] The placement of ABHLTH in the row and ABPOOR in the column fields is arbitrary because neither has been identified as the independent or dependent variable. In this instance, our goal is not hypothesis testing, but merely to show that approval for abortion varies by the reason. Consequently, we could have switched the placement of the variables in the table.

You will notice that there are several other options available in the Crosstabs dialog box. We are going to explore these more later on. For now, once your window looks like the one above, you can click **OK**. After a few seconds, you'll be rewarded with the following data in your Output window.

ABHLTH WOMANS HEALTH SERIOUSLY ENDANGERED * ABPOOR LOW INCOME--CANT AFFORD MORE CHILDREN Crosstabulation

Count

		ABPOOR LOW INCOME--CANT AFFORD MORE CHILDREN		
		1 YES	2 NO	Total
ABHLTH WOMANS HEALTH SERIOUSLY ENDANGERED	1 YES	403	389	792
	2 NO	6	109	115
Total		409	498	907

SPSS Command 8.3 Producing Crosstabs[6]

> Click **Analyze** → **Descriptive Statistics** → **Crosstabs** . . .
>
> Highlight **variable name** → click on **arrow** pointing toward Row(s): box →
>
> Highlight **variable name** → click on **arrow** pointing toward Column(s):
>
> box → Click **OK**

Notice that the crosstabs table demonstrates the logic of the command we asked you to make. By specifying ABPOOR as the Column variable, we have caused it to appear across the top of the table with its attributes of "Yes" and "No" representing the two columns of figures.

ABHLTH, the Row variable, appears to the left of the table, and its attributes constitute the rows of the table.

More important, this table illustrates a logic that operates within the system of attitudes that people hold about abortion. First, we notice that 403 people say they would support a woman's right to choose abortion if her health were seriously endangered or if she were poor and felt she couldn't afford more children. At the opposite corner of the table, we find 109 people who would oppose abortion in both cases.

Another 389 respondents said they would support the right to choose if the woman's health were seriously endangered, but not on the basis of poverty. There are probably two elements involved in this pattern. On the one hand, threats to the woman's life are probably seen as more serious than the suffering presented by another mouth to feed in a poor family. At the same time, few, if any, would hold a woman responsible for ending a pregnancy that seriously threatened her health. Some people, however, do blame the poor for their poverty and would probably say that the woman in question should have avoided getting pregnant if she knew that it would be hard for her to feed another child. As a consequence, then, 389 of the respondents oppose abortion under some circumstances but are willing to make an exception in the case of a woman's health being threatened.

You may also have noticed that six respondents said they would support abortion on the basis of poverty but deny it on the basis of health. Although there may be some people who actually hold such a seemingly inconsistent attitude, the inconsistency is more likely due to a failure of the respondent to understand the questions or a failure of the researcher to accurately record respondents' responses.

There is additional information in the SPSS table that will become more useful to us in later analyses. The rightmost column in the table, for example, tells us that a total of 792 of those with an opinion said that they would approve an abortion for a woman whose health was seriously endangered, and 115 said they would not. The bottom row of numbers in the table gives us the breakdown regarding the other variable.

Let's try another example of the same phenomenon. The threat of a birth defect was considered a more compelling reason for abortion by the respondents than was the fact that the woman was not married. Why don't you run that table now? Use

---

[6] While the dependent variable normally goes in the Row(s): box and the independent variable goes in the Column(s): box, we have not introduced this or some of the options available in the Crosstabs dialog box yet because our primary goal in this chapter is to use this technique to highlight the complexity of attitudes (i.e., to help students/users understand the necessity of/usefulness of composite measures introduced in Chapter 9). Part IV, Chapters 11-13 are devoted to a more in-depth discussion of crosstabulation.

Analyze → **Descriptive Statistics** → **Crosstabs** . . . to get to the Crosstabs window. If ABHLTH and ABPOOR are still specified as the Row(s): and Column(s): variables, simply click **Reset** or **highlight** them and transfer them to the list of variables on the left-hand side of the dialog box using the **left-pointing arrows**. Now specify **ABDEFECT** as the row variable and **ABSINLGE** as the column variable.

Click **OK** and here's what the output should look like.

ABDEFECT STRONG CHANCE OF SERIOUS DEFECT * ABSINGLE NOT MARRIED Crosstabulation

Count

		ABSINGLE NOT MARRIED		
		1 YES	2 NO	Total
ABDEFECT STRONG CHANCE OF SERIOUS DEFECT	1 YES	375	323	698
	2 NO	8	187	195
Total		383	510	893

This table presents a strikingly similar picture. We see that 375 support the woman's right to choose in both situations, and 187 oppose abortion in both instances. Of those who would approve abortion in only one of the two situations, almost all of them (323) make the exception for the threat of birth defects. Only 8 respondents would allow abortion for a single woman but deny it in the case of birth defects. What are we to make of the 8 people who responded in this way? One possibility is that these respondents misunderstood one or both of the questions, or perhaps they have some complex point of view that demands such answers. Either way, they are few enough in number that they will not seriously affect the analysis of this topic.

We could continue examining tables like these, but the forthcoming conclusion remains the same: There are three major positions regarding abortion. One position approves it unconditionally on the basis of the woman's choice; another position opposes it under all circumstances; and the third position approves abortion only in certain circumstances – those involving medical complications or rape.

While we have used the crosstabs procedure to examine the structure of abortion attitudes in more depth, keep in mind that we could also (and will) use this procedure beginning in Part IV to test hypotheses. For instance, we will move beyond crosstabulating two attitudes and begin exploring questions such as whether women are more supportive of abortion than men by crosstabulating one of our measures of attitudes toward abortion with SEX. Before we do that, however, we want to conclude our discussion in this section by learning how to combine two or more indicators of a concept to create a composite index (Chapter 9). Then in Chapter 10 we will offer suggestions for further univariate analyses before we refocus our attention on how the crosstabs procedure can be used to examine the relationship between two variables and test hypotheses.

Conclusion

In this initial analysis of abortion attitudes, we have had an opportunity to explore the structure of attitudes on this controversial topic. Although abortion is generally discussed as an all-or-nothing proposition, we've seen that relatively few Americans reject abortion completely. A sizable minority appear to have reservations about abortion but are willing to make exceptions in certain circumstances.

We are going to explore this structuring of attitudes further in Chapter 9, where you will learn how to create a new kind of variable called an index that captures the variation in attitudes toward abortion.

Main Points

- This chapter is to introduces a new technique, crosstabulation, which helps explore the complexity of attitudes toward a controversial issue such as abortion.
- The file DEMO.SAV contains seven abortion items.
- In this chapter we reviewed two ways you can use SPSS to identify the abbreviated variable names of each of these items.
- You can produce frequency tables for all these items at once by following the commands listed in SPSS Command 8.2.
- The frequency tables for the abortion variables show that attitudes toward abortion fall into three main categories.
- A minority of respondents (12 percent) would not support abortion under any circumstances.
- 44 percent of respondents would support a woman's right to choose under any circumstances, whereas the remainder of the population would support abortion only in the case of a medical emergency or rape.
- The crosstabs procedure is used to create crosstabulations.
- Crosstabulations allow you to cross-classify respondents in terms of their answers to more than one question.
- While we used this procedure primarily to examine the structure of abortion attitudes in more depth, beginning in Part IV we are going to begin to use this procedure to test hypotheses when we focus on bivariate analyses in more depth.

Key Terms

Univariate analysis
Bivariate distributions
Bivariate analysis
Contingency tables

Crosstabulations
Two-way frequency distributions
Crosstabs

SPSS Commands Introduced in This Chapter

8.1 Identifying Variables – File Info

8.2 Running Frequencies for Several Variables (Not Clustered)

8.3 Producing Crosstabs

Review Questions

1. If you wanted to identify the names of the abortion items in your DEMO.SAV file, would you use the Utilities → File . . . command or the Analyze Descriptive Statistics . . . command?

2. In this chapter we found that there are three major positions on abortion. Briefly describe those positions.

3. List the abbreviated variable names for the abortion items in your DEMO.SAV file.

4. Which abortion variable is most likely to garner support from respondents?

5. Which abortion variable is least likely to garner support from respondents?

6. A researcher produced a crosstabulation analyzing the relationship between the answers people gave to the question about whether a woman should be able to have an abortion if her pregnancy was the result of rape (ABRAPE) and if she was married but did not want any more children (ABNOMORE). Based on what you know about the structure of abortion attitudes, estimate generally what you think the table would display in terms of levels of support for abortion in both cases? How about levels of support for abortion in the case of rape but not in the case of a married woman who does not want more children?

7. Thinking back to the crosstabulation discussed in Question 6, approximately how many respondents would you estimate are likely to support abortion in the case of a married woman who wants no more children but not in the case of a pregnancy that resulted from rape? Do you think the number would be closer to 5, 50, or 500?

8. If respondents answered that they support abortion in the case of a married woman who wants no more children, but not in the case of a pregnancy that resulted from rape, how might you explain these answers?

9. Thinking back again to the crosstabulation discussed in Question 6, what would the column of numbers on the far right of the table indicate?

10. What would the row of numbers on the bottom of the table indicate?

11. While we don't normally ask you to access SPSS for purposes of the Review Questions, if you have access to SPSS go ahead and generate a crosstab between ABRAPE and ABNOMORE to check your answers to the previous series of Questions (6-10). Write a short paragraph noting how accurate (or inaccurate) your predictions were.[7]

---

[7] Requires access to SPSS.

NAME _____

CLASS _____

INSTRUCTOR _____

DATE _____

To complete the following exercises, you need to load the data file EXER.SAV. You will find answers to Questions 1-14 in Appendix B.

1. List the abbreviated variable names and a short description of the five items in your EXER.SAV data set that measure whether or not respondents would approve of a police officer striking a citizen and, if so, under what circumstances.

Abbreviated Variable   *Description*
Name

A. _____ _____
B. _____ _____
C. _____ _____
D. _____ _____
E. _____ _____

Run Frequencies for all five variables listed above at once and then use the results to answer the following questions.[8]

2. (POLHITOK) _____% [Valid %] of respondents said they can imagine a situation in which they would approve of a police officer striking a citizen.

3. (POLHITOK) _____% [Valid %] of respondents said they would not approve of a police officer striking a citizen under any circumstances.

4. Excluding POLHITOK, which two items enjoy the most support (i.e., under what circumstances would the majority of respondents approve of a police officer striking a citizen)? List the variable name and the percentage of those who responded "Yes" for both variables.

Variable Name   *% Answered "Yes" [Valid %]*
A. _____ _____
B. _____ _____

5. Excluding POLHITOK, which two items enjoy the least support?

Variable Name   *% Answered "Yes" [Valid %]*
A. _____ _____
B. _____ _____

6. In the space provided below, construct a table that summarizes four of the frequency tables we just examined (POLABUSE, POLATTAK, POLESCAP, POLMURDR). Your new table should be titled:

[8] For each of the five variables, the values 0, 8, and 9 should be defined as missing.

"Percentage Who Support a Police Officer Striking a Citizen when . . . "
[conditions under which support police officer striking citizen]
[% of respondents who support]

A.

B.

C.

D.

7. Write a short paragraph describing the conditions under which respondents approve or disapprove of police officers striking citizens. How does the strength of approval vary by condition(s)? Approval is strongest in what situation(s)? Disapproval is greatest in what situation(s)? What explanation can you offer for the similarities and differences in support?

Run Crosstabs to analyze the relationship between the answers people gave to the question about whether they would support a police officer striking a citizen if the citizen attacked the officer with his fists (POLATTAK – row variable) and if the citizen said vulgar and obscene things (POLABUSE - column variable). Then use your table to answer the questions below (Questions 8-13).

8. _____ respondents said they would support a police officer striking a citizen in both cases.

9. _____ respondents said they would support a police officer striking a citizen if the citizen attacked the officer with his fists, but not if the citizen said vulgar and obscene things.

10. _____ respondents said they would not support a police officer striking a citizen in either situation.

11. _____ respondents said they would support an officer striking a citizen if the citizen said vulgar and obscene things, but not if the citizen attacked the officer with his fists.

12. _____ of those with an opinion said they would approve of a police officer striking a citizen if the citizen attacked the officer with his fists, whereas _____ said they would not.

13. _____ of those with an opinion said they would approve of a police officer striking a citizen if the citizen said vulgar and obscene things, whereas _____ said they would not.

14. There was more support for a police officer striking a citizen if the citizen was trying to escape custody than if the citizen was being questioned as a murder suspect. Run Crosstabs for POLESCAP (row variable) and POLMURDR (column variable). How many

NAME _____

CLASS _____

INSTRUCTOR _____

DATE _____

respondents approved and disapproved of an officer striking a citizen under specific conditions? What insights can we draw from the differences?

15. In the chapter we noted that there are three major positions on abortion (unconditional approval, conditional approval, and unconditional disapproval). How many positions are there on the issue of a police officer striking a citizen? Describe each of the major positions on this issue.

Chapter 9 **Creating Composite Measures**

*Exploring Attitudes Toward
Abortion in More Depth*

Now that you've had a chance to become familiar with univariate analysis, we're going to add a little more sophistication to the process.

You will recall that in the last chapter we used seven separate variables to examine the complexity of attitudes toward abortion. By running Crosstabs we were able to distinguish between three major positions on this issue: unconditional approval, conditional approval, and unconditional disapproval. We were also able to see that many respondents make fine distinctions between those situations in which they would and would not support abortion.

While the separate abortion items were helpful in this regard, they also made it difficult for us to get a clear picture of how Americans feel about abortion overall. Consequently, to explore attitudes toward abortion further, it may be useful for us to have a single variable, a *composite measure*, which captures the complexities of attitudes towards abortion overall - in other words, a single variable that takes into account the complexity of attitudes by capturing the three major positions on this issue.

Now that we have raised the issue, you will probably not be surprised to learn that SPSS allows us to create such a variable or composite measure made up of multiple indicators of a single concept. By employing the *Count* command we can use the scores on two or more variables to compute a new variable that summarizes attitudes toward a complicated issue or ambiguous concept such as abortion, sexual permissiveness, religiosity, prejudice, and so on. We will begin this chapter with a fairly simple two item index indicating anti-abortion attitudes and then move to a somewhat more sophisticated measure indicating pro-abortion attitudes.

Index — A Form of Composite Measure

An *index* is a form of composite measure, composed of more than one indicator of the variable under study. The score on a multiple-choice quiz is an example of a very simple index. Each question is an "item" that indicates some of the student's knowledge of the subject matter. Together, all the items form an index of the student's knowledge. Just as we would not think a single-question quiz would give us a very accurate assessment of a student's knowledge, so it is also when we measure attitudes. We do a better job measuring respondents' attitudes with multiple items.

In addition, there are two other advantages to using an index. First, they include multiple dimensions of the subject under study. In this case, an index composed of ABDEFECT and ABSINGLE will combine two aspects of the debate over abortion rather than being limited to only one (e.g., the impact of birth defects).

Second, composite measures tap into a greater range of variation between the extremes of a variable. If we were to simply use one of the abortion items, we would distinguish two groups of respondents: the pros and the antis. Combining two items will allow us to distinguish three groups. A later example will extend this range of variation even further.

ABORT Index

As we noted, the Count command allows us to create a new summary variable based on information from existing variables. The new variable can then be saved in your data set and used like any other variable.[1]

The COUNT command scans a list of variables for each respondent and counts the number of variables containing a particular code. For instance, the abortion variables, have been consistently coded "1" to indicate approval of abortion and "2" to indicate disapproval of abortion. When the time comes, we will instruct COUNT to count either the number of 1s or 2s depending on whether or not we want our index to reflect overall approval or disapproval of abortion.

Our first index will be based on the two variables mentioned above: ABDEFECT and ABSINGLE. As you probably recall, ABDEFECT measures respondents' support for abortion if there is a chance of serious defect in the baby, whereas ABSINGLE measures respondents' support for abortion if the woman is not married and does not want to marry the man. You may want to refer to the Codebook (Appendix A) to find the exact wording of each question. If you do that, you will notice that both items are coded as follows:

Value/Code		Value Label
0	-	NAP [Missing Value]
1	-	Yes
2	-	No
8	-	DK [Missing Value]
9	-	NA [Missing Value]

ABORT Index Scores

We are going to treat ABDEFECT and ABSINGLE as if they were items on a quiz designed to find out how much our respondents disapprove of abortion. On this quiz, we will only count the "right" answers, those who answered "No."

---

[1] If you follow the demonstrations and exercises in this chapter, you will be asked to compute a handful of new variables. Anyone using the Student Version of SPSS should be sensitive to the 50 variables limitation.

Consequently, a respondent who answered "No" to both questions would get 2 points. Someone answering "No" to only one question and "Yes" to the other would get 1 point, and a respondent answering "Yes" to both would get a score of 0. On this quiz then, the higher the score, the more respondents disapprove of abortion.

We will use the Count command to instruct SPSS to create a new variable (ABORT) based on respondents' scores on ABDEFECT and ABSINGLE. Our index (ABORT) will be made up of three possible scores as discussed above:

0 - Respondent approves of abortion in both cases (if there is a chance of a serious birth defect and if the woman is single).

1 - Respondent approves of abortion in one circumstance (primarily birth defects) but not the other.

2 - Respondent disapproves of abortion in both cases (if there is a chance of a serious birth defect and if the woman is single).

When we are done, if a respondent had a 1 ("Yes") on both ABDEFECT and ABSINGLE, her score will be a 0 on our new index. If a respondent had a 1 ("Yes") on ABDEFECT and a 2 ("No") on ABSINGLE (or vice versa), his score will be a 1 on our new index. And if a respondent had a 2 ("No") for both component variables, her score will be 2 on our index.

Demonstration 9.1: ABORT Index

Before we get started, you should check to make sure the values **0**, **8**, and **9** are defined as **missing** for both **ABDEFECT** and **ABSINGLE**.

Once you have done that, go ahead and click **Transform** in the menu bar and then select **Count ...** in the drop-down menu. This will open the "Count Occurrences of Values within Case ... " dialog box as shown below.

In the upper-left hand corner of the box you will see a rectangle labeled "Target Variable:," where you can type the name of your new variable (**ABORT**). To the right, you will see another rectangle labeled "Target Label:" where you can type a descriptive label for your new variable, such as "**Simple Abortion Index.**"

Once you have typed the variable name and label, transfer both **ABDEFECT** and **ABSINGLE** from the variable list to the Numeric Variables: field. Remember you can do this by highlighting the **variable name** and then clicking on the **right-pointing arrow**. Alternatively, you can transfer both variables at the same time by using the **Ctrl** key on your keyboard.

Whichever method you choose, your screen should look like this once you are done.

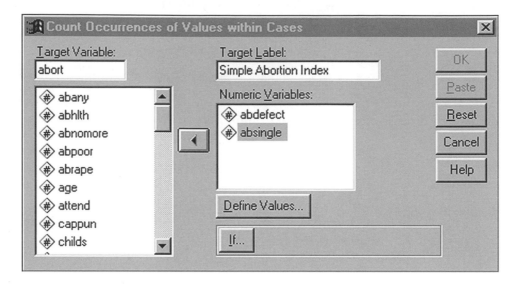

So far all we have done is tell SPSS the variables for which specified values will be counted. We have not, however, told SPSS which value(s) to count. To do that, we need to open the "Count Values within Cases: Values to Count dialog box by clicking on the **Define Values . . .** option. Use this dialog box to tell SPSS which value(s) of ABDEFECT and ABSINGLE to count. For this index, we want SPSS to count the value of 2 or the number of respondents who said they do not support a woman's right to have an abortion in either case (if there is a chance of a birth defect and if the woman is single).

To do this, type **2** in the **Value:** field on the left, then click on the **Add** button. You should now see that the value of 2 is displayed in the large box labeled "Values to Count:."

Count Values within Cases: Values to Count	

Value
- ⊙ Value:
- ○ System-missing
- ○ System- or user-missing
- ○ Range: [ ] through [ ]
- ○ Range: Lowest through [ ]
- ○ Range: [ ] through highest

Add   Change   Remove

Values to Count:
2

Continue   Cancel   Help

Now click **Continue** to return to the "Count Occurrences . . . " dialog box.

We are almost ready to set SPSS on its task. Before we do that, however, we have to deal with "missing values." Remember, before we started we made sure the values of 0 (NAP), 8 (DK), and 9 (NA) for ABDEFECT and ABSINGLE were defined as missing. Since we do not want SPSS to count respondents with missing codes, we have to tell it to count only respondents who answered 1 (Yes) or 2 (No) on both questions.

In order to remove the people with missing value codes from consideration, click **If . . .** This opens the "Count Occurrences: If Cases" dialog box.

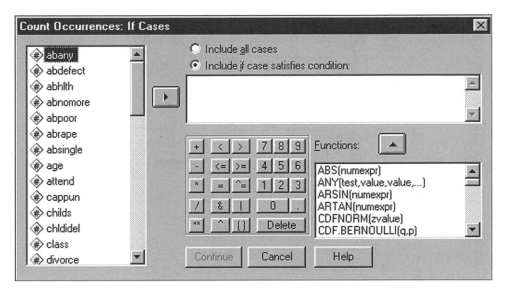

Begin by clicking the **button** next to the "**Include if case satisfies condition**" box. Now you can either **type** or **paste** the following expression in the box under the "Include if case satisfies condition" box:

nmiss (abdefect,absingle)=0

You can do this by clicking in the box and then using your key pad to type the expression. Alternatively, you can paste the expression by following the directions below:

- **Scroll** through the **Functions: list** on the bottom right hand side of the dialog box until you locate the NMISS(variable . . .) function. This function[2] is used to count the number of variables with missing value codes. Once you have located **NMISS(variable . . .)**, **highlight** it and click on the **arrow** above the list to move it to the empty field.
- The blinking question mark (?) shows that SPSS is waiting for you to specify the names of the variables. To do this, simply highlight **ABDEFECT** in the variable list, then transfer it with the right pointing **arrow**. You will notice that ABDEFECT has replaced the blinking question mark.
- Type a **comma** (,) then follow the same process to transfer the variable **ABSINGLE**
- Now you can use the calculator below to finish the expression by clicking **=0**

---

[2] SPSS contains an extensive library of functions for data manipulation and statistical computations that cannot be accomplished with procedures found on the **Data** and **Transform** drop down menus. Detailed information about functions may be found by clicking **Help→Index** and looking under "functions."

The expression, as shown below, tells SPSS to count only when the values 1 or 2 are present for both variables. If respondents answered 0, 8, or 9 for either variable, the index ABORT will be set to missing.

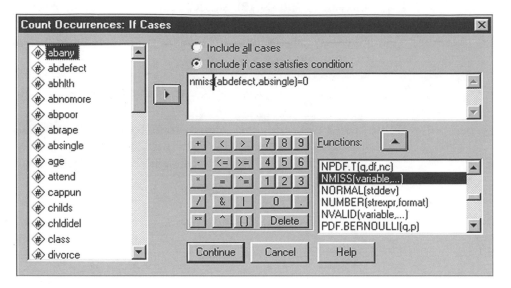

Now click **Continue** and then **OK** in the "Count Occurrences…" dialog box to set SPSS off on its assigned task.

You should now be back in the **Data View** portion of the Data Editor. **Scroll to the far right-side** and you will see your new ABORT variable in the last column. You may notice that many respondents (cases number 3 and 4, for instance) have a dot (.) as opposed to a value for ABORT. That is okay, it is just SPSS's way of telling you that this person had a missing value (0, 8, or 9) on either ABDEFECT or ABSINGLE, and therefore did not receive a score on our new index.

Demonstration 9.2: Defining ABORT

You may also notice that unlike other variables on our data file, the scores for ABORT include decimal places. If this is true, it is because the default number of decimals for your copy of SPSS has been set to two. The unused decimal places may be discarded when you define ABORT.

To do that, simply click on the **Variable View** tab.

Once you are in the Variable View window, **scroll down** until you see ABORT in the last row.

Now define your new index, similar to the way we defined new recoded variables in Chapter 6. In this case:

- set the decimals at 0
- set the width at 1
- you should already have a variable label, but you can change that if you prefer
- add values and labels as shown below
  0 = Yes/Approve (in both cases)
  1 = Conditional Support (yes in one case, no in one case)
  2 = No/Disapprove (in both cases)
- set the level of measurement to ordinal

Demonstration 9.3: Checking New Index – Comparing Scores on Old and New Variables

After you have defined your new variable, go back to the Data View portion of the Data Editor and locate ABORT in the far right-hand column. You will see that the decimal places are gone and each respondent has one of three scores: 0, 1, or 2.

Now we want to check our new index or verify that we created it correctly.

One simple way to determine whether we constructed our index properly is to compare a few respondents scores on the original variables (ABDEFECT and ABSINGLE) to their scores on our Index (ABORT).

For instance, determine how the first five respondents listed (case/row numbers #1-5) answered ABDEFECT and ABSINGLE. We have done it ourselves and listed their responses below:

	ABDEFECT	ABSINGLE	Expected Index Score	Actual ABORT Score
Case #1	1	2	1	1
Case #2	1	2	_____	_____
Case #3	0	0	Missing	Missing
Case #4	0	0	_____	_____
Case #5	1	2	_____	_____

Now without looking at your data file, determine what score each respondent should have gotten on your new ABORT index. If we constructed the index correctly their expected score should match their actual score on ABORT. As you can see above, Case #1 responded Yes (1) on ABDEFECT and No (2) on ABSINGLE, so he/she should get a score of 1 on our new index ABORT.

Similarly, since Case #3 has a 0 for ABDEFECT and a 0 for ABSINGLE, he/she should be labeled as Missing on our new index ABORT.

Now go ahead and determine the expected ABORT scores for Cases/Rows #2, 4, and 5.

Once you have done that, compare the expected Index scores to the actual ABORT scores. If you constructed the index properly, the expected and actual scores should match.

Demonstration 9.4: Running Frequencies for ABORT

An even better way to see if we really accomplished what we set out to do is to run **Frequencies** for the variable ABORT. Once you do that, you should see the following table.

ABORT Simple Abortion Index

		Frequency	Percent	Valid Percent	Cumulative Percent
Valid	0 yes, approve	375	25.0	42.0	42.0
	1 conditional support	331	22.1	37.1	79.1
	2 No/Disapprove	187	12.5	20.9	100.0
	Total	893	59.5	100.0	
Missing	System	607	40.5		
Total		1500	100.0		

If you compare the index score in this table with the crosstabs of the two component variables we ran in the last chapter, you'll see a logical correspondence. In the earlier table, 187 people disapproved of abortion under both of the specified conditions; here we find that 187 people scored 2 on the index. We also found that 323 people would approve abortion for birth defects but not for a single woman, and 8 had the reverse view; the index shows 331 people (323 + 8) with a score of 1. Finally, the 375 people who approved of abortion in both cases previously have a score of 0 on the index. Notice also that 607 people were excluded on the basis of missing data.

Congratulations! You've just created a composite index. We realize you may still be wondering why that's such good news. After all, it wasn't your idea to create the thing in the first place.

SPSS Command 9.1: Creating a Simple Index using COUNT

> *Creating Index*
>
> Click **Transform** → **Count** . . . →
>
> Type new **variable name** in **Target Variable:** field →
>
> Type new **variable label** in **Target Label:** field →
>
> **Transfer variables** for which specified values will be counted to **Numeric Variables:** field →
>
> Click **Define Values** . . . → Intert **Value(s)** to be counted → click **Add** → **Continue** →
>
> Click **If** . . . → click **Include if case satisfies condition:** → **Type or paste Expression** (ex. nmissing(abdefect,absingle)=0) → click **Continue** → **OK**
>
> *Defining New Variable*
>
> Access **Variable View** tab → scroll to **new variable** in last row → set **Type, Width, Values, Measure** →
>
> *Checking New Variable*
>
> Compare Expected and Actual Index scores →
>
> Run **Frequencies** for new variable →

Demonstration 9.5: Validating ABORT

To get a clearer idea of the value of such a composite measure, let's move on to the next step in the process we've launched. Let's validate the index; that is, let's make sure it really measures what we are attempting to measure. If you recall the earlier discussion of validity and reliability in Chapter 3, you'll see the link to this discussion of index validation.

In creating this simple index, we've tried to put respondents in one of three groups: those very supportive of abortion, those very opposed, and those in the middle. If we've succeeded in that effort, the scores we've assigned people on the new index, ABORT, should help us to predict how people answered other abortion items in the questionnaire. Let's begin with their answers to ABHLTH: approving abortion for a woman whose health is in danger.

To undertake this test of the index's validity, we'll return to the Crosstabs command, introduced in Chapter 8. As you'll see, it has some additional features that can be used to good effect. In this instance, we want to cross-classify people in terms of their scores on the index and on the variable ABHLTH.

Run the **Crosstabs** command with **ABHLTH** as the **row** variable and **ABORT** as the **column** variable (if you need to review the Crosstabs command, refer to the discussion in Chapter 8).[3] Here's the result you should get:

ABHLTH WOMANS HEALTH SERIOUSLY ENDANGERED * ABORT Simple Abortion Index Crosstabulation

Count

| | | ABORT Simple Abortion Index | | | |
		0 yes/approve	1 conditional support	2 no/disapprove	Total
ABHLTH WOMANS HEALTH SERIOUSLY ENDANGERED	1 YES	372	311	82	765
	2 NO	3	14	93	110
Total		375	325	175	875

You may be able to look at this table and see the relationship between the index and ABHLTH, but the analysis will be much simpler if we convert the data in the table to percentages. Let's express the assumption of validity that we are testing in terms of percentages. If those with a score of 0 on the index are the most supportive of abortion, then we should expect to find a higher percentage of them approving abortion in the case of the woman's health being endangered than we would find among the other groups.

Those who scored 2 on the index, by contrast, should be the least likely - the smallest percentage - to approve abortion based on the woman's health.

Looking first at those who scored 0, in the leftmost column of the table, we would calculate the percentage as follows. Of the 375 people who scored 0, we see that 372 approved of abortion in the case of ABHLTH. Dividing 372 by 375 indicates that those 372 people are 99.2 percent of the total 375. Looking at those with a score of 2, in the rightmost column, we find that the 82 who approve represent 46.85 percent of the 175 with that score. These two percentages support the assumption we are making about the index.

Happily, SPSS can be instructed to calculate these percentages for us. In fact, we are going to be looking at percentage tables for the most part in the rest of this book.

Go back to the **Crosstabs** window. Your previous request should still be in the appropriate fields. Notice a button at the bottom of this window called **Cells** . . . Click it. This will take you to a new window, as shown below:

---

[3] For the variable ABHTLH, the values 0, 8, and 9 should be defined as missing.

Notice that you can choose to have SPSS calculate percentages for you in one of three ways: using row totals, column totals, or the total number of cases. Click **Column** and then select **Continue** and **OK** in the Crosstabs window to have SPSS run the table for you. Your reward should look like the following:

ABHLTH WOMANS HEALTH SERIOUSLY ENDANGERED * ABORT Simple Abortion Index Crosstabulation

			ABORT Simple Abortion Index			
			0 yes, approve	1 conditional support	2 No/Disap prove	Total
ABHLTH WOMANS HEALTH SERIOUSLY ENDANGERED	1 YES	Count	372	311	82	765
		% within ABORT Simple Abortion Index	99.2%	95.7%	46.9%	87.4%
	2 NO	Count	3	14	93	110
		% within ABORT Simple Abortion Index	.8%	4.3%	53.1%	12.6%
Total		Count	375	325	175	875
		% within ABORT Simple Abortion Index	100.0%	100.0%	100.0%	100.0%

Take a moment to examine the logic of this table. For each score on the index, we have calculated the percentage saying they support (yes) or oppose (no) a woman's right to an abortion if her health is seriously endangered. It is as though we limited our attention to one of the index-score groups (those who scored 0, for example) and described them in terms of their attitudes on the abortion item; then we repeated the process for each of the index-score groups. Once we've described each of the subgroups, we can compare them.

When you have created a table with the percentages totaling 100 down each column, the proper way to read the table is across the rows. Rounding off the percentages to simplify matters, we would note, in this case (reading across the first two rows of the table), that

99 percent of those with a score of 0 on the index,

96 percent of those with a score of 1 on the index, and

47 percent of those with a score of 2 on the index

said they would approve of abortion if the woman's health were seriously endangered. This table supports our assumption that the index measures levels of support for a woman's freedom to choose abortion.

Now let's validate the index using the other abortion items not included in the index itself. Repeat the **Crosstabs** command, substituting the four abortion items — **ABNOMORE, ABRAPE, ABPOOR,** and **ABANY** — for ABHLTH.[4]

Run the Crosstabs command now and see what results you get. Look at each of the four tables and see what they say about the ability of the index to measure attitudes toward abortion. Here is an abbreviated table format that you might want to construct from the results of that command. SPSS doesn't create a table like this, but it's a useful format for presenting data in a research report.

Percentage Who Approve of Abortion When	0	1	2
the woman was raped	100	85	32
the couple can't afford more children	93	15	3
the couple doesn't want more children	94	14	4
the woman wants an abortion	89	13	3

ABORT Index

Whereas the earlier table showed the percentages who approved and those who disapproved of abortion in a specific situation, this table presents only those who approved. The first entry in the table, for example, indicates that 100 percent of those with a score of 0 on the index approved of abortion in the case of rape. Of those with a score of 1 on the index, 85 percent approved of abortion for this reason, and 32 percent of those with a score of 2 approved.

As you can see, the index accurately predicts differences in responses to each of the other abortion items. In each case, those with lower scores on the index are more likely to support abortion under the specified conditions than are those with higher scores on the index.

By building this composite index, we've created a more sophisticated measure of attitudes toward abortion. Whereas each of the individual items allows only for approval or disapproval of abortion under various circumstances, this index reflects three positions on the issue: unconditional disapproval (2), conditional approval (1), and unconditional approval (0).

---

[4] For the variables ABNOMORE, ABRAPE, ABPOOR, and ABANY, the values 0, 8, and 9 should be defined as missing.

SPSS Command 9.2: Producing Crosstabs with Column Percentages

Click **Analyze** → **Descriptive Statistics** → **Crosstabs** . . . →

Highlight variable name → click **arrow** pointing to the **Row(s)**: box →

Highlight **variable name** → click **arrow** pointing to the **Column(s)**: box →

Click **Cells** . . . → choose **Column** in Percentages box → **Continue** → OK

ABINDEX – Index Based on Six Abortion Variables

While our first index was created from only two of the abortion items, we can easily create a more thorough index using more items. In addition to providing us with a wider range of scores, having more items will increase our confidence in the index. As with quizzes, we'd have more confidence in a six item quiz than a two item quiz. For our new index, we will use all the abortion items except for ABANY, supporting a woman's unrestricted choice.

For this index, we will ask SPSS to count the number of times respondents approve (1 = YES) of abortion. Unlike the previous index, the more supportive respondents are of abortion, the higher the scores will be. Respondents who disapprove of abortion will have lower scores.

The ABINDEX scores will range from 0 (disapprove of abortion in all instances) to 6 (approve of abortion in all cases), with some respondents falling in between depending on their support/disapproval in various circumstances.

Usually before we begin we would ask you to make sure the appropriate values (0, 8, and 9) for each variable are defined as missing. Since we used these variables in the previous demonstrations, they should be ready to use.

Demonstration 9.6: ABINDEX

Since we are following the same basic procedures we used previously, the steps should be somewhat familiar to you. As a guide, we've outlined the process in brief below.

- Click **Transform** → **Count** . . . →
- Click **Reset** to remove all previous settings →
- Type new variable name **(ABINDEX)** in **Target Variable**: →
- Type a label for new variable **(descriptive variable label** of your choice) in **Target Label**: →
- Transfer six abortion variables **(ABDEFECT, ABHLTH, ABNOMORE, ABPOOR, ABRAPE, ABSINGLE)** to **Numeric Variables**: field[5] →
- Click **Define Values** . . . →
- Click **button** next to **Value**: →
- Type **1** → click **Add** → click **Continue** →
- Click **If** . . . →
- Click **button** next to **Include if case satisfies condition**: →

---

[5] If the previous index ABORT is still in the variable list, be careful that you do NOT transfer it to the Numeric Variables: field as well.

- Type or paste expression **NMISS(abdefect,abhlth,abnomore,abpoor, abrape,absingle)=0**
- Click **Continue → OK**

Now all we have to do is tidy up our new variable, ABINDEX, by accessing the **Variable View tab** and setting the **Decimals, Width, Values,** and level of measurement (**Measure**).

Once you have done that, you may want to return to the **Data View** portion of the Data Editor and check your new index by **comparing** the **Expected and Actual ABINDEX scores** for a few respondents/cases chosen at random.

Demonstration 9.7: Running Frequencies

Better yet, let's go ahead and run a **Frequency** distribution for **ABINDEX**. Here's what you should find.

		Frequency	Percent	Valid Percent	Cumulative Percent
Valid	0 no support	72	4.8	8.7	8.7
	1	59	3.9	7.1	15.8
	2	79	5.3	9.5	25.4
	3	201	13.4	24.3	49.6
	4	44	2.9	5.3	55.0
	5	43	2.9	5.2	60.1
	6 high support	330	22.0	39.9	100.0
	Total	828	55.2	100.0	
Missing	System	672	44.8		
Total		1500	100.0		

ABINDEX Abortion Index

This table shows the distribution of scores on the new index, ABINDEX. As you can see, there are 330 people — 40 percent of those with opinions — who support abortion in all the specified circumstances (score 6 on the index). A total of 72 disapprove of abortion in any of those circumstances (score 0 on the index). The rest are spread out according to the number of conditions they feel would warrant abortion.

Demonstration 9.8: Validating ABINDEX

For validation purposes, this time we have only one item not included in the index itself: ABANY. Let's see how well the index predicts respondents' approval of a woman's unrestricted choice of abortion. If necessary, click **Reset** before running Crosstabs.

In the **Crosstabs** dialog box specify:
- **ABANY** as the **row** variable
- **ABINDEX** as the **column** index
- **Cells** to be percentaged by **column**

ABANY ABORTION IF WOMAN WANTS FOR ANY REASON * ABINDEX Abortion Index Crosstabulation									
			ABINDEX Abortion Index						
			0 no support	1	2	3	4	5	6 high support	Total
ABANY ABORTION IF WOMAN WANTS FOR ANY REASON	1 YES	Count		2	5	15	22	18	306	368
		% within ABINDEX Abortion Index		3.4%	6.4%	7.7%	50.0%	43.9%	93.9%	45.2%
	2 NO	Count	72	56	73	181	22	23	20	447
		% within ABINDEX Abortion Index	100.0%	96.6%	93.6%	92.3%	50.0%	56.1%	6.1%	54.8%
Total		Count	72	58	78	196	44	41	326	815
		% within ABINDEX Abortion Index	100.0%	100.0%	100.0%	100.0%	100.0%	100.0%	100.0%	100.0%

As we can see, answers to ABANY are closely related to scores on ABINDEX.

Writing Box 9.1: Description of ABINDEX

Respondents' attitudes toward abortion have been summarized in the form of an index, ABINDEX. Scores on the index, which range from 0 to 6, are based on responses to six items asked in the questionnaire, each of which indicates some degree of support for a woman's right to choose an abortion (or opposition to it). The six items were presented as different circumstances in which you might approve or disapprove of abortion as a choice:

Strong chance of serious defect (ABDEFECT)
Woman's health seriously endangered (ABHLTH)
Married—wants no more children (ABNOMORE)
Low income—can't afford more children (ABPOOR)
Pregnant as result of rape (ABRAPE)
Not married (ABSINGLE)
(GSS variable names for items are presented in parentheses.)

Respondents were given one point for each circumstance they felt justified letting a woman choose abortion. Thus, respondents who scored 6 on the index (40% of the sample) felt each of the circumstances was sufficient justification. Those who scored 0 on the index (9% of the sample) were unconditionally opposed to abortion. A person who scored 3 on the index felt three of the circumstances warranted abortion but that the other three did not.

None of the people who scored 0 on ABINDEX favored a woman's right to an abortion for any reason. For scores 1 through 6, the percentage continues increasing across the index until we find that 93.9 percent of those who scored 6 on the index say a woman has the unconditional right to an abortion.

Once again, we find the index validated. This means that if we wish to analyze peoples' attitudes toward abortion further (and we will), we have the choice of using a single item to represent those attitudes or using a composite measure.

That is enough for now. However, before ending this session, make sure you **Save** both of your new variables (**ABORT** and **ABINDEX**) on your **DEMOPLUS** file so we can use them later (see Chapter 6).[6] It is important to reiterate that anyone using the Student Version of SPSS has to be sensitive to the fact that it is

---

[6] At the end of Chapters 6 and 7 we recommended you save your recoded variables on a file named DEMOPLUS so we can use these variables in later analysis.

limited to 50 variables. Consequently, you may need to follow the instructions in Chapter 6 regarding saving your data. For those of you using the Professional Version of SPSS, this is obviously not an issue.

Conclusion

In this chapter, we've seen that it is often possible to measure social scientific concepts in a number of ways. Sometimes, the data set contains a single item that does the job nicely. Measuring gender by asking people for their gender is a good example.

In other cases, the mental images that constitute our concepts (e.g., religiosity, political orientations, prejudice) are varied and ambiguous. Typically, no single item in a data set provides a complete representation of what we have in mind. Often, we can resolve this problem by combining two or more indicators of the concept into a composite index. As we've seen, SPSS offers the tools necessary for such data transformations.

If you continue your studies in social research, you will discover that there are many more sophisticated techniques for creating composite measures. However, the simple indexing techniques you have learned in this chapter will serve you well in the analyses that lie ahead.

Main Points

- Concepts can be measured in a number of different ways.
- In some cases a single item is enough to measure a concept.
- In the case of a controversial and emotionally charged issue such as abortion, where opinion is varied and intricate, no one item is capable of capturing the complexity of opinion.
- In such cases, composite measures made up of multiple indicators of a single concept can be very useful.
- There are a variety of advantages to using composite measures.
- An index is a form of composite measure.
- The Count command allows us to create a new summary variable or index based on the scores of existing variables.
- We created one fairly simple index (ABORT) and one more complicated index (ABINDEX) with Count. Both indices were designed to measure overall feelings about abortion.
- After creating variables, it is important to check your work by running frequencies and to validate your work by requesting Crosstabs with percentages.
- When saving your new recoded variables, those working with the Student Version of SPSS must be aware of the variable limit, those working with the Professional Version of SPSS are NOT limited in terms of the number of variables they can save.

Key Terms

Composite measure   Index
Count

SPSS Commands Introduced in This Chapter

9.1   Creating a Simple Index Using COUNT

9.2   Producing Crosstabs with Column Percentages

Review Questions

1. What is a composite measure?

2. What is an index?

3. Why do researchers create indexes? What are the advantages of using an index?

4. In this chapter we created indexes using which command: Analyze, Compute, Count, or Recode?

5. What dialog box do we use to specify which value(s) of certain variables are to be counted?

6. After creating an index, you access the Variable View tab for what purpose(s)?

7. How do we test an index's validity?

8. What are the SPSS commands used to run Crosstabs with column percentages?

9. In addition to percentagizing by column, how else can we percentagize crosstab tables?

10. Can indexes be based on the scores of more than two variables?

11. Can the procedure used to create indexes in this chapter be used if the variables are not coded the same way?

12. What is one disadvantage of using COUNT to create an index?

13. In this chapter we created two indexes that helped summarize American attitudes toward abortion. Setting this issue aside, for a moment, what other complicated issues or ambiguous concepts are you personally interested in investigating further? Identify three issues or concepts, at least one of which can be investigated using either your DEMO.SAV or EXER.SAV files.

NAME _____

CLASS _____

INSTRUCTOR _____

DATE _____

In this exercise you will be given an opportunity to create two indexes. In order to complete the exercises, you should access the EXERPLUS.SAV file we asked you to create at the end of SPSS Lab Exercise 6.1. If you did not save the recoded variables, don't worry; when we use them in later exercises, you can simply go back and recode them following the commands in SPSS Lab Exercise 6.1. At the end of this exercise we will ask you to save the indexes you create on your EXERPLUS file, so if you are working in a lab setting, make sure you have a disk handy.

The first index is based on two variables contained in your EXERPLUS.SAV data file, POLABUSE and POLATTAK. Simply follow the steps below and supply the information requested. You will find answers to Questions 1-3, 5-6, 8, 10, 12-15 in Appendix B.

1. What does the variable POLABUSE measure?

2. What does the variable POLATTAK measure?

3. List the values and labels for POLABUSE and POLATTAK.

   Value   . *Label*

   _____   _____

   _____   _____

   _____   _____

   _____   _____

   _____   _____

4. Define 0, 8, and 9 as "missing" for the variables POLABUSE, POLATTAK, POLESCAP, POLHITOK, and POLMURDR.
   Our new variable/index will be named POLIN (for POLice INdex)
   POLIN scores are:
   0 - Approve/Yes in both cases.
   1 - Conditional Approval/Yes in one case, but not the other.
   2 - Disapprove/No in both cases.

5. The _____ [higher/lower] the index score, the *more the respondent agrees* that there are situations in which they would approve of a police officer striking an adult male citizen.

6. The _____[higher/lower] the index score, the *less the respondent agrees* that there are situations in which they would approve of a police officer striking an adult male citizen.

7. Compute new variable/index – POLIN [Hint: Click **Transform** → **Count**] Then define your new variable [Hint: Access **Variable View** tab, then set **decimals**, **width**, **values**/labels, and **measure**).

8. Access the **Data View** tab. Use the information in the Matrix to complete the first two columns indicating the values for the variables POLABUSE and POLATTAK (Respondents Case #1-6).

   After completing first two columns, use the information to fill in the "Expected Index score" for each case.

   Now compare the Expected Index score to the actual POLIN score for each Case. Based on this "test," use the space below to indicate whether your Index appears by this method at least, to have been completed properly, or whether you need to go back and reconstruct the index.

	Value on *POLABUSE*	*Value on* *POLATTAK*	*Expected* *Index Score*	*Actual* *POLIN Score*
Case #1				
Case #2				
Case #3				
Case #4				
Case #5				
Case #6				

9. Run and print Frequencies for POLIN.

10. Of those who answered,
    _____ % received a score of 0 on the index.
    _____ % received a score of 1 on the index.
    _____ % received a score of 2 on the index.

11. Now validate your index by cross-classifying people in terms of their response to **POLIN** and the following variables: **POLESCAP**, **POLHITOK**, and **POLMURDR**.
    *Run **Crosstabs** with **column percentages**
    *Specify **POLIN** as the **Column variable**
    [Hint: **Analyze** → **Descriptive Statistics** → **Crosstabs** ...]

12. POLESCAP by POLIN
    _____ % of those with a score of 0 on the index
    _____ % of those with a score of 1 on the index
    _____ % of those with a score of 2 on the index
    agree that it is okay for a police officer to hit someone if he is trying to escape from custody.

NAME _____

CLASS _____

INSTRUCTOR _____

DATE _____

13. POLMURDR by POLIN

_____% of those with a score of 0 on the index

_____% of those with a score of 1 on the index

_____% of those with a score of 2 on the index

agree that it is okay for a police officer to hit someone if he is being questioned as a murder suspect.

14. POLHITOK by POLIN

_____ % of those with a score of 0 on the index

_____ % of those with a score of 1 on the index

_____ % of those with a score of 2 on the index

say that they can imagine a situation in which they would approve of a policeman striking an adult male citizen.

15. Was the POLIN index validated? If so, what does it tell you about American attitudes towards law enforcement officials and the use of force? Explain.

16. Now it is time to compute an index on your own. Create a more complex index (POLFORCE) based on the following four variables: POLABUSE, POLATTAK, POLESCAP, and POLMURDR. After you construct and define your index:

- Run frequencies.
- Validate your index by running Crosstabs (using POLFORCE as the column variable).
- Print both your frequencies and Crosstabs, and attach them to this sheet.
- Describe your findings below. You may want to indicate, for instance, whether your index was validated, as well as what this index reveals about Americans' attitudes toward the use of force by police officers.
- Save the indexes you created in this Lab Exercise on your EXERPLUS.SAV file so we can use them in later analysis.

Chapter 10 **Suggestions for Further Analysis**

In the preceding chapters, we've given you a number of research possibilities to begin exploring based on the variables contained in your DEMO.SAV file. The topics we have focused on so far include religion, politics, and abortion. In the event that you've exhausted those possibilities and want to look beyond them, here are some additional topics for you to consider.

Desired Family Size

One of the major social problems facing the world today is that of overpopulation. A brief summary of population growth on the planet should illustrate what we mean.

Year	Population	Doubling Time
0	25 billion	—
1650	50 billion	1,650 years
1850	1.00 billion	200 years
1930	2.00 billion	80 years
1975	4.00 billion	45 years
1994	5.64 billion	39 years
1998	5.93 billion	49 years
2002	6.27 billion	54 years

These data show several things. For example, the world's population has increased more than 20-fold since the beginning of the Christian era. More important, until recently the rate of growth has been increasing steadily. This is most easily seen in the rightmost column above, showing what demographers call the *doubling time*. It took 1,650 years for the world's population to increase from a quarter of a billion people to half a billion. The time required to double dramatically shortened until 1994. As of 1998, the doubling time increased to about 49 years. However, even with the slight increase in doubling time, today's children can expect to live out their older years in a world with nearly 12 billion people.

This astounding increase in the pace of population growth has been caused by the fact that during most of human existence, extremely high death rates have been matched by equally high birth rates. During the past few generations, however, death rates have plummeted around the world because of improved public health measures, medical discoveries, and improved food production.

The current pace of population growth simply cannot go on forever. Although scientists may disagree on the number of people the planet can support, there is simply no question that there is some limit. At some point, population growth must be slowed even more and stopped—perhaps even reversed.

There are two ways to end population growth: Either death rates can be returned to their former high levels or birth rates can be reduced. Because most of us would choose the latter solution, demographers have been very interested in variables that measure desired family size.

Demonstration 10.1:
Respondents' Ideal Family Size (CHLDIDEL)

Your data set contains a variable, CHLDIDEL, that presents responses to the question, "What do you think is the ideal number of children for a family to have?" If every family had only two children, then births and deaths would eventually roughly balance each other out, producing a condition of population stabilization, or zero population growth (excluding the effect of migration). What percentage of the population do you suppose chose that as the ideal? Some favored larger families, and others said they thought only one child was the ideal. Why don't you find out what the most common response was by running frequencies and the appropriate measure of central tendency.[1]

CHLDIDEL IDEAL NUMBER OF CHILDREN

		Frequency	Percent	Valid Percent	Cumulative Percent
Valid	0	13	.9	1.3	1.3
	1	36	2.4	3.7	5.1
	2	516	34.4	53.3	58.3
	3	233	15.5	24.0	82.4
	4	89	5.9	9.2	91.5
	5	9	.6	.9	92.5
	6	3	.2	.3	92.8
	7 SEVEN+	1	.1	.1	92.9
	8 AS MANY AS WANT	69	4.6	7.1	100.0
	Total	969	64.6	100.0	
Missing	-1 NAP	484	32.3		
	9 DK,NA	47	3.1		
	Total	531	35.4		
Total		1500	100.0		

Later in this book when we focus on bivariate analysis, you may want to explore the causes of people's attitudes about ideal family size. For instance, it may be interesting to consider whether the number of siblings that respondents have (SIBS) impacts their conception of ideal family size (CHLDIDEL).

---

[1] Throughout the chapter, be sure to define the appropriate values for each variable under consideration as "missing."

Writing Box 10.1

Half the respondents (53%) say two children would be ideal, with a fourth (24%) saying three. Seven percent offer an ambiguous answer, saying "as many as you want" is the ideal number. Five percent of the sample say they want fewer than two children, and the rest want four or more. Clearly, the two-child family has become the norm. Both the median and mode are 2 children, and the mean is 2.83.

Child Training

What do you think are the most important qualities for children to develop as they grow up? Respondents to the General Social Survey were asked that question also. To frame the question more specifically, they were presented with several of the answers people commonly give and were asked how important each was. If you had to choose, which thing on this list would you pick as the most important for a child to learn to prepare him or her for life?

The interviewer read the following list (which we've annotated with the GSS variable names):

OBEY	to obey
POPULAR	to be well-liked or popular
THNKSELF	to think for himself or herself
WORKHARD	to work hard
HELPOTH	to help others when they need help

Once the respondents indicated which of these they felt were most important, they were asked:

Which comes next in importance?
Which comes third?
Which comes fourth?

This set of responses allowed the researchers to code the final responses as "Least important."

Demonstration 10.2: Important Qualities for Children

As with earlier topics, take a moment to notice how you feel about such matters. Then see if you can anticipate what public opinion is on these qualities of children. It will be useful, by the way, to observe your reasoning process as you attempt to anticipate public opinion. What observations, clues, or cues prompt you to think OBEY is the most important, or POPULAR, or whichever one you picked as the one most people would choose?

Then you can see how people actually responded to the questions. You can use either of the univariate techniques reviewed in earlier chapters (Frequencies or Graphs) to examine how respondents to the 2000 GSS answered these questions. In this case, let's go ahead and run appropriate graphs and charts for these variables.

Once you've done that, you should review your earlier reasoning, either to confirm your predictions or to figure out where you went wrong. What can you infer from the differences among your opinions, your predictions, and the actual results?

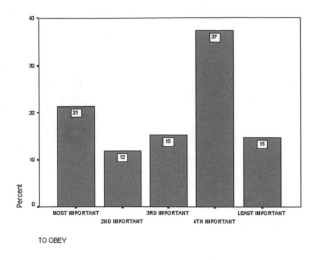

TO OBEY

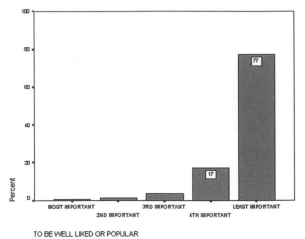

TO BE WELL LIKED OR POPULAR

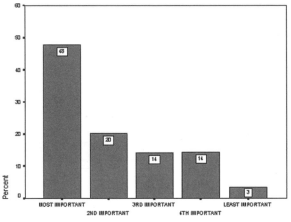

TO THINK FOR ONES SELF

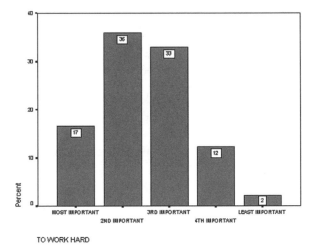

TO WORK HARD

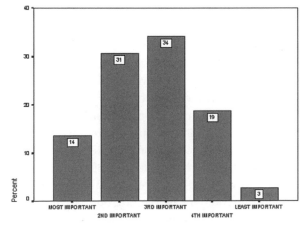

TO HELP OTHERS

Writing Box 10.2

These graphs paint a pretty clear picture of what people say they value in their children. Thinking for themselves is clearly the most prized, whereas being well-liked or popular is in the basement. Hard work and helping others are both valued, and they evidence a normal distribution—minorities at the two extremes and most saying they are somewhat important.

The issue of obedience in children is the most interesting, perhaps. There is a bipolar response: with large numbers at the extremes and fewer in the middle. This indicates that there are two relatively strong and opposing points of view among Americans on this issue. (A similar pattern exists in attitudes toward homosexuality - see HOMOSEX below.)

Attitudes About Sexual Behavior

As with most other things, Americans differ in their feelings about sexual behavior. We thought you might be interested in this area of public opinion, so we've included three GSS variables dealing with two different kinds of sexual behavior.

HOMOSEX asks about homosexual sex relations while PREMARSX focuses on premarital sex. Both variables measure respondents' attitudes toward the behavior of others. Either might be taken as an indication of overall orientation, but it is important always to remember exactly what variables represent. One question this raises, however, is whether self-reports of behavior can be considered generally reliable? A second question you may want to think about is whether this method of data collection (surveys) should be used primarily to measure opinions and attitudes rather than behavior, or doesn't it matter?

We realize that you may very well have strong opinions about each of these issues. Your job as a social science researcher, however, is to find out what Americans as a whole think and do. Which do you think people tolerate more: premarital sex or homosexuality? Give it some thought and then check it out using one of the techniques we covered earlier.

It's not too early to begin asking yourself what would cause people to be more tolerant or less so in these regards. When we turn to bivariate analysis later on, you'll have a chance to test some of your expectations.

Demonstration 10.3: Index of Sexual Permissiveness

Here's an idea that could take you deeper into this general topic. See if you can use the **Transform → Count . . .** command to create a composite measure of sexual permissiveness, combining the two items so that the higher the index score, the more likely respondents will be sexually permissive.

Go ahead and construct an index called **SEXPERM**. As always, you will need to make sure the nonresponses for **HOMOSEX** and **PREMARSX** (codes 0, 5, 8, and 9) are defined as missing. Since response code 4, "Not Wrong" indicates permissiveness, you will need to tell COUNT to count the 4's for both variables. Use the NMISS function to assure only those cases that have responses for both questions are used to construct the index.

After you have created **SEXPERM**, run frequencies to check your index. What conclusions would you draw about the sexual attitudes and behavior of Americans? Are they generally permissive or not? You can check your findings against ours shown below.

SEXPERM sexual permissiveness					
		Frequency	Percent	Valid Percent	Cumulative Percent
Valid	0 neither	236	15.7	53.2	53.2
	1 one	136	9.1	30.6	83.8
	2 both	72	4.8	16.2	100.0
	Total	444	29.6	100.0	
Missing	System	1056	70.4		
Total		1500	100.0		

Writing Box 10.3: Description of SEXPERM Index

SEXPERM is an index of sexual permissiveness, based on two indicators. HOMOSEX asks respondents whether "sexual relations between two adults of the same sex . . . is always wrong, almost always wrong, wrong only sometimes, or not wrong at all." Those who chose either of the last two responses received one point on the index.

The other item in the index, PREMARSX, asked a similar question about a man and a woman having "sex relations before marriage" and was scored the same as HOMOSEX. Thus, respondents who approved of both homosexuality and premarital sex received a score of 2 on the index, those who disapproved of both were scored 0. Those who approved of only one (usually premarital sex) were scored 1.

The sexual permissiveness index has a range of 0 to 2. A majority of respondents (53%) had a score of zero, meaning they disapproved of both PREMARSX and HOMOSEX. Thirty-one percent scored 1, indicating they were permissive toward one of the two behaviors. A minority of respondents (16%) had a score of 2 indicating approval of both PREMARSX and HOMOSEX behavior.

Prejudice

Prejudice is a topic that has concerned social scientists for a long time, and the persistence of the problem keeps it a topic of interest and research. Your disk includes three items from the GSS that deal with aspects of anti-Black prejudice: RACMAR, RACPUSH, and RACDIF4. All three items deal with different components of prejudice and racial attitudes. RACMAR measures respondents' attitudes toward the legality of interracial marriage, RACPUSH measures attitudes toward Black-White relations, whereas RACDIF4 deals with the causes of differences in socioeconomic status. You may want to look at Appendix A for the exact wording of these questions. Remember, it's always important to know exactly how survey questions were asked in order to understand what the responses really mean.

These items present you with an interesting picture of racial attitudes and prejudice in the United States. Where, for instance, do you think the majority of adult Americans stand on the issue of interracial marriage? Do you think most respondents feel that interracial marriage should be outlawed or not?

You may be able to guess that general opposition to interracial marriage has decreased over the years. Before you look at this variable, however, take a moment to try to guess what the level of public support for making interracial marriage illegal might be. Then use one of the techniques introduced in earlier chapters to see how well you've been able to anticipate opinion on this issue.

Next, try to estimate overall opinion on the other two variables: RACPUSH and RACDIF4. It may be somewhat more difficult for you to estimate opinion on these issues, but after you have come up with an estimate, check to see whether you were correct by running frequencies.

You may want to consider creating a composite measure of prejudice called PREJIND, from three of the variables: RACMAR, RACPUSH, and RACDIF4. Remember, as in the last demonstration, you need to do a few things before you start constructing your index:

- Define appropriate values for each variable as missing.
- Take into account that the values/labels for RACPUSH are different than the values/labels for the other two variables. Consequently, in order to create an index using COUNT, you should recode RACPUSH to create RECRAC as follows:

Old values/labels	*New values/labels*
1 Agree Strongly	1 Yes/Agree
2 Agree Slightly	
3 Disagree Slightly	2 No/Disagree
4 Disagree Strongly	

In this case you want to give respondents 1 point for each of the following responses:

RACMAR: 1 - Yes, oppose interracial marriage
RECRAC: 1 - Yes/Agree "Blacks shouldn't push themselves where they're not wanted."
RACDIF4: 1 - Yes, agree with statement Blacks "have worse jobs, income, and housing" than White people because they "just don't have the motivation or willpower to pull themselves up out of poverty."

For your new index (PREJIND), respondents will receive between 0-3 points, with higher scores indicating higher degrees of prejudice

- Afterwards, be sure to define your new variable and then run frequencies and crosstabs to check and validate your findings.

Writing Box 10.4

PREJIND is an index intended to measure respondents' levels of prejudice. Respondents received one point for each of the following responses (GSS code names are in parentheses):

- opposing interracial marriage (RACMAR)
- strongly agreeing or agreeing with the statement "Blacks shouldn't push themselves where they're not wanted" (RECRAC, recoded RACPUSH)
- saying Blacks "have worse jobs, income, and housing than white people" because they "just don't have the motivation or will power to pull themselves up out of poverty" (RACDIF4)

Thus, respondents could get between 0 and 3 points on the index, with higher scores representing higher degrees of prejudice.

Thirty-eight percent of the respondents had PREJIND scores of 0, while 29% indicated prejudice by responding affirmatively to one item. Twenty-five percent responded affirmatively to two items. Only 8% showed prejudice by responding positively to all three items.

Conclusion

There are several other variables in the data set. As you no doubt recall from our discussion in Chapter 8 (SPSS Command 8.1), you can get an overview of the whole thing by the command **Utilities → Variables** . . . Once you see the list of variables on the left side of the window, you can click on any of the **variable names** to get short descriptions and the codes used for categorical responses.

By the time you finish this chapter, you should be feeling fairly comfortable with SPSS and the GSS data set. Now you can add more strength to the facility you are developing. In Part IV, you are going to try your hand at bivariate analysis, which lets you start to search for the reasons people are the way they are.

Main Points

- DEMO.SAV contains a variety of variables that open up a number of different research possibilities.
- In addition to religion, politics, and abortion, the data set also contains variables that deal with issues such as desired family size, child training, attitudes toward sexual behavior, and prejudice.
- Overpopulation is an issue of grave concern that can be dealt with in two primary ways.
- Because most people prefer a solution that deals with decreasing birth rates as opposed to increasing death rates, public opinion regarding ideal family size is an issue of great interest to many researchers.
- If you are interested in child development and child rearing, public attitudes regarding child training may be of particular interest to you.
- Attitudes toward sexual behavior can be combined to create an interesting measure of sexual permissiveness.
- It is important to note that while two of the variables dealing with sexual behavior measure public attitudes toward the behavior of others, the third variable focuses on the respondents' own behavior.
- Three variables deal with different aspects of prejudice, specifically anti-Black prejudice.
- You can use several of the techniques reviewed in earlier chapters to examine these and other topics in more depth.
- Some of the key techniques we have covered so far include: frequencies, measures of central tendency and dispersion, recoding, graphs and charts, crosstabs, and index construction.

Key Term

Doubling time

SPSS Commands Introduced in This Chapter

No new commands were introduced in this chapter.

Review Questions

1. What topics besides religion, politics, and abortion are represented by the variables contained in your DEMO.SAV file?

2. List the variables on your DEMO.SAV file that pertain to ideal family size.

3. List two SPSS techniques reviewed previously that you could use to determine how respondents to the 2000 GSS feel about this issue.

4. List the variables on your DEMO.SAV file that pertain to child training.

5. List two SPSS techniques reviewed earlier that you could use to determine which qualities respondents value in children.

6. List the variables on your DEMO.SAV file that pertain to attitudes about sexual behavior.

7. Which of the variable(s) listed in response to Question 6 measure attitudes and which measure behavior?

8. Why might some researchers argue that a measure of self-reported behavior is potentially unreliable?

9. List the variables on your DEMO.SAV file that pertain to prejudice.

10. List two SPSS techniques reviewed previously that you could use to examine either the topic of sexual attitudes/behavior OR prejudice in more depth.

11. Of the four new topics introduced in this chapter, which would you be most interested in examining further and why?

NAME _____

CLASS _____

INSTRUCTOR _____

DATE _____

Your EXER.SAV data file contains a number of additional topics and research possibilities for you to consider, including sex roles, police, environment, mass media use, national government spending priorities, teen sex, and affirmative action.

In this exercise, you will be asked to choose and examine one of these topics in more depth. Our goal is to allow you to use and apply several of the SPSS techniques introduced in earlier chapters. In addition, we want you to gain more practice not only using SPSS, but interpreting your findings and writing up research results. Throughout the last few chapters we have periodically supplied you with "Writing Boxes" which illustrate how a social scientist might communicate findings in writing. Remember the ability to interpret and communicate your findings in writing is crucial. While this is a skill that is as difficult to teach as it is to master, our experience has been that the more you read research reports in the media, scholarly journals, and the like, and the more you practice creating your own research reports, the better your chances of success.

1. Choose a topic or issue you are interested in investigating further from the list provided above.

2. Use the **Utilities → Variables . . .** command to identify the variables in your EXER.SAV file which pertain to this issue/topic. Then list the abbreviated variable name and variable label for each item in the space provided below. [SPSS Command 8.1 - Chapter 8][2]

   Abbreviated Variable Name   *Description*

---

[2] If you have trouble recalling how to accomplish a particular task, please refer to the relevant SPSS commands referenced throughout this lab exercise.

3. Using the world wide web, the library or another research tool, investigate the issue/topic you have chosen. Then write a few short paragraphs (similar to those in Chapter 10) which accomplish the following:
   - provide a general overview or introduction to this issue/topic
   - state why the issue/topic is of interest to you (as well as others)
   - highlight at least one of the central questions and controversies that make this issue/topic ripe for social research and further investigation

NAME _____

CLASS _____

INSTRUCTOR _____

DATE _____

4. In the space provided below, list the abbreviated variable names, values and labels for each variable listed in response to Question #2. [SPSS Command 5.6 - Chapter 5]

Then indicate which of the values for each variable should be defined as missing.

Once you have done that, use SPSS to define the appropriate values for each variable as missing. [SPSS Command 6.12 - Chapter 6; SPSS Command 7.6 – Chapter 7]

5. Run frequencies for each variable listed in response to Question #2. Then summarize your findings in a paragraph or two in the space provided below. Be sure to print your findings and attach them to this sheet. [SPSS Commands 6.4, 6.9 – Chapter 6]

NAME _____

CLASS _____

INSTRUCTOR _____

DATE _____

6. Run the appropriate graphs/charts for each variable listed in response to Question #2. Then summarize your findings in a few short paragraphs in the space below. Be sure to include a title on each of your charts, print out your findings and attach them to this sheet. [SPSS Commands 7.1-7.5, 7.7 – Chapter 7]

7. Choose two of the following techniques:
   - Running measures of central tendency and dispersion [SPSS Commands 6.10-6.11 – Chapter 6]
   - Recoding [SPSS Command 6.13 – Chapter 6]
   - Crosstabulation [SPSS Command 8.3 – Chapter 8; SPSS Command 9.2 – Chapter 9]
   - Index construction [SPSS Command 9.1 – Chapter 9]

Then use the techniques to investigate the issue/topic you are considering in more depth. After examining the issue/topic:

   - summarize your findings below
   - print and attach your output to this sheet [SPSS Command 6.14 – Chapter 6]

Part IV Bivariate Analysis

This set of chapters adds another dimension to your analyses. By moving from the analysis of one variable, univariate analysis, to the analysis of two variables at a time, bivariate analysis, we open the possibility of exploring matters of cause and effect. Thus, in Chapter 11, we'll begin to examine what factors cause some people to be more religious than others. In this analysis, we'll be guided by an earlier analysis, which put forward a "deprivation theory" of church involvement.

In Chapter 12, we'll begin to discover why some people are liberal and others conservative, as well as why some are Democrats, others Republicans, and still others Independents. In addition, we'll begin to explore some of the consequences of political orientations. What differences do they make in terms of other attitudes and orientations?

Chapter 13 is going to take us deep inside the hotly controversial issue of abortion. You probably already have a few ideas about why some people are supportive of a woman's right to choose an abortion and others are opposed. Now you are going to have an opportunity to test your expectations and learn something about the roots of different points of view in this national debate.

In Chapters 11 through 13, we are going to limit our analyses to percentage tables, a basic format for investigations in social research. However, there are many other methods for measuring the extent to which variables are related to one another. We'll examine some of these in Chapter 14, where we focus on some common measures of association such as lambda, gamma, Pearson's *r*, and simple regression. You'll learn the logic that lies behind these measures, as well as how they help us assess the strength (and in some cases, the direction) of association between variables.

Chapter 15 adds another set of techniques for your use in assessing the associations that you discover among variables. Whenever samples have been chosen from a larger population, as is the case with the GSS data, there is always some danger that the associations we discover among variables in our sample are merely results of sampling error and do not represent a genuine pattern in the larger population. Chapter 15 will demonstrate several techniques used by social researchers to guard against being misled in that fashion.

Finally, as we did in Part III, we'll conclude our examination of bivariate analysis in Chapter 16 with suggestions for other lines of inquiry.

Chapter 11 Examining the Sources of Religiosity

You may recall that in Chapter 8, we gave you a sense of bivariate analysis by showing you how to run Crosstabs, an important bivariate technique. You may also recall that while we utilized this technique to examine attitudes toward abortion in more depth, we noted that it is primarily used to examine the relationships between variables and to test hypotheses.

Consequently, in this chapter we are going to turn our attention to Crosstabs once again, paying particular attention to how this technique can be used to help us understand why some people are more religious than others.

Except for our brief foray into Crosstabs, up to this point we have largely limited our discussion to *unviariate analysis*, the analysis of one variable. Now, however, we are going to turn our attention to *bivariate analysis*, the analysis of two variables at a time. This will allow us to shift our focus from description (mainly the province of univariate analysis) to the more exciting world of explanation.

It may be useful for you to think about the differences between univariate and bivariate analyses in terms of the number of variables, major questions, and primary goals.

	Univariate Analysis	Bivariate Analysis
Number of Variables	1	2
Major Question	What?	Why?
Primary Goal	Description	Explanation

Consequently, whereas in the previous section we looked at the extent of people's religiosity, we now turn our attention to trying to explain "why": *Why* are some people more religious than others? What *causes* some people to be more religious than others? How can we *explain* the fact that some people are more religious than others?

The Deprivation Theory of Religiosity

The reading titled "A Theory of Involvement," by Charles Y. Glock, Benjamin R. Ringer, and Earl R. Babbie, on the CD that accompanies this text, presents one explanation for differing degrees of religiosity. In it, the authors explain their social deprivation theory of religiosity. Simply put, they say that people who are denied gratification within the secular society will be more likely to turn to the church as an alternative source of gratification.

In their analysis, they looked for variables that distinguished those who were getting more gratification in the secular society from those who were getting less. For example, they reasoned that the United States is still a male-dominated society, meaning that women are denied the level of gratification enjoyed by men. Women often earn less for the same work, are denied equal access to prestigious occupations, are underrepresented in politics, and so on. According to the deprivation theory, therefore, women should be more religious than men.

The data analyses done by Glock et al., based on a sample of Episcopalian church members, confirmed their hypothesis. The question we might now ask is whether the same is true of the general U.S. population? Our data allow us to test that hypothesis.

Testing Our Hypothesis — Correlating Religiosity and Gender

You may recall that at the end of Chapter 6 we asked you to save your recoded variables in a file named DEMOPLUS. Since we want to use some of our recoded variables in this chapter, go ahead and open the **DEMOPLUS** file. If you did not save your recoded variables, don't worry. You can easily recode the necessary variables (ATTEND → CHATT; AGE → AGECAT) by following the recode commands in Chapter 6.

As we noted earlier, this analysis requires us to advance our analytic procedures to bivariate analysis, involving two variables: a cause and an effect. If you think back to our discussion of theory and hypotheses in Chapter 2, you may recall that in this case religiosity would be the effect or *dependent variable* and gender the cause or *independent variable*. This means that your gender causes — to some extent — your degree of religiosity. Based on this notion we might construct a *hypothesis* that states:

> You are more likely to be religious [dependent variable] if you are a woman [category of independent variable — gender] than if you are a man [category of independent variable — gender].

It is often easy to confuse the *categories of the variable* with the variable itself. Keep in mind that in this case, "woman" and "man" are categories of the independent variable, "gender."

To test this hypothesis, we need measures of both the independent and dependent variables. The independent variable (gender) is easy: The variable SEX handles that nicely. But what about our dependent variable (religiosity)? As you'll recall from our earlier discussion, there are several measures available to us. For the time being, let's use church attendance as our measure, even though we've noted that it is not a perfect indicator of religiosity in its most general meaning.

You will remember that when we looked at ATTEND in Chapter 6, it had nine categories. If we were to crosstabulate ATTEND and SEX without recoding ATTEND, we would expect a table with 18 (9 × 2) cells. To make our table more manageable, we are going to use the recoded CHATT as our measure of church attendance.[1]

Once we have identified the independent variable (SEX) and dependent variable (CHATT), we are going to ask SPSS to construct a crosstab or crosstabulation. A *crosstab* is a table that shows the distribution of one variable for each category of a second variable. For an example, look back at some of the crosstabs we created in Chapters 8 and 9.

Crosstabs are powerful tools because they allow us to determine whether there is an association between the two variables under consideration. In this case, for instance, is gender (SEX) related to or associated with church attendance (CHATT)?

Demonstration 11.1:
Running Crosstabs to Test Our Hypothesis

When running **Crosstabs** it is customary to specify the dependent variable as the row variable and the independent variable as the column variable. We will follow this convention by accessing the Crosstabs dialog box (**Analyze → Descriptive Statistics → Crosstabs . . .**) and then specifying:

- **CHATT** (dependent variable) as the **row** variable
- **SEX** (independent variable) as the **column** variable
- **Cells** to be percentaged by **column**

If you execute this command, you should get the following result.

CHATT Recoded Church Attendance * SEX RESPONDENTS SEX Crosstabulation

| | | | SEX RESPONDENTS SEX | | |
			1 MALE	2 FEMALE	Total
CHATT Recoded Church Attendance	1 About weekly	Count	160	273	433
		% within SEX RESPONDENTS SEX	25.1%	33.1%	29.6%
	2 About monthly	Count	96	144	240
		% within SEX RESPONDENTS SEX	15.0%	17.5%	16.4%
	3 Seldom	Count	237	253	490
		% within SEX RESPONDENTS SEX	37.1%	30.7%	33.5%
	4 Never	Count	145	155	300
		% within SEX RESPONDENTS SEX	22.7%	18.8%	20.5%
Total		Count	638	825	1463
		% within SEX RESPONDENTS SEX	100.0%	100.0%	100.0%

---

[1] If you did not save the recoded variable CHATT, simply go back to Chapter 6 and follow the recode commands to create CHATT before moving ahead with the demonstrations in this chapter.

Table 11.1   Tips for Identifying Independent and Dependent Variables[a]

Remember, when running crosstabs on SPSS it is important that you first determine which variable is the independent and which is the dependent. Then specify the independent as the column variable and the dependent as the row variable. Sometimes identifying independent and dependent variables can sometimes be tricky. If you are having difficulty determining the independent and dependent variables, try using one of the following "hints":[b]

1. Restate the hypothesis as an "If _____ [independent variable], then _____ [dependent variable]" statement.

   Example: If you are female [independent variable - gender], then you are more likely to be religious [dependent variable - religiosity]

2. The independent variable "influences" the dependent variable.

   Example: Ask yourself if religiosity can "influence" gender. Once you have reasoned that the answer is no, switch it around. Can gender "influence" religiosity? Since in this case the answer is maybe, you know that gender is the independent variable and religiosity is the dependent variable.

3. The independent variable is the one that comes first in time (i.e., "before" the dependent variable).

   Example: Ask yourself which came first, gender or religiosity. Since gender is determined before religiosity, you know that gender is the independent variable.

a. For further discussion, see Russell K. Schutt, *Investigating the Social World: The Process and Practice of Research*, 3rd Edition (Thousand Oaks, CA: Pine Forge Press, 2001), 39-41; Chava Frankfort-Nachmias and Ana Leon-Guerrero, *Social Statistics for a Diverse Society*, 2nd Edition (Thousand Oaks, CA: Pine Forge Press, 2000), 6-8.

b. If it isn't clear which variable is the independent or dependent, it may be that you are dealing with an ambiguous relationship or a case in which either variable could be treated as the independent. We examine this possibility in the next chapter.

Examining Your Output

Take a moment to examine the crosstab you created. You should notice that as requested, the categories of the independent variable (Male and Female - SEX) are displayed across the top in the columns. The categories of the dependent variable (About weekly, About monthly, Seldom, Never - CHATT) are displayed down the left side of the table in the rows.

Now look at the numbers in each of the squares or *cells*. You can see there are two sets of numbers in each cell: the *frequency* (or *count*) and *column percentage*.

If you look in the first cell in the upper left corner of the table, you see there are 160 males who attend church about weekly. Below the frequency or count, you find the column percentage. In this instance, we know that 25.1 percent of male respondents reported attending church about weekly. The column percentage is calculated by dividing the cell frequency (160) by the *column total* (638) and then multiplying by 100.

In contrast, 273 or 33.1 percent of female respondents reported attending church about weekly. Once again, the column percentage (33.1) was calculated by dividing the cell frequency (273) by the column total (825) and then multiplying by 100. Luckily, you do not have to go through the process of calculating the column percentages by hand because you have SPSS to do the work for you.

If we want, we can also note that 40.1 percent of the men attend church about monthly (25.1 + 15.0, "About weekly" + "About monthly"). Note also that 50.6 percent of the women attend about monthly (33.1 + 17.5, "About weekly" + "About monthly").

In addition to the cell frequencies and column percentages, the table also contains *row* and *column totals* (sometimes called *marginals*). These are the frequencies for each variable. In this case the column totals or marginals tell us that 638 of the respondents are male and 825 are female, while the row totals or marginals tell us that 433 respondents attend church about weekly, 240 about monthly, 490 seldom, and 300 never.

The column and row totals are followed by the *column* and *row marginal percentages*. The column marginal percentages are 100 percent for each column. While the row marginal percentages tell us what percentage of all respondents attend church about weekly (29.6%), about monthly (16.4%), seldom (33.5%) and never (20.5%).

The *Total* (**N**) in the bottom right side tells us that a total of 1463 of our 1500 respondents gave valid responses to both the SEX and CHATT (recoded ATTEND) questions.

SPSS Command 11.1: Running Crosstabs - Specifying the Dependent and Independent Variables

Click **Analyze** → **Descriptive Statistics** → **Crosstabs** . . . →

Highlight **dependent variable** → Click **arrow** pointing to **Row(s):** box →

Highlight **independent variable** → Click **arrow** pointing to

Column(s): box →

Click **Cells** . . . → Select **Column** in the Percentages box →

Click **Continue** → **OK**

Interpreting Crosstabs

The demonstration asked you to run crosstabs to test a hypothesis with two variables, one which is ordinal (CHATT – dependent variable) and one which is nominal (SEX – independent variable). While we can run crosstabs with either nominal or ordinal variables, as a practical matter, the larger the number of categories, the more tricky it becomes to read or interpret your table.[2]

To start, we'll keep it simple by focusing on a table with two nominal variables and limited to two categories each. Then we will look at a few crosstabs with variables that have more than two categories.

Interpreting Crosstabs: Association, Strength, and Direction

As we noted earlier, we run crosstabs to determine whether there is an *association* between two variables. In addition, crosstabs may tell us other important

---

[2] If you have trouble recalling the distinction between variables at different levels of measurement or variables of different types, refer back to the discussion in Chapter 3.

things about the relationship between the two variables, namely the *strength* of the association and *in some cases*, the *direction* of association. We should stress that you can only determine the direction of association when both the variables in your table greater than nominal, that is, capable of "greater than" "less than" relationships. If your table contains one or more nominal variables, it is *not* possible to determine the direction.

Once you have created your crosstab, you should ask yourself the following questions:

1. Is there an *association* between the two variables?
   IF THE ANSWER TO QUESTION 1 IS YES (OR MAYBE) . . .
2. What is the *strength of association* between the two variables?
   IF BOTH VARIABLES ARE ORDINAL . . .
3. What is the *direction of association*?

Demonstration 11.2:
Interpreting a Crosstab with Limited Categories

Since we have been focusing on the relationship between religiosity and gender, let's run a crosstab with an indicator of religiosity (POSTLIFE) and gender (SEX). POSTLIFE measures respondents' belief in life after death and it is measured at the nominal level. In accordance with the deprivation theory, we may hypothesize that women are more likely than men to believe in life after death. Consequently, POSTLIFE is the dependent variable and SEX is once again the independent variable.

Before running crosstabs, make sure to define the values **0, 8**, and **9** as **missing** for the variable **POSTLIFE**.

Now go ahead and request **crosstabs** specifying **POSTLIFE** (dependent variable) as the **row** variable, **SEX** (independent variable) as the **column** variable, and **cells** to be percentaged by **column**. If you are doing this all in one session, remember to click **Reset** or move **CHATT** back to the **variable list** before proceeding.

POSTLIFE BELIEF IN LIFE AFTER DEATH * SEX RESPONDENTS SEX Crosstabulation			SEX RESPONDENTS SEX		
			1 MALE	2 FEMALE	Total
POSTLIFE BELIEF IN LIFE AFTER DEATH	1 YES	Count	379	521	900
		% within SEX RESPONDENTS SEX	78.0%	83.8%	81.2%
	2 NO	Count	107	101	208
		% within SEX RESPONDENTS SEX	22.0%	16.2%	18.8%
Total		Count	486	622	1108
		% within SEX RESPONDENTS SEX	100.0%	100.0%	100.0%

First Question: Is There an Association?

As we noted earlier, the first question you want to ask is whether there is an association between the variables. In examining a crosstab to determine if there is an *association* between two variables, what we are really trying to determine is whether knowing the value of one variable helps us predict the value of the other variable. In other words, if gender is associated with belief in the after-life, knowing the independent variable (SEX) should help us predict the value of the dependent variable (POSTLIFE). If gender and belief in the after-life are *not* related or associated, knowing the value of SEX will *not* help us predict the value of POSTLIFE.

In order to determine whether SEX and POSTLIFE are associated, we read across the rows of the dependent variable to see if there are differences in the column percentages.[3] Let's go ahead and do that for the table we just created. By reading across the first row we see that women (84%) are somewhat more likely than men (78%) to believe in life after death.

You can also examine the second category of the dependent variable or the second row (those who do not believe in life after death). Here we see that a somewhat higher percentage of men (22%) are likely to report that they do not believe in life after death than women (16%).

Consequently, the crosstab seems to suggest that women are just a little more likely to believe in the after-life than men, but knowing respondents' gender helps us very little in predicting whether or not they believe in life after death.

Second Question:
How Strong is the Association?

If there seems to be an association between the variables, the next logical question is: How strong is the association? In Chapter 14 we provide you with statistical techniques that provide measures of strength for associations. For now, we'll provide a crude method of assessing the strength of associations by examining the size of the differences in the percentages. One general rule to keep in mind is that the larger the percentage difference across the categories, the stronger the association. Conversely, the smaller the percentage differences across categories, the weaker the association between the variables.

Some researchers use a *rough "10 percentage point rule."* That is, if the percentage point difference is 10 percent or more, the relationship between the variables is probably worth examining further. Of course, the larger the percentage point difference, the stronger the association. Keep in mind, this "rule of thumb" is just a rough indicator. Whereas some researchers may see a 6 or 8% point difference as an indication of a potentially noteworthy relationship, others may not.

In the case of our crosstab between POSTLIFE and SEX, we have a 6% point difference (84%-78%; 22%-16%). Based on the 10% rule, the relationship would be judged to be weak. However, bear in mind that just because the percentage point difference is not 10%, some researchers may still feel that a 6% point difference is noteworthy enough to warrant further investigation.

Finally, because POSTLIFE and SEX are nominal variables, we cannot ask the third question regarding the direction of association. That question only applies when *both* of the variables in your table are measured at the ordinal level or higher.

---

[3] One useful rule to keep in mind is when the table is percentagized down (as it is in this case, and will be for the remainder of the text) you read across. Conversely, if the table is percentagized across, you read down.

Demonstration 11.3: Correlating Another Measure of Religiosity and Gender

Your file contains a third measure of religiosity that we can use to continue our examination, PRAY. As the name implies, this variable measures how often respondents pray: several times a day, once a day, several times a week, etc. . . .

Take a moment to examine the response categories for the variable PRAY. Remember you can do this in a number of ways (accessing **the Variable View tab** and then clicking on **Values**; using the **Utilities → Variables . . .** ; or **Utilities → File Info** commands).

Based on your examination it should be clear that **PRAY** is measured at the ordinal level. It should also be apparent that before running crosstabs, you need to define the values **0, 8,** and **9** for this variable as missing.

Once you have done that, go ahead and run crosstabs, specifying **PRAY** as the **row** variable, **SEX** as the **column** variable, with **cells** percentaged by **column**. Once again, if you are doing this all in one session, you should click **Reset** or move **POSTLIFE** back to the **variable list** before you begin.

PRAY HOW OFTEN DOES R PRAY * SEX RESPONDENTS SEX Crosstabulation

			SEX RESPONDENTS SEX		Total
			1 MALE	2 FEMALE	
PRAY HOW OFTEN DOES R PRAY	1 SEVERAL TIMES A DAY	Count	76	135	211
		% within SEX RESPONDENTS SEX	23.2%	32.1%	28.2%
	2 ONCE A DAY	Count	70	146	216
		% within SEX RESPONDENTS SEX	21.4%	34.8%	28.9%
	3 SEVERAL TIMES A WEEK	Count	44	53	97
		% within SEX RESPONDENTS SEX	13.5%	12.6%	13.0%
	4 ONCE A WEEK	Count	28	25	53
		% within SEX RESPONDENTS SEX	8.6%	6.0%	7.1%
	5 LT ONCE A WEEK	Count	104	59	163
		% within SEX RESPONDENTS SEX	31.8%	14.0%	21.8%
	6 NEVER	Count	5	2	7
		% within SEX RESPONDENTS SEX	1.5%	.5%	.9%
Total		Count	327	420	747
		% within SEX RESPONDENTS SEX	100.0%	100.0%	100.0%

Now take a moment to examine your table. Remember, because one of your variables (SEX) is measured at the nominal level it is not possible to determine the direction of association between the variables. It is possible however, to draw some tentative conclusions regarding whether there is a relationship between the variables, and if so, the strength of the association.

Once you have examined your table, compare your answer to the description that follows. Keep in mind that because crosstabs give us only a rough indication of the strength of association, your interpretation may be somewhat different than the one below.

Writing Box 11.1

As we see in the table, women pray more often than men. For example, 67% of the women in the sample say they pray at least once a week, compared to 67% of the men. Or, looking at the other end of the table, we see that men are more likely (33%) to say they pray less than once a week than are women (15%).

Drawing Conclusions Carefully: Reassessing Our Original Hypothesis

Now that we have had a chance to examine three crosstabs involving gender and religiosity, it is important to go back to our original hypothesis. Would you say that we have found support for the thesis put forth by Glock and his co-authors? Remember, we began with a hypothesis based on the deprivation theory which suggested that people who were deprived of gratification in the secular society would be more likely to turn to religion as an alternative source of gratification. Based on our analysis, would you say that we have found evidence that supports the thesis with regard to gender differences — that women are still deprived of gratification in American society in comparison with men? Why or why not?

It is important to note that while we may have found relationships between some of the religiosity variables and gender that are worth investigating further, we still have not *proven* our theory. For instance, while there seems to be a fairly strong association between PRAY and SEX, this association is probably best looked at as *evidence of, not proof of,* a causal relationship. Because two variables can be associated without it necessarily being a causal relationship, we need to proceed with care when interpreting our findings.

Demonstration 11.4: Interpreting a Crosstab With Ordinal Variables – Religiosity and Age

Now that you've had a chance to practice interpreting crosstabs with variables measured at the nominal level, we will consider a case in which both variables are measured at the ordinal level. As we noted earlier, the greater the number of categories, the more difficult it is to interpret your output.

In addition to focusing on gender, Glock et al. also argue that the United States is a youth-oriented society, with gratification being denied to old people. Whereas some traditional societies tend to revere their elders, this is not the case in the United States. The deprivation thesis, then, would predict that older respondents would be more religious than younger ones. The researchers confirmed this expectation in their data from Episcopalian church members.

Let's check out the relationship between age and religiosity. To make the table manageable, we'll use the recoded AGECAT variable created earlier in Chapter 6.[4]

So, request a **Crosstab** using:[5]

---

[4] If you did not save the recoded variable AGECAT, simply go back to Chapter 6 and follow the recode commands to create AGECAT before moving ahead with the demonstrations in this chapter.

[5] If you are doing this all in one session, remember to click **Reset** before specifying your Row and Column variables for this demonstration.

- **CHATT** (our dependent variable) as a **row** variable
- **AGECAT** (our independent variable) as a **column** variable
- **Cells** to be percentaged by **column**

The resulting table should look like this:

CHATT Recoded Church Attendance * AGECAT Recoded Age Categories Crosstabulation							
			AGECAT Recoded Age Categories				
			1 Under 21	2 21-39	3 40-64	4 65 and older	Total
CHATT Recoded Church Attendance	1 About weekly	Count	8	115	197	112	432
		% within AGECAT Recoded Age Categories	18.6%	20.4%	32.6%	45.5%	29.6%
	2 About monthly	Count	8	105	94	32	239
		% within AGECAT Recoded Age Categories	18.6%	18.7%	15.5%	13.0%	16.4%
	3 Seldom	Count	22	221	190	53	486
		% within AGECAT Recoded Age Categories	51.2%	39.3%	31.4%	21.5%	33.4%
	4 Never	Count	5	122	124	49	300
		% within AGECAT Recoded Age Categories	11.6%	21.7%	20.5%	19.9%	20.6%
Total		Count	43	563	605	246	1457
		% within AGECAT Recoded Age Categories	100.0%	100.0%	100.0%	100.0%	100.0%

Interpreting Crosstabs With Ordinal Variables

Because our table contains two ordinal variables, our method of interpretation varies slightly from what it was when we were looking at a table with at least one nominal variable.

Consider the following hypothetical example of a crosstab with two ordinal variables (variable A and B):

Table 11.2   Hypothetical Example of a Positive Association

Variable B (dependent)	Variable A (independent)		
	Low	Medium	High
Low	50%	25%	25%
Medium	25%	50%	25%
High	25%	25%	50%
Total	100%	100%	100%

Notice that we have identified the highest percentage in each row of our hypothetical table. Because the highest percentages occur in the three cells that form a diagonal from the upper left, to the lower right, this is an indication of a *positive association* between variables A and B.

Positive associations are ones in which increases in one variable are related to increases in the other variable. You may be able to think of some variables that you suspect are positively related. One common example is level of education and income. The more education you have, the more money you are likely to earn. If this is truly the case, these variables are positively related or associated. In terms of religiosity, you may hypothesize that church attendance and the amount that you pray are positively related, meaning that the more you attend church the more likely you are to pray.

Now consider another table depicting a negative relationship between two hypothetical variables.

Table 11.3   Hypothetical Example of a Negative Association

| | Variable A (independent) | | |
Variable B (dependent)	Low	Medium	High
Low	25%	25%	50%
Medium	25%	50%	25%
High	50%	25%	25%
Total	100%	100%	100%

Once again you will notice that we have indicated the highest percentage in each row. However, in this case the higher percentages occur in the three cells that form a diagonal line from the bottom left to the upper right side of the table. This indicates a *negative association* between the variables—an increase in one variable is associated with a decrease in the other variable.

Can you think of two variables that you suspect may be negatively related? How about levels of education and prejudice? Students' alcohol consumption and GPA? If the variables are negatively associated, you would find that as education increases, the level of prejudice decreases. Similarly, as alcohol consumption increases, GPA decreases.

Examining Your Output

Of course as we move from hypothetical tables to tables with "real social data" we seldom if ever find such clear positive or negative relationships.

Look back at your crosstab of AGECAT and CHATT. If you take a moment to identify the highest percentage in each row you will quickly notice that it does not form a diagonal line depicting a positive or negative association such as the ones we mentioned earlier. Instead, as is typical when you are dealing with real-life data, the relationship is a little more "messy."

Nevertheless, with some slight variations, we can see that older respondents are more likely to report that they attend church than younger respondents. This would tend to support the deprivation thesis in terms of age, at least to some extent. You should be aware that some variations like this become more common as the number of groups being compared increases.

Once again, while the table gives us an indication of association and strength, other statistics, such as measures of association that we discuss in Chapter 14, are a much better indication of the strength and direction of the association.

Demonstration 11.5: Correlating Other Measures of Religiosity and Age

We can request more than one table in our Crosstab window. You will notice that the commands for this procedure are the same as those listed in SPSS Command 11.1, except that in this case we are going to click on two dependent variables and place them both in the Row(s): field.

Once you open your **Crosstabs** window, highlight **POSTLIFE** and move it to the **Row(s):** field. Then do the same with **PRAY**, placing it in the **Row(s):** field directly below POSTLIFE. Now go ahead and move **AGECAT** to the **Column(s):** field, request that your **cells** be percentaged by **column** and then click **OK**.[6]

POSTLIFE BELIEF IN LIFE AFTER DEATH * AGECAT Recoded Age Categories Crosstabulation

			AGECAT Recoded Age Categories				
			1 Under 21	2 21-39	3 40-64	4 65 and older	Total
POSTLIFE BELIEF IN LIFE AFTER DEATH	1 YES	Count	27	347	377	143	894
		% within AGECAT Recoded Age Categories	81.8%	80.7%	81.3%	81.7%	81.1%
	2 NO	Count	6	83	87	32	208
		% within AGECAT Recoded Age Categories	18.2%	19.3%	18.8%	18.3%	18.9%
Total		Count	33	430	464	175	1102
		% within AGECAT Recoded Age Categories	100.0%	100.0%	100.0%	100.0%	100.0%

PRAY HOW OFTEN DOES R PRAY * AGECAT Recoded Age Categories Crosstabulation

			AGECAT Recoded Age Categories				
			1 Under 21	2 21-39	3 40-64	4 65 and older	Total
PRAY HOW OFTEN DOES R PRAY	1 SEVERAL TIMES A DAY	Count	2	54	99	53	208
		% within AGECAT Recoded Age Categories	9.1%	19.2%	31.4%	43.1%	28.1%
	2 ONCE A DAY	Count	12	79	83	41	215
		% within AGECAT Recoded Age Categories	54.5%	28.1%	26.3%	33.3%	29.0%
	3 SEVERAL TIMES A WEEK	Count	2	47	37	11	97
		% within AGECAT Recoded Age Categories	9.1%	16.7%	11.7%	8.9%	13.1%
	4 ONCE A WEEK	Count	1	23	21	7	52
		% within AGECAT Recoded Age Categories	4.5%	8.2%	6.7%	5.7%	7.0%
	5 LT ONCE A WEEK	Count	5	76	70	11	162
		% within AGECAT Recoded Age Categories	22.7%	27.0%	22.2%	8.9%	21.9%
	6 NEVER	Count		2	5		7
		% within AGECAT Recoded Age Categories		.7%	1.6%		.9%
Total		Count	22	281	315	123	741
		% within AGECAT Recoded Age Categories	100.0%	100.0%	100.0%	100.0%	100.0%

Now take a moment to examine your tables. As you do this keep in mind that one table has an ordinal and a nominal variable, while the other contains two ordinal variables.

While examining the tables you may want to consider the following types of questions: does there appear to be an association between age and belief in the after-life? How about age and prayer? Are older people more likely to believe in the after-life than younger people? Do younger people report praying less often than elderly people, more often, or about the same? Based on your interpretation what conclusions might you draw in regard to our original hypothesis regarding the relationship between age and religiosity? Is there support for the notion that the older you are the more religious you are likely to be? Why or why not?

Once you have taken a few minutes to examine these tables, compare your interpretation to that in Writing Box 11.2.

---

[6] Don't forget to click Reset or move CHATT back to the variable list before proceeding with this demonstration.

Writing Box 11.2

Age appears to have no impact on belief in a life after death. Approximately four out of five hold this belief in each of the age groups.

The relationship between age and prayer is more complex than other relationships we've examined. If we only look at praying several times a day, we find a strong, linear relationship: as age increases, so does the likelihood of frequent prayer.

However, if we combine the first two response categories — representing prayer at least once a day — the relationship is curvilinear. Nearly two-thirds (64 percent) of the youngest group say they pray at least once a day. This drops to 47 percent among the 21-39 group, rises to 58 percent among the 40-64 group, and reaches 76 percent in the oldest group.

Epsilon

Before concluding our initial examination of crosstabs, we want to mention one simple statistic that you may find useful. *Epsilon* is a statistic often used to summarize percentage differences such as those in the tables above. Epsilon is calculated by identifying the largest and smallest percentages in either row and then subtracting the smallest from the largest.

For example, look back at the first crosstab we ran in this chapter (Demonstration 11.1) comparing gender and church attendance. In comparing men and women in terms of "About weekly" church attendance, the percentage difference (epsilon) is 8 points (33.1 - 25.1). This simple statistic is useful because it gives us a tool for comparing sex differences on other measures of religiosity.

When discussing epsilon, it is important to note that technically, tables that have more than two columns have several epsilons, one for each pair of cells being compared. In these cases, researchers will often use epsilon to refer to the largest difference in any row of cell percentages.

These data then seem to show that women are somewhat more likely than men to attend church frequently. This would seem to support the deprivation theory of religiosity to a limited extent. Take a moment to determine epsilon for the other tables we created in this chapter and see if they produce a similar result.

This completes our initial foray into the world of bivariate analysis. We hope you've gotten a good sense of the potential for detective work in social research.

Conclusion

In this chapter, we made a critical logical advance in the analysis of social scientific data. Up to now, we have focused our attention on description. With this examination of religiosity, we've crossed over into explanation. We've moved from asking what to asking why.

Much of the excitement in social research revolves around discovering why people think and act as they do. You've now had an initial exposure to the logic and computer techniques that make such inquiries possible.

Let's apply your new capabilities to other subject matter. In the next two chapters, we're going to examine, respectively, the sources of different political orientations and why people feel as they do about abortion.

Main Points

- In this chapter we shifted our focus from univariate analysis to bivariate analysis.
- Univariate analysis is the analysis of one variable at a time.
- Bivariate analysis is the analysis of two variables.
- You can think of the differences between univariate and bivariate analysis in terms of the number of variables, major questions, and primary goals.
- We began our bivariate analysis by considering why some people are more religious than others.
- In this analysis we were guided by the social deprivation theory of religiosity, first discussed in Chapter 2.
- We used this theory to develop a hypothesis stating that women are more likely to be religious than men.
- This hypothesis contains two variables: gender (independent variable/cause) and religiosity (dependent variable/effect).
- It is important not to confuse the categories of a variable with the variable itself.
- We tested this hypothesis by running Crosstabs with column percentages.
- When running Crosstabs, it is customary to specify the dependent variable as the row variable and the independent variable as the column variable.
- Throughout the chapter we ran several crosstabs correlating religiosity (as measured by CHATT, PRAY, and POSTLIFE) with gender (as measured by SEX) and then age (as measured by AGECAT).
- While you can run crosstabs with both nominal and ordinal variables, as a general rule the more categories you are dealing with, the more difficult it becomes to interpret your table.
- When interpreting crosstabs we are generally looking to see whether there is an association between two variables.
- We do this by reading across categories of the dependent variable.
- A percentage point difference of 10% or more is sometimes taken as an indication that there may be an association between the variables that is worth investigating further. However, this is just a general rule of thumb.
- In addition to looking for an association between the variables, crosstabs also give us a rough indication of the strength, and in some cases the direction, of association.
- Bear in mind, however, that the measures of association we focus on in Chapter 14 give us a much better basis for drawing conclusions about the nature, strength, and direction of association between variables.
- Finding an association between variables is best looked at as evidence of, not proof of, a causal relationship.
- Epsilon is a simple statistic used to summarize percentage differences.

Key Terms

Univariate analysis	Cells
Hypothesis	Epsilon
Column percentage	Independent variable
Bivariate analysis	Frequency or count
Categories of the variable	Association
10% point rule	Positive association
Dependent variable	Negative association

SPSS Command Introduced in This Chapter

11.1 Running Crosstabs - Specifying the Dependent and Independent Variables

Review Questions

1. What is univariate analysis?

2. What is bivariate analysis?

3. What are the major differences between univariate and bivariate analysis in terms of the number of variables, major questions, and primary goals?

4. In a hypothesis, the variable that is said to "cause" (to some extent) variation in another variable is referred to as what type of variable?

5. What three general questions might you ask yourself when examining a crosstab with two ordinal variables?

Identify the independent and dependent variables in the following hypotheses (Questions 6 and 7):

6. Those employed by companies with more than twenty employees are more likely to have some form of managed-choice health care than those employed by companies with fewer employees.

7. In the United States, women are more likely to vote Democratic than men are.

8. What are the categories of the independent variable in the hypothesis in Question 7?

9. When running Crosstabs, is it customary to specify the dependent variable as the row or column variable?

10. If you were running Crosstabs to test the relationship between the variables in the hypothesis in Question 6, which variable would you specify as the row variable and which would you specify as the column variable?

11. If you produce a crosstab for the variables SEX and PARTYID (party identification, with the following categories: Democrat, Republican, Independent, Other) is it possible to determine the direction of association between these two variable? Why or why not?

12. A researcher produces a crosstab for the variables AGECAT and level of happiness (with the following categories: low, medium, and high) and finds that there is a negative relationship between these two variables. Does this mean that the older you are the more happy you are likely to be or the older you are the less happy you are likely to be?

13. A researcher produces a crosstab for the variables class (with the following categories: lower, working, middle, and upper) and level of contentment (with the following categories: low, medium, and high) and finds that the upper class are more likely to be content than the middle, working, and lower class. Based on this hypothetical example, how would you describe the direction of association between these variables?

14. What is epsilon?

15. How is epsilon calculated?

16. Can there be more than one epsilon in a table that has more than two columns?

17. If you run Crosstabs and find a strong relationship between the independent and dependent variable in your hypothesis, are you better off looking at this association as evidence of or proof of a causal relationship?

NAME _____

CLASS _____

INSTRUCTOR _____

DATE _____

To complete the following exercises, you need to load the data file EXER.SAV.
You can find answers to Questions #1-10 in Appendix B.

A number of studies have addressed the relationship between race and attitudes
toward sex roles. In a 1992 study Jill Grisby argued that Whites are more likely than
Blacks to believe that if a woman works it has a detrimental impact on her children.
We are going to test this hypothesis using the variables RACE (as a measure of race)
and FECHLD (as a measure of opinions regarding the impact of working women on
their children). Simply follow the steps listed below and supply the information
requested in the spaces provided (Questions 1-10).

1. Restate the hypothesis linking RACE and FECHLD.

2. Identify the independent and dependent variables in the hypothesis.

3. When running Crosstabs, which variable should you specify as the
   row variable?

4. When running Crosstabs, which variable should you specify as the
   column variable?

5. What is the level of measurement for RACE?

6. What is the level of measurement for FECHLD?

7. Now run Crosstabs with column percentages to test the hypothesis (do not forget to define 0, 8, and 9 as missing values for FECHLD before you begin). When you have produced your table, present your results by filling in the following information:
   A. List the categories of the independent variable in the spaces provided on Line A.
   B. List the percentage of respondents who "Strongly agree" and "Agree" with the statement that the fact that a woman works does not hurt children in the spaces provided on Line B (i.e., sum of those who "Strongly agree" + "Agree" on FECHLD).

   FECHLD by RACE

   LINE A _____ _____ _____
   LINE B _____ _____ _____

8. Are the results consistent with your hypothesis as stated in response to Question 1? Explain.

9. Compare Blacks and Whites in terms of agreement ("Strongly agree" + "Agree") with the statement that the fact that a woman works does not hurt children and give the percentage difference (epsilon) below.

NAME _____

CLASS _____

INSTRUCTOR _____

DATE _____

10. Do your findings show that there is evidence of a causal relationship between RACE and FECHLD? Explain.

Continue to research the causes of differing attitudes toward sex roles by selecting one independent and one dependent variable from the following lists:

Independent variables: SEX, RACE, CLASS [select one]

Dependent variables: FEFAM, FEHELP, FEPRESCH [select one]

As before, run Crosstabs with column percentages to test your hypothesis and then fill in the information requested in the spaces provided. (Questions 11-18)

11. State and explain your hypothesis involving the [one] independent variable and [one] dependent variable you chose from the lists above.

12. Identify the independent and dependent variables in your hypothesis.

13. When running Crosstabs, which variable should you specify as the column variable and which should you specify as the row variable?

14. Identify the level of measurement for each of the variables in your hypothesis.

15. Now run Crosstabs with column percentages to test your hypothesis. Remember to define the appropriate values as missing for both of your variables. Then complete the exercise below:
    A. List the abbreviated variable names of your independent and dependent variables on Line A.
    B. List the categories of the independent variable in the spaces provided on Line B (use only as many blank spaces as necessary).
    C. List the percentage of respondents who "Strongly agree" and "Agree" for either FEFAM, FEHELP, or FEPRESCH on Line C (i.e., sum of those who "Strongly agree" + "Agree" for the variable you have chosen); use only as many blank spaces as necessary.

    LINE A _____ by _____
              [Dependent Variable]   [Independent Variable]
    LINE B _____ _____ _____ _____ _____ _____
    LINE C _____ _____ _____ _____ _____ _____

16. Are these results consistent with your hypothesis as stated in response to Question 11 above? Explain.

17. Compute epsilon.

NAME _____

CLASS _____

INSTRUCTOR _____

DATE _____

18. Do your findings show that there is evidence of a causal relationship between your independent and dependent variables? Explain.

Continue to research the causes of differing attitudes toward sex roles by selecting one independent and one dependent variable from the following lists:

Independent variables: AGE, EDUC   [select one]

Dependent variables: FEFAM, FEHELP, FEPRESCH   [select one]

This time, however, recode the independent variable before proceeding. Then run Crosstabs with column percentages to test your hypothesis and fill in the information requested in the spaces provided. (Questions 19-23)

19. State and explain your hypothesis involving the [one recoded] independent variable and [one] dependent variable you chose from the lists above.

20. Identify the independent and dependent variables in your hypothesis.

21. When running Crosstabs, which variable should you specify as the column variable and which should you specify as the row variable?

22. Identify the level of measurement for each of the variables in your hypothesis.

NAME _____

CLASS _____

INSTRUCTOR _____

DATE _____

23. Now run Crosstabs with column percentages to test your hypothesis. Then print and attach a copy of your table to this sheet. (Remember to define the appropriate values as missing before proceeding.)

   Analyze and then write a short description of your findings below (similar to those in Writing Box 11.1). In particular you may want consider whether the results are consistent with your hypothesis; whether there appears to be an association between the variables; if so, how strong is the association; and if applicable, what is the direction of association? Based on your examination, is this association worth investigating further? Why or why not?

24. Access the SPSS Help feature Tutorial

Hint: Click **Help** → **Tutorial** → Click on the **Table of Contents** button/icon on the bottom right side of the screen (icon that looks like a house) →
Once you have opened the Table of Contents, work your way through the following aspect of the tutorial: Crosstabulation Tables
To exit or close the Tutorial, click on the "**X**" (Close button) or click **File** → **Close**.

Chapter 12 Political Orientations as Cause and as Effect

In looking for the sources of religiosity, we worked with a coherent theory (the deprivation theory). As we noted in Chapter 2, this process is called *deduction*, and it is usually the preferred approach to data analysis. Sometimes, however, it's appropriate to take a less structured route beginning with data and then proceeding to theory. As you may recall, this process is known as *induction*. As we turn our attention to politics in this chapter, we're going to be more inductive than deductive so that you can become familiar with this approach as well.

In Chapter 7, we examined two GSS variables: POLVIEWS and PARTYID. In the analyses to follow, we'll look at the relationship between these variables. You can do that now that you understand the Crosstabs command. Next, we'll explore some of the variables that cause differences in political philosophies and party identification, such as age, religion, gender, race, education, class, and marital status. Finally, we'll look at POLVIEWS and PARTYID as independent variables to determine what impact they have on other variables.

The Relationship Between POLVIEWS and PARTYID

Let's begin with the recoded forms of our two key political variables, POLVIEWS and PARTYID. You may recall that when we recoded these items in Chapter 7, we named them POLREC and PARTY. We then recommended that you save these variables on a file named DEMOPLUS. Go ahead and **open** your **DEMOPLUS** file now. If you did not save the recoded variables, don't worry. Simply follow the recode commands listed in Chapter 7 before continuing.

As we indicated earlier, there is a consensus that Democrats are more liberal than Republicans and that Republicans are more conservative than Democrats, although everyone recognizes the existence of liberal Republicans and conservative Democrats.

The GSS data allow us to see what the relationship between these two variables actually is. Because neither is logically prior to the other, we could treat either as the independent variable. For our present purposes, it is probably useful to explore both possibilities: (a) political philosophy causes party identification (political philosophy as the independent variable), and (b) party identification causes political philosophy (party identification as the independent variable).

Demonstration 12.1: POLREC by PARTY

To begin, then, let's see if Democrats are more liberal or more conservative than Republicans. Before beginning your examination, make sure you define the value 4 ("Other") for the variable **PARTY** as **missing**. Now go ahead and run Crosstabs specifying:

- **POLREC** as the **row** variable
- **PARTY** as the **column** variable
- **Cells** to be percentaged by **Column**

POLREC Recoded polviews * PARTY Recoded partyid Crosstabulation

			PARTY Recoded partyid			
			1 Democrat	2 Independent	3 Republican	Total
POLREC Recoded polviews	1 Liberal	Count	163	149	30	342
		% within PARTY Recoded partyid	35.1%	26.3%	8.6%	24.8%
	2 Moderate	Count	204	267	119	590
		% within PARTY Recoded partyid	44.0%	47.1%	34.1%	42.8%
	3 Conservative	Count	97	151	200	448
		% within PARTY Recoded partyid	20.9%	26.6%	57.3%	32.5%
Total		Count	464	567	349	1380
		% within PARTY Recoded partyid	100.0%	100.0%	100.0%	100.0%

The data in this table confirm the general expectation. Of the Democrats in the GSS sample, 35 percent describe themselves as liberals in contrast to 9 percent of the Republicans. The Independents fall halfway between the two parties, with 26 percent saying they are liberals. The relationship can also be seen by reading across the bottom row of percentages: 21 percent of the Democrats, versus 57 percent of the Republicans, call themselves conservatives.

Demonstration 12.2: PARTY by POLREC

We can also turn the table around logically and ask whether liberals or conservatives are more likely to identify with the Democratic party (or which are more likely to say they are Republicans). You can get this table by simply reversing the location of the two variable names in the earlier command. Run the **Crosstabs** procedure again, only this time make **PARTY** the **row** variable and **POLREC** the **column** variable. Here's what you'll get:

PARTY Recoded partyid * POLREC Recoded polviews Crosstabulation

			POLREC Recoded polviews			
			1 Liberal	2 Moderate	3 Conservative	Total
PARTY Recoded partyid	1 Democrat	Count	163	204	97	464
		% within POLREC Recoded polviews	47.7%	34.6%	21.7%	33.6%
	2 Independent	Count	149	267	151	567
		% within POLREC Recoded polviews	43.6%	45.3%	33.7%	41.1%
	3 Republican	Count	30	119	200	349
		% within POLREC Recoded polviews	8.8%	20.2%	44.6%	25.3%
Total		Count	342	590	448	1380
		% within POLREC Recoded polviews	100.0%	100.0%	100.0%	100.0%

Again, the relationship between the two variables is evident. Liberals are more likely (47 percent) to say they are Democrats than are moderates (35 percent are Democrats) or conservatives (only 22 percent are Democrats).

Now, why don't you state the relationship between these two variables in terms of the likelihood that they will support the Republican party? Either way of stating the relationship is appropriate.

In summary, then, there is an affinity between liberalism and the Democrats and between conservatism and the Republicans. At the same time, it is not a perfect relationship, and you can find plenty of liberal Republicans and conservative Democrats in the tables.

Now, let's switch gears and see if we can begin to explain why people are liberals or conservatives, Democrats or Republicans. Whereas in the last chapter when we began our discussion of bivariate analyses we examined why some people are more religious than others, in this chapter we are going to ask similar questions regarding political orientation and party identification: Why are some people more liberal (or conservative) than others? Why do some people identify themselves as Democrats, while others identify themselves as Republicans, Independents, or "Other"? What causes people to be liberals or conservatives, Democrats or Republicans?

Age and Politics

Often the search for causal variables involves the examination of *demographic* (or background) *variables*, such as: age, religion, sex, race, education, class, and marital status. Such variables often have a powerful impact on attitudes and behaviors. Let's begin with age.

There is a common belief that young people are more liberal than old people — that people get more conservative as they get older. As you can imagine, liberals tend to see this as a trend toward stodginess, whereas conservatives tend to explain it as a matter of increased wisdom. Regardless of the explanation you might prefer, let's see if it's even true that old people are more conservative than young people.

Demonstration 12.3: POLREC by AGECAT

To find out, run **Crosstabs**. In this case, age (as measured by AGECAT) would be the independent variable and political views (as measured by POLREC) would be the dependent variable.[1] Consequently, you should specify **POLREC** as the **row** variable and **AGECAT** as the **column** variable. Here's what you should get:

---

[1] If you did not save the recoded variable AGECAT, go back to Chapter 6 and follow the recode commands before continuing.

POLREC Recoded polviews * AGECAT Recoded Age Categories Crosstabulation

			AGECAT Recoded Age Categories				
			1 Under 21	2 21-39	3 40-64	4 65 and older	Total
POLREC Recoded polviews	1 Liberal	Count	14	151	149	40	354
		% within AGECAT Recoded Age Categories	33.3%	27.9%	25.4%	17.2%	25.2%
	2 Moderate	Count	18	220	243	112	593
		% within AGECAT Recoded Age Categories	42.9%	40.6%	41.4%	48.3%	42.3%
	3 Conservative	Count	10	171	195	80	456
		% within AGECAT Recoded Age Categories	23.8%	31.5%	33.2%	34.5%	32.5%
Total		Count	42	542	587	232	1403
		% within AGECAT Recoded Age Categories	100.0%	100.0%	100.0%	100.0%	100.0%

Which of the following statements is a more accurate interpretation of the table above?

Older age groups appear to be more conservative than younger age groups.

Older age groups appear to be more liberal than younger age groups.

If you chose the first answer, you have just won the right to continue with the analysis. (Oh, never mind—you can continue even if you got it wrong.)

Notice, however, that the relationship is not terribly strong.

Demonstration 12.4: PARTY by AGECAT

What would you expect to find in terms of political party identification (as measured by PARTY)? If that relationship corresponds to the one we've just examined, we'd expect to find growing strength for Republicans as people grow older. Young people should be more likely to identify themselves as Democrats. Here's an opportunity to test common sense. Why don't you try it yourself and see what you get? And then compare your table to the following one.

PARTY Recoded partyid * AGECAT Recoded Age Categories Crosstabulation

			AGECAT Recoded Age Categories				
			1 Under 21	2 21-39	3 40-64	4 65 and older	Total
PARTY Recoded partyid	1 Democrat	Count	7	154	218	107	486
		% within AGECAT Recoded Age Categories	16.3%	27.5%	36.2%	42.3%	33.3%
	2 Independent	Count	32	275	234	78	619
		% within AGECAT Recoded Age Categories	74.4%	49.0%	38.8%	30.8%	42.4%
	3 Republican	Count	4	132	151	68	355
		% within AGECAT Recoded Age Categories	9.3%	23.5%	25.0%	26.9%	24.3%
Total		Count	43	561	603	253	1460
		% within AGECAT Recoded Age Categories	100.0%	100.0%	100.0%	100.0%	100.0%

Interpreting Your Table: The Relationship Between Age and Party Identification

How would you interpret this table? What's the relationship between age and party identification? See if you can interpret this table yourself before moving on.

As you can see, the relationship between AGECAT and PARTY is not as clear as the relationship between AGECAT and POLREC.

In fact, as you probably noticed, the first row of percentages goes directly contrary to our expectations: Older people are substantially more likely to call themselves Democrats than are young people. When we examine the Republicans, however, we discover virtually the same thing, although it is not as clear. How can this be?

One explanation may be found among those identifying themselves as Independents. This identification is much more common among the young than it is among the old. The clearest relationship in this table is that the likelihood of identifying with some political party increases dramatically with age in the table, but there is no clear tendency for that identification to favor one party over another.

Realize that the observed pattern is amenable to more than one explanation. It could be that people become more likely to identify with the major parties as they grow older. On the other hand, the relationship might reflect a trend phenomenon: a disenchantment with the major parties in recent years, primarily among young people. To test these competing explanations, you would need to analyze *longitudinal data*, those representing the state of affairs at different points in time. Because the GSS has been conducting surveys since 1972, we have such data extending back more than a quarter century.

Religion and Politics

In the United States, the relationship between religion and politics is somewhat complex, especially with regard to Roman Catholics. Let's begin with political philosophies. We will ask SPSS to run Crosstabs connecting RELIG with POLREC.

Demonstration 12.5: POLREC by RELIG

Before we run Crosstabs, however, we need to make our measure of religious affiliation (RELIG) more manageable. You may recall from our discussion in Chapter 6 that RELIG contains 16 categories. Because we are primarily interested in the 4 largest categories (Protestant, Catholic, Jewish, Agnostics/Atheists) as opposed to the smaller categories labeled "Other" (Mormon, Buddhist, Moslem), we want to instruct SPSS to define the latter as "Missing."

You can review the labels and values for this item by accessing the **Variable View** tab and then double-clicking in the **rectangle** that corresponds with RELIG and Values (or by looking at the Codebook in Appendix A). Do that now and you will see that we want to define the values 0, 5-13, 98, and 99 as missing.

Now go ahead and define these **values** as **missing** by using the **Range plus one discrete missing value** option (to review these commands, see Chapter 7, SPSS Command 7.6). In this case we want to list the range of values as **5** through **99** and the discrete value as **0**.

Now we are ready to run your Crosstabs connecting **RELIG** (independent/ **column** variable) and **POLREC** (dependent/**row** variable).

POLREC Recoded polviews * RELIG RS RELIGIOUS PREFERENCE Crosstabulation							
			RELIG RS RELIGIOUS PREFERENCE				
			1 PROTES TANT	2 CATHOLIC	3 JEWISH	4 NONE	Total
POLREC Recoded polviews	1 Liberal	Count	152	74	14	85	325
		% within RELIG RS RELIGIOUS PREFERENCE	19.9%	21.6%	48.3%	43.8%	24.4%
	2 Moderate	Count	336	146	11	72	565
		% within RELIG RS RELIGIOUS PREFERENCE	43.9%	42.7%	37.9%	37.1%	42.5%
	3 Conservative	Count	277	122	4	37	440
		% within RELIG RS RELIGIOUS PREFERENCE	36.2%	35.7%	13.8%	19.1%	33.1%
Total		Count	765	342	29	194	1330
		% within RELIG RS RELIGIOUS PREFERENCE	100.0%	100.0%	100.0%	100.0%	100.0%

We did not define "None" as a missing because, as you can see, it is a very meaningful category. Notice that agnostics and atheists ("None," 44%) are almost as likely as Jews (48%) to identify themselves as politically liberal. It makes sense then that among the three religious categories, Jews are the least conservative (14 percent) followed by those having no religious preference (19%). Protestants and Catholics, on the other hand, are among the most conservative.

If you were to make a gross generalization about the relationship between religious affiliation and political philosophy, it would place Protestants and Catholics on the right end of the political spectrum and Jews and "Nones" on the left.

Demonstration 12.6: PARTY by RELIG

Political party identification, however, is a somewhat different matter. Like the Jews, Roman Catholics have been an ethnic minority throughout much of U.S. history, and the Democratic party, in the last century at least, has focused more on minority rights than has the Republican party. That would explain the relationship between religion and political party. Why don't you run that table now? Make **PARTY** the **row** variable and **RELIG** the **column** variable.

PARTY Recoded partyid * RELIG RS RELIGIOUS PREFERENCE Crosstabulation							
			RELIG RS RELIGIOUS PREFERENCE				
			1 PROTES TANT	2 CATHOLIC	3 JEWISH	4 NONE	Total
PARTY Recoded partyid	1 Democrat	Count	260	131	18	59	468
		% within RELIG RS RELIGIOUS PREFERENCE	32.5%	36.4%	60.0%	29.8%	33.7%
	2 Independent	Count	291	148	10	123	572
		% within RELIG RS RELIGIOUS PREFERENCE	36.4%	41.1%	33.3%	62.1%	41.2%
	3 Republican	Count	248	81	2	16	347
		% within RELIG RS RELIGIOUS PREFERENCE	31.0%	22.5%	6.7%	8.1%	25.0%
Total		Count	799	360	30	198	1387
		% within RELIG RS RELIGIOUS PREFERENCE	100.0%	100.0%	100.0%	100.0%	100.0%

As we see in the table, Jews are the most likely to identify themselves with the Democratic party. While Catholics are slightly more likely to identify themselves as Democrats than are Protestants, there is not a meaningful difference between the two groups in this regard.

If you are interested in these two variables, you might want to explore the relationship between politics and the other religious variables we've examined: POSTLIFE and PRAY.

On the other hand, you could look for other consequences of RELIG. What else do you suppose might be affected by differences of religious affiliation?

Gender and Politics

Gender is a demographic variable associated with a great many attitudes and behaviors. Take a minute to think about the reasons women might be more liberal or more conservative than men.

Demonstration 12.7: PARTY and POLREC by SEX

Once you've developed expectations regarding this relationship, use SPSS to examine the actual association between these variables.

POLREC Recoded polviews * SEX RESPONDENTS SEX Crosstabulation

| | | | SEX RESPONDENTS SEX | | |
			1 MALE	2 FEMALE	Total
POLREC Recoded polviews	1 Liberal	Count	155	200	355
		% within SEX RESPONDENTS SEX	24.9%	25.4%	25.2%
	2 Moderate	Count	244	354	598
		% within SEX RESPONDENTS SEX	39.2%	45.0%	42.4%
	3 Conservative	Count	223	233	456
		% within SEX RESPONDENTS SEX	35.9%	29.6%	32.4%
Total		Count	622	787	1409
		% within SEX RESPONDENTS SEX	100.0%	100.0%	100.0%

PARTY Recoded partyid * SEX RESPONDENTS SEX Crosstabulation

| | | | SEX RESPONDENTS SEX | | |
			1 MALE	2 FEMALE	Total
PARTY Recoded partyid	1 Democrat	Count	179	312	491
		% within SEX RESPONDENTS SEX	28.2%	37.5%	33.5%
	2 Independent	Count	273	347	620
		% within SEX RESPONDENTS SEX	43.0%	41.7%	42.3%
	3 Republican	Count	183	173	356
		% within SEX RESPONDENTS SEX	28.8%	20.8%	24.3%
Total		Count	635	832	1467
		% within SEX RESPONDENTS SEX	100.0%	100.0%	100.0%

Although a slightly larger percentage of men are likely to identify themselves as conservative, and a larger percentage of women are likely to identify as moderate, the relationship between gender and political philosophy is still fairly weak.

While the association between party identification and gender is somewhat stronger, it is perhaps not as meaningful as you may have expected. Although slightly more women are more likely to identify with the Democratic party (38 percent) than are men (28 percent), this may reflect the fact that the Democratic party has been more explicit in its support for women's issues in recent years than has the Republican party. Still, the relationship is not a particularly strong one.

Race and Politics

Given our brief discussion above about politics and ethnic minority groups such as Jews and Roman Catholics, what relationship do you expect to find between politics and race? The variable available to you for analysis (RACE) codes only "White," "Black," and "Other," so it's not possible to examine this relationship in great depth, but you should be able to make some educated guesses about how Caucasians and African Americans might differ politically.

Demonstration 12.8: POLREC by RACE

After you've thought about the likely relationship between race and politics, why don't you run the tables and test your ability to predict such matters?

POLREC Recoded polviews * RACE RACE OF RESPONDENT Crosstabulation

| | | | RACE RACE OF RESPONDENT | | | |
			1 WHITE	2 BLACK	3 OTHER	Total
POLREC Recoded polviews	1 Liberal	Count	277	59	19	355
		% within RACE RACE OF RESPONDENT	24.7%	26.9%	27.9%	25.2%
	2 Moderate	Count	466	100	32	598
		% within RACE RACE OF RESPONDENT	41.5%	45.7%	47.1%	42.4%
	3 Conservative	Count	379	60	17	456
		% within RACE RACE OF RESPONDENT	33.8%	27.4%	25.0%	32.4%
Total		Count	1122	219	68	1409
		% within RACE RACE OF RESPONDENT	100.0%	100.0%	100.0%	100.0%

The first table shows that Whites are somewhat more conservative (34 percent) than Blacks (27 percent). Interestingly, both groups are about equally liberal (although Blacks are just slightly more liberal than Whites). This can be explained by the fact that Blacks identify themselves as somewhat more moderate (46 percent) than Whites (42 percent).

Demonstration 12.9: PARTY by RACE

PARTY Recoded partyid * RACE RACE OF RESPONDENT Crosstabulation						
			RACE RACE OF RESPONDENT			
			1 WHITE	2 BLACK	3 OTHER	Total
PARTY Recoded partyid	1 Democrat	Count	321	139	31	491
		% within RACE RACE OF RESPONDENT	27.8%	58.4%	41.3%	33.5%
	2 Independent	Count	498	86	36	620
		% within RACE RACE OF RESPONDENT	43.2%	36.1%	48.0%	42.3%
	3 Republican	Count	335	13	8	356
		% within RACE RACE OF RESPONDENT	29.0%	5.5%	10.7%	24.3%
Total		Count	1154	238	75	1467
		% within RACE RACE OF RESPONDENT	100.0%	100.0%	100.0%	100.0%

While the correlation between political views and race may not have been as pronounced as you might have expected, the relationship between race and political party identification is very strong, reflecting the Democratic party's orientation toward minority groups.

Education and Politics

Education, a common component of social class, is likely to be of interest to you, especially if you are currently a college student. From your own experience, what would you expect to be the relationship between education and political philosophy?

Demonstration 12.10: Recoding EDUC → EDCAT

Before we test the relationship between these variables, we need to **Recode** our measure of education (**EDUC**) to make it more manageable. We will create a new variable called **EDCAT** and **save** it on our **DEMOPLUS.SAV** file.

Before you begin recoding, make sure to define the values **97**, **98**, and **99** for **EDUC** as **missing**. Then follow the instructions listed below:[2]

Old Values	New Values	Labels
Lowest through 11	→1	Less than high school
12	→2	High school graduate
13 through 15	→3	Some college
16	→4	College graduate
17 through 20	→5	Graduate studies (beyond college)

---

[2] If you have any trouble recoding, you may want to review the discussion in Chapter 6, SPSS Command 6.13.

After you have successfully recoded and labeled EDCAT, check your results by running Frequencies on the new variable. Your table should look like the one below:

EDCAT Recoded EDUC

		Frequency	Percent	Valid Percent	Cumulative Percent
Valid	1 Less than HS	243	16.2	16.2	16.2
	2 HS grad	463	30.9	30.9	47.2
	3 Some College	428	28.5	28.6	75.8
	4 College grad	195	13.0	13.0	88.8
	5 Graduate studies	167	11.1	11.2	100.0
	Total	1496	99.7	100.0	
Missing	System	4	.3		
Total		1500	100.0		

Demonstration 12.11: POLREC by EDCAT

Now we are ready to run the **Crosstabs** for **EDCAT** (independent/**column** variable) and **POLREC** (dependent/**row** variable), so you can find out whether your expectations regarding the relationship between these variables are accurate.

POLREC Recoded polviews * EDCAT Recoded EDUC Crosstabulation

			EDCAT Recoded EDUC					
			1 Less than HS	2 HS grad	3 Some College	4 College grad	5 Graduate studies	Total
POLREC Recoded polviews	1 Liberal	Count	51	88	89	59	68	355
		% within EDCAT Recoded EDUC	24.3%	20.5%	21.6%	30.9%	42.0%	25.3%
	2 Moderate	Count	97	219	176	62	40	594
		% within EDCAT Recoded EDUC	46.2%	50.9%	42.7%	32.5%	24.7%	42.3%
	3 Conservative	Count	62	123	147	70	54	456
		% within EDCAT Recoded EDUC	29.5%	28.6%	35.7%	36.6%	33.3%	32.5%
Total		Count	210	430	412	191	162	1405
		% within EDCAT Recoded EDUC	100.0%	100.0%	100.0%	100.0%	100.0%	100.0%

As you can see, while liberalism seems to increase with education, this does not mean that conservatism declines with increasing education. Instead, the rise in liberalism is accounted for by a decline in the number of moderates as education increases.

Demonstration 12.12: PARTY by EDCAT

But how about political party? You decide how to structure your Crosstabs instruction to obtain the following table.

PARTY Recoded partyid * EDCAT Recoded EDUC Crosstabulation								
			EDCAT Recoded EDUC					
			1 Less than HS	2 HS grad	3 Some College	4 College grad	5 Graduate studies	Total
PARTY Recoded partyid	1 Democrat	Count	84	150	142	63	50	489
		% within EDCAT Recoded EDUC	35.1%	33.2%	34.0%	32.8%	30.9%	33.4%
	2 Independent	Count	112	200	172	75	59	618
		% within EDCAT Recoded EDUC	46.9%	44.2%	41.1%	39.1%	36.4%	42.2%
	3 Republican	Count	43	102	104	54	53	356
		% within EDCAT Recoded EDUC	18.0%	22.6%	24.9%	28.1%	32.7%	24.3%
Total		Count	239	452	418	192	162	1463
		% within EDCAT Recoded EDUC	100.0%	100.0%	100.0%	100.0%	100.0%	100.0%

The relationship here is fairly consistent, but it is possibly in the opposite direction from what you expected. We've seen throughout these analyses that the association of liberalism with the Democratic party is hardly a perfect one, and these latest two tables point that out very clearly.

Whereas liberalism increases somewhat with rising educational levels, Democratic party identification decreases for all educational categories. Why do you suppose that would be the case? Think about this, and we'll return to this issue in Chapter 18, when you have the ability to analyze multivariate tables.

Some Surprises — Class, Marital Status, and Politics

Sometimes the inductive method of analysis produces some surprises. As an example, you might take a look at the relationship between our political variables and the demographic variables CLASS and MARITAL.[3]

Social Class

You might expect that social class is related to political philosophy and party identification because the Democratic party has traditionally been strong among the working class, whereas the well-to-do have seemed more comfortable as Republicans. If you are so inclined, why don't you check to see if this relationship still holds true? You can use the variable CLASS, which is a measure of subjective social class, asking respondents how they view themselves in this regard.

After you have done that, try to interpret your tables in much the same way we did with the tables above. What do your tables show? Is there a relationship between subjective social class and political philosophy or party identification? Are the results consistent with your expectations or are they surprising in some way?

Marital Status

In addition, you may also want to take a look at the relationship between marital status and political orientations. If even the suggestion that there is a relationship between marital status and political orientations sounds far-fetched to you, the results of this analysis may be surprising.

---

[3] Remember to define appropriate values for each of the variables as missing.

Once you've run the tables, try to interpret them and think of any good reasons for the observed differences. Here's a clue: Try to think of other variables that might account for the patterns you've observed. Then, in Chapter 18, when we engage in multivariate analysis, you'll have a chance to check out some of your explanations.

The Impact of Party and Political Philosophy

Let's shift gears now and consider politics as an independent variable. What impact do you suppose political philosophy and/or political party might have in determining people's attitudes on some of the political issues we looked at earlier?

Ask yourself where liberals and conservatives would stand on the following issues. Then run the tables to find out if your hunches are correct.

GUNLAW   registration of firearms

CAPPUN   capital punishment

Remember, when POLREC is the independent variable, you need to alter its location in the Crosstabs command, making it the column variable.

After you've examined the relationship between political philosophies and these more specific political issues, consider the impact of political party. In forming your expectations in this latter regard, you might want to review recent political platforms of the two major parties or the speeches of political candidates from the two parties. Then see if the political party identification of the American public falls along those same lines.

Saving Recoded Variable – EDCAT

Before concluding your SPSS session, be sure to **save** the recoded variable **EDCAT** on your **DEMOPLUS file** so we can use it later on.

Conclusion

We hope this chapter has given you a good look at the excitement possible in the detective work called social science research. We're willing to bet that some of the results you've uncovered in this chapter pretty much squared with your understanding of American politics, whereas other findings came as a surprise.

The skills you are learning in this book, along with your access to SPSS and the GSS data, make it possible for you to conduct your own investigations into the nature of American politics and other issues that may interest you. In the chapter that follows, we're going to return to our examination of attitudes toward abortion. This time, we want to learn what causes differences in attitudes on this hotly controversial topic.

Main Points

- While in the last chapter we began with a theory of religiosity, in this chapter we took a more inductive approach.
- We examined the causes (and effects) of political orientations by focusing primarily on the recoded forms of our two main political variables: POLVIEWS and PARTYID.
- After looking at the relationship between these two variables in their recoded form (POLREC and PARTY), we concluded that there is an affinity between liberalism and Democrats and conservatism and Republicans, although it is by no means a perfect relationship.
- We then resumed our focus on bivariate analyses by examining what causes some people to be liberals or conservatives, Democrats or Republicans.
- In searching for causal variables, we focused primarily on demographic items such as age, religion, gender, race, education, class, and marital status.
- In some cases our results did not match our expectations.
- The bulk of the chapter was devoted to explaining what causes people to hold various political views or to identify with one political party or another. In these analyses we identified POLREC and PARTY as dependent variables.
- It is also possible to look at political views and party identification as independent variables to see what role they might have in determining people's attitudes on political issues such as gun control and capital punishment.

Key Terms

Deduction	Induction
Demographic variables	Longitudinal data

SPSS Commands Introduced in This Chapter

No new commands were introduced in this chapter

Review Questions

1. What is the difference between deductive and inductive data analysis?

2. Which approach did we use in Chapter 11 to examine religiosity?

3. Which approach did we use to examine political orientations in this chapter (Chapter 12)?

4. What did we find when we crosstabulated POLREC and PARTY?

5. Do our findings suggest that all conservatives are Republican and all liberals are Democrats?

6. Name three demographic variables in either your DEMO.SAV or EXER.SAV files.

7. Is the variable CAPPUN a demographic variable? How about INCOME98?

8. Our findings show that older age groups appear to be slightly more conservative than younger age groups. Does this mean that older age groups are more likely than younger age groups to identify themselves as Republicans?

9. Of the three religious categories we examined, which is the most liberal? Which is the most conservative?

10. Summarize the relationship between gender and our political variables.

11. There is a strong relationship between race and party identification, with 58 percent of Blacks identifying themselves as Democrats, compared to 28 percent of Whites. Can we conclude from this that there is an equally strong relationship between race and political views?

12. Why do you suppose Democratic party identification decreases with rising educational levels?

13. Summarize the relationship between marital status and political orientation. How can we explain these results?

14. Does either political philosophy or party identification determine attitudes about issues such as gun control or capital punishment?

NAME _____

CLASS _____

INSTRUCTOR _____

DATE _____

To complete the following exercises you need to load the EXERPLUS data file. You can find answers to Questions 1-2, 12-13 in Appendix B.

In Questions 1-7 we are going to examine what causes some people to feel that the national government is spending too little on improving and protecting Americans' health. Remember to define the appropriate values as missing for each relevant variable before proceeding with your analysis.

1. Run Crosstabs with NATHEAL as your dependent variable, HEALTH as your independent variable, and cells to be percentaged by column. After you run Crosstabs, print your output.[4]

    Then on Line A below write the names of the categories of HEALTH using as many spaces as necessary. On Line B, fill in the spaces noting the percentage who answered "Too little" on NATHEAL for each category of HEALTH.

                            NATHEAL by HEALTH

    Line A _____   _____   _____   _____   _____
    Line B _____   _____   _____   _____   _____

2. Do the column percentages in the summary table above change, suggesting that there is a relationship between the variables?

3. Choose one demographic variable from your data file EXER.SAV and state your expectations regarding the relationship between that variable (as the independent variable) and NATHEAL (as the dependent variable). (Depending on which variable you chose, you may need to recode it to make it more manageable.)

---

[4] Define the values 0, 8, and 9 as missing for both NATHEAL and HEALTH

4. Was it necessary for you to recode the demographic variable you chose as your independent variable? If so, explain how you recoded the variable by listing the name of the variable you recoded, the name of the new (recoded) variable, the old value labels, and the new value labels.

5. Run Crosstabs with NATHEAL as your dependent variable and the variable you chose as the independent variable and print your table. Then on Line A below write the name of your independent variable. On Line B write the names of the categories of your independent variable using as many spaces as necessary. On Line C, fill in the spaces noting the percentage who answered "Too little" on NATHEAL for each category of the independent variable.

    Line A NATHEAL by _____
    Line B _____ _____ _____ _____ _____
    Line C _____ _____ _____ _____ _____

6. Do the column percentages in the summary table you created above change, suggesting that there is a relationship between the variables?

7. Summarize and explain your findings below. You may want to note, for instance, whether the findings match your expectations and whether you were surprised by the findings.

8. Choose one of the following variables as your dependent variable: NATEDUC, NATRACE, or NATFARE and note the name of the variable you chose and what it measures below.

NAME _____

CLASS _____

INSTRUCTOR _____

DATE _____

9. Now choose a second variable from your data set as your independent variable. Note the name of the variable and what it measures below. If it is necessary to recode your variable, note how you did that below.

10. What are your expectations regarding the relationship between your independent and dependent variables?

11. Run Crosstabs and print your table. Then summarize and explain your findings below. You may want to note, for instance, whether there is a relationship between your independent and dependent variables? Do the findings match your expectations? Were you at all surprised by the results? If so, why? If not, why not?

In Chapter 12 we examined the relationship between PARTY and POLREC in two ways: (a) PARTY as the "cause" or independent variable and (b) POLREC as the "cause" or independent variable. In the following exercise, we are going to consider the relationship between two variables on your EXERPLUS file (GRNEXAGG and RECGRNT), both of which can be examined as the "cause" and as the "effect." You may recall that RECGRNT is the recoded form of the variable GRNTAXES we created earlier. If you did not save this variable on your EXERPLUS file, simply refer back to the recode instructions in SPSS Lab Exercise 6.1 (Question #15) before proceeding with the follow exercises.

12. What does the variable GRNEXAGG measure?

13. What does the variable RECGRNT measure?

14. Before proceeding, define the values **0, 8,** and **9** as **missing** for **GRNEXAGG**.

    Now **recode GRNEXAGG** to create **RECEXAG** as follows:

Old Value	New Value	New Label
1-21	→	**Agree**
32	→	**Neither (Agree nor Disagree)**
4-53	→	**Disagree**

15. Construct a hypothesis in which RECGRNT is the independent variable and RECEXAG is the dependent variable.

16. Using your recoded variables, test your hypothesis in response to Question 15 by running Crosstabs. Print and attach your output to this sheet. Then in the space provided below, analyze your findings. You may want to consider questions such as: How does the dependent variable change with changes in the independent variable? How strong is the relationship between the variables?

NAME _____

CLASS _____

INSTRUCTOR _____

DATE _____

17. Now construct a hypothesis in which RECGRNT is the dependent variable and RECEXAG is the independent variable.

18. Use your recoded variables to test the hypothesis listed in response to Question 17 by running Crosstabs. Print and attach your output to this sheet. Then in the space provided below, analyze your findings. You may want to consider questions such as: How does the dependent variable change with changes in the independent variable? How strong is the relationship between the variables?

19. Now choose two other variables on your EXERPLUS file that can be treated as the "cause" and as the "effect." [For instance, you may want to consider the relationship between RECEXAG and another one of the environmental variables GRNPRICE.] Once you have identified the variables, make sure you define the appropriate values for each variable as missing, and recode if necessary. Then run Crosstabs to examine the relationship between the variables. Remember, you should examine each variable as the "cause" (or independent variable). Once you have run Crosstabs, print your output and attach it to this sheet. Then write a short description of your findings below. Your

primary goal is to identify and describe the general pattern (and any exceptions to that pattern) in the tables (i.e. those who believe the environmental threat is exaggerated are less likely to support paying higher taxes . . .). In addition, you may want to ask yourself: what is the nature of association between the variables in each table? How does the dependent variable change with changes in the independent variable? How strong is the association between the variables? What general pattern(s) is/are evident in each table? Are there any exceptions to this pattern that are worth noting? Is one variable "better" viewed as the "cause" or independent variable?

Chapter 13 What Causes Different Attitudes Toward Abortion?

One of the most controversial issues of recent years has concerned whether a woman has the right to have an abortion. Partisans on both sides of this issue are often extremely vocal and demonstrative.

As we saw in Chapter 8, there appear to be three main positions on this issue among the GSS respondents in 2000. Just under 45 percent support a woman's right to have an abortion for any reason, whereas 12 percent oppose abortion under all circumstances, and the rest are opposed to unrestricted abortions but are willing to make exceptions when pregnancy results from rape when it risks the mother's health or is likely to result in serious birth defects.

In this chapter, we're going to use your new analytic skills to begin exploring the causes of these different points of view on abortion. Whereas in the last two chapters we focused on running and interpreting Crosstabs, in this chapter we want to use our output to create summary tables which help us to understand the causes of different attitudes toward abortion. Why are some people permissive and others not? As we pursue this question, we can profit from an excellent review of the research on abortion attitudes: Cook, Jelen, and Wilcox's *Between Two Absolutes: Public Opinion and the Politics of Abortion* (1992). Chapter 2 from that book is reprinted on your CD to serve as background for the analyses we'll undertake in this chapter and to suggest additional directions of analysis if you would like to pursue this topic beyond these first steps.

Demonstration 13.1: Gender and Abortion

Go ahead and **open** your **DEMOPLUS** file so we can use some of the variables we created earlier.

As you think about possible causes of different attitudes about abortion, the first one that probably comes to mind is gender, given that abortion affects women more directly than it does men. In a quote that has become a popular pro-choice bumper sticker, Florynce Kennedy put it this way several years ago: "If men could get pregnant, abortion would be a sacrament." There is reason to believe, therefore, that women would be more supportive of abortion than men. Let's see.

Here is a table that summarizes attitudes toward abortion by gender. It is *not* SPSS output, but we've *created* it from several SPSS tables. Your task

231

is to figure out how to get the SPSS tables that would allow you to create this table.[1]

Percentage Approving of Abortion Under the Following Conditions		Men	Women
ABHLTH	woman's health endangered	89	87
ABRAPE	resulted from rape	84	78
ABDEFECT	serious defect likely	82	76
ABPOOR	too poor for more children	48	41
ABNOMORE	family wants no more	48	40
ABSINGLE	woman is unmarried	46	38
ABANY	for any reason	43	41

Contrary to what we expected, women are not more supportive of abortion than men. Actually, men are consistently more supportive, representing a difference of as little as two percentage points on ABHLTH and ABANY, and as much as seven to eight percent in the cases of ABPOOR, ABNOMORE, ABSINGLE.

We used the individual items concerning abortion for this analysis because it was possible that men and women would differ on some items but not on others. For example, we might have expected women to be more supportive on the item concerning the woman's health, but this was not the case. As an alternative strategy for examining the sources of attitudes toward abortion, let's make use of the index ABORT that we created by combining responses to ABDEFECT and ABSINGLE. At the end of Chapter 9 we asked you to save ABORT on your DEMOPLUS file. If you didn't, you need to follow the recode commands in Chapter 9 again before continuing.

Based on the summary table above, we would expect men to exhibit a little more support for abortion than women. And our modified expectations are more accurate, as you'll discover when you create the following table.

ABORT Simple Abortion Index * SEX RESPONDENTS SEX Crosstabulation

			SEX RESPONDENTS SEX		Total
			1 MALE	2 FEMALE	
ABORT Simple Abortion Index	0 yes/approve	Count	188	187	375
		% within SEX RESPONDENTS SEX	46.8%	38.1%	42.0%
	1 conditional support	Count	143	188	331
		% within SEX RESPONDENTS SEX	35.6%	38.3%	37.1%
	2	Count	71	116	187
		% within SEX RESPONDENTS SEX	17.7%	23.6%	20.9%
Total		Count	402	491	893
		% within SEX RESPONDENTS SEX	100.0%	100.0%	100.0%

---

[1] If you are having trouble figuring out how to access the information used to create this table, don't worry, the commands are as follows: Run **Crosstabs** for the **seven abortion variables** (**row** variables) and **SEX** (**column** variable), **cells** to be percentagized by **column**. You should get seven crosstabs that can be used to create this table (i.e. the percent of men and women who responded "Yes" to each item). Make sure you are clear as to how this table was created before moving ahead because we will ask you to set-up similar tables later in the chapter.

Recall that a score of 0 on the index represents those who supported a woman's right to have an abortion in both circumstances: if there was a chance of a birth defect and if she was single. Overall, 42 percent of the sample took that position. As we suspected, this table indicates a small difference between men and women, with men somewhat *more likely* (47 percent) to score 0 on the index than women (38 percent).

So far, then, we have learned that while men are somewhat more likely to be supportive of abortion, gender is not the sole explanation for differences in attitudes toward abortion. Let's see if age has an impact.

Demonstration 13.2: Age and Abortion

As Cook and her colleagues (1992) point out, abortion is somewhat more relevant to young people because they are more likely to experience unwanted pregnancies than are older people. What would that lead you to expect in the way of a relationship between age and support for abortion? Think about that, and then use SPSS to run the tables that answer the question for you.

Recall that we recoded AGE into AGECAT in Chapter 6 and saved the variable on our DEMOPLUS file. We'll want to use **AGECAT** for our examination of the relationship between age and abortion attitudes.[2]

Now you can request the SPSS tables that relate age to abortion attitudes. Here's a summary of the tables you should have created.

Percentage Approving of Abortion Under the Following Conditions		Under 21	21-39	40-64	Over 64
ABHLTH	woman's health endangered	94	89	86	90
ABRAPE	resulted from rape	90	82	78	82
ABDEFECT	serious defect likely	78	80	78	80
ABPOOR	too poor for more children	38	47	43	40
ABSINGLE	woman is unmarried	36	42	43	39
ABNOMORE	family wants no more	34	48	43	41
ABANY	for any reason	30	47	42	34

Take a minute to look over the data presented in this summary table. How do the analytic results square with your expectations?

These data suggest that younger people are slightly more likely than older people to support abortion if a woman's health is at risk and if the pregnancy resulted from rape, although there is a great deal of support for abortion in these situations across all age groups. Interestingly, those under 21 are slightly less likely to support abortion if the woman is poor, single, doesn't want any more children, or if she wants an abortion for any reason. Nevertheless, this table shows that as in the case of gender, there is little or no relationship between age and the other abortion items.

---

[2] If you did not save the recoded variable AGECAT, simply follow the commands in Chapter 6 before moving ahead with the demonstration.

Now let's run Crosstabs using our ABORT index and AGECAT to see what we find.

			AGECAT Recoded Age Categories				
			1 Under 21	2 21-39	3 40-64	4 65 and older	Total
ABORT Simple Abortion Index	0 yes/approve	Count	11	146	155	62	374
		% within AGECAT Recoded Age Categories	35.5%	42.2%	42.6%	41.6%	42.0%
	1 conditional support	Count	13	132	130	55	330
		% within AGECAT Recoded Age Categories	41.9%	38.2%	35.7%	36.9%	37.1%
	2 no/disapprove	Count	7	68	79	32	186
		% within AGECAT Recoded Age Categories	22.6%	19.7%	21.7%	21.5%	20.9%
Total		Count	31	346	364	149	890
		% within AGECAT Recoded Age Categories	100.0%	100.0%	100.0%	100.0%	100.0%

ABORT Simple Abortion Index * AGECAT Recoded Age Categories Crosstabulation

This table indicates that there is no relationship between age and abortion as measured by our ABORT index. Based on the analyses above then, we could say that there is not convincing evidence of a strong relationship between age and abortion attitudes. Or, perhaps it is just more complex than we have been allowing for in these analyses. We'll find out once we are able to undertake multivariate analysis in Part V.

Demonstration 13.3: Religion and Abortion

If we began this analysis by asking you what variable you thought might account for attitudes toward abortion, there is a good chance that you would have guessed religion, given the unconditional and public opposition of the Roman Catholic church. Your growing facility with SPSS and the GSS data make it possible for you to test that expectation.

Let's start with the possible impact of religious affiliation. Here's a summary of what you should discover if you run the several abortion items by **RELIG**. Remember to define the values **0, 5-99** as **missing** for the variable **RELIG** before running **Crosstabs** and creating your summary table.

Percentage Approving of Abortion Under the Following Conditions		*Prot.*	*Cath.*	*Jew.*	*None*
ABHLTH	woman's health endangered	87	86	95	91
ABRAPE	resulted from rape	80	76	95	90
ABDEFECT	serious defect likely	77	75	95	89
ABNOMORE	family wants no more	40	36	90	63
ABPOOR	too poor for more children	39	36	95	62
ABANY	for any reason	38	36	95	58
ABSINGLE	woman is unmarried	37	36	95	55

There are several observations you might make about these data. To begin with, the expectation that Catholics would be the most opposed to abortion is not confirmed. In fact, Protestants are just as likely, if not slightly more likely to disapprove of abortion under any of the conditions asked about. Based on our summary table we can conclude that roughly three-quarters of both Protestants and Catholics are likely to approve of abortion in cases of health, rape and birth defect, while just under 40 percent are likely to support it in the other cases.

You might also note that the level of support for abortion among American Catholics is greatly at variance with the church's official position. Under the traumatic conditions summarized at the top of the table, 75 to 86 percent of the Catholics say they would approve abortion. Even under the less traumatic conditions, 36 percent of the Catholics would support a woman's right to an abortion.

In contrast, Jews and those with no religion are consistently more supportive of a woman's right to an abortion. It is interesting to note that 90 percent or more of the Jewish respondents said they would support abortion in all seven cases, including if the woman is poor, single, or doesn't want any more children.

To examine this relationship further, you could also use the index ABORT to see if this pattern is reflected in scores on a composite measure. Your table should look like the one below.

ABORT Simple Abortion Index * RELIG RS RELIGIOUS PREFERENCE Crosstabulation

| | | | RELIG RS RELIGIOUS PREFERENCE | | | | |
			1 PROTESTANT	2 CATHOLIC	3 JEWISH	4 NONE	Total
ABORT Simple Abortion Index	0 yes/approve	Count	185	77	20	67	349
		% within RELIG RS RELIGIOUS PREFERENCE	37.5%	35.8%	95.2%	56.3%	41.2%
	1 conditional support	Count	196	83		38	317
		% within RELIG RS RELIGIOUS PREFERENCE	39.8%	38.6%		31.9%	37.4%
	2 no/disapprove	Count	112	55	1	14	182
		% within RELIG RS RELIGIOUS PREFERENCE	22.7%	25.6%	4.8%	11.8%	21.5%
Total		Count	493	215	21	119	848
		% within RELIG RS RELIGIOUS PREFERENCE	100.0%	100.0%	100.0%	100.0%	100.0%

In our earlier examinations of religion, we've sometimes gone beyond affiliation to examine the measure of religiosity, or religiousness. How do you suppose church attendance would relate to abortion attitudes? To find out, let's use **CHATT**, the recoded variable created in Chapter 6.[3]

Run the appropriate tables. Here's a summary of what you should have learned.

_____
[3] If you did not save the recoded variable CHATT, simply follow the commands in Chapter 6 before moving ahead with the demonstration.

Percentage Approving of Abortion Under the Following Conditions		Weekly	Monthly	Seldom	Never
ABHLTH	woman's health endangered	80	89	92	91
ABDEFECT	serious defect likely	64	83	86	85
ABRAPE	resulted from rape	61	84	90	90
ABPOOR	too poor for more children	26	43	52	56
ABSINGLE	woman is unmarried	24	40	51	52
ABNOMORE	family wants no more	24	42	54	56
ABANY	for any reason	23	40	52	53

What does this table tell you about religion and abortion attitudes? The overall relationship is pretty clear: Increased church attendance is related to decreased support for abortion. There is a substantial difference, however, between those who attend church about weekly and those who attend less often. Those who attend one to three times per month are almost twice as likely to support unconditional abortion as those who attend church weekly. Even in the case of the traumatic conditions at the top of the table, only those who attend church weekly stand out in their comparatively low level of support.

The fact that the other three groups do not differ much from one another, by the way, is a result of what we call a *ceiling effect*. Whenever the overall percentage of people agreeing with something approaches 100 percent, it's not possible for there to be much variation among subgroups.

In the extreme case, if everyone agreed on something, there would be no way for men and women to differ because 100 percent of both would have to agree. Similarly, there could be no differences among age groups, religions, and so on. When the overall percentage approaches zero, a similar situation occurs that we call a *floor effect*.

Now check the relationship between CHATT and the abortion index, ABORT, and then compare your results with ours below.

ABORT Simple Abortion Index * CHATT Recoded Church Attendance Crosstabulation

			CHATT Recoded Church Attendance				
			1 About weekly	2 About monthly	3 Seldom	4 Never	Total
ABORT Simple Abortion Index	0 yes/approve	Count	60	60	147	97	364
		% within CHATT Recoded Church Attendance	24.8%	37.7%	51.2%	52.7%	41.7%
	1 conditional support	Count	92	74	101	59	326
		% within CHATT Recoded Church Attendance	38.0%	46.5%	35.2%	32.1%	37.4%
	2 no/disapprove	Count	90	25	39	28	182
		% within CHATT Recoded Church Attendance	37.2%	15.7%	13.6%	15.2%	20.9%
Total		Count	242	159	287	184	872
		% within CHATT Recoded Church Attendance	100.0%	100.0%	100.0%	100.0%	100.0%

Are these results consistent with those in the summary table we created? Do you find evidence of a ceiling effect in this table as well?

The GSS data we've provided for your use permit you to explore this general topic even further, if you wish. Why don't you check out the effect of **POSTLIFE** and **PRAY** on abortion attitudes? Before running the tables, however, take some time to reflect on what might logically be expected. How should beliefs about an afterlife affect support for or opposition to abortion? You may be surprised by what you learn. Then again, maybe you won't be surprised.

Writing Box 13.1

It might seem ironic that those who believe in a life after death are less likely to support abortion than those who do not — and vice versa — but that's what the data indicate. Of those who believe in an afterlife, only 36 percent give unconditional support to a woman's right to have an abortion, contrasted to 50 percent of those who disbelieve in an afterlife.

Religiosity, as measured by prayer, also affects attitudes toward abortion. Among those who pray several times a day, only 25 percent give unconditional support for abortion, as do about a third of those in the three categories representing prayer once a day to once a week. The real difference shows up among those who pray less than once a week: 64 percent support for abortion when the two final categories are combined.

Demonstration 13.4: Politics and Abortion

There is a strong and consistent relationship between political philosophy and abortion attitudes. What do you suppose that relationship is? Who would you expect to be the more supportive of abortion: liberals or conservatives? To carry out this investigation, you'll probably want to use the recoded variable, **POLREC**.[4]

Now you can examine the relationship between political philosophy and abortion attitudes to see if your hunch is correct. Here's a summary of what you should discover.

Percentage Approving of Abortion Under the Following Conditions		Liberal	Moderate	Conservative
ABHLTH	woman's health endangered	91	91	83
ABRAPE	resulted from rape	87	87	70
ABDEFECT	serious defect likely	85	85	68
ABPOOR	too poor for more children	61	46	30
ABNOMORE	family wants no more	60	45	31
ABSINGLE	woman is unmarried	57	42	30
ABANY	for any reason	56	45	28

How would you describe these results? Try your hand at writing a sentence or two to report on the impact of political philosophy on abortion attitudes before reading ahead.

One way to summarize the relationship between political philosophy and abortion attitudes is to say the following: Liberals are strongly and consistently more supportive of a woman's right to an abortion than are conservatives, with moderates falling in between.

To pursue this relationship further, you may want to use the ABORT index.

---

[4] If you did not save the recoded variable POLREC, simply follow the commands in Chapter 7 before moving ahead with this demonstration.

ABORT Simple Abortion Index * POLREC Recoded polviews Crosstabulation			POLREC Recoded polviews			
			1 Liberal	2 Moderate	3 Conservative	Total
ABORT Simple Abortion Index	0 yes/approve	Count	125	148	85	358
		% within POLREC Recoded polviews	55.3%	42.3%	31.3%	42.2%
	1 conditional support	Count	71	149	98	318
		% within POLREC Recoded polviews	31.4%	42.6%	36.0%	37.5%
	2 no/disapprove	Count	30	53	89	172
		% within POLREC Recoded polviews	13.3%	15.1%	32.7%	20.3%
Total		Count	226	350	272	848
		% within POLREC Recoded polviews	100.0%	100.0%	100.0%	100.0%

Are these results consistent with those in the summary table above? Does the interpretation of the relationship between political philosophy and abortion attitudes as strong and consistent hold up?

Another direction you might want to follow in investigating the relationship between politics and abortion attitudes concerns political party identification. As you no doubt realize, the Democratic party has been generally more supportive of a woman's right to have an abortion than has the Republican party. This difference was dramatically portrayed by the presidential and vice presidential candidates during the 1996 and 2000 elections.

How do you suppose the official differences separating the parties show up in the attitudes of the rank and file? Among the general public, who do you suppose are the most supportive of abortion: Democrats or Republicans? See if you can find out for yourself by creating a summary table similar to those above and then running **Crosstabs** with **PARTY** (as our measure of party identification) and **ABORT** (our index of abortion attitudes).[5] Once you have done that, see if the findings are consistent with your expectations.

Writing Box 13.2

The relationship between political party identification and support for abortion is what you may have anticipated, based on official party platforms and the pronouncements of party spokespersons. Forty-four percent of the Democrats give unconditional support to a woman's right to an abortion. Among Republicans, only 32 percent do so. Interestingly, Independents are almost identical to Democrats in this regard, with 45 percent giving unconditional support for abortion.

Demonstration 13.5: Sexual Attitudes and Abortion

Recalling that abortion attitudes are related to differences in political philosophy, it might occur to you that other philosophical differences might be relevant as

---

[5] If you did not save the recoded variable PARTY, simply follow the commands in Chapter 7 before moving ahead with this demonstration.

well. As you may recall from Chapter 10, the GSS data set contains three items dealing with sexual permissiveness/restrictiveness:[6]

PREMARSX   attitudes toward premarital sex

HOMOSEX   attitudes toward homosexual sex relations

XMOVIE   attendance at an X-rated movie during the year

Here's the relationship between attitudes toward premarital sex (**PREMARSX**) and toward abortion. Notice how permissiveness on one is related to permissiveness on the other.

ABORT Simple Abortion Index * PREMARSX SEX BEFORE MARRIAGE Crosstabulation

| | | | PREMARSX SEX BEFORE MARRIAGE | | | | |
			1 ALWAYS WRONG	2 ALMST ALWAYS WRG	3 SOMETIMES WRONG	4 NOT WRONG AT ALL	Total
ABORT Simple Abortion Index	0 yes/approve	Count	31	11	43	89	174
		% within PREMARSX SEX BEFORE MARRIAGE	23.1%	30.6%	40.2%	52.4%	38.9%
	1 conditional support	Count	48	19	47	67	181
		% within PREMARSX SEX BEFORE MARRIAGE	35.8%	52.8%	43.9%	39.4%	40.5%
	2 no/disapprove	Count	55	6	17	14	92
		% within PREMARSX SEX BEFORE MARRIAGE	41.0%	16.7%	15.9%	8.2%	20.6%
Total		Count	134	36	107	170	447
		% within PREMARSX SEX BEFORE MARRIAGE	100.0%	100.0%	100.0%	100.0%	100.0%

Now, why don't you check to see if the same pattern holds for the other sexual permissiveness items?

ABORT Simple Abortion Index * HOMOSEX HOMOSEXUAL SEX RELATIONS Crosstabulation

| | | | HOMOSEX HOMOSEXUAL SEX RELATIONS | | | | |
			1 ALWAYS WRONG	2 ALMST ALWAYS WRG	3 SOMETIMES WRONG	4 NOT WRONG AT ALL	Total
ABORT Simple Abortion Index	0 yes/approve	Count	138	11	35	155	339
		% within HOMOSEX HOMOSEXUAL SEX RELATIONS	28.9%	32.4%	52.2%	65.1%	41.5%
	1 conditional support	Count	197	17	25	65	304
		% within HOMOSEX HOMOSEXUAL SEX RELATIONS	41.2%	50.0%	37.3%	27.3%	37.2%
	2 no/disapprove	Count	143	6	7	18	174
		% within HOMOSEX HOMOSEXUAL SEX RELATIONS	29.9%	17.6%	10.4%	7.6%	21.3%
Total		Count	478	34	67	238	817
		% within HOMOSEX HOMOSEXUAL SEX RELATIONS	100.0%	100.0%	100.0%	100.0%	100.0%

---

[6] Use the "**Range plus one optional discrete missing value option**" to define the values **0, 5, 8** and **9** as **missing** for the variables **PREMARSX** and **HOMOSEX**. In addition, remember to define the values **0, 8,** and **9** as **missing** for the variable **XMOVIE**.

ABORT Simple Abortion Index * XMOVIE SEEN X-RATED MOVIE IN LAST YEAR Crosstabulation			XMOVIE SEEN X-RATED MOVIE IN LAST YEAR		Total
			1 YES	2 NO	
ABORT Simple Abortion Index	0 yes/approve	Count	61	136	197
		% within XMOVIE SEEN X-RATED MOVIE IN LAST YEAR	56.0%	41.7%	45.3%
	1 conditional support	Count	33	113	146
		% within XMOVIE SEEN X-RATED MOVIE IN LAST YEAR	30.3%	34.7%	33.6%
	2 no/disapprove	Count	15	77	92
		% within XMOVIE SEEN X-RATED MOVIE IN LAST YEAR	13.8%	23.6%	21.1%
Total		Count	109	326	435
		% within XMOVIE SEEN X-RATED MOVIE IN LAST YEAR	100.0%	100.0%	100.0%

As you probably expected, abortion attitudes are related to attitudes toward homosexuality and to attendance at an X-rated movie. In other words, those who are sexually permissive tend to be permissive in the area of abortion as well.

Other Factors You Can Explore on Your Own

There are a number of other factors that can affect attitudes toward abortion. We'll suggest a few more demographic variables for you to check out. You may want to review the excerpt from Cook et al. on the CD for further ideas.

You might suspect that education is related to abortion attitudes. If so, which direction do you suppose that relationship goes? Why do you suppose that is?

Race is another standard demographic variable that might be related to abortion attitudes. You should examine the relationship between attitudes toward abortion in particular circumstances and race carefully, because race may have slightly different effects on different items.

Finally, you might like to explore the relationship between abortion attitudes and some family variables. How do you suppose abortion attitudes relate to respondents' views of the ideal number of children to have?

The family variable that may surprise you in its relationship to abortion attitudes is MARITAL. You may recall that we also uncovered a surprising effect of marital status on political philosophy. Check this one out, and we'll take a more in-depth look once we begin our multivariate analyses.

Conclusion

In this chapter, you've had an opportunity to search for explanations for the vast differences in people's feelings about abortion. We've found that religion and politics, for example, are powerful influences. We've also just seen that permissiveness and restrictiveness regarding abortion are strongly related to permissiveness and restrictiveness on issues of sexual behavior.

Thus far, we've opened up the search only for explanations, limiting ourselves to bivariate analyses. In the analyses to come, we'll dig ever deeper into the reasons for differences in the opinions people have. Ultimately, you should gain a well-rounded understanding of the logic of social scientific research as well as master some of the fundamental techniques for acting on that logic through SPSS.

Main Points

- This chapter focused on the causes of differing attitudes toward abortion.
- Cook, Jelen, and Wilcox's book *Between Two Absolutes* was used as a starting point for our analysis.
- Throughout the chapter we examined the relationship between attitudes toward abortion and several potential independent or causal variables.
- In addition to examining SPSS output (primarily crosstabs), we also created our own summary tables based on several SPSS tables. These summary tables made it easy to examine the relationship between attitudes toward abortion and several independent variables.
- Gender and age are not related to attitudes toward abortion, whereas religion, politics, and sexual attitudes are.
- In the case of religion, for example, we found that those who attend church weekly are much less likely to support abortion than those who attend less often.
- We also found that those attending less often (monthly, seldom, or never) do not differ much from one another. Here we see evidence of what we call a ceiling effect.
- You may also want to try looking for relationships between attitudes toward abortion and other demographic variables such as race, education, and family.

Key Terms

Ceiling effect
Floor effect

SPSS Commands Introduced in This Chapter

No new commands were introduced in this chapter.

Review Questions

1. One way we explored the relationship between attitudes toward abortion and several potential independent variables was by constructing a summary table based on SPSS output. How were these tables constructed?

2. What are the commands used to instruct SPSS to construct a table looking at the relationship between our abortion index ABORT and gender?

3. Do our findings support the contention that women are more likely to be supportive of abortion than men?

4. Why did we use the recoded variable AGECAT as opposed to the variable AGE to examine the relationship between age and attitudes toward abortion?

5. Summarize the relationship between abortion attitudes and religious affiliation.

6. Do the majority of American Catholics differ from the Catholic church on abortion in particular circumstances? If so, what circumstances?

7. What is the ceiling effect?

8. What is the floor effect?

9. We found that liberals are more likely than conservatives to support abortion. Does this mean that Democrats are more likely to support abortion than Republicans?

10. Are those favoring small families more or less likely to support abortion?

11. Is there any difference between those who are separated and those who are divorced in terms of their unconditional support for abortion?

12. Is there a relationship between attitudes toward sexual behavior and attitudes toward abortion?

NAME _____

CLASS _____

INSTRUCTOR _____

DATE _____

To complete the following exercises, you need to retrieve the data file EXERPLUS. Answers to Questions 1-2, 5-10 can be found in Appendix B.

We are going to begin by looking at what causes people to be permissive (or restrictive) in the area of teen sex. We will focus primarily on the three variables from your EXER.SAV file that deal with this issue: PILLOK, SEXEDUC, and TEENSEX.

1. What do each of the following variables measure?
   A. PILLOK

   B. SEXEDUC

   C. TEENSEX

2. List the values and labels of each of the following variables in the spaces provided below. Then define NAP (0), DK (8), and NA (9) as missing for the variable PILLOK. Define NAP (0), Depends (3), DK (8), and NA (9) as missing for SEXEDUC. Finally, define NAP (0), Other (5), DK (8), and NA (9) as missing for the variable TEENSEX. Hint: use the "Range plus one optional discrete missing value" option to define values as missing for both SEXEDUC and TEENSEX.

   A.   PILLOK
   Value   Label

   _____   _____
   _____   _____
   _____   _____
   _____   _____
   _____   _____
   _____   _____
   _____   _____

   B.   SEXEDUC
   Value   Label

   _____   _____
   _____   _____

———	————————————————
———	————————————————
———	————————————————
———	————————————————

C.   TEENSEX
Value   Label

———	————————————————
———	————————————————
———	————————————————
———	————————————————
———	————————————————
———	————————————————
———	————————————————
———	————————————————

3. Recode the variables PILLOK and TEENSEX as indicated below.
   A. PILLOK recode to create PILLREC

1-2	→	1	Permissive
3-4	→	2	Restrictive

   B. TEENSEX recode to create TEENREC

3-4	→	1	Permissive
1-2	→	2	Restrictive

4. Relabel SEXEDUC in the following manner. Hint: access the Variable View tab → click the cell corresponding with SEXEDUC and the column Values → remove the label (1 – Favor; 2 – Oppose) and add new labels as listed below.
   1 Permissive (favor)
   2 Restrictive (oppose)

5. Use SEX and our three measures of permissiveness on teen sex (PILLREC, TEENREC, and SEXEDUC) to instruct SPSS to run tables that can be used to fill in the summary table below.

Percentage Permissive on Teen Sex Given the Following Situations	Men	Women
PILLREC	_____	_____
SEXEDUC	_____	_____
TEENREC	_____	_____

6. What does this table tell you about the strength of the relationship between gender and permissiveness on teen sex? Do the column percentages change? If so, specify how the dependent variable changes with changes in the independent variable.

NAME _____

CLASS _____

INSTRUCTOR _____

DATE _____

7. Now we will move away from demographic variables. Try using FEFAM (which as you may recall is one of our measures of attitudes toward family and sex roles) and our three measures of permissiveness on teen sex (PILLREC, TEENREC, and SEXEDUC) to instruct SPSS to run tables that can be used to fill in the summary table below. (Don't forget to define 0, 8, and 9 as missing for FEFAM.)

Percentage Permissive on Teen Sex Given the Following Situations

	Strongly Agree	Agree	Disagree	Strongly Disagree
PILLREC	_____	_____	_____	_____
SEXEDUC	_____	_____	_____	_____
TEENREC	_____	_____	_____	_____

8. What does this table tell you about the strength of the relationship between attitudes toward family/sex roles and permissiveness on teen sex? Do the column percentages change? If so, specify how the dependent variable changes with changes in the independent variable.

9. Use FEPRESCH and our three measures of permissiveness on teen sex (PILLREC, TEENREC, and SEXEDUC) to instruct SPSS to run tables that can be used to fill in the following summary table. (Don't forget to define 0, 8, and 9 as missing for FEPRESCH.)

Percentage Permissive on Teen Sex Given the Following Situations

	Strongly Agree	Agree	Disagree	Strongly Disagree
PILLREC	_____	_____	_____	_____
SEXEDUC	_____	_____	_____	_____
TEENREC	_____	_____	_____	_____

10. What does this table tell you about the strength of the relationship between attitudes toward family/sex roles and permissiveness on

teen sex? Do the column percentages change? If so, specify how the dependent variable changes with changes in the independent variable.

11. Now choose another variable that you think may be related to permissiveness on teen sex. Write the name of the variable and explain why you chose it (i.e., how it might be related to permissiveness on teen sex).

12. List the values and labels of the item you chose and indicate whether it is necessary to recode/relabel. If so, explain how you did that below. Remember, you may also need to define values as missing for your variable.

13. Examine the relationship between the variable you chose and our three measures of permissiveness on teen sex (PILLREC, SEXEDUC, and TEENREC). Then fill in the following summary table below with the results of your analysis. If you need more space, use a separate sheet of paper. (Don't forget, depending on which variable you choose, you may have to designate DK as missing.)

Percentage Permissive on Teen Sex
LABELS OF
VARIABLE CHOSEN _____

PILLREC

SEXEDUC

TEENREC

14. What does this table tell you about the strength of the relationship between _____ [name of variable you chose] and

NAME _____

CLASS _____

INSTRUCTOR _____

DATE _____

permissiveness on teen sex? Do the column percentages change? If so, specify how the dependent variable changes with changes in the independent variable.

15. In previous SPSS Lab Exercises we examined several variables on your data file that ask respondents under which circumstances, if any, they would support a police officer striking an adult male (POLABUSE, POLATTAK, POLESCAP, POLIIITOK, POLMURDR). In Lab Exercise 9.1 we created an index, named POLIN, based on two of these items. In the following exercises we want you to explore these variables further, specifically by asking why some people are more supportive of the use of violence by police officers than others.

A. To begin, choose two of the demographic variables from your file that you think may be associated with attitudes towards the use of force. List the abbreviated variable names and explain why you think these variables may be related to attitudes towards the use of force by police officers.

B. Is it necessary to recode either of the demographic variables to make them more amenable to examination? If so, recode the variable(s) and show how you did that in the space below. If necessary, define appropriate values for each variable as missing.

C. Use SPSS to explore the association between these demographic variables and the five variables (POLABUSE, POLATTAK, POLESCAP, POLHITOK, POLMURDR). Then create two summary tables similar to those we focused on in the Demonstrations in Chapter 13. Your tables should be entitled:
"Percentage Approving of Police Officer Striking a Citizen under the Following Conditions"
Demographic/Independent Variable 1_____
                Categories/Labels
                of Demographic/Independent Variable

_____   _____   _____   _____

POLABUSE

POLATTAK

POLESCAP

POLHITOK

POLMURDR

You should use a separate sheet to create two summary tables, one for each "demographic/independent variable" you are working with.

D. After creating your summary tables, write a few sentences showing what each table tells us about the relationship between the independent/demographic variables you are working with and POLABUSE, POLATTAK, POLESCAP, POLHITOK, POLMURDR.

NAME _____

CLASS _____

INSTRUCTOR _____

DATE _____

E. Now, examine the relationship between the two demographic variables you chose and POLIN. If you did not save POLIN on your EXERPLUS file, simply follow the instructions in SPSS Lab Exercise 9.1 to create the index before moving ahead. Once you have run your Crosstabs, print and attach your output to this sheet. Then summarize your findings in a few sentences. What do your findings tell us about the relationship between the variables? Are the variables associated? If so, how strongly?

Reminder: Before ending this session, be sure to save your new recoded variables on your EXERPLUS file.

Chapter 14 **Measures of Association**

In the preceding analyses, we depended on percentage tables as our format for examining the relationships among variables. While crosstabs are a useful way to examine the relationship between two variables, it is often difficult to get a clear sense of how strong the association between the variables is. While there may appear to be a relationship between POLREC and PARTY, it can be difficult to say how strong the association actually is. In this chapter, we are going to explore some measures that allow us to determine more precisely the strength of a relationship. By and large, these techniques, called *measures of association*, summarize relationships (strength and in some cases direction) in contrast to the way percentage tables lay out the details.

Another way you might think of measures of association is in contrast to the statistics (measures of central tendency and dispersion) we introduced in Chapter 6. Both are considered *descriptive statistics*, but measures of central tendency and dispersion summarize the distribution of categories of a single variable, whereas measures of association summarize the strength of association between two variables. Additionally, when two variables are at either the ordinal or interval/ratio level of measure, measures of association also indicate the direction of association. These capabilities enable us to use measures of association to answer two important questions:

1. How strong is the association or relationship between two variables?

2. And, for ordinal and interval/ratio variables, what is the direction of association between two variables?

We begin our discussion with a thought experiment designed to introduce you to the logic of statistical association. We will then focus on four of the most commonly used measures of association, each of which is appropriate for variables at different levels of measurement: lambda, gamma, Pearson's *r*, and regression. In each case we will begin by introducing the logic of the measure and then show you how it can be calculated using SPSS. Finally, we will briefly discuss measures appropriate for mixed types of variables.

The Logic of Statistical Association: Proportionate Reduction of Error (PRE)

To introduce the logic of statistical association, we would like you to take a minute for a "thought experiment." Imagine that there is a group of 100 people in a lecture hall, and you are standing in the hallway outside the room. The people will come out of the room one at a time, and your task will be to guess the gender of each before he or she comes into view. Take a moment to consider your best strategy for making these guesses.

If you know nothing about the people in the room, there really is no useful strategy for guessing—no way to make educated guesses. But now suppose you know that 60 of the people in the room are women. This would make educated guesses possible: You should guess "woman" every time. By doing this, you would be right 60 times and wrong 40 times.

Now suppose that every time a person prepares to emerge from the room, his or her first name is announced. This would probably improve your guessing substantially. You'd guess "woman" for every Nancy or Joanne and "man" for every Joseph and Wendell. Even so, you probably wouldn't be totally accurate, given the ambiguity of names like Pat, Chris, and Leslie.

It is useful to notice that we could actually calculate how much knowing first names improved your guessing. Let's say you would have made 40 errors out of 100 guesses without knowing names and only 10 errors when you knew the names. You would have made 30 fewer mistakes. Out of an original 40 mistakes, that's a 75 percent improvement. Statisticians refer to this as a *proportionate reduction of error*, which they abbreviate as *PRE*. The measures of association we are going to focus on are largely based on this logic.

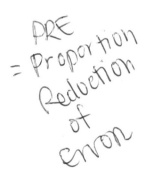

Lambda: A Measure Appropriate for Nominal Variables

Lambda is a measure of association appropriate for use with two nominal variables, and it operates on the PRE logic. Essentially, this means that the two variables are related to one another to the extent that knowing a person's attribute on one will help you guess his or her attribute on the other (i.e., the extent to which one variable is "associated" with, affects, or has an impact on, another variable).

An Indication of Strength of Association

The value of lambda, which can vary between 0.00 and 1.00, indicates the *strength* of association or relationship between two nominal variables. The closer the value of lambda is to 1.00, the stronger the relationship between the variables. Conversely, the closer the value of lambda is to 0.00, the weaker the relationship between the variables.

You'll remember that nominal variables are just sets of categories with no greater-than or less-than relationships between them. Based on that, you have probably already correctly surmised that lambda provides *no* indication of the direction of association. In the absence of an order between categories, there can be no direction of relationship. Even if there were a strong relationship between eye color and hair color, it would make no sense to say it was positive or negative.

Measure of Association	Lambda
Type of variables	Nominal × Nominal
Values (strength)	0 to +1.00
	0 = no association
	1.00 = perfect association
Direction	Not applicable

Example 1: The Logic of Lambda[1]

Here's a very simple example of lambda. Suppose that we have data on the employment status of 1,000 people. Half are employed; half are unemployed. If we were to begin presenting you with person after person, asking you to guess whether each was employed or not, you'd get about half wrong and half right by guessing blindly. So, the logic of lambda begins with the assumption that you'd make 500 errors in this case. Let's call these your "uneducated errors."

Now, take a look at the table below, which gives you additional information: the ages of the subjects.

	Young	*Old*	*Total*
Employed	0	500	500
Unemployed	500	0	500
Total	500	500	1,000

Suppose now that we were to repeat the guessing exercise. This time, however, you would know whether each person is young or old. What would be your strategy for guessing employment status?

Clearly, you should make an educated guess of "unemployed" for every young person and "employed" for every old person. Do that and you'll make no errors. You will have reduced your errors by 500, in comparison with the first attempt. Given that you will have eliminated all your former errors, we could also say that you have reduced your errors by 100 percent.

Here's the simple equation for lambda that allows you to calculate the reduction of errors:

$$\frac{\text{(uneducated errors)} - \text{(educated errors)}}{\text{(uneducated errors)}} = \frac{500 - 0}{500} = 1.00$$

Notice that the calculation results in 1.00, which we treat as 100 percent in the context of lambda.

Example 2: The Logic of Lambda

To be sure the logic of lambda is clear to you, let's consider another hypothetical example, similar to the previous example:

---

[1] Throughout this chapter we review how measures of association are computed in an effort to provide the rationale for matching the measure to the level of their data. Instructors and students who would rather focus on interpretation are encouraged to skip these sections and proceed directly to the demonstrations.

	Young	Old	Total
Employed	250	250	500
Unemployed	250	250	500
Total	500	500	1,000

In this new example, we still have half young and half old, and we also have half employed and half unemployed. Notice the difference in the relationship between the two variables, however. Just by inspection, you should be able to see that they are independent of one another. In this case, age has no impact on employment status.

The lack of a relationship between age and employment status here is reflected in the "educated" guesses you would make about employment status if you knew a person's age. It wouldn't help you at all, and you would get half the young people wrong and half the old people wrong. You would have made 500 errors in uneducated guesses, and you wouldn't have improved by knowing their ages.

Lambda reflects this new situation:

$$\frac{\text{(uneducated errors)} - \text{(educated errors)}}{\text{(uneducated errors)}} = \frac{500 - 500}{500} = 0.00$$

Knowing age would have reduced your errors by zero percent.

Demonstration 14.1:
Instructing SPSS to Calculate Lambda

The real relationships between variables are seldom this simple, of course, so let's look at a real example using SPSS and the General Social Survey data. You'll be pleased to discover that you won't have to calculate the errors or the proportion of reduction because SPSS does it for you.

Go ahead and **open** your **DEMOPLUS** file. Then set up a **Crosstabs** request using **ABANY** as the **row** variable and **RELIG** as the **column** variable.[2] For the time being, it will be useful to request **no percentaging of** the **cells** in the table.[3] Click on **Cells . . .** , and **turn off** "Column" if that's still selected. Then return to the Crosstabs window by clicking **Continue**. Before executing the Crosstabs command, however, click the **Statistics . . .** button. Here's what you should see:

---

[2] Define the values **0, 8**, and **9** as "**missing**" for the variable **ABANY**. Define the values **0, 5-99** as "**missing**" for the variable **RELIG**.

[3] Usually percentages are requested in order to see how the column percentages change or move. We omitted them here only to make the table somewhat easier to read.

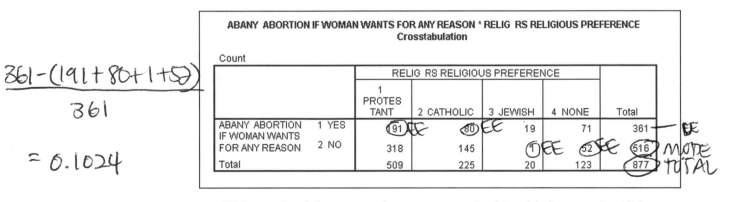

You will notice that SPSS gives you a variety of options, including some of the measures of association we are going to introduce in this chapter (as well as some we will not introduce, but which you may want to explore on your own). You can see that lambda is listed in the box on the left-hand side under Nominal because, as we know, lambda is a measure of association used for two nominal variables. Click **Lambda** and a check mark will appear in the small box to the left. Once you have done that, you can leave the Statistics window by clicking **Continue** and then execute the Crosstabs command by selecting **OK**. Here's the result that should show up in your Output window:

$$\frac{361-(191+80+1+52)}{361}$$

$$= 0.1024$$

ABANY ABORTION IF WOMAN WANTS FOR ANY REASON * RELIG RS RELIGIOUS PREFERENCE Crosstabulation

Count

		RELIG RS RELIGIOUS PREFERENCE				
		1 PROTES TANT	2 CATHOLIC	3 JEWISH	4 NONE	Total
ABANY ABORTION IF WOMAN WANTS FOR ANY REASON	1 YES	91	80	19	71	361
	2 NO	318	145	1	52	516
Total		509	225	20	123	877

We've omitted the request for percentages in this table because it will be useful to see the actual number of cases in each cell of the table. However, keep in mind that in most cases you want to request percentages to see how the column percentages change or move. At the far right of the table, notice that 361 people supported the idea of a woman being able to get an abortion just because she wanted one; 516 were opposed. If we were to make uneducated guesses about people's opinions on this issue, we'd do best always to guess "opposed." But by doing that, we would make 361 errors.

If we knew each person's religion, however, we would improve our record somewhat. Here's what would happen.

Religion	Guess	Errors
Protestant	No	191
Catholic	No	80
Jewish	Yes	1
None	· Yes	52
Total		324

Compare this table to your output to ensure that you understand how we created it. To calculate lambda, then,

$$\frac{\text{(uneducated errors)} - \text{(educated errors)}}{\text{(uneducated errors)}} = \frac{361 - 324}{361} = .102493$$

This indicates, therefore, that we have improved our guessing of abortion attitudes by 10 percent as a result of knowing religious affiliation. Here's how SPSS reports this result:

Directional Measures

			Value	Asymp. Std. Error[a]	Approx. T[b]	Approx. Sig.
Nominal by Nominal	Lambda	Symmetric	.051	.016	3.111	.002
		ABANY ABORTION IF WOMAN WANTS FOR ANY REASON Dependent	.102	.031	3.111	.002
		RELIG RS RELIGIOUS PREFERENCE Dependent	.000	.000	.[c]	.[c]
	Goodman and Kruskal tau	ABANY ABORTION IF WOMAN WANTS FOR ANY REASON Dependent	.050	.011		.000[d]
		RELIG RS RELIGIOUS PREFERENCE Dependent	.010	.004		.000[d]

SPSS reports more information than we need right now, so let's focus our attention on the second row of numbers. Because we have been testing whether we could predict abortion attitudes (ABANY) by knowing religion, that makes ABANY the dependent variable. As you can see, the value of lambda in that instance is 0.102, the value we got by calculating it for ourselves.

Knowing a person's religious affiliation, then, allows us to predict his or her attitude on abortion 10 percent more accurately. The implicit assumption in this analysis is that religious affiliation is associated with or to some extent "causes," attitudes toward abortion. We use the value of lambda as an indication of how strong the causal link is.

However, it is important that you bear in mind that *association alone does not prove causation*. When we observe a statistical relationship between two variables, that relationship strengthens the probability that one causes the other, but it is not sufficient proof. To be satisfied that a causal relationship exists, social scientists also want the link to make sense logically (in this case, the role of churches and clergy in the abortion debate offer that reasoning). And finally, we want to be sure that the observed relationship is not an artifact produced by the effects of a third variable. This latter possibility will be examined in Part V on multivariate analysis.

For curiosity's sake, notice the third row, which treats RELIG as the dependent variable. This deals with the possibility that we might be able to guess people's religions by knowing where they stand on abortion. Take a moment to look at the crosstabulation above.

If we were to make uneducated guesses about people's religions, we'd always guess Protestant, because Protestants are by far the largest group. Knowing attitudes toward abortion wouldn't help matters, however. In either case, we'd still guess Protestant, even among those who were in favor of abortion rights.

If RELIG were the dependent variable, then, knowing ABANY would improve our guessing by zero percent, which is the calculation presented by SPSS.

Interpreting Lambda and Other Measures

After all this discussion about lambda, you may still be wondering what a value of .102, for instance, actually means in terms of the strength of the relationship between these two variables. Does it signify a strong, relatively strong, moderate, or weak association? Is it something worth noting or does it indicate such a weak relationship that it is not even worth paying attention to? Unfortunately, there are no easy answers to these questions. While we are going to say more about statistical significance in the next chapter, we do want to give you some (albeit general) basis for interpreting these values.

We can say for certain that not only for lambda, but also for all the PRE measures of association we are considering in this chapter, a value of 1.00 (positive or negative in the case of gamma and Pearson's r) indicates a perfect association or the strongest possible relationship between two variables. Conversely, with the exception noted above, a value of 0.00 indicates no relationship between the variables. We can also say that the closer the value is to 1.00 (positive or negative in the case of gamma and Pearson's r), the stronger the relationship. And the closer the value is to 0.00, the weaker the relationship.

Determining whether or not a relationship is noteworthy depends on what other researchers have found. If other researchers had not discovered any variables that related to abortion attitudes, then our lambda of .102 would be important. As you will see later, there are variables that have much stronger relationships to abortion than religion, so strong that they make our .102 quite unremarkable. In short, all relationships must be interpreted in the context of other findings in the same general area of inquiry.

That said, in order to give you a sense of one way you can approach these statistics, we include some general guidelines for interpreting the strength of association between variables in Table 14.1. As the title of the table clearly indicates, these are merely loose guidelines with arbitrary cut-off points that must

Table 14.1 Some General Guidelines for Interpreting Strength of Association (Lambda, Gamma, Pearson's *r* . . .)

Strength of Association	Value of Measures of Association (Lambda, Gamma, Pearson's r . . .)
None	0.00
Weak/Uninteresting association	±.01 to .09
Moderate/Worth noting	±.10 to .29
Evidence of strong association/ Extremely interesting	±.30 to .99
Perfect/Strongest possible association	±1.00

This table is adapted from a more in-depth discussion in Healey et al. (1999, 84). In the text the authors note that whereas "this scale may strike you as too low . . . [r]emember that, in the social sciences, we deal with probabilistic causal relationships . . . expecting measures of association to approach 1 is unreasonable. Given the complexity of the social world the (admittedly arbitrary) guideline presented is serviceable in most instances." In comparison to other similar guides to interpretation, the scale presented here is fairly low. Frankfort-Nachmias et al. (2000, 259) for instance, include a table which gives the following guide to interpretation: .00 (no relationship); +/−.20 (weak relationship); +/−.40 (moderate relationship); +/−.60 (strong relationship); +/−.80 (very strong relationship); +/−1.00 (perfect relationship). They go on to note that "these are only rough guidelines."

be understood within the context of our discussion above regarding the absence of any absolute "rules" of interpretation.

You will note that Table 14.1 lists the possible values as positive or negative. While the value of lambda is, as we noted, always a positive value between 0.00 and 1.00, the values of the other measures that we will discuss later in this chapter (see discussions of gamma and Pearson's *r* below) run from −1.00 to +1.00, and thus include both positive and negative values.

Caveat: Interpreting Lambdas of 0.0

Now that we have told you quite firmly that lambdas of 0.0 always indicate there is no association between the variables, we need to revise our statement just slightly. Lambdas of 0.0 must be treated with great caution. When one of the totals for the dependent variable is much larger then the rest, lambda can take on the value zero even when an inspection of the percents indicate a strong relationship. To be safe, lambda should only be used when the marginal totals are relatively equal in magnitude. If they are not, a chi square based measure of association, such as Cramer's V, should be used.[4]

Based on these general guidelines, what might you say about the strength of the relationship between ABANY and RELIG? Take a moment to develop your answer, then compare your response to Writing Box 14.1 below.

---

[4] A more complete discussion may be found in Hubert M. Blalock's *Social Statistics*, (McGraw-Hill, 1960) 310-311.

Writing Box 14.1

The relationship between ABANY and RELIG can be summarized by a value of .102 on lambda. This means that if we wanted to predict how someone felt about abortion, we'd make only about 10% fewer errors if we knew their religious affiliation than we'd make without knowing that.

Now, why don't you choose two nominal variables and then experiment with instructing SPSS to calculate lambda? If you need help recalling how to run lambda on SPSS, refer to SPSS Command 14.1 below.

SPSS Command 14.1: Running Crosstabs and Lambda

Click **Analyze → Descriptive Statistics → Crosstabs . . . →**

Specify **dependent variable** as the **Row(s):** variable →

Specify **independent variable** as the **Column(s):** variable →

Click **Cells . . . →**

[Make sure "Column" under "Percentages" is not selected (there should not be a check mark next to "Column")][5]

Click **Continue→**

Click **Statistics . . . → Lambda → Continue → OK**

Gamma: A Measure Appropriate for Ordinal Variables

Whereas lambda is used to examine the association between two nominal variables, *gamma* is a measure of association based on the logic of proportionate reduction of error appropriate for two ordinal variables.

An Indication of Strength and Direction (with a Caveat) of Association

Unlike lambda, gamma not only indicates the *strength of association* but it also indicates the direction of association between two ordinal variables. With each variable having a greater than/less than between its categories, we can observe whether or not high values of one variable are associated with high values of the other (a **positive association**) or if high values of one variable are associated with low values of the other (a **negative association**). The values of gamma range from −1.00 to 1.00.

---

[5] Usually percentages are requested in order to see how the column percentages change or move. We purposefully omitted the percentages in Demonstration 14.1 in order to make the table easier to read.

Table 14.2 Direction of Association: Using Class and Prejudice as an Example

Negative association	*Value of gamma is negative (−)*
	As social class increases, prejudice decreases
	↑ Social Class, ↓ Prejudice
	OR
	As social class decreases, prejudices increases
	↓ Social Class, ↑ Prejudice
Positive association	*Value of gamma is positive (+)*
	As social class increases, so too does prejudice
	↑ Social Class, ↑ Prejudice
	OR
	As social class decreases, so too does prejudice
	↓ Social Class, ↓ Prejudice

In terms of the ***strength of association***, the closer to −1.00 or 1.00, the stronger the relationship between the two variables, whereas the closer to 0.00, the weaker the association between the variables.

In terms of the ***direction of association***, a negative sign indicates a ***negative association***; as one variable increases, the other decreases (the items change in opposite directions). Conversely, a positive sign indicates a ***positive association***; both items change in the same direction (they both either increase or decrease).

A negative association between social class and prejudice, for instance, indicates that the variables change in opposite directions: As one increases, the other decreases. Conversely, a positive association between social class and prejudice indicates that the variables change in the same direction: They both either increase or decrease (see Table 14.2).

We want to underscore the fact that you can only determine the direction of association between two variables if they are both measured on scales that express greater than/less than relationships between their points. Furthermore, if an ordinal variable's values have been arbitrarily assigned in such a way that high numbers or values indicate an absence of what is being measured and low numbers or values indicate a presence of the phenomenon, the sign (− or +) of the relationship will be reversed.

For an example of what we mean by *arbitrary* values, think back to when we reduced the number of ordinal categories on the variable ATTEND to create CHATT. In that case, we chose the value of 1 to represent "About weekly," 2 to represent "About monthly," and so on. These are arbitrary values in the sense that we could just as easily have arranged the categories in the opposite direction so that 1 represented "Never," 2 represented "Seldom," 3 represented "About monthly," and 4 represented "About weekly." With reversed codes, you need to keep in mind that a negative value for gamma in this case would not correctly indicate a direction of association, it would merely be a result of the way we arbitrarily arranged the categories of an item.

Measure of Association	Gamma
Type of variables	Ordinal × Ordinal
Values (strength)	−1.00 to +1.00
	0 = no association
	−1.00 = perfect (negative) association
	+1.00 = perfect (positive) association
Direction	+indicates positive association (variables change or move in same direction i.e. both ↓↓ OR both ↑↑)
	−indicates negative association (variables change or move in opposite directions i.e. as one goes ↑, other goes ↓ OR as one goes ↓, other goes ↑)
	caveat – have the values been arbitrarily assigned? If so, +/− sign may be reversed

Example 1: The Logic of Gamma

We judge two variables to be related to each other to the extent that knowing what a person is like in terms of one variable helps us to guess what he or she is like on the other. Whereas the application of this logic in the case of lambda lets us make predictions for individuals (e.g., if a person is Protestant, we guess he or she is also Republican), the logic is applied to pairs of people in the case of gamma.

To see the logic of gamma, let's consider the following nine people, placed in a matrix that indicates their social class standing and their level of prejudice: two ordinal variables.

Prejudice	Lower Class	Middle Class	Upper Class
Low	Jim	Tim	Kim
Medium	Mary	Harry	Carrie
High	Nan	Jan	Fran

Our purpose in this analysis is to determine which of the following best describes the relationship between social class and prejudice:

1. The higher your social class, the more prejudiced you are.

2. The higher your social class, the less prejudiced you are.

3. Your social class has no effect on your level of prejudice.

To begin our analysis, we should note that the only pairs who are appropriate to our question are those who differ in both social class and prejudice. Jim and Harry are an example; they differ in both social class and level of prejudice. Here are the 18 pairs that qualify for analysis:

Jim-Harry	Kim-Mary	Harry-Nan
Jim-Carrie	Kim-Harry	Harry-Fran
Jim-Jan	Kim-Nan	
Jim-Fran	Kim-Jan	
Tim-Mary	Mary-Jan	Carrie-Nan
Tim-Nan	Mary-Fran	Carrie-Jan
Tim-Carrie		
Tim-Fran		

Gamma helps us determine whether how 2 people differ on an attribute would reduce the # of errors.

Take a minute to assure yourself that no other pair of people satisfies the criterion that they differ in both social class and prejudice.

If you study the table, you should be able to identify pairs of people who would support conclusions 1 and 2; we'll come back to conclusion 3 a little later.

Suppose now that you have been given the list of pairs, but you've never seen the original table. Your task is to guess which member of each pair is the more prejudiced. Given that you will simply be guessing blind, chances are that you'll get about half right and half wrong: nine correct answers and nine errors. Gamma helps us determine whether knowing how two people differ on social class would reduce the number of errors we'd make in guessing how they differ on prejudice.

Let's consider Jim-Harry for a moment. If they were the only two people you could study, and if you had to reach a conclusion about the relationship between social class and prejudice, what would you conclude? Notice that Harry is higher in social class than Jim (middle class versus lower class), and Harry is also higher in prejudice (medium versus low). If you were to generalize from this single pair of observations, there is only one conclusion you could reach: "The higher your social class, the more prejudiced you are."

As we noted earlier, this is referred to as a positive association: The higher on one variable, the higher on the other. In the more specific language of gamma, we'll refer to this as a *same pair*: The direction of the difference between Jim and Harry on one variable is the same as the direction of difference on the other. Harry is higher than Jim on both.

Suppose you had to base your conclusion on the Jim-Jan pair. What would you conclude? Look at the table and you'll see that Jan, like Harry, is higher than Jim on both social class and prejudice. This pair would also lead you to conclude that the higher your social class, the more prejudiced you are.

Jim-Jan, then, is another same pair in the language of gamma.

Suppose, on the other hand, we observed only Tim and Mary. They would lead us to a very different conclusion. Mary is lower than Tim on social class, but she is higher on prejudice. If this were the only pair you could observe, you'd have to conclude that the higher your social class, the lower your prejudice. In the language of gamma, Tim-Mary is an *opposite pair*: The direction of their difference on one variable is the opposite of their difference on the other.

Now, we hope you've been feeling uncomfortable about the idea of generalizing from only one pair of observations, although that's what many people often do in everyday life. In social research, however, we would never do that.

Moving a little bit in the direction of normal social research, let's assume that you have observed all nine of the individuals in the table. What conclusion would you draw about the association between social class and prejudice? Gamma helps you answer this question.

Let's see how well each of the alternative conclusions might assist you in guessing people's prejudice based on knowing about their social class. If you operated on the basis of the conclusion that prejudice increases with social class, for example, and I told you Fran is of a higher social class than Harry, you would correctly guess that Fran is more prejudiced. If, on the other hand, I told you that Harry is higher in social class than Nan, you would incorrectly guess that he is more prejudiced.

Take a minute to go through the list of pairs above and make notations of which ones are same pairs and which ones are opposite. Once you've done that, count the numbers of same and opposite pairs.

You should get nine of each type of pair. This means that if you assume that prejudice increases with social class, you will get the nine opposite pairs wrong; if you assume prejudice decreases with social class, you will get the nine same pairs wrong. In other words, neither strategy for guessing levels of prejudice based on knowing social class will do you any good in this case. In either case, we make as many errors as we would have made if we didn't know the social class differences in the pairs. Gamma gives us a method for calculating that result.

The formula for gamma is as follows:

$$\frac{\text{same} - \text{opposite}}{\text{same} + \text{opposite}}$$

To calculate gamma, you must first count the number of same pairs and the number of opposite pairs. Once you've done that, the mathematics is pretty simple.

Now, you can complete the formula as follows:

$$\frac{9 - 9}{9 + 9} = \frac{0}{18} = 0$$

In gamma, this result is interpreted as 0 percent, meaning that knowing how two people differ on social class would improve your guesses as to how they differ on prejudice by 0—or not at all.

Consider the following modified table, however. Suppose for the moment that there are only three people to be studied:

Prejudice	Lower Class	Middle Class	Upper Class
Low	Jim		
Medium		Harry	
High			Fran

Just by inspection, you can see how perfectly these three people fit the pattern of a positive association between social class and prejudice. Each of the three pairs—Jim-Harry, Harry-Fran, Jim-Fran—is a same pair. There are no opposite pairs. If we were to give you each of these pairs, telling you who was higher in social class, the assumption of a positive association between the two variables would let you guess who was higher in social class with perfect accuracy.

Let's see how this situation would look in terms of gamma.

$$\frac{\text{same} - \text{opposite}}{\text{same} + \text{opposite}} = \frac{3 - 0}{3 + 0} = 1.00 \text{ or } 100 \text{ percent}$$

In this case, we would say gamma equals 1.00, with the meaning that you have reduced the number of errors by 100 percent. To understand this meaning of gamma, we need to go back to the idea of guessing prejudice differences without knowing social class.

Recall that if you were guessing blind, you'd be right about half the time and wrong about half the time. In this hypothetical case, you'd be wrong 1.5 times (that would be your average if you repeated the exercise hundreds of times). As we've seen, however, knowing social class in this instance lets us reduce the number of errors by 1.5—down to zero. It is in this sense that we say we have reduced our errors by 100 percent.

Now, let's consider a slightly different table.

Prejudice	Lower Class	Middle Class	Upper Class
Low			Nan
Medium		Harry	
High	Kim		

Notice that in this case we could also have a perfect record if we use the assumption of a negative association between social class and prejudice: The higher your social class, the lower your prejudice. The negative association shows up in gamma as follows:

$$\frac{\text{same} - \text{opposite}}{\text{same} + \text{opposite}} = \frac{0 - 3}{0 + 3} = -1.00 \text{ or } -100 \text{ percent}$$

Once again, the gamma indicates that we have reduced our errors by 100 percent. The minus sign in this result simply signals that the relationship is negative.

Example 2: The Logic of Gamma

We are finally ready for a more realistic example. Just as you would not want to base a generalization on as few cases as we've been considering so far, neither would it make sense to calculate gamma in such situations. Notice how gamma helps you assess the relationship between two variables when the results are not as obvious to the nonstatistical eye.

Prejudice	Lower Class	Middle Class	Upper Class
Low	200	400	700
Medium	500	900	400
High	800	300	100

In this table, the names of individuals have been replaced with the numbers of people having a particular social class and level of prejudice. There are 200 lower-class people in the table, for example, who are low on prejudice. On the other hand, there are 100 upper-class people who are high on prejudice.

Perhaps you can get a sense of the relationship in this table by simple observation. The largest cells are those lying along the diagonal running from lower left to upper right. This would suggest a negative association between the two variables (*direction of association*). Gamma lets us determine with more confidence whether that's the case and gives us a yardstick for measuring how strong the relationship is (*strength of association*).

In the simpler examples, every pair of cells represented one pair because there was only one person in each cell. Now it's a little more complex. Imagine for a moment just one of the people in the upper left cell (lower class, low prejudice). If we match that person up with the 900 people in the center cell (middle class, medium prejudice), we'd have 900 pairs. The same would result from matching each of the people in the first cell with all those in the second. We can calculate the total number of pairs produced by the two cells by simple multiplication: 200 times 900 gives us 180,000 pairs. Notice, by the way, that these are same pairs.

As a further simplification, notice that there are 900 + 400 + 300 + 100 people who will match with the upper left cell to form same pairs. That makes a total of 1,700 * 200 = 340,000. Here's an overview of all the "same" pairs in the table:

$200 \times (900 + 300 + 400 + 100) = 340,000$
$500 \times (300 + 100) = 200,000$
$400 \times (400 + 100) = 200,000$
$900 \times 100 = 90,000$
Total same pairs = 830,000

Following the same procedure, here are all the opposite pairs:

$700 \times (500 + 800 + 900 + 300) = 1,750,000$
$400 \times (800 + 300) = 440,000$
$400 \times (500 + 800) = 520,000$
$900 \times 800 = 720,000$
Total opposite pairs = 3,430,000

Even though this procedure produces quite a few more pairs than we've been dealing with, the formula for gamma still works the same way:

$$\frac{(\text{same} - \text{opposite})}{(\text{same} + \text{opposite})} = \frac{830,000 - 3,430,000}{830,000 + 3,430,000} = \frac{-2,6000,000}{4,260,000} = -.61$$

The minus sign in this result confirms that the relationship between the two variables is a negative one (direction). The numerical result indicates that knowing the social class ranking in each pair reduces our errors in predicting their ranking in terms of prejudice by 61 percent (strength).

Suppose, for the moment, that you had tried to blindly predict differences in prejudice for each of the 4,260,000 pairs. You would have been wrong about 2,130,000 times. By assuming that the person with higher social class is less prejudiced, you would have made only 830,000 errors, or 2,130,000 − 830,000 = 1,300,000 fewer errors. Dividing the 1,300,000 improvement by the 2,130,000 baseline gives .61, indicating you have reduced your errors by 61 percent.

Demonstration 14.2: Instructing
SPSS to Calculate Gamma – Example 1

Now, here's the good news. Although it's important for you to understand the logic of gamma, it is no longer necessary for you to do the calculations by hand. Whenever you run Crosstabs in SPSS, you can request that gamma be calculated by making that request when you set up the table.

Go to **Crosstabs**. Make **EDCAT** the **column** and **CLASS** the **row** variable.[6] Then click on **Statistics . . .**

Notice that **Gamma** is appropriately a choice for ordinal data. **Click** it. If **Lambda** still has a **check mark** next to it, **turn it off** before selecting **Continue** to return to the main window. Once you have returned to the Crosstabs window, you can instruct SPSS to run the procedure by selecting **OK**. You should get the following table and report on gamma.

---

[6] We walked through the steps of **recoding EDUC** to create the new variable **EDCAT** in Chapter 12. If you did not save EDCAT on your **DEMOPLUS** file, simply refer back to the recode commands in Chapter 12 before continuing with this demonstration. For the variable **CLASS** the values **0**, **5**, **8** and **9** should be defined as **missing**.

CLASS SUBJECTIVE CLASS IDENTIFICATION * EDCAT Recoded EDUC Crosstabulation

Count

		EDCAT Recoded EDUC					
		1 Less than HS	2 HS grad	3 Some College	4 College grad	5 Graduate studies	Total
CLASS SUBJECTIVE CLASS IDENTIFICATION	1 LOWER CLASS	31	23	17	4	4	79
	2 WORKING CLASS	129	268	219	62	42	720
	3 MIDDLE CLASS	74	153	182	110	104	623
	4 UPPER CLASS	8	19	9	17	13	66
Total		242	463	427	193	163	1488

Symmetric Measures

		Value	Asymp. Std. Error[a]	Approx. T[b]	Approx. Sig.
Ordinal by Ordinal	Gamma	.325	.032	9.852	.000
N of Valid Cases		1488			

Notice that gamma is reported as .325. This means that knowing a person's level of education would improve our estimate of his class by 33 percent. Based on our "general guidelines" for interpreting measures of association, you can see that this value of gamma is fairly high and evidence of a strong, extremely interesting association between these two variables.

Remember that in addition to indicating the strength of the association between two variables, which in this case is fairly high, gamma also tells us the direction of association. In this instance, the positive sign indicates a positive association between the variables. That is, as level of education rises, so too does class.

Writing Box 14.2

Education is a powerful predictor of social class, as these data illustrate. The gamma value of +.325 indicates that our ability to accurately predict which of two people has the higher social class is improved by almost a third if we know their respective educational levels.

Demonstration 14.3: Running Gamma – Example 2 (Reverse Scoring Case)

Now that you are fairly comfortable requesting gamma, let's look at an example that makes the reverse scoring case. An instance in which the arbitrary arrangement of the categories means that you cannot rely on the positive or negative sign as an indication of the direction of association between the variables.

For this example let's look at the association between CHATT and AGECAT. Go ahead and run **Crosstabs**, then make **CHATT** the **row** variable and **AGECAT** the **column** variable. Once you have done that, click on **Statistics . . .** and request **gamma**. Your output should look like the table below:

CHATT Recoded Church Attendance * AGECAT Recoded Age Categories Crosstabulation

Count

		AGECAT Recoded Age Categories				Total
		1 Under 21	2 21-39	3 40-64	4 65 and older	
CHATT Recoded Church Attendance	1 About weekly	8	115	197	112	432
	2 About monthly	8	105	94	32	239
	3 Seldom	22	221	190	53	486
	4 Never	5	122	124	49	300
Total		43	563	605	246	1457

Symmetric Measures

		Value	Asymp. Std. Error[a]	Approx. T[b]	Approx. Sig.
Ordinal by Ordinal	Gamma	-.172	.032	-5.257	.000
N of Valid Cases		1457			

Notice that gamma is reported as −.172. This means that knowing a person's age would improve our estimate of his or her church attendance by 17 percent.

Although you might think the negative sign means there is a negative relationship between age and church attendance, we know now that this is not the case. In this example the minus sign results from our choosing to arbitrarily arrange attendance categories from the most frequent at the top to the least frequent at the bottom. If we had arranged the categories in the opposite direction, the gamma would have been positive.

Whenever you ask SPSS to calculate gamma, it is important that you note how the variable categories are arranged. If coding is not consistent—that is, if low codes indicate low amounts of what is being measured and vice versa—gamma's signs will be reversed. You can also determine the direction of the association by inspecting the table. Looking at the first row in the table above, it is fairly clear that church attendance tends to increase as age increases; hence the relationship between the two variables is a positive one.

Now take a moment to compare the two tables we just created: CLASS-EDCAT and CHATT-AGECAT. You can see that in the first case the values of CLASS run down the left-hand side from lowest (top) to highest (bottom), whereas the values of EDCAT run across the top from the lowest education level (left-side) to the highest (far right side). Because the categories are arranged in this way, you can be sure that the sign (positive in this case) is meaningful.

Example 1: CLASS × EDCAT

	EDCAT				
	Less than HS	*HS*	*Some College*	*College Grad*	*Grad Stds+*
CLASS	*LOWEST education level* → *HIGHEST education level*				
Lower	*LOWEST*				
Working	*class*				
Middle	↓				
Upper	*HIGHEST*				
	class				

To the contrary, if you examine the second example (CHATT-AGECAT) you can see a major difference. In this case, CHATT is arranged down the left side from the most frequent attendance (top) to the least frequent attendance (bottom). Whereas AGECAT is arrayed across the top from the youngest (left-side) to the oldest (right-side). As a result in this case the sign is reversed. If we rearranged the categories for CHATT, we would get the opposite sign. However instead of recoding the variable, it is easier just to make sure you are careful when reading the table and pay attention to cases like this in which the sign is reversed.

Example 2:   CHATT × AGECAT

| | **AGECAT** | | | |
	Under 21	*21-39*	*40-64*	*65 and older*
CHATT	*YOUNGEST age category → OLDEST age category*			
About Weekly	*Attend*			
About Monthly	*MOST often*			
Seldom	*↓*			
Never	*Attend*			
	LEAST			
	often			

To gain some more experience with gamma, why don't you select two ordinal variables that interest you and examine their relationships with one another by using gamma? Remember to pay attention to cases like the one we just reviewed in which the scoring is reversed.

SPSS Command 14.2: Running Crosstabs and Gamma

Click **Analyze → Descriptive Statistics → Crosstabs . . . →**

Specify **dependent variable** as the **Row(s):** variable →

Specify **independent variable** as the **Column(s):** variable →

Click **Cells . . . →**

[Make sure "Column" under "Percentages" is not selected (there should not be a check mark next to "Column")][7]

Click **Continue →**

Click **Statistics . . . → Gamma → Continue → OK**

---

[7] Usually percentages are requested in order to see how the column percentages change or move. We purposefully omitted the percentages in Demonstrations 14.2 and 14.3 in order to make the table easier to read.

INTERVAL/RATIO

Pearson's *r*: A Measure Appropriate for I/R Variables

Finally, we are going to work with **Pearson's *r*,** also known as a *product-moment correlation coefficient*. Pearson's *r* is a measure of association that reflects the PRE logic and is appropriate to continuous, interval-ratio (I/R) variables such as age, education, and income.

An Indication of Strength and Direction of Association

Like gamma, the value of Pearson's *r* ranges from −1.00 to +1.00, indicating both the strength and direction of the relationship between two I/R variables. Once again, a −1.00 indicates a perfect negative association, a +1.00 indicates a perfect positive association, and a 0.00 indicates no association.

Measure of Association	Pearson's *r*
Type of variables	IR x IR
Values (strength)	−1.00 to +1.00
	0 = no association
	−1.00 = perfect (negative) association
	+1.00 = perfect (positive) association
Direction	+ indicates positive association (variables change or move in same direction, i.e. both ↓↓ OR both ↑↑)
	− indicates negative association (variables change or move in opposite directions i.e., as one goes ↑, other goes ↓ OR as one goes ↓, other goes ↑)

Example 1: The Logic of Pearson's *r*

Although this measure also reflects the PRE logic, its meaning in that regard is not quite so straightforward as it is for the discrete variables analyzed by lambda and gamma. Although it made sense to talk about "guessing" someone's gender or employment status and being either right or wrong, there is little chance that we would ever guess someone's annual income in exact dollars or his or her exact age in days. Our best strategy would be to guess the mean income, and we'd be wrong almost every time. Pearson's *r* lets us determine whether knowing one variable would help us come closer in our guesses of the other variable and calculates how much closer we would come.

To understand *r*, let's take a simple example of eight young people and see whether there is a correlation between their heights (in inches) and their weights (in pounds). To begin, then, let's meet the eight subjects.

	Height	Weight
Eddy	68	144
Mary	58	111
Marge	67	137
Terry	66	153

Albert	61	165
Larry	74	166
Heather	67	92
Ruth	61	128

Take a minute to study the heights and weights. Begin with Eddy and Mary, at the top of the list. Eddy is both taller and heavier than Mary. If we were forced to reach a conclusion about the association between height and weight based only on these two observations, we would conclude there is a positive correlation: The taller you are, the heavier you are. We might even go a step further and note that every additional inch of height corresponds to about 3 pounds of weight.

On the other hand, if you needed to base a conclusion on observations of Eddy and Terry, see what that conclusion would be. Terry is 2 inches shorter but 9 pounds heavier. Our observations of Eddy and Terry would lead us to just the opposite conclusion: The taller you are, the lighter you are.

Sometimes, it's useful to look at a *scattergram*, which graphs the cases at hand in terms of the two variables.[8] The diagram on the next page presents the eight cases in this fashion. Notice that there seems to be a general pattern of increasing height being associated with increasing weight, although there are a couple of cases that don't fit that pattern.

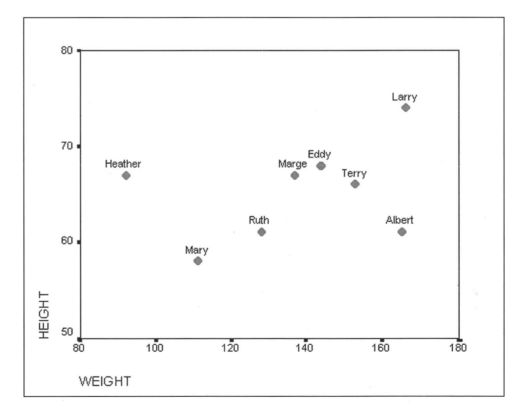

---

[8] We are going to review how you can instruct SPSS to produce a scattergram (also called a scatterplot) toward the end of this chapter.

Pearson's *r* allows for the fact that the relationship between height and weight may not be completely consistent, but nevertheless it lets us discover any prevailing tendency in that regard. In the gamma logic presented above, we might consider a strategy of guessing who is heavier or lighter on the basis of who is taller or shorter, assuming either a positive (taller means heavier) or negative (taller means lighter) relationship between the two variables. With *r*, however, we'll take account of *how much* taller or heavier.

To calculate *r*, we need to know the mean value of each variable. As you recall, this is calculated by adding all the values on a variable and dividing by the number of cases. If you do these calculations in the case of height, you'll discover that the eight people, laid end to end, would stretch 522 inches, for a mean height of 65.25 inches. Do the same calculation for their weights, and you'll discover that the eight people weigh a total of 1,096 pounds, for a mean of 137 pounds.

From now on, we are going to focus less on the actual heights and weights of our eight people and deal more with the extent to which they differ from the means. The table below shows how much each person differs from the means for height and weight. Notice that plus and minus signs have been used to indicate whether a person is above or below the mean. (If you want to check your calculations in this situation, you should add all the deviations from height and notice they total 0; the same is true for deviations from mean weight.)

	Height	Weight	H-dev	W-dev
Eddy	68	144	+2.75	+7
Mary	58	111	−7.25	−26
Marge	67	137	+1.75	0
Terry	66	153	+0.75	+16
Albert	61	165	−4.25	+28
Larry	74	166	+8.75	+29
Heather	67	92	+1.75	−45
Ruth	61	128	−4.25	−9
Means	65.25	137		

As our next step, we want to determine the extent to which heights and weights vary from their means overall. Although we have shown the plus and minus signs above, it is important to note that both +2.00 and −2.00 represent deviations of 2 inches from the mean height. For reasons that will become apparent shortly, we are going to capture both positive and negative variations by squaring each of the deviations from the means. The squares of both +2.00 and − 2.00 are the same: 4.00. The table below shows the squared deviations for each person on each variable. We've also totaled the squared deviations and calculated their means.

	Height	Weight	H-dev	W-dev	Sq H-dev	Sq W-dev
Eddy	68	144	+2.75	+7	7.5625	49
Mary	58	111	−7.25	−26	52.5625	676
Marge	67	137	+1.75	0	3.0625	0
Terry	66	153	+0.75	+16	0.5625	256
Albert	61	165	−4.25	+28	18.0625	784
Larry	74	166	+8.75	+29	76.5625	841
Heather	67	92	+1.75	−45	3.0625	2,025
Ruth	61	128	−4.25	−9	18.0625	81
Means =	65.25	137		Totals =	179.5000	4,712

Now we're going to present a couple of steps that would require more complicated explanations than we want to subject you to in this book, so if you can simply hear what we say without asking why, that's sufficient at this point. (If you are interested in learning the logic of the intervening steps, that's great. You should check discussions of variance and standard deviations in statistics textbooks.)

Dividing the sum of the squared deviations by 1 less than the number of cases (N − 1) yields a quantity statisticians call the *variance*. With a large number of cases, this quantity is close to the mean of the sum of squared deviations.

The variances in this case are 25.643 for height and 673.143 for weight. The square root of the variance is called the *standard deviation*. (Perhaps you are already familiar with these concepts, or perhaps you have heard the terms but haven't known what they mean.) Thus, the standard deviation for height is 5.063891; for weight, 25.94499.

Now, we are ready to put all these calculations to work for us. We are going to express all the individual deviations from mean height and mean weight in units equal to the standard deviations. For example, Eddy was +2.75 inches taller than the average. Eddy's new deviation from the mean height becomes +0.54 (+2.75 _ 5.064). His deviation from the mean weight becomes +0.27 (+7 ÷ 25.945).

Our purpose in these somewhat complex calculations is to standardize deviations from the means of the two variables because the values on those variables are of very different scales. Whereas Eddy was 2.75 inches taller than the mean and 7 pounds heavier than the mean, we didn't have a way of knowing whether his height deviation was greater or lesser than his weight deviation. By dividing each deviation by the standard deviation for that variable, we can now see that Eddy's deviation on height is actually greater than his deviation in terms of weight. These new measures of deviation are called *z scores*. The table below presents each person's z score for both height and weight.

	Height	Weight	zheight	zweight	zcross
Eddy	68	144	.54	.27	.15
Mary	58	111	−1.43	−1.00	1.43
Marge	67	137	.35	.00	.00
Terry	66	153	.15	.62	.09
Albert	61	165	−.84	1.08	−.91
Larry	74	166	1.73	1.12	1.93
Heather	67	92	.35	−1.73	−.60
Ruth	61	128	−.84	−.35	.29
				Total	2.38

You'll notice that there is a final column of the table called "zcross." This is the result of multiplying each person's z score on height by the z score on weight. You'll notice we've begun rounding off the numbers to two decimal places. That level of precision is sufficient for our present purposes.

Thanks to your perseverance, we are finally ready to calculate Pearson's r product-moment correlation. By now, it's pretty simple.

r = sum of (z scores for height × z scores for weight) divided by N − 1

In our example, this amounts to

r = 2.38 ÷ 8 − 1 = .34.

There is no easy, commonsense way to represent the meaning of r. Technically, it has to do with the extent to which variations in one variable can explain variations in the other. In fact, if you square r, .12 in this case, it can be interpreted as follows: 12 percent of the variance in one variable can be accounted for by the variance in the other. Recall that the variance of a variable reflects the extent to which individual cases deviate from the mean value. Reverting to the logic of PRE, this means that knowing a person's height reduces by 12 percent the extent of our errors in guessing how far he or she is from the mean weight.

In large part, r's value comes with use. When you calculate correlations among several pairs of variables, the resulting r's will tell which pairs are more highly associated with one another than is true of other pairs.

Demonstration 14.4:
Instructing SPSS to Calculate Pearson's r

Here's the really good news. Your reward for pressing through all the calculations above, in order to gain some understanding of what r represents, is that you'll never have to do it again. SPSS will do it for you.

Let's consider the possible relationship between two of the continuous variables in the data set: AGE and RINCOM98. If you think about it, you should expect that people tend to earn more money as they grow older, so let's check the correlation between age and respondents' incomes. (Note: RINCOM98 is the respondent's personal income; INCOME98 is total family income.)

You might be reluctant to calculate the deviations, squared deviations, and so on for the 1,500 respondents in your data set (if not, you need a hobby), but computers thrive on such tasks.

Demonstration 14.5:
Recoding RINCOM98 → RECRINC

Before we tell SPSS to take on the task of computing correlations for us, we need to do a little housekeeping.

		Frequency	Percent	Valid Percent	Cumulative Percent
RINCOM98 RESPONDENTS INCOME					
Valid	1 UNDER $1 000	28	1.9	2.7	2.7
	2 $1 000 TO 2 999	20	1.3	1.9	4.7
	3 $3 000 TO 3 999	18	1.2	1.7	6.4
	4 $4 000 TO 4 999	22	1.5	2.1	8.5
	5 $5 000 TO 5 999	11	.7	1.1	9.6
	6 $6 000 TO 6 999	23	1.5	2.2	11.8
	7 $7 000 TO 7 999	15	1.0	1.5	13.3
	8 $8 000 TO 9 999	35	2.3	3.4	16.7
	9 $10000 TO 12499	57	3.8	5.5	22.2
	10 $12500 TO 14999	49	3.3	4.8	27.0
	11 $15000 TO 17499	49	3.3	4.8	31.7
	12 $17500 TO 19999	50	3.3	4.8	36.6
	13 $20000 TO 22499	60	4.0	5.8	42.4
	14 $22500 TO 24999	52	3.5	5.0	47.4
	15 $25000 TO 29999	73	4.9	7.1	54.5
	16 $30000 TO 34999	100	6.7	9.7	64.2
	17 $35000 TO 39999	54	3.6	5.2	69.4
	18 $40000 TO 49999	82	5.5	8.0	77.4
	19 $50000 TO 59999	55	3.7	5.3	82.7
	20 $60000 TO 74999	56	3.7	5.4	88.2
	21 $75000 - $89999	17	1.1	1.6	89.8
	22 $90000- $109999	13	.9	1.3	91.1
	23 $110 000 OVER	22	1.5	2.1	93.2
	24 REFUSED	70	4.7	6.8	100.0
	Total	1031	68.7	100.0	
Missing	0 NAP	429	28.6		
	98 DK	25	1.7		
	99 NA	15	1.0		
	Total	469	31.3		
Total		1500	100.0		

There are two problems with using RINCOM98 the way it has been coded. First we need to be sure codes 0 (NAP), 24 (REFUSED), 98 (DK), and 99 (NA) are not included in our analysis. They may be eliminated by recoding them "system missing."

Secondly, the code categories are not equal in width. Code category 8 includes respondents whose incomes were between $8,000 and $9,999, whereas code category 9 includes incomes between $10,000 and $12,499. The categories form an ordinal scale that is not appropriate for use with Pearson's r.

We can use Recode to improve on the coding scheme used for recording incomes.[9] If we assume incomes are spread evenly across categories, then we can simply substitute the midpoints of the interval widths for the codes used in RINCOM98. That way, we can approximate an I/R scale and rid ourselves of the problems created by the interval widths not being equal. Code 23, $110,000 or

[9] The authors greatly appreciate the suggestion of this analysis by Professor Gilbert Klajman, Montclair State College.

more, has no upper limit. We just took a guess that the midpoint would be about $130,000. Even though we don't have each respondent's actual income, this approach will enable us to use Pearson's *r* to search for relationships between income and other variables. As SPSS commands, the recoding looks like this:

Transform → Recode → Into Different Variables . . .

Old Variable	→	New Variable
RINCOM98	→	RECRINC

Old and New Values

Old		New
0	→	**System-missing**
1	→	**500**
2	→	**2,000**
3	→	**3,000**
4	→	**4,000**
5	→	**5,000**
6	→	**6,000**
7	→	**7,000**
8	→	**8,000**
9	→	**11,250**
10	→	**13,750**
11	→	**16,250**
12	→	**18,750**
13	→	**21,250**
14	→	**23,750**
15	→	**27,500**
16	→	**32,500**
17	→	**37,500**
18	→	**45,000**
19	→	**55,000**
20	→	**67,500**
21	→	**82,500**
22	→	**100,000**
23	→	**130,000**
24	→	**System-missing**
98	→	**System-missing**
99	→	**System-missing**

Once you have completed the recode, access the **Variable View** tab and **define** your new variable **RECRINC** (i.e., set the **width**, **decimals**, etc . . .). Also, don't forget to **save** your recoded variable on your **DEMOPLUS** file so we can use it later on.

Now go ahead and run **Frequencies** for **RECRINC**. Here's what the recoded variable looks like:

RECRINC Recoded rincom98

		Frequency	Percent	Valid Percent	Cumulative Percent
Valid	500	28	1.9	2.9	2.9
	2000	20	1.3	2.1	5.0
	3000	18	1.2	1.9	6.9
	4000	22	1.5	2.3	9.2
	5000	11	.7	1.1	10.3
	6000	23	1.5	2.4	12.7
	7000	15	1.0	1.6	14.3
	8000	35	2.3	3.6	17.9
	11250	57	3.8	5.9	23.8
	13750	49	3.3	5.1	28.9
	16250	49	3.3	5.1	34.0
	18750	50	3.3	5.2	39.2
	21250	60	4.0	6.2	45.5
	23750	52	3.5	5.4	50.9
	27500	73	4.9	7.6	58.5
	32500	100	6.7	10.4	68.9
	37500	54	3.6	5.6	74.5
	45000	82	5.5	8.5	83.0
	55000	55	3.7	5.7	88.8
	67500	56	3.7	5.8	94.6
	82500	17	1.1	1.8	96.4
	100000	13	.9	1.4	97.7
	130000	22	1.5	2.3	100.0
	Total	961	64.1	100.0	
Missing	System	539	35.9		
Total		1500	100.0		

Demonstration 14.6: Using SPSS to Compute *r*

Now make sure codes 98 and 99 are defined as missing for AGE.

With the housekeeping out of the way, you need only move through this menu path to launch SPSS on the job of computing *r*. Unlike the previous measures we have discussed, Pearson's *r* is *not* available in the Crosstabs window. Instead it is appropriately available in the Bivariate Correlations dialog box. To access this window simply follow the steps below:

Analyze → Correlate → Bivariate . . .

This will bring you to the following window:

Transfer **AGE** and **RECRINC** to the **Variables:** field. (Be sure to use AGE and not AGECAT, because we want the uncoded variable.) Below the Variables: list, you'll see that we can choose from among three forms of correlation coefficients. Our discussion above has described Pearson's r, so click **Pearson** if it is not selected already.

Did you ever think about what we would do if we had an AGE for someone, but we did not know his or her RECRINC? Because we would have only one score, we would have to throw that person out of our analysis. But suppose we had three variables and we were missing a score on a case? Would we throw out just the pair that had a missing value, or would we throw out the whole case?

SPSS lets us do it either way. Click on **Options . . .** , and you will see that we can choose to exclude cases either *pairwise* or *listwise*. If we exclude pairwise, we discard a pair only when either score is missing, but with listwise exclusion, we discard the entire case if only one pair is missing. We will use pairwise exclusion. Given the time and money it takes to collect data, it's usually best to keep as much of it as we can. Unless there is a specific reason for using listwise exclusion, it is best to preserve as much of the data as possible by using pairwise deletion.

Once you have selected **Exclude cases pairwise**, click on **Continue** and then **OK**. Your reward will be a *correlation matrix*, a table that shows the correlations among all variables (including, as we will see, the correlation of each item with itself).

Correlations[a]		AGE AGE OF RESPONDENT	RECRINC Recoded rincom98
AGE AGE OF RESPONDENT	Pearson Correlation	1	.241**
	Sig. (2-tailed)	.	.000
RECRINC Recoded rincom98	Pearson Correlation	.241**	1
	Sig. (2-tailed)	.000	.

**. Correlation is significant at the 0.01 level (2-tailed).

a. Listwise N=958

The Pearson's r product-moment correlation between AGE and RECRINC is .241.[10] Notice that the correlation between AGE and itself is perfect (1), which makes sense if you think about it.

You now know that the .241 is a measure of the extent to which deviations from the mean income can be accounted for by deviations from the mean of age. By squaring r, we learn that about 5.8 percent of the variance in income can be accounted for by how old people are.

We are going to ignore the references to "Significance" until the next chapter. This indicates the *statistical significance* of the association.

SPSS Command 14.3: Producing a Correlation Matrix and Pearson's r

Click **Analyze** → **Correlate** → **Bivariate** . . . →

Highlight **variable name** → Click **right-pointing arrow** to transfer variable to "Variables:" field →

Repeat previous step until all variables have been transferred →

Click **Pearson** →

Click **Options** . . . → **Exclude cases** either **listwise** OR pairwise →

Continue → OK

Demonstration 14.7: Requesting Several Correlation Coefficients

What else do you suppose might account for differences in income? If you think about it, you might decide that education is a possibility. Presumably, the more education you get, the more money you'll make. Your understanding of r through SPSS will let you check it out.

---

[10] See Table 14.1 for some general guidelines you can use to interpret the value of Pearson's r.

The Correlations command allows you to request several correlation coefficients at once. Go back to the **Bivariate Correlations** window and add **EDUC** to the list of variables being analyzed.[11] Once again, **exclude cases listwise** before executing the command.

Here's what you should get in your Output window. (Hint: If you didn't get this, go back and make sure you defined the values **97, 98,** and **99** as **missing** for the variable **EDUC** and then try it again.)

Correlations

		AGE AGE OF RESPONDENT	RECRINC Recoded rincom98	EDUC HIGHEST YEAR OF SCHOOL COMPLETED
AGE AGE OF RESPONDENT	Pearson Correlation	1	.241**	-.156**
	Sig. (2-tailed)	.	.000	.000
	N	1493	958	1489
RECRINC Recoded rincom98	Pearson Correlation	.241**	1	.397**
	Sig. (2-tailed)	.000	.	.000
	N	958	961	960
EDUC HIGHEST YEAR OF SCHOOL COMPLETED	Pearson Correlation	-.156**	.397**	1
	Sig. (2-tailed)	.000	.000	.
	N	1489	960	1496

**. Correlation is significant at the 0.01 level (2-tailed).

Take a moment to examine your new correlation matrix. It is slightly more complex than the previous example. The fact that each variable correlates perfectly with itself should offer assurance that we are doing something right.

The new matrix also tells us that there is a stronger correlation between EDUC and RECRINC: .397. Squaring the r tells us that 15.7 percent of the variance in income can be accounted for by how much education people have.

Writing Box 14.3

Respondent's years of education are more strongly related to income than their ages. While age is only moderately related to income ($r = .241$), highest year of school completed is strongly related to income ($r = .397$). Interestingly, an inverse relation ($r = -.156$) exists between age and highest year of school. Older people have fewer years of education. This, in part, accounts for the somewhat weaker relationship found between age and income than education and income.

A Note of Caution

We'll be using the Correlations command and related statistics as the book continues. In closing this discussion, we'd like you to recall that Pearson's r is appropriate only for I/R variables. It would not be appropriate in the analysis of

---

[11] Make sure to define the values **97, 98,** and **99** for **EDUC** as **missing** before continuing with this demonstration.

nominal variables such as RELIG and MARITAL, for example. But what do you suppose would happen if we asked SPSS to **correlate r** for those two variables? This time, **exclude cases pairwise** before you execute the command.

Correlations

		MARITAL MARITAL STATUS	RELIG RS RELIGIOUS PREFERENCE
MARITAL MARITAL STATUS	Pearson Correlation	1	.129**
	Sig. (2-tailed)	.	.000
	N	1499	1416
RELIG RS RELIGIOUS PREFERENCE	Pearson Correlation	.129**	1
	Sig. (2-tailed)	.000	.
	N	1416	1416

**. Correlation is significant at the 0.01 level (2-tailed).

As you can see, SPSS does not recognize that we've asked it to do a stupid thing. It stupidly complies. It tells us there is a somewhat significant (see next chapter) relationship between a person's marital status and the religion he or she belongs to, whereas the correlation calculated here has no real meaning.

SPSS has been able to do the requested calculation because it stores "Married" as 1 and "Widowed" as 2 and stores "Protestant" as 1, "Catholic" as 2, and so on, but these numbers have no numerical meaning in this instance. Catholics are not "twice" Protestants, and widowed people are not "twice" married people.

Here's a thought experiment we hope will guard against this mistake: (a) Write down the telephone numbers of your five best friends; (b) add them up and calculate the "mean" telephone number; (c) call that number and see if an "average" friend answers. Or go to a Chinese restaurant with a group of friends and have everyone in your party select one dish by its number in the menu. Add all those numbers and calculate the mean. When the waiter comes, get several orders of the "average" dish and see if you have any friends left.

Pearson's *r* is designed for the analysis of relationships among continuous, interval/ratio variables. We have just entrusted you with a powerful weapon for understanding. Use it wisely. Remember: Statistics don't mislead—those who calculate statistics stupidly mislead.

Regression

The discussion of Pearson's *r* correlation coefficient opens the door for discussion of a related statistical technique that is also appropriate for I/R level variables: *regression*. When we looked at the scattergram of weight and height in the hypothetical example that introduced the discussion of correlation, you will recall that we tried to "see" a general pattern in the distribution of cases. Regression makes that attempt more concrete.

Example 1: The Logic of Regression

To begin, let's imagine an extremely simple example that relates the number of hours spent studying for an examination and the grades students got on the exam. Here are the data in a table:

Student	Hours	Grade
Fred	0	0
Mary	2	25
Sam	4	50
Edith	6	75
Earl	8	100

First question: Can you guess which of us prepared this example? Second question: Can you see a pattern in the data presented?

The pattern, pretty clearly, is this: The more you study, the better the grade you get. Let's look at these data in the form of a graph. (This is something you can do by hand, using graph paper.)

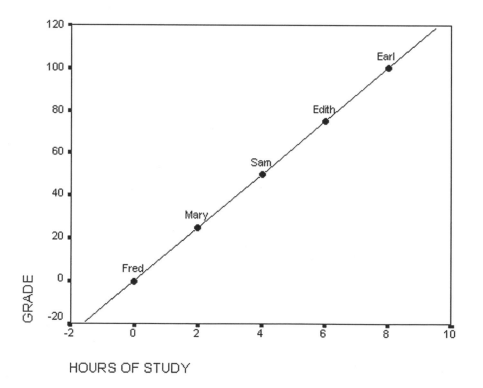

HOURS OF STUDY

As you can see, the five people in this example fall along a straight line across the graph. This line is called the *regression line*. As you may recall from plane geometry, it is possible to represent a straight line on a graph in the form of an equation. In this case the equation would be as follows:

Grade = 12.5 × Hours

To determine a person's grade using this equation, you need only multiply the number of hours he or she studied by 12.5. Multiply Earl's 8 hours of study by 12.5 and you get his grade of 100. Multiply Edith's 6 hours by 12.5 and you get 75. Multiply Fred's 0 hours by 12.5 and, well, you know Fred.

Whereas correlation considers the symmetrical association between two variables, regression adds the notion of causal direction. One of the variables is the *dependent variable*—grades, in this example—and the other is the *independent variable* or cause—hours of study. Thus, the equation we just created is designed to predict a person's grade based on how many hours he or she studied. If we were to tell you that someone not included in these data studied 5 hours for the exam, you could predict that that person got a 62.5 on the exam (5 × 12.5).

If all social science analyses produced results as clear as these, you probably wouldn't need SPSS or a book like this one. In practice, however, the facts are usually a bit more complex, and SPSS is up to the challenge.

Given a set of data with an imperfect relationship between two variables, SPSS can discover the line that comes closest to passing through all the points on the graph. To understand the meaning of the notion of coming close, we need to recall the squared deviations found in our calculation of Pearson's *r*.

Suppose Sam had gotten 70 on the exam, for example. Here's what he would look like on the graph we just drew.

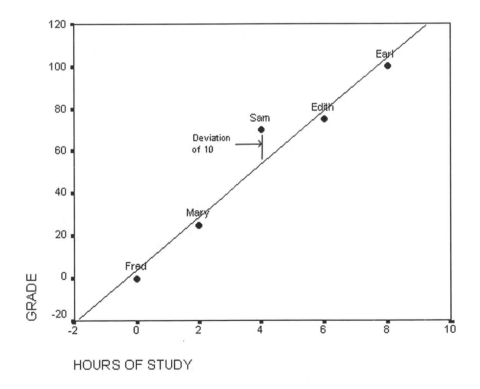

Notice that the improved Sam does not fall on the original regression line: His grade represents a deviation of 10 points. With a real set of data, most people fall to one side or the other of any line we might draw through the data. SPSS, however, is able to determine the line that would produce the smallest deviations overall—measured by squaring all the individual deviations and adding them. This calculated regression line is sometimes called the *least-squares regression line*.

Requesting such an analysis from SPSS is fairly simple. To use this technique to real advantage, you need more instruction than is appropriate for this book. However, we wanted to introduce you to regression because it is a popular technique among many social scientists.

Demonstration 14.8: Regression

To experiment with the regression technique, let's make use of a new variable: SEI. This variable rates the socioeconomic prestige of respondents' occupations on a scale from a low of 0 to a high of 100, based on other studies that have asked a sample from the general population to rate different occupations.

Here's how we would ask SPSS to find the equation that best represents the influence of EDUC on SEI. You should realize that there are a number of ways to request this information, but we'd suggest you do it as follows. (Just do it this way and nobody gets hurt, okay?)

Under **Analyze**, select **Regression → Linear . . .** Here's what you get.

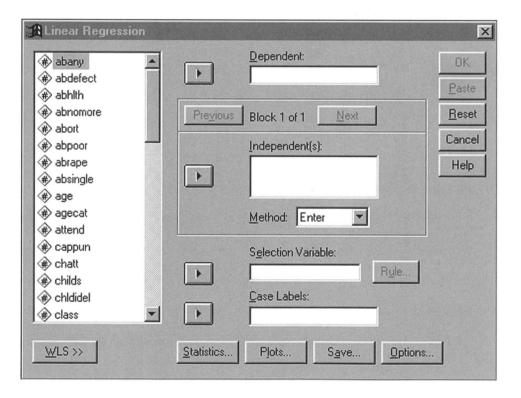

Select **SEI** as the **Dependent:** variable and **EDUC** as the **Independent(s):** variable. Click **OK**, and SPSS is off and running. Here's the output you should get in response to this instruction.

Model Summary

Model	R	R Square	Adjusted R Square	Std. Error of the Estimate
1	.570[a]	.324	.324	15.5977

a. Predictors: (Constant), EDUC HIGHEST YEAR OF SCHOOL COMPLETED

ANOVA[b]

Model		Sum of Squares	df	Mean Square	F	Sig.
1	Regression	165855.6	1	165855.559	681.726	.000[a]
	Residual	345468.6	1420	243.288		
	Total	511324.1	1421			

a. Predictors: (Constant), EDUC HIGHEST YEAR OF SCHOOL COMPLETED

b. Dependent Variable: SEI

Coefficients[a]

Model		Unstandardized Coefficients		Standardized Coefficients		
		B	Std. Error	Beta	t	Sig.
1	(Constant)	-2.635	2.023		-1.303	.193
	EDUC HIGHEST YEAR OF SCHOOL COMPLETED	3.868	.148	.570	26.110	.000

a. Dependent Variable: SEI

The key information we are looking for is contained in the final table titled "Coefficients": the *intercept* (−2.635) and the *slope* (3.868). These are the data we need to complete our regression equation. Use them as follows:

$$SEI = -2.635 + (EDUC \times 3.868).$$

This means that we would predict the occupation prestige ranking of a high school graduate (12 years of schooling) as follows:

$$SEI = -2.635 + (12 \times 3.868) = 43.781.$$

On the other hand, we would predict the occupational prestige of a college graduate (16 years of schooling) as

$$SEI = -2.635 + (16 \times 3.868) = 59.253.$$

SPSS Command 14.4: Regression

Click **Analyze** → **Regression** → **Linear . . .** →

Highlight **dependent variable** and click **right-pointing arrow** to transfer it to Dependent: field →

Highlight **independent variable** and click **right-pointing arrow** to transfer it to Independent(s): field →

Click **OK**

Demonstration 14.9: Presenting Data Graphically: Producing a Scatterplot with Regression Line

Another way to explore the relationship between SEI and EDUC is to instruct SPSS to produce a *scatterplot* with a *regression line*. Scatterplot is a term SPSS uses to identify what we referred to earlier in our discussion of Pearson's *r* as a scattergram. A scatterplot/scattergram is simply a graph with a *horizontal (x) axis* and a *vertical (y) axis*. As you saw earlier, each dot on the graph represents the point of intersection for each individual case. It is the "scatter" of dots taken as a whole which, along with the regression line, indicate the strength and direction of association between the variables.

Instructing SPSS to produce a scatterplot with a regression line allows us to see the distribution and array of cases, while saving us the time-consuming task of creating the graph on our own (which as you can imagine with approximately 1,500 cases would be quite a daunting task).

To produce a scatterplot, all you have to do is open the Scatterplot window by clicking **Graphs** and then choosing **Scatter . . .** in the drop-down menu.

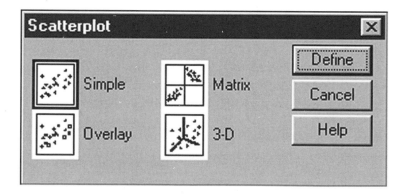

When you have opened the Scatterplot box as shown above, select **Simple** if it is not already highlighted and then click **Define**. You should now be looking at the Simple Scatterplot dialog box as shown below:

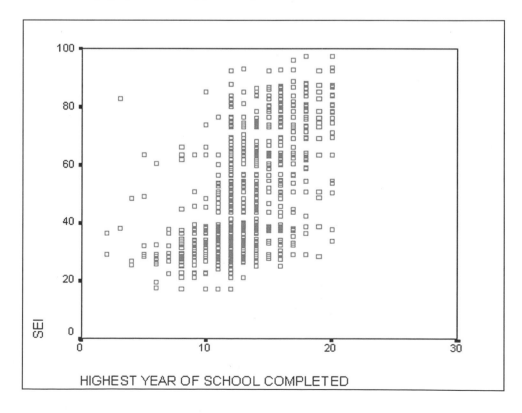

Following the example we used above, place **EDUC** (the independent variable) along the **x axis:**. And then place **SEI** (the dependent variable) along the **y axis:**. When you are finished with this process you can hit **OK** and very shortly the following graph should appear on your screen.

As requested, our independent variable EDUC is arrayed along the x (horizontal) axis and our dependent variable SEI is arrayed along the y (vertical) axis. You can also see the splatter of dots on the graph, each representing a particular case.

Now **double-click** on the **graph** and the SPSS Chart Editor will appear.

We are going to use the Chart Editor to add our regression line, which, as we saw earlier, is simply a single straight line that will run through our scatterplot and come as close as possible to touching all the "dots" or data points.

Now click on the **Chart Options** button, which is the second button from the right on the lower button bar (the icon that looks a little bit like the Eiffel Tower). Once you have done that the Scatterplot Options dialog window will open as shown below.

Click on the box next to **Total** in the upper right-hand side of the window below Fit Line. Once a check mark appears in the box, you can click **OK**. You will soon see that the regression line we requested has been added to your scatterplot as shown below. To close the Chart Editor, simply click the close button in the upper-right hand corner (**X**) or select **File → Close**.

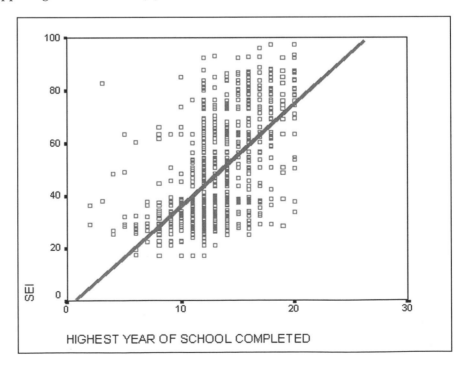

An Indication of Direction and Strength of Association

The scatterplot and regression line serve as a visual indication of the direction and strength of association between EDUC and SEI.

The direction of association can be determined based on the way the regression line sits on the scatterplot. Generally, when the line moves from the bottom left-hand side of the graph to the upper right-hand side of the graph (uphill), this indicates a positive association between the variables (they both either increase or decrease in the same direction), whereas a regression line that runs from the upper left to the lower right side of the scatterplot (downhill) indicates a negative association between the items (as one increases, the other decreases).

The strength of association can be estimated based on the extent to which the dots (cases) are scattered around the regression line. The closer the dots are to the regression line, the stronger the association between the variables (in the case of a "perfect relationship," the dots will sit exactly on the regression line, indicating the strongest possible association between the variables). Conversely, the further spread out or scattered the dots are, the weaker the relationship between the items.

We want to emphasize that although this type of visual representation allows us to estimate the strength of association between variables, there is no agreement regarding what constitutes a "strong" versus a "moderate" or "weak" association. Consequently, your best option may be to use the scatterplot with a regression line in conjunction with a measure such as Pearson's r, which allows you to obtain a value that summarizes the association between variables more precisely than just the scatterplot and regression line do. Keep in mind that because both options are appropriate for continuously distributed I/R variables, they can be used to examine the same types of items.

Now try to see if you can describe the strength and direction of association between EDUC and SEI as shown in the scatterplot with a regression line above. What is the direction of association? Are the variables positively or negatively related (i.e., does the regression line run uphill or downhill)? What can you estimate in terms of the strength of association between EDUC and SEI? Are the dots or cases clustered around the regression line or spread out?

Writing Box 14.4

The positive relationship between education and socioeconomic status can be seen by inspection of the scattergram. While the many cases are widely dispersed, there is a discernible pattern concentrating on the lower left and upper right quadrants. Adding the regression line confirms that assessment.

SPSS Command 14.5:   Producing a Scatterplot with Regression Line

> Click **Graphs** → **Scatter** . . . → **Simple** → **Define** →
>
> Highlight **independent variable** → click **right-pointing arrow** to transfer to
> X Axis: →
>
> Highlight **dependent variable** → click **right-pointing arrow** to transfer to
> Y Axis: →
>
> Click **OK** →
>
> *To Add Regression Line:*
>
> **Double click** on **Scatterplot** to open the SPSS Chart Editor →
>
> Click **Chart Options** icon → **Total** → **OK** →
>
> Click **Close** button (X) *OR* **File** → **Close** to close the SPSS Chart Editor

That's enough fun for now. We'll return to regression later, when we discuss multivariate analysis in Chapter 17.

Additional Measures of Association

The measures of association we have focused on are each appropriate for variables at a particular level of measurement. For instance, lambda is used to examine the association between two nominal variables, whereas gamma is used to explore the relationship between two ordinal variables and Pearson's *r* and regression are appropriate for two I/R items. Table 14.3 lists the measures we have reviewed along with their appropriate level of measurement.

Table 14.3 Measures of Association Reviewed in This Chapter

Level of Measurement	Measure of Association (Range of Values) of Each Variable
Nominal	Lambda [0 to +1]
Ordinal	Gamma [−1 to +1]
I/R	Pearson's *r* [−1 to +1]
	Regression

Keep in mind, however, that the measures we reviewed are just a few of the most popular measures available. In Table 14.4 below we list some other measures applicable for variables at particular levels of measurement. You can access many of these (and other measures) on SPSS. However we want to caution you that you should use these measures with caution because like the others we reviewed in the chapter, each has its own peculiar benefits and limitations.

Table 14.4   Additional Measures of Association

Level of Measurement	
Nominal	Goodman and Kruskal's tau
	Phi
	Cramer's V
Ordinal	Somer's *d*
	Kendall's tau-*b*
	Kendall's tau-*c*

Analyzing the Association Between Variables at Different Levels of Measurement

In some cases you may discover that you want to analyze the association between variables at different levels of measurement: for instance, nominal by ordinal, nominal by I/R, and so on. While there are specialized bivariate measures of association for use when two variables have different levels of measurement, the safest course of action for the novice is to use a measure of association that meets the assumptions for the variable with the lowest level of measurement. This usually means that one variable will have to be recoded to reduce its level of measurement. For instance, when we examined the relationship between church attendance (ordinal) and age (I/R), we recoded people's ages into ordinal categories.

While it would not be appropriate to use Pearson's *r* to correlate our CHATT and AGE, it is perfectly legitimate to use gamma to correlate CHATT with AGECAT.

While it is beyond the scope of this chapter to review all the statistical measures appropriate for each particular situation, those of you who are interested in pursuing the relationship between mixed variables may want to consult a basic statistics or research methods text for a discussion of appropriate measures.[12] Keep in mind that a variety of basic statistics texts can now be accessed quite easily on the world wide web.[13] In addition, you may want to access some of the many web sites that have been established in recent years to help students identify

---

[12] Among the many basic statistics texts you may want to consult are: Freeman's *Elementary Applied Statistics* (1968); Siegel and Castellan's *Nonparametric Statistics for the Behavioral Sciences* (1998); and Frankfort-Nachmias et al.'s *Social Statistics for a Diverse Society*. Alreck and Settle's (1985, 287-362, Table 10-5, 303) *The Survey Research Handbook* contains a table titled "Statistical Measures of Association," which, depending on the type of independent and dependent variables you are working with (i.e., categorical or continuous), specifies appropriate measures of association. The table is accompanied by a discussion of statistical analysis and interpretation.

[13] See for instance: William M. Trochim's *Research Methods Knowledge Base* at http://trochim.human.cornell.edu/kb/index.htm; David M. Lane's *Hyperstat Online: An Introductory Statisics Book . . .* at http://davidmlane.com/hyperstat/index.html; and David M. Stockburger's *Introductory Statistics: Concepts, Models, and Applications* at http://www.psychstat.smsu.edu/.

appropriate statistical tests. The following are just two examples of the numerous sites available:

"Selecting Statistics"

http://trochim.human.cornell.edu/selstat/ssstart.htm

"HyperStat Online"

http://davidmlane.com/hyperstat/index.html

Conclusion

In this chapter, we've seen a number of statistical techniques that can be used to summarize the degree of relationship or association between two variables. We've seen that the appropriate technique depends on the level of measurement represented by the variables involved. Lambda is appropriate for nominal, gamma for ordinal, and Pearson's r product-moment correlation and regression for I/R variables.

We realize that you may have had trouble knowing how to respond to the results of these calculations. How do you decide, for example, if a gamma of .25 is high or low? Should you get excited about it or yawn and continue looking? The following chapter on statistical significance offers one basis for making such decisions.

Main Points

- In this chapter we looked at new ways to examine the relationships among variables.
- Measures of association summarize the strength (and in some cases the direction) of association between two variables in contrast to the way percentage tables lay out the details.
- This chapter focuses on only some of the many measures available: lambda, gamma, Pearson's r, and regression.
- The measures are largely based on the logic of PRE.
- Lambda is appropriate for two nominal variables; its values range from 0 to 1.
- Gamma is appropriate for two ordinal variables; its values range from −1 to +1.
- Pearson's r is appropriate for two I/R items; its values range from −1 to +1.
- The closer the value is to positive or negative 1, the stronger the relationship between the items (with +1 or −1 indicating a perfect association). The closer the value is to 0, the weaker the relationship between the items (with 0 indicating no association between the items).
- There are no set rules for interpreting strength of association.
- Like Pearson's r, regression is also appropriate for I/R variables.
- Another way to explore the strength and direction of association between two I/R variables is to produce a scatterplot with a regression line.
- There are a variety of appropriate statistics for examining the relationship between mixed types of variables.

Key Terms

Measures of association	Strength of association
Variance	Least-squares regression line
PRE (proportionate reduction of error)	Direction of association
Standard deviation	Intercept
Lambda	Same pair
z scores	Slope
Gamma	Opposite pair
Correlation matrix	Regression line
Positive association	Pearson's r
Statistical significance	x (horizontal) axis
Negative association	Scattergram (scatterplot)
Regression	y (vertical) axis

SPSS Commands Introduced in This Chapter

14.1   Running Crosstabs and Lambda

14.2   Running Crosstabs and Gamma

14.3   Producing a Correlation Matrix and Pearson's r

14.4   Regression

14.5   Producing a Scatterplot with Regression Line

Review Questions

1. If two variables are strongly associated, does that mean that they are necessarily causally related?

2. What is PRE?

3. List three measures of association.

4. Measures of association give us an indication of the _____ of association and (if the variables are ordinal or higher) the _____ of association between two variables.

5. Lambda is appropriate for variables at which level of measurement?

6. Gamma is appropriate for variables at which level of measurement?

7. Pearson's r is appropriate for variables at which level of measurement?

8. List the range of values for each of the following measures:

   *lambda

   *gamma

   *Pearson's r

9. The closer to _____ or _____ (value) the stronger the relationship between the variables.

10. The closer to _____ (value), the weaker the relationship between the variables.

11. A value of _____ or _____ indicates a perfect (or the strongest) relationship between the variables.

12. What does a positive association between two variables indicate? What does a negative association between two variables indicate?

13. Does a negative value for gamma necessarily indicate that the variables are negatively associated? Explain.

14. Regression is appropriate for two variables at which level of measurement?

15. What type of graph did we review in this chapter which allows us to examine the strength and direction of association between two I/R variables?

16. Name one measure of association you might use to examine the strength of association between the variable CHATT (ordinal) and SEX (nominal)?

NAME _____

CLASS _____

INSTRUCTOR _____

DATE _____

To complete these exercises, load your data file EXERPLUS. You will find answers to selected Questions (1-7, 13-20, and 27-36) in Appendix B.

Run Crosstabs with column percentages for the variables RACE (independent) and POLHITOK (dependent). Then request the appropriate measure of association and answer Questions 1-7. Be sure to define the values 0, 8, and 9 as missing for POLHITOK.

1. What is the level of measurement for the variable RACE?

2. What is the level of measurement for the variable POLHITOK?

3. What measure of association is appropriate to examine the relationship between these variables?

4. Record the percentage of respondents who said "Yes" to POLHITOK for each category of the variable RACE.

	Race		
	White	*Black*	*Other*
Yes	____	____	____

5. Do the column percentages change or move, signifying a relationship between RACE and POLHITOK? Explain.

6. The strength/value of _____ (measure of association) is _____ (value/strength of measure of association).

7. Would you characterize the relationship between these two variables as weak, moderate, or strong? Explain.

Choose two nominal variables from your data set. Run Crosstabs with column percentages for the variables. Then request the appropriate measure of association and answer Questions 8-12. Reminder: Be sure to define the appropriate values as missing for each of your variables.

8. List the two variables you chose, designating one as the independent and one as the dependent variable. Then state briefly why you chose them and what you expect to find in terms of the relationship between these variables (i.e., construct a hypothesis relating your variables).

9. What measure of association is appropriate to examine the relationship between these variables?

10. Do the column percentages change or move, signifying a relationship between these variables? Explain.

NAME _____

CLASS _____

INSTRUCTOR _____

DATE _____

11. The strength/value of _____ (measure of association) is _____ (value/strength of measure of association).

12. Would you characterize the relationship between these two variables as weak, moderate, or strong? Explain.

Run Crosstabs with column percentages for the variables RACWORK (independent) and DISCAFF (dependent). Then request the appropriate measure of association and answer Questions 13-20. Before proceeding with your analysis, remember to define the values 0, 6, 8, 9 as missing for RACWORK. In addition, be sure to define 0, 8, and 9 as missing for DISCAFF.

13. What is the level of measurement for the variable RACWORK?

14. What is the level of measurement for the variable DISCAFF?

15. What measure of association is appropriate to examine the relationship between these variables?

16. Record the percentage of respondents who said "Very likely" and "Somewhat likely" to DISCAFF for each category of the variable RACWORK.

17. Do the column percentages change or move, signifying a relationship between RACWORK and DISCAFF? Explain.

18. The strength/value of _____ (measure of association) is _____ (value/strength of measure of association).

19. Would you characterize the relationship between these two variables as weak, moderate, or strong? Explain.

20. What is the direction of association between these variables?

Choose two ordinal variables from your data set. Run Crosstabs with column percentages for the variables. Then request the appropriate measure of association and answer Questions 21-26. Reminder: Be sure to label appropriate values for each variable as missing.

NAME _____

CLASS _____

INSTRUCTOR _____

DATE _____

21. List the two variables you chose, designating one as the independent and one as the dependent variable. Then state briefly why you chose them and what you expect to find in terms of the relationship between these variables (i.e., construct a hypothesis relating your variables).

22. What measure of association is appropriate to examine the relationship between these variables?

23. Do the column percentages change or move, signifying a relationship between these variables? Explain.

24. The strength/value of _____ (measure of association) is _____ (value/strength of measure of association).

25. Would you characterize the relationship between these two variables as weak, moderate, or strong? Explain.

26. What is the direction of association between these variables?

Produce a correlation matrix, exclude cases pairwise, and request Pearson's r for the variables AGE (independent) and SEI (dependent). Then answer Questions 27-30. Remember to define the values 98 and 99 as missing for the variable AGE.

27. What is the level of measurement for the variable AGE?

28. What is the level of measurement for the variable SEI?

29. Pearson's *r* for AGE and SEI is _____.

30. Would you characterize the relationship between these two variables as weak, moderate, or strong? Explain.

Produce a scatterplot with a regression line for the variables EDUC (independent) and TVHOURS (dependent). Then answer Questions 31-36. Before proceeding with your analysis, be sure to define the values 97, 98, and 99 as missing for the variable EDUC. In addition, define the values –1, 98, and 99 as missing for the variable TVHOURS.

31. What is the level of measurement for the variable EDUC?

NAME _____

CLASS _____

INSTRUCTOR _____

DATE _____

32. What is the level of measurement for the variable TVHOURS?

33. What is the direction of the relationship between the variables?

34. As years of education increases, does the number of hours of television watched increase or decrease?

35. The relationship of the "dots" or cases to the regression line suggests what about the strength of the relationship between these two variables?

36. Produce a correlation matrix with Pearson's *r*, exclude cases pairwise, and then further describe the strength of the relationship between EDUC and TVHOURS by noting what the value of Pearson's *r* is and whether the relationship is weak, moderate, or strong.

37. Now choose two variables from your data set that you think may be associated. After defining appropriate values for each variable as missing, analyze the relationship between the variables by instructing SPSS to calculate the appropriate measure of association. If you want to recode either of your variables, feel free to do so. Remember, if you choose two variables at different levels of measure, you can follow our suggestion toward the end of the chapter that you use a measure that meets the assumptions for the variable with the lowest level of measurement. If you choose two I/R variables, also produce a scatterplot with a regression line.

Once you have completed your analysis, print your output and attach it to this sheet. Then, take a few moments to describe your findings in the space provided below. In particular, you may want to consider noting: what variables you chose and why, the levels of measurement of each, whether you had to recode either item or designate any values as missing, what measure of association you instructed SPSS to calculate, the value of that measure, what it indicates about the relationship between these variables (strength and direction), etc . . . If you are having any trouble producing an analysis of your findings in prose, you may want to re-read the Writing Boxes throughout Chapter 14.

Chapter 15 **Tests of Significance**

Thus far, in Chapters 11 through 14, we've been looking at the relationships between pairs of variables. In all that, you may have been frustrated over the ambiguity as to what constitutes a "strong" or a "weak" relationship. As we noted in the last chapter, ultimately there is no absolute answer to this question. The strength and significance of a relationship between two variables depend on many things.

If you are trying to account for differences among people on some variable, such as prejudice, the explanatory power of one variable, such as education, needs to be contrasted with the explanatory power of other variables. Thus you might be interested in knowing whether education, political affiliation, or region of upbringing has the greatest impact on a person's prejudice.

Sometimes the importance of a relationship is based on practical policy implications. Thus the impact of some variable in explaining (and potentially reducing) auto theft rates, for example, might be converted to a matter of dollars. Other relationships might be expressed in terms of lives saved, students graduating from college, and so forth.

Statistical Significance

In this chapter, we're going to introduce you to another standard for judging the relationships among variables—one that is commonly used by social scientists. Whereas in Chapter 14 we discussed measures of association that allow us to examine the strength (and in the case of ordinal and I/R variables, the direction) of association, in this chapter we explore tests that will allow you to estimate *statistical significance*. Tests of statistical significance allow us to estimate the likelihood that a relationship between variables in a sample actually exists in the population as opposed to being an illusion due to chance or sampling error.

For instance, whenever analyses are based on random samples selected from a population rather than on data collected from everyone in that population, there is always the possibility that what we learn from the samples may not truly reflect the whole population. Thus we might discover in a sample that women are more religious than men, but that could be simply an artifact of our sample: We happened to pick too many religious women and/or too few religious men. Tests of significance allow us to estimate the likelihood that our finding, a relationship between gender and religiosity in this case, could have happened by chance. If the chances of our finding are very unlikely, say only about five in a hundred, then we have the confidence needed to generalize our finding from the sample to the population from which it was drawn.

Significance Tests: Part of the Larger Body of Inferential Statistics[1]

Significance tests are part of a larger body of statistics known as inferential statistics. **Inferential statistics** can probably best be understood in contrast to **descriptive statistics**, which you are already familiar with. Together, descriptive and inferential statistics constitute two of the main types of statistics that social researchers use. Up to this point (Chapters 6 through 14) our focus has been largely on descriptive statistics that allow us to describe or summarize the main features of our data or the relationships between variables in our data set. In contrast, inferential statistics allows us to go a step further by making it possible to draw conclusions or make inferences that extend beyond the items in our particular data set to the larger population. In short, we can use inferential statistics to help us learn what our sample tells us about the population from which it was drawn. In the case of tests of significance, for instance, we can estimate whether an observed association between variables in our sample is generalizable to the larger population.

Statistical Significance Versus Measures of Association

Social scientists often test the statistical significance of relationships discovered among variables. Although these tests do not constitute a direct measure of the strength of a relationship, they tell us the likelihood that the observed relationship could have resulted from the vagaries of probability sampling, which we call **sampling error**. These tests relate to the strength of relationships in that the stronger an observed relationship, the less likely it is that it could be the result of sampling error. Correspondingly, it is more likely that the observed relationship represents something that exists in the population as a whole.

You will find that social scientists use measures of association and tests of significance in conjunction with one another because together they allow us to address three important questions about the relationships between variables:

1. *How strong is the relationship?* (Measures of Association/Descriptive Statistics such as lambda, gamma, etc. . . . Chapter 14)

2. In the case of ordinal and I/R variables, *what is the direction of association?* (Measures of Association/Descriptive Statistics such as gamma, Pearson's *r*, etc. . . . Chapter 14)

3. *Is the relationship statistically significant?* (Tests of Significance/Inferential Statistics such as chi-square, *t* test, etc. . . .)

---

[1] For a brief and accessible introduction to inferential statistics (among other things) see: "Research Methods Knowledge Base," at http://trochim.human.cornell.edu/kb/. The site contains a useful introduction to some of the basic inferential statistics reviewed in this chapter. Another useful site is "HyperStat Online," at http://davidmlane.com/hyperstat. Chapter 1 of the "HyperStat Online Textbook," for instance, contains a brief overview of inferential statistics.

In this chapter we turn our attention to Question 3 and some of the measures that can be used to estimate statistical significance, primarily chi-square, *t* tests, and ANOVA.

Chi-Square

To learn the logic of statistical significance, let's begin with a measure, *chi-square*, that is based on the kinds of crosstabulations we've been examining in previous chapters. Chi-square is a test of significance that is most appropriate for nominal items, although it can be used with ordinal variables or a combination of nominal and ordinal variables. Chi-square, one of the most widely used tests of significance, estimates the probability that the association between variables is a result of random chance or sampling error by comparing the actual or observed distribution of responses with the distribution of responses we would expect if there were absolutely no association between two variables.

To help make this more clear, let's take some time now to look at the logic of statistical significance in general and chi-square in particular.

The Logic of Statistical Significance: Chi-Square

For a concrete example, let's return to one of the tables that examines the relationship between religion and abortion attitudes.

Let's reexamine the relationship between religious affiliation and unconditional support for abortion.

Do a **Crosstabs** of **ABANY** (**row** variable) and **RELIG** (**column** variable) and request Cells percentaged by **column.**[2]

ABANY ABORTION IF WOMAN WANTS FOR ANY REASON * RELIG RS RELIGIOUS PREFERENCE Crosstabulation							
			RELIG RS RELIGIOUS PREFERENCE				
			1 PROTESTANT	2 CATHOLIC	3 JEWISH	4 NONE	Total
ABANY ABORTION IF WOMAN WANTS FOR ANY REASON	1 YES	Count	191	80	19	71	361
		% within RELIG RS RELIGIOUS PREFERENCE	37.5%	35.6%	95.0%	57.7%	41.2%
	2 NO	Count	318	145	1	52	516
		% within RELIG RS RELIGIOUS PREFERENCE	62.5%	64.4%	5.0%	42.3%	58.8%
Total		Count	509	225	20	123	877
		% within RELIG RS RELIGIOUS PREFERENCE	100.0%	100.0%	100.0%	100.0%	100.0%

The question this table (which contains the actual or observed frequencies) is designed to answer is whether a person's religious affiliation affects his or her attitude toward abortion. You'll recall that we concluded it does: Catholics and Protestants are the most opposed to abortion, and Jews and those with no religion are the most supportive. The question we now confront is whether the observed differences point to some genuine pattern in the U.S. population at large or whether they result from a quirk of sampling.

---

[2] Define the following values as **missing** for each variable: **ABANY - 0, 8,** and **9; RELIG – 0, 5-99.**

To assess the *observed relationship* as shown in the table above, we are going to begin by asking what we should have *expected* to find if there were no relationship between religious affiliation and abortion attitudes. An important part of the answer lies in the rightmost column in the preceding table. It indicates that 41 percent of the whole sample supported a woman's unconditional right to an abortion (Yes), and 59 percent did not (No).

If there were no relationship between religious affiliation and abortion attitudes, we should expect to find 41 percent of the Protestants approving (Yes), 41 percent of the Catholics approving, 41 percent of the Jews approving, and so forth. But we recall that the earlier results did not match this perfect model of no relationship, so the question is whether the disparity between the model and our observations would fall within the normal degree of sampling error.

To measure the extent of the disparity between the model and what's been observed, we need to calculate the number of cases we'd expect in each cell of the table if there were no relationship. The table below shows how to calculate the expected cell frequencies.

ABANY	Protestant	Catholic	Jewish	None
Yes	509	225	20	123
	x.41	x.41	x.41	x.41
No	509	225	20	123
	x.59	x.59	x.59	x.59

Make sure you know how we constructed this table before moving ahead.

Consequently, if there were no relationship between religious affiliation and abortion attitudes, we would expect 41 percent of the 509 Protestants (509 × .41 = 209) to approve and 59 percent of the 509 Protestants (509 × .59 = 300) to disapprove. If you continue this series of calculations, you should arrive at the following set of *expected cell frequencies*.

ABANY	Protestant	Catholic	Jewish	None
Yes	209	92	8	50
No	300	133	12	73

The next step in calculating chi-square is to calculate the difference between expected and observed values in each cell of the table. For example, if religion had no affect on abortion, we would have expected to find 209 Protestants approving; in fact, we observed only 191. Thus the discrepancy in that cell is −18. The discrepancy for Catholics approving is −12 (observed - expected = 80 − 92). The table below shows the discrepancies for each cell.

ABANY	Protestant	Catholic	Jewish	None
Yes	-18	-12	11	21
No	18	12	-11	-21

Finally, for each cell we square the discrepancy and divide it by the expected cell frequency. For the Protestants approving of abortion, then, the squared discrepancy is 324 (–18 × –18). Dividing it by the expected frequency of 209 yields 1.55. When we repeat this for each cell, we get the following results.

ABANY	Protestant	Catholic	Jewish	None
Approve	1.55	1.57	15.13	8.82
Disapprove	1.08	1.08	10.08	6.04

Chi-square is the sum of all these latest cell figures: 45.35. We have calculated a summary measure of the discrepancy between what we would have expected to observe if religion did not affect abortion and what we actually observed. Now the only remaining question is whether that resulting number should be regarded as large or small. Statisticians often speak of the *goodness of fit* in this context: How well do the observed data fit a model of two variables being unrelated to each other?

The answer to this latest question takes the form of a probability: the probability that a chi-square this large could occur as a result of sampling error. A probability of .05 in this context would mean that it should happen five times in 100 samples. A probability of .001 would mean it should happen only one time in 1,000 samples.

To evaluate our chi-square of 45.35, we need to look it up in a table of chi-square values, which you'll find in the back of any statistics textbook. Such tables have several columns marked by different probabilities (e.g., .30, .20, .10, .05, .01, .001). The tables also have several rows representing different *degrees of freedom* (df).

If you think about it, you'll probably see that the larger and more complex a table is, the greater the likelihood that there will be discrepancies from the perfect model of expected frequencies. We take account of this by one final calculation.

Degrees of freedom are calculated from the data table as (rows – 1) × (columns – 1). In our table, there are four columns and two rows, giving us (3 × 1) degrees of freedom. Thus, we would look across the third row in the table of chi-square values, which would look, in part, like this:

df	05	.01	.001
3	7.815	11.341	16.268

These numbers tell us that a chi-square as high as 7.815 from a table like ours would occur only 5 times in 100 samples if there were no relationship between religious affiliation and abortion attitudes among the whole U.S. population. A chi-square as high as 11.341 would happen only once in 100 samples, and a chi-square as high as 16.268 would only happen once in 1,000.

Thus we conclude that our chi-square of 45.35 could result from sampling error less than once in 1,000 samples. This is often abbreviated as p <.001: The probability is less than 1 in 1,000.

They have no magical meaning, but the .05 and .001 levels of significance are often used by social scientists as a convention for concluding that an observed relationship reflects a similar relationship in the population rather than arising from sampling error. Most social scientists agree that relationships with significance values of .05 or less are so unlikely to have occurred by chance that they can be called significant. The lower the probability, the more statistically significant the relationship. Accordingly, if a relationship is significant at the .001 level, we can be more confident of our conclusion than if it is significant only at the .05 level.

Going back to our example then, if the value of chi-square is greater than the value printed in the reference table for the appropriate degree of freedom and at the probability level of .05 or less, then the relationship between the variables can be considered statistically significant.

As we noted, in our example the value of chi-square is 45.35, which is greater than the value printed in the reference table for the appropriate *df* at the probability of .05, .01, and .001. This then tells us that the relationship between our variables (ABANY and RELIG) can be considered statistically significant.

There you have it: far more than you ever thought you'd want to know about chi-square. By sticking it out and coming to grasp the logical meaning of this statistical calculation, you've earned a reward.

Demonstration 15.1:
Instructing SPSS to Calculate Chi-Square

Rather than going through all the preceding calculations, we could have simply modified our **Crosstabs** request slightly (and after seeing how easy it is to instruct SPSS to run chi-square, you will probably wish we had just done this much earlier). In the Crosstabs window, click **Statistics ...** and select **Chi-Square** in the upper left corner of the Statistics window. Then click **Continue** and **OK** to run the Crosstabs request.

Chi-Square Tests			
	Value	df	Asymp. Sig. (2-sided)
Pearson Chi-Square	43.567[a]	3	.000
Likelihood Ratio	46.266	3	.000
Linear-by-Linear Association	21.207	1	.000
N of Valid Cases	877		

a. 0 cells (.0%) have expected count less than 5. The minimum expected count is 8.23.

Reading Your Output

We are interested primarily in the first row of figures in this report. Notice that the 43.567 value of chi-square is slightly different from our hand calculation. This is because of our rounding off in our cell calculations, and it shouldn't worry you. Notice that we're told that there are three degrees of freedom. Finally, SPSS has calculated the probability of getting a chi-square this high with three degrees of freedom and has run out of space after three zeros to the right of the decimal point. Thus the probability is far less than .001, as we determined by checking a table of chi-square values.

The reference to a *minimum expected frequency* of 8.23 is worth noting. Because the calculation of chi-square involves divisions by expected cell frequencies, it can be greatly inflated if any of them are very small. By convention, adjustments to chi-square should be made if more than 20 percent of the expected cell frequencies are below 5. You should check a statistics text if you want to know more about this.

SPSS Command 15.1: Producing Crosstabs with Chi-Square

> Click **Analyze** → **Descriptive Statistics** → **Crosstabs** . . . →
>
> Highlight **dependent** variable → Click **arrow** to transfer to **Row(s):** field →
>
> Highlight **independent** variable → Click **arrow** to transfer to **Column(s):** field →
>
> Click **Cells** . . . → Click **Column** in Percentages box → **Continue** →
>
> **Statistics** . . . → **Chi-Square** → **Continue** → **OK**

Practice Running Chi-Square

While it is fresh in your mind, why don't you have SPSS calculate some more chi-squares for you? You may recall that sex had little impact on abortion attitudes. Why don't you see what the chi-square is? Once you have done so, compare your interpretation of your findings to that in Writing Box 15.1.

Writing Box 15.1

With a chi-square of only .395, we note that the slight relationship observed between sex and abortion attitudes in the sample would be found about half the time (p = .530) due to sampling error alone if there were no relationship whatever between the two variables in the population.

To experiment more with chi-square, you might rerun some of the other tables relating various demographic variables to abortion attitudes. Notice how chi-square offers a basis for comparing the relative importance of different variables in determining attitudes on this controversial topic.

Significance and Association

It bears repeating here that tests of significance are different from measures of association, although they are related to one another. The stronger an association between two variables, the more likely it is that the association will be judged statistically significant—that is, not a simple product of sampling error. Other factors also affect statistical significance, however. As we've already mentioned, the number of degrees of freedom in a table is relevant. So is the size of the sample: The larger the sample, the more likely it is that an association will be judged significant.

Researchers often distinguish between *statistical significance* (examined in this section) and *substantive significance*. The latter refers to the importance of an association, and it can't be determined by empirical analysis alone. As we suggested at the outset of this chapter, substantive significance depends on practical and theoretical factors. All this notwithstanding, social researchers often find statistical significance a useful device in gauging associations.

Table 15.1   A Guide to Interpreting Tests of Association and Significance

Strength of Association	Statistical Significance	Interpretation	Comment
Strong	Significant	Knowledge of the independent variable improves prediction of dependent variable and relationship can be generalized from the sample to the population.	Look what I've discovered.
Strong	Not Significant	Although knowledge of the independent variable improves prediction of dependent variable in the sample, the relationship cannot be generalized to the population.	Close, but no banana.
Weak	Significant	Knowledge of the independent variable is of little help in predicting the dependent variable but may be generalized to the population.	That's no big thing.
Weak	Nonsignificant	Knowing about the independent variable provides little help in the prediction of the dependent variable in the sample and cannot be generalized to the population.	Back to the drawing board.

That said, you may still be wondering how you should interpret findings which show, for instance, that there is a strong but not statistically significant relationship between two variables. Or, conversely, what you should say if you find that there is a fairly weak but nonetheless statistically significant relationship between two items. Table 15.1 is intended to help as you approach the sometimes daunting task of interpreting tests of significance and association. While there are no "rules" of interpretation, this table can be looked at as a general guide of sorts to help you as you begin to bring together the concepts of association and significance. However, we do want to add one note of caution. This table is meant to serve only as a general guide to interpreting tests of association and significance. Consequently, you may (and probably should) find that you do not agree with the interpretation offered in every instance.

For instance, if your findings show that the association between two variables is strong and statistically significant, you can look across the first row of the table to get some guidance in interpreting these results.

Whereas chi-square operates on the logic of the contingency table, which you've grown accustomed to through the crosstabs procedure, we're going to turn next to a test of significance based on means.

t Tests

Who do you suppose lives longer, men or women? Whichever group lives longer should, as a result, have a higher average age at any given time.

Regardless of whether you know the answer to this question for the U.S. population as a whole, let's see if our GSS data can shed some light on the issue.

We could find the average ages of men and women in our GSS sample with the simple command path:

Analyze → Compare Means → Means . . .

Because age is the characteristic on which we want to compare men and women, **AGE** is the **dependent** variable; **SEX** the **independent**.[3] Transfer those variables to the appropriate fields in the window. Then click **OK**.

Report

AGE AGE OF RESPONDENT

SEX	Mean	N	Std. Deviation
1 MALE	44.77	648	16.695
2 FEMALE	46.93	845	18.016
Total	45.99	1493	17.482

As you can see, our sample reflects the general population in that women have a mean age of 46.93, compared with the mean age of 44.77 for men. The task facing us now parallels the one pursued in the discussion of chi-square. Does the observed difference reflect a pattern that exists in the whole population, or is it simply a result of a sampling procedure that happened to get too many old

---

[3] Define the values **98** and **99** as "**missing**" for the variable **AGE**.

women and/or too many young men this time? Would another sample indicate that men are older than women or that there is no difference?

In the last section we ran Crosstabs with chi-square to estimate the statistical significance of the observed association between gender and religiosity, two nominal variables. We will not rely on crosstabs and chi-square here because our dependent variable, AGE, is an I/R item that contains many categories. Consequently, the Crosstabs procedure would produce a table that is too large and unwieldy to analyze easily. Instead we will rely on one of the most commonly used inferential statistics – *t* tests. While there are three types of t tests available on SPSS, we are going to utilize the *Independent-samples t test (two sample t test)*.

Given that we've moved very deliberately through the logic and calculations of chi-square, we are going to avoid such details in the present discussion. The *t test*, which is best suited for dependent variables at the I/R level of measurement, examines the distribution of values on one variable (AGE) among different groups (men and women - two categories of one variable SEX) and calculates the probability that the observed difference in means results from sampling error alone. As with chi-square, it is customary to use the value of .05 or less to identify a statistically significant association.

Demonstration 15.2:
Instructing SPSS to Run Independent-Samples *t* Test

To request a *t* test from SPSS to examine the relationship between AGE and SEX, you enter the following command path:

Analyze → Compare Means → Independent-Samples T Test . . .

You will notice that the drop-down menu lists the three types of t tests available on SPSS: One-Sample T Test . . . , Independent-Samples T Test. . , and Paired-Samples T Test . . . . As noted above, we are interested in the Independent-Samples T Test . . . option. After following the command path above, you should see the following screen:

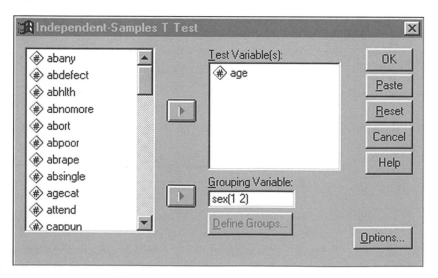

In this window, we want to enter **AGE** as the **Test Variable(s):** and **SEX** as the **Grouping Variable:**. This means that SPSS will group respondents by sex and then examine and compare the mean ages of the two gender groups.

Notice that when you enter the Grouping Variable, SPSS puts "SEX[??]" in that field. Although the comparison groups are obvious in the case of SEX, it might not be so obvious with other variables so SPSS wants some guidance. Click **Define Groups** . . .

Define Groups

- (•) Use specified values
  - Group 1: 1
  - Group 2: 2
- ( ) Cut point:

[Continue] [Cancel] [Help]

Type **1** (male) into Group 1: and **2** (female) into Group 2:. Click **Continue**, then **OK**.

Group Statistics

	SEX RESPONDENTS SEX	N	Mean	Std. Deviation	Std. Error Mean
AGE AGE OF RESPONDENT	1 MALE	648	44.77	16.695	.656
	2 FEMALE	845	46.93	18.016	.620

Independent Samples Test

		Levene's Test for Equality of Variances		t-test for Equality of Means					95% Confidence Interval of the Difference	
		F	Sig.	t	df	Sig. (2-tailed)	Mean Difference	Std. Error Difference	Lower	Upper
AGE AGE OF RESPONDENT	Equal variances assumed	6.951	.008	-2.381	1491	.018	-2.15	.911	-3.940	-.364
	Equal variances not assumed			-2.385	1438.877	.017	-2.15	.902	-3.922	-.382

Reading Your Output

The program gives you much more information than you need for the present purposes, so let's identify the key elements. Some of the information is a repeat of what we got earlier from the Means command: means, standard deviations, and standard errors for men and women.

In the Group Statistics box under Mean, for example, we see once again that the average age is 44.77 for men and 46.93 for women.

The results regarding significance that we are most interested in now are given in the box below labeled "Independent Samples Test," under the heading "t- test for Equality of Means." If you look there under the subheading "Sig. (2-tailed)," in the top row labeled Equal variances assumed, you will see the probability we are looking for: .018.

As you will anticipate, .018 in this context indicates a probability of 18 in 1,000. The "2-tailed" notation requires just a little more explanation.

In our sample, the average age for women is 2.16 years higher than for men (46.93 – 44.77). SPSS has calculated that about 18 times in 1,000 samples, sampling error might produce a difference this great in either direction. That is, if the average

age of men and the average age of women in the population were exactly the same, and we were to select 1,000 samples like this one, we could expect 18 of those samples to show women at least 2.16 years older than men or men as much as 2.16 years older than women.

When you don't have theoretical reasons to anticipate a particular relationship, it is appropriate for you to use the "2-tailed" probability in evaluating differences in means like these. In some cases—when you have deduced specific expectations from a theory, for example—you might come to the data analysis with a hypothesis that "women are older than men." In such a case, it might be more appropriate to note that there is a probability of 9 in 1,000 (p = .009) that sampling error would have resulted in women being as much as 2.16 years older than men. For our purposes, however, we'll stick with the 2-tailed test.

SPSS Command 15.2: Running *t* Test (Independent Samples *t* Test)

Click **Analyze → Compare Means → Independent-Samples T Test . . . →**

Highlight **test variable** in variable list →

Click **arrow** pointing to the **Test Variable(s):** box →

Highlight name of **grouping variable** in variable list →

Click **arrow** pointing to the **Grouping Variable:** box →

Click **Define Groups . . . →** Define **Group 1:** and **Group 2: →**

Continue → OK

Demonstration 15.3: *t* Test—EDUC by SEX

Some of the variables in your GSS data set allow you to explore this issue further. For example, it would be reasonable for better-educated workers to earn more than poorly educated workers, so if the men in our sample have more education than the women, that might explain the difference in pay. Let's see.

Return to the **T Test window** and substitute **EDUC** for AGE as the Test Variable(s):[4] Leave "SEX[1 2]" as the Grouping Variable:. Run the new *t* test.

Group Statistics

	SEX RESPONDENTS SEX	N	Mean	Std. Deviation	Std. Error Mean
EDUC HIGHEST YEAR OF SCHOOL COMPLETED	1 MALE	652	13.54	3.051	.119
	2 FEMALE	844	13.10	2.585	.089

Independent Samples Test

		Levene's Test for Equality of Variances		t-test for Equality of Means						95% Confidence Interval of the Difference	
		F	Sig.	t	df	Sig. (2-tailed)	Mean Difference	Std. Error Difference	Lower	Upper
EDUC HIGHEST YEAR OF SCHOOL COMPLETED	Equal variances assumed	20.421	.000	2.995	1494	.003	.44	.146	.151	.723
	Equal variances not assumed			2.933	1271.417	.003	.44	.149	.145	.729

---

[4] Define the values **97, 98,** and **99** as **"missing"** for the variable **EDUC.**

What conclusion do you draw from these latest results? Notice first that the men and women in our sample have very similar mean number of years of education (men = 13.54, women = 13.10). The difference is very small, and it is one we could expect to find in 3 of 1,000 samples.

With such a small difference between men's and women's educational backgrounds, it is unlikely that education can be used as a "legitimate reason" for women earning less than men. That's not to say that there aren't other legitimate reasons that may account for the difference in pay. For instance, it is often argued that women tend to concentrate in less prestigious jobs than men: nurses rather than doctors, secretaries rather than executives, teachers rather than principals. Leaving aside the reasons for such occupational differences, that might account for the differences in pay. As you may recall, your GSS data contain a measure of socioeconomic status (SEI). We used that variable in our experimentation with Correlations. Let's see if the women in our sample have lower-status jobs, on average, than the men.

Demonstration 15.4: *t* Test—SEI by SEX

Go back to the **T Test window** and replace EDUC with **SEI**. Run the procedure, and you should get the following result.

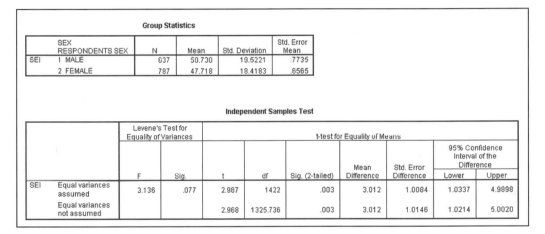

Group Statistics

SEX RESPONDENTS SEX		N	Mean	Std. Deviation	Std. Error Mean
SEI	1 MALE	637	50.730	19.5221	.7735
	2 FEMALE	787	47.718	18.4183	.6565

Independent Samples Test

		Levene's Test for Equality of Variances		t-test for Equality of Means					95% Confidence Interval of the Difference	
		F	Sig.	t	df	Sig. (2-tailed)	Mean Difference	Std. Error Difference	Lower	Upper
SEI	Equal variances assumed	3.136	.077	2.987	1422	.003	3.012	1.0084	1.0337	4.9898
	Equal variances not assumed			2.968	1325.736	.003	3.012	1.0146	1.0214	5.0020

The mean difference in occupational prestige ratings of men and women is 3.012 on a scale from 0 to 100. SPSS tells us that such a difference could be expected just as a consequence of sampling error in only about 3 samples in 1,000 (p = .003). How would you interpret this finding? Do you think this difference is statistically significant enough to have any social significance?

Writing Box 15.2

Our comparison of mean scores on occupational prestige (*p* = .003) suggests the observed difference probably exists in the whole population, rather than being a fluke of sampling error. At the same time, it suggests the gap (3.012) separating men and women in this instance is not that great.

To pursue this line of inquiry further, you will need additional analytic skills that will be covered shortly in the discussion of multivariate analysis.

Analysis of Variance

The *t* test is limited to the comparison of two groups at a time (for example, male and female). If we wanted to compare the levels of education of different religious groups, we'd have to compare Protestants and Catholics, Protestants and Jews, Catholics and Jews, and so forth. And if some of the comparisons found significant differences and other comparisons did not, we'd be hard pressed to reach an overall conclusion about the nature of the relationship between the two variables.

The *analysis of variance* (*ANOVA*) is a technique that resolves the shortcoming of the *t* test. It examines the means of subgroups in the sample and analyzes the variances as well. That is, it examines more than whether the actual values are clustered around the mean or spread out from it.

If we were to ask ANOVA to examine the relationship between RELIG and EDUC, it would determine the mean years of education for each of the different religious groups, noting how they differed from one another. Those "between-group" differences would be compared with the "within-group" differences (variance): how much Protestants differed among themselves, for example. Both sets of comparisons are reconciled by ANOVA to calculate the likelihood that the observed differences are merely the result of sampling error.

Demonstration 15.5: Instructing SPSS to Run ANOVA

To get a clearer picture of ANOVA, ask SPSS to perform the analysis we've been discussing. You can probably figure out how to do that, but here's a hint.

Analyze → General Linear Model → Univariate . . .[5]

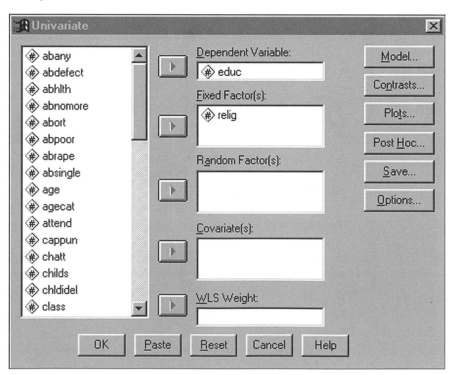

---

[5] If you have used earlier versions of SPSS you may notice a difference here. The simple factorial ANOVA procedure has been replaced with the GLM univariate procedure (General Factorial). This allows for ANOVA tables but does not require a defined range of factor variables.

Put **EDUC** into the **Dependent Variable:** field and **RELIG** in the **Fixed Factor(s):** field. Next, open the Univariate Options box by clicking on the **Options** button.

Put a check mark next to **Homogeneity tests** by clicking the empty box. Then click **Continue** and **OK** to run the analysis.

Levene's Test of Equality of Error Variances[a]

Dependent Variable: EDUC HIGHEST YEAR OF SCHOOL COMPLETED

F	df1	df2	Sig.
2.577	3	1409	.052

Tests the null hypothesis that the error variance of the dependent variable is equal across groups.

a. Design: Intercept+RELIG

Tests of Between-Subjects Effects

Dependent Variable: EDUC HIGHEST YEAR OF SCHOOL COMPLETED

Source	Type III Sum of Squares	df	Mean Square	F	Sig.
Corrected Model	143.106[a]	3	47.702	6.281	.000
Intercept	72406.109	1	72406.109	9533.971	.000
RELIG	143.106	3	47.702	6.281	.000
Error	10700.704	1409	7.595		
Total	258960.000	1413			
Corrected Total	10843.810	1412			

a. R Squared = .013 (Adjusted R Squared = .011)

Reading Your Output

Here's the SPSS report on the analysis. Again, we've gotten more information than we want for our present purposes.

The first table, "Levene's Test of Error Variances," tests whether or not the variances between the groups are the same. In our table, we are checking to see if the variability in education is the same for each of the categories of religion. If they differed significantly in variability, then our test of differences in means could be distorted by variability between the groups rather then differences between the means. The Levene statistic tests for equal amounts of variation within the groups. If they are significantly different, the ANOVA should not be used. We know significance level of the Levene test by looking at the probability labeled "Sig." on the table. If the significance level is .05 or less, the variances are considered significantly different and the ANOVA test should not be used. If the significance level is greater than .05, the variances are considered equal and the ANOVA can be used. In our example, the significance level is .052, just barely above the criteria required to consider the variances equal.

Once the variances are determined to be equal, we can proceed to the table titled "Tests of Between-Subjects Effects" and simply look at the row titled Corrected Model. This refers to the amount of variance in EDUC that can be explained by variations in RELIG. Because our present purpose is to learn about tests of statistical significance, let's move across the row to the statistical significance of the explained variance. You can see that the value listed here is .000. This means that if religion and education were unrelated to each other in the population, we might expect samples that would generate this amount of explained variance less than once in 1,000 samples.

Perhaps you will find it useful to think of ANOVA as something like a statistical broom. We began by noting a lot of variance in educational levels of our respondents; imagine people's educations spread all over the place. In an attempt to find explanatory patterns in that variance, we use ANOVA to sweep the respondents into subgroups based on religious affiliation (stay with us on this). The questions are whether variations in education are substantially less within each of the piles than we originally observed in the whole sample, and whether the mean years of education in each of the subgroups are quite different from one another. Imagine a set of tidy piles that are quite distant from one another. ANOVA provides a statistical test of this imagery.

SPSS Command 15.3: ANOVA (GLM Univariate)

Click **Analyze** → **General Linear Model** → **Univariate** . . . →

Highlight **dependent variable** → Click **arrow** pointing to **Dependent Variable:** field →

Highlight **factor variable** → Click **arrow** pointing to **Fixed Factor(s):** field →

Click **Options** → check **box** next to **Homogeneity tests** → **Continue** → **OK**

It is also possible for ANOVA to consider two or more independent variables, but that goes beyond the scope of this book. We have introduced you to ANOVA

Table 15.2   A Statistical Toolbox

Statistics for Measuring:	Level of Measurement		
	Nominal	Ordinal	I/R
DESCRIPTIVE STATISICS			
Central Tendency	**MODE**	**MEDIAN**	**MEAN**
Dispersion		**RANGE**	**VARIANCE**
		Interquartile Range	**STANDARD DEVIATION**
Association	**LAMBDA**	**GAMMA**	r^2
(PRE and non-PRE)	Cramer's V	Somer's D	Pearson's r
	Phi	Tau B	beta
	Contingency Coefficient		
INFERENTIAL STATISTICS			
Tests of Significance	**CHI-SQUARE**	**CHI-SQUARE**	**INDEPENDENT SAMPLES t TEST ANOVA**

because we feel it is useful, and we wanted to open up for you the possibility of your using this popular technique; however, you will need more specialized training in the performance of analysis of variance to use it effectively.

A Statistical Toolbox: A Summary

As we near the end of our discussion of bivariate analysis, we think it may be useful as a review and summary of sorts, to provide you with a table listing descriptive and inferential statistics by their appropriate level of measurement.

You will note that those statistics we reviewed in depth are listed in bold. In addition, we included a few references to some basic statistics we did not cover, but which you may find useful as you pursue your own research.

Please keep in mind that this table is not exhaustive. It references only a few of the many statistics social researchers find useful when working with items at various levels of measurement.

Conclusion

This chapter has taken on the difficult question of whether the observed relationship between two variables is important or not. It is natural that you would want to know whether and when you have discovered something worth writing home about. No one wants to shout, "Look what I've discovered!" and have others say, "That's no big thing."

Ultimately, there is no simple test of the substantive significance of a relationship between variables. If we found that women earn less than men, who can say if that amounts to a lot less or just a little bit less? In a more precise study, we could calculate exactly how much less in dollars, but we would still not be in a position to say absolutely whether that amount was a lot or a little. If women made a dollar a year less than men on the average, we'd all probably agree that was not an important difference. If men earned a hundred times as much as women, on the other hand, we'd probably all agree that was a big difference. However, few of the differences we discover in social science research are that dramatic.

In this chapter, we've examined a very specific approach that social scientists often take in addressing the issue of significance. As distinct from notions of *substantive* significance, we have examined *statistical* significance. In each of the measures we've examined—chi-square, *t* test, and analysis of variance – we've asked how likely it would be that sampling error could produce the observed relationship if there were actually no relationship in the population from which the sample was drawn.

This assumption of "no relationship" is sometimes referred to as the **null hypothesis**. The tests of significance we've examined all deal with the probability that the null hypothesis is correct. If the probability is relatively high, we conclude that there is no relationship between the two variables under study in the whole population. If the probability is small that the null hypothesis could be true, then we conclude that the observed relationship reflects a genuine pattern in the population.

Main Points

- In this chapter we introduced tests of statistical significance.
- As opposed to measures of association that focus on the strength and direction of the relationship, tests of significance allow us to estimate whether the relationship can be considered statistically significant.
- Statistical significance generally refers to the likelihood that an observed relationship between variables in a sample could have occurred as a result of chance or sampling error.
- Tests of significance also allow you to determine whether or not an observed association between items in a sample is likely to exist in the population.
- In this chapter we moved from focusing primarily on descriptive statistics to inferential statistics.
- The three tests of significance we reviewed are part of the larger body of inferential statistics: chi-square, *t* tests, and ANOVA.
- Chi-square is most appropriate for nominal variables, although it can be used with ordinal variables.
- Traditionally, a chi-square with a probability of .05 or less is considered significant.
- The *t* test is most appropriate if the dependent variable is at the I/R level of measurement.
- ANOVA builds on the shortcomings of the t test.
- There is an important difference between substantive and statistical significance.

Key Terms

Statistical significance

Substantive significance

Inferential statistics

Independent samples *t* Test

Descriptive statistics

(two sample *t* test)

Sampling error

t test

Chi-square

Analysis of variance (ANOVA)

Goodness of fit

Null hypothesis

Degrees of freedom (*df*)

SPSS Commands Introduced in This Chapter

15.1 Producing Crosstabs with Chi-Square

15.2 Running *t* Test (Independent Samples *t* Test)

15.3 ANOVA (GLM Univariate)

Review Questions

1. What does the term statistical significance mean?

2. If you are interested in estimating the strength of association between variables, would you rely on tests of significance or measures of association?

3. If you are interested in determining whether or not an observed relationship between variables in your sample is likely to exist in the population, would you rely on tests of significance or measures of association?

4. What are inferential statistics?

5. How do they differ from descriptive statistics?

6. Chi-square is considered appropriate for variables at what level of measurement?

7. Chi-square is based on a comparison of _____ frequencies and _____ frequencies.

8. If a chi-square has a probability level greater than .05, is it generally considered significant by traditional social science standards?

9. Would a chi-square with a probability of .01 be considered significant by traditional social science standards?

10. Would we have more confidence if an association was significant at the .05 or .001 level?

11. The *t* test is considered appropriate if your dependent variable is at what level of measurement?

12. Does the *t* test allow us to determine whether the means, the variances, or both the means and variances of two groups are statistically different from each other?

13. How does ANOVA resolve the shortcomings of the t test? Explain.

14. Does ANOVA examine the means, variances, or both the means and variances of subgroups in a sample?

15. In this chapter we have focused primarily on statistical significance. How does this differ from substantive significance?

NAME _____

CLASS _____

INSTRUCTOR _____

DATE _____

To complete the following exercises you need to load the data file EXERPLUS. You will find answers to Questions 2-15, 17-18 in Appendix B.

1. Define the values 0, 8, and 9 as "missing" for AFFRMACT. Then recode AFFRMACT as follows to create a new variable AFFREC. When you have done that, be sure to set the decimal places for AFFREC to "0" and add value labels.

Old Values	New Values	New Value Labels
1 - 2	→ 1	Support
3 - 4	→ 2	Oppose
System or user-missing	→ System-missing	

Run Crosstabs listing RACE and SEX as the independent variables and AFFREC as the dependent variable. Request column percentages and chi-square. Then answer Questions 2-8.

2. Record the percentage of respondents who said they "Support" preferences (AFFREC) for each independent variable (RACE and SEX).

	White	Black	Other	Chi-Square Asymp. Sig.
Percentage Support	_____	_____	_____	_____

	Male	Female	Chi-Square Asymp. Sig.
Percentage Support	_____	_____	_____

3. (RACE) Do the percentages change or move, signifying a relationship between RACE and AFFREC? Explain how you know.

4. (RACE) What is the significance of chi-square? Is it less than, equal to, or more than .05?

5. (RACE) Is the relationship between RACE and AFFREC statistically significant?

6. (SEX) Do the percentages change or move, signifying a relationship between SEX and AFFREC? Explain how you know.

7. (SEX) What is the significance of chi-square? Is it less than, equal to, or more than .05?

8. (SEX) Is the relationship between SEX and AFFREC statistically significant?

Run the t test, specifying AGE, SEI, and EDUC as the Test Variables and RACE as the Grouping Variable.[6] Keep in mind that you will have to ask SPSS to limit the comparison to Whites and Blacks, omitting the "Other" category. Once you have run the procedure, complete Questions 9-16.

9. Fill in the blanks with the appropriate information.

		RACE	
		White	Black
AGE			
	Mean	_____	_____
	Sig. (2-Tailed)	_____	
EDUC			
	Mean	_____	_____
	Sig. (2-Tailed)	_____	

---

[6] Insure that the following values for each variable are defined as "missing": AGE – 0, 98, 99; EDUC – 97, 98, 99; SEI - .0, 99.8, 99.9.

NAME _____

CLASS _____

INSTRUCTOR _____

DATE _____

SEI

Mean   _____   _____

Sig.

(2-Tailed)   _____

10. (AGE) Is the mean age of Whites higher than, lower than, or the same as Blacks?

11. (AGE) Is the difference significant? Why or why not? Explain.

12. (EDUC) Is the mean education of Whites higher than, lower than, or the same as Blacks?

13. (EDUC) Is the difference significant? Why or why not? Explain.

14. (SEI) Is the mean SEI of Whites higher than, lower than, or the same as Blacks?

15. (SEI) Is the difference significant? Why or why not? Explain.

16. On the basis of these results, what conclusions if any can you draw about racial inequality in the United States in 2000? How much inequality is there? Is there inequality in education, the work force, or both? Do your data indicate that Whites have a higher average age, suggesting that they live longer? What if anything does this say about racial inequality today?

NAME _____

CLASS _____

INSTRUCTOR _____

DATE _____

Define the following values as missing for the variable CLASS: 0, 5, 8, and 9. Then run ANOVA, putting EDUC in the Dependent Variable: field and CLASS in the Fixed Factor(s): field.

17. What is the significance level of the Levene test and does it meet the criteria required to consider the variances equal?

18. Based on your findings, is it appropriate to use ANOVA in this case?

19. Run ANOVA, putting AGE in the Dependent Variable: field and CLASS in the Fixed Factor(s): field. Summarize your findings below.

Chapter 16 Suggestions for Further Bivariate Analyses

By now, you've amassed a powerful set of analytic tools. In a world where people make casual assertions about sociological topics, you're now in a position to determine the facts. You can determine how the U.S. population feels about a variety of topics, and with your new bivariate skills, you can begin to explain why they feel as they do.

Remember, in Chapters 11-15 we introduced you to a number of techniques that make this type of analyses possible, including: Crosstabs (Chapters 11-13), Measures of association – lambda, gamma, Pearson's r, regression (Chapter 14), and Tests of Significance – Chi-square, *t*-test, ANOVA (Chapter 15). Our goal in this chapter is to encourage you to use these techniques to explore some of the other variables contained on your data files.

To get you started, we are going to suggest some analyses you might undertake. In Chapter 10, we suggested some topics, drawn from the items on your DEMOPLUS file, which you might pursue with the techniques of univariate analysis. Let's start by returning to those topics.

Demonstration 16.1: Desired Family Size

Your **DEMOPLUS** file contains the variable CHLDIDEL, which asked respondents what they considered the ideal number of children for a family. A little more than half of the respondents said that two was best. Because that is also the number of children that would represent population stabilization, you might want to begin by recoding this variable to create two response categories. If you are having difficulty with this, here is a "hint" to point you in the right direction:

Select **Transform → Recode → Into Different Variables . . .**

Then recode CHLDIDEL to create a new variable CHLDNUM with the following values and labels:[1]

---

[1] Before proceeding, define the following values as "missing" for CHLDIDEL: -1, and 9.

CHLDIDEL Old Values	NEW VARIABLE New Values	CHLDNUM Label
0 through 2	1	0-2
3 through 8	2	3 or more

Once you've recoded **CHLDIDEL** into the more manageable variable **CHLDNUM**, you can use some of the bivariate techniques you learned to examine the causes of differences. As a start, for instance, you might want to see if the variables we examined in relation to abortion attitudes are related to opinions about ideal family size.

We found that gender was basically unrelated to abortion attitudes. How about ideal family size? Do you think men and women differ in their images of the perfect family? If you think so, in which direction do you think that difference goes?

How about age? Support for small families is a fairly recent development in the United States, against a historical backdrop of large farm families. Does this mean that young people would be more supportive of small families than older people? You find out.

The better-educated members of the population are generally more concerned about environmental issues. Are they also more committed to small families?

Religion and race are good candidates for shaping opinions about ideal family size because the nature of family life is often central to subcultural patterns. We saw that Catholics and Protestants were resistant to abortion. How do they feel about limiting family size in general? You can know the answer in a matter of minutes.

Several family variables may very well relate to attitudes toward ideal family size. Marital status and whether respondents have ever been divorced might be relevant. Can you see why that would be worth exploring? What would you hypothesize?

Of possibly direct relevance, the data set contains SIBS (the number of brothers and sisters the respondent has). You might want to see if the experience of having brothers and sisters has any impact on opinions about what's best in family size.

Once you have explored one or more of these possibilities, take a moment to describe your findings in a few sentences or paragraphs.

In Writing Box 16.1 we provide you with an example of how a social scientist examining the relationship between ideal family size (**CHLDNUM**) and church attendance (**CHATT**) might describe her findings in prose. We created CHATT, recoded church attendance, in Chapter 6. CHATT should be saved on your DEMOPLUS.SAV file.

Take a moment to consider which measure of association and test of statistical significance is appropriate in this case. If you have trouble making this determination, refer back to the discussion in Chapters 14 and 15.

Now that you have done the hard work, you are ready to determine if there is a relationship between religious affiliation and ideal family size. After you have completed your analysis and written a short description of your findings, compare it to the discussion in Writing Box 16.1.

Writing Box 16.1

The relationship between the number of children people have and their church attendance appears significant (< .001), whether measured by chi-square or gamma. Moreover, the gamma (−.232) points to a negative relationship as the variables are coded. However, since the higher scores on CHATT represent less frequent attendance at worship services, the ultimate interpretation is that church attendance increases with the number of children: the more children, the more frequent attendance.

If you would like to explore the issue of ideal family size further, you might want to read Judith Blake's *Family Size and Achievement*.

Child Training

In Chapter 10, we took an initial look at different opinions about what was important in the development of children. The key variables were as follows:

OBEY	to obey
POPULAR	to be well-liked or popular
THNKSELF	to think for himself or herself
WORKHARD	to work hard
HELPOTH	to help others when they need help

If you examined these variables, you discovered some real differences in how people want their children to turn out. Now let's see what causes those differences, because opinions on this topic can reflect some more general attitudes and worldviews.

Once again, such demographic variables as sex, age, race, and religion might make a difference. OBEY, for example, reflects a certain authoritarian leaning. Perhaps it is related to political variables, such as PARTYID and POLVIEWS; perhaps not. There's only one way to find out.

HELPOTH measures an altruistic dimension. That's something religions often encourage. Maybe there's a relation between this variable and some of the religion variables.

Also consider the variable THNKSELF, which values children's learning to think for themselves. What would you expect to influence this? Education, perhaps? How about age and sex? Do you think older respondents would be relatively cool to children thinking for themselves? Would men or women be more supportive? Don't rule out religious and political variables. Some of these results are likely to confirm your expectations; some are not.

When it comes to the value of children thinking for themselves, you may find some of the other attitudinal variables in the GSS data set worth looking at. Consider those who have told us they are permissive on premarital sex and homosexuality. Do you think they would be more or less likely to value children's learning to think for themselves?

There are any number of directions you might want to pursue in looking for the causes of different attitudes toward the qualities most valued for children. For more ideas in this arena, you might want to look at Duane Alwin's *Changes in Qualities Valued in Children* (1989).

Attitudes About Sexual Behavior

You may want to focus on the three sexual variables. What do you suppose would cause differences of opinion regarding premarital sexual relations and homosexuality? What do you suppose determines who goes to X-rated movies? You have the ability and the tools to find out for yourself.

Near the end of the movie *Casablanca*, the police chief instructs his officers to "round up the usual suspects." You might do well to round up the usual demographic variables as a way of beginning your examination of sexual attitudes: age, gender, race, religion, education, social class, and marital status, for example.

Before examining each of these relationships, take some time to think about any links you might logically expect. Should men or women be more permissive about homosexuality? Should married, single, or divorced people be more supportive of premarital sex? How do you expect young and old people to differ?

As you investigate these attitudes, be careful about assuming that the three items are just different dimensions of the same orientation. The kinds of people who are permissive about premarital sex are not necessarily the same ones who are permissive about homosexuality.

Demonstration 16.2:
Investigating Sexual Permissiveness Further

Another possibility is to use the index of sexual permissiveness (SEXPERM) we created in Chapter 10 to explore why some people are more permissive when it comes to attitudes toward sex than others.

Writing Box 16.2 contains an example of how a social scientist examining this issue might convey his findings in prose. In this case, we examined the possibility that two basic demographic variables may be related to sexual permissiveness: AGE (as represented by the recoded variable AGECAT) and SEX. After making sure to define appropriate values for each variable as missing, determine which measure of association and test of statistical significance is appropriate to examine the relationship between SEXPERM, AGECAT, and SEX. After exploring the relationship between these variables, take some time to describe your findings in prose. Then compare your analysis to the short description in Writing Box 16.2 that follows.

Writing Box 16.2

The relationship between gender (SEX) and sexual permissiveness (SEXPERM) is neither strong nor significant when measured by lambda (.015) and chi-square. Consequently, knowing a person's gender will not help you predict whether they are permissive.

To the contrary, however, a person's age is related to how permissive they are. The relationship between AGECAT and SEXPERM is significant when measured chi-square ($p = < .001$). Moreover, the gamma (−.311) indicates a negative relationship between the variables: older people are less likely to be permissive than younger people.

If you are interested in exploring this topic further, you may want to consult Tom Smith's *The Polls: A Report: The Sexual Revolution?* (1990) or Kaye Wellings et al.'s *Sexual Attitudes* (1994).

Prejudice

At least two items in your DEMOPLUS file address different aspects of racial prejudice about African-Americans. RACMAR measures respondents' attitudes toward the legality of interracial marriage, whereas RACPUSH measures attitudes toward Black-White relations.

Certainly, RACE is the most obvious variable to examine, and you probably won't be surprised at what you find. Don't stop there, however. There are other variables that provide even more dramatic relationships.

Education, politics, and social class offer fruitful avenues for understanding the roots of attitudes on these variables. You may be surprised by the impact of religious variables.

As a different approach, you might look at the opinion that homosexuality is morally wrong, as is prejudice against gays and lesbians. It's worth checking whether responses to that item are related to prejudice against African Americans.

To get a sense of how other researchers have explored racial prejudice, you may want to see Edward Carmines et al.'s *The Changing Content of American Racial Attitudes: A Fifty Year Portrait* (1990) or Howard Schuman et al.'s *Racial Attitudes in America: Trends and Interpretations* (1985).

Additional Resources

Throughout the chapter we recommended some sources you may want to consult if you are interested in pursuing one of these topics further. In addition, the National Opinion Research Center (NORC) maintains a web site that not only has a complete Codebook for the General Social Survey (1972-2000), but a fairly extensive bibliography. This is a particularly useful resource if you want to identify studies, reports, books, and articles that use the GSS variables you are working with.

You can access the site at http://www.icpsr.umich.edu/GSS. From here you have several options. You may, for instance, search the reference section directly by clicking "Bibliography." This, however, may not be particularly useful unless you know exactly what you are looking for.

A better alternative may be to search by either Subject or Mnemonic (an index of abbreviated variable names). For example, if you are interested in pursuing the subject of "Child Training" further. Simply access the NORC site, then click Subject → C (for Children) Children → Abbreviated Variable Name → OBEY (for instance, or any of the other abbreviated variables names pertaining to Child Training) → Links.

If you scroll toward the bottom of the screen you will see a fairly extensive bibliography referencing studies, articles, reports, and books pertaining to "Child Training" in general (and the variable OBEY in particular).

If you wish to search an abbreviated variable name directly, once you access the site, click on Mnemonic → O (for OBEY) → OBEY → Links. Once again, if you scroll to the bottom of your screen you will see a Bibliography of studies which pertain to Child Training and utilize the variable OBEY.

Conclusion

The preceding suggestions should be enough to keep you busy, but you shouldn't feel limited by them. The most fruitful guides to your analyses should be your own personal interests. Consequently, while we have focused our suggestions on the DEMO.SAV (or DEMPLUS) file(s), we encourage you to explore the EXER.SAV (or EXERPLUS) file(s) as well. Keep in mind the EXER.SAV file contains a number of additional variables, covering issues such as environment, mass media use, national government spending priorities, sex roles, law enforcement, teen sex, and equalization. Think about what topics from either the DEMO.SAV file or the EXER.SAV file interest or concern you. Now you have a chance to learn something about them on your own. You don't have to settle for polemical statements about "the way things are." You now have the tools you need to find out for yourself.

In examining these bivariate relationships, you may want to begin with Crosstabs, because that technique gives you the most detailed view of the data. At the same time, you should use this exercise as an opportunity to experiment with the other bivariate techniques we've examined. Try chi-squares where appropriate, for example. As you find interesting relationships between variables, you may want to test their statistical significance to get another view of what they mean.

What you've learned so far may be sufficient for most of your day-to-day curiosities. Now you can learn what public opinion really is on a given topic, and you can determine what kinds of people hold differing views on that topic. In the remaining chapters of this book, however, we are going to show you an approach to understanding that goes much deeper. As we introduce you to multivariate analysis, you're going to have an opportunity to sample a more complex mode of understanding than most people are even aware of.

Main Points

- Now that you are capable of describing both what Americans think about a variety of issues and why, we suggest some additional bivariate analyses for you to pursue on your own.
- We focus specifically on four topics drawn from the items in your DEMO.SAV file as examples of the types of investigations you may want to pursue: desired family size, child training, attitudes about sexual behavior, and prejudice.
- Don't be limited by these suggestions, however. Pursue topics and issues that interest or concern you. After all, this is your adventure.
- Keep in mind that your DEMO.SAV and EXER.SAV files each contain more than forty GSS items covering a number of important and controversial issues and topics in American life.
- When pursuing relations between two variables, you should begin with Crosstabs, then experiment with the other techniques we reviewed in this section, including measures of association and tests of statistical significance.

Key Terms

No new terms were introduced in this chapter.

SPSS Commands Introduced in This Chapter

No new commands were introduced in this chapter.

Review Questions

Discuss how you might apply the techniques and procedures we covered in Part IV (Chapters 11-16) on bivariate analysis (i.e., crosstabs, measures of association, and tests of statistical significance) to examine the following topics.

1. Desired family size

2. Child training

3. Attitudes toward sexual behavior

4. Prejudice

NAME _____

CLASS _____

INSTRUCTOR _____

DATE _____

In Lab Exercise 10.1 we asked you to use univariate techniques to examine one of the topics from your EXERPLUS file in more depth: sex roles, law enforcement, environment, mass media (use and confidence), national government spending priorities, teen sex, affirmative action, or equalization.

In this Exercise you will be given an opportunity to expand your analysis of this issue by applying some of the bivaraite techniques discussed in Chapters 11-15.

1. List the general topic/issue you examined in Lab Exercise 10.1.

2. List the variables in your EXERPLUS file that pertain to this topic/issue?

3. In Lab Exercise 10.1 (Question 7), did you either RECODE or create an INDEX based on any of the variables you were working with? If so, list the abbreviated variable name(s) below.

4. Choose one of the variables listed in response to Questions 2 and/or 3 above. Make sure it is an item that you are interested in examining further and list it in the space below.

   Dependent variable_____

5. List the names of two other items (independent variables) from the DEMOPLUS file which you think may be causally related to or associated with your dependent variable.

Independent variable 1 _____

Independent variable 2 _____

6. Write two hypotheses linking your dependent (Question 4) and independent variables (Question 5).

Hypothesis 1:

List the dependent variable in Hypothesis 1 _____

List the independent variable in Hypothesis 1 _____

Hypothesis 2:

NAME _____

CLASS _____

INSTRUCTOR _____

DATE _____

List the dependent variable in Hypothesis 2_____

List the independent variable in Hypothesis 2_____

7. From the list of bivariate techniques below, circle the procedures that are appropriate for examining the relationship in Hypothesis 1 (Question 6) further. [Hint: you should circle at least one technique in each "group" (A) Chapters 11-13; (B) Chapter 14; (C) Chapter 15]

   (A) Chapters 11-13: Crosstabs
         Crosstabs
   (B) Chapter 14: Measures of Association
         Lambda
         Gamma
         Correlation Matrix with Pearson's r
         Regression
         Scatterplot with Regression Line
   (C) Chapter 15: Tests of Significance
         Chi-square
         t-Test
         ANOVA

8. From the list of bivariate techniques reviewed in Chapters 11-15, circle the procedures that are appropriate for examining the relationship in Hypothesis 2 (Question 6) further. [Hint: you should circle at least one technique in each "group" (A) Chapters 11-13; (B) Chapter 14; (C) Chapter 15]

   (A) Chapters 11-13: Crosstabs
         Crosstabs
   (B) Chapter 14: Measures of Association
         Lambda
         Gamma
         Correlation Matrix with Pearson's r
         Regression
         Scatterplot with Regression Line
   (C) Chapter 15: Tests of Significance
         Chi-square
         t-Test
         ANOVA

9. Now use the techniques you identified as appropriate in response to Question 7 to examine the relationship between the variables in Hypothesis 1. After you have completed your analysis:

- Print and attach a copy of your output to this sheet
- Summarize your findings in prose below.

10. Now use the techniques you identified as appropriate in response to Question 8 to examine the relationship between the variables in Hypothesis 2. After you have completed your analysis:

- Print and attach a copy of your output to this sheet
- Summarize your findings in prose below

NAME _____

CLASS _____

INSTRUCTOR _____

DATE _____

Part V Multivariate Analysis

Now that you've mastered the logic and techniques of bivariate analysis, we are going to take you one step further: to the examination of three or more variables at a time, known as ***multivariate analysis***.

In Chapter 17, we'll delve more deeply into religious orientations to gain a more comprehensive understanding of this variable. Chapter 18 will pick up some loose threads of our bivariate analysis and pursue them further with our new analytic capability.

In Chapter 19, we will set as our purpose the prediction of attitudes toward abortion. We'll progress, step-by-step, through a number of variables previously found to have an impact on abortion attitudes, and we'll accumulate them in a composite measure that will offer a powerful predictor of opinions.

Finally, Chapter 20 launches you into uncharted areas of social research, which you should now be empowered to chart for yourself.

Chapter 17 **Multiple Causation**

Examining Religiosity in Greater Depth

In the last section we focused primarily on the relationship between two variables: a single independent and a single dependent variable. If we continued to limit ourselves solely to the examination of two variables at a time, our understanding of the social world would remain incomplete, not to mention dissatisfying. Bivariate analysis alone cannot help us understand the social world, because in the "real world" two or more factors often have an impact on, influence, or cause variation in a single dependent variable. Consequently, to understand the complexities of the social world, we need to introduce a more sophisticated form of statistical analysis that allows us to examine the impact of more than one independent variable on a single dependent variable.

Social scientists refer to this type of analysis as *multivariate analysis*, the *simultaneous* analysis of three or more variables. Multivariate analysis is the next step beyond bivariate analysis. By helping us move beyond the limitations of unviariate and bivariate analysis, it allows us to develop a more complete understanding of the complexities of the social world.

We are going to begin our introduction to multivariate analysis by looking at the simplest of outcomes, multiple causation.

Multiple Causation

In Chapter 11, we discussed several variables that might affect the levels of respondents' religiosity. Women, we found, were more religious than men. Older people were more religious than younger people.

It is often the case with social phenomena that people's attitudes and behaviors are affected by more than one factor. It is the task of the social scientist, then, to discover all those factors that influence the dependent variable under question and discover how those factors work together to produce a result. If both age and gender affect religiosity independently, perhaps a combination of the two would predict it even better.

Demonstration 17.1:
The Impact of Age and Sex on Religiosity

To begin our multivariate analysis, let's see how well we can predict religiosity if we consider AGE and SEX simultaneously. Does religiosity increase with age among both men and women separately? Moreover, do the two variables have a cumulative effect on religiosity? That is, are older women the most religious and younger men the least?

To being our exploration of this topic, let's open our **DEMOPLUS.SAV** file and access the **Crosstabs** dialog box. In this case, we want to use **CHATT** as the **dependent/row** variable, and **AGECAT** (recoded AGE) as the **independent/ column** variable.

Now select **SEX** in the list of variables. Notice that the arrows activated would let you transfer SEX to the row or column fields — but don't do that! Instead, transfer it to the third field, near the bottom of the window.[1]

---

[1] This SPSS procedure is sometime referred to as *controlling for a third variable*, and often used to elaborate on bivariate relationships. *Elaboration* is a technique that helps us examine the relationship between two variables (an independent and dependent) while controlling for a third variable. In this example, for instance, we specified CHATT as our dependent variable, AGECAT as our independent variable, and SEX as our *control* or *third variable*. This will allow us to examine the relationship between church attendance and age, while controlling for sex. Consequently, our output will be two tables: one showing the relationship between CHATT and AGECAT for men, and the other showing the relationship between CHATT and AGECAT for women. While the elaboration model is beyond the scope of this text, for a complete discussion of this technique see Chapter 16 of Earl Babbie's *The Practice of Social Research* 9th ed. (Belmont, CA: Wadsworth, 2001).

We have now told SPSS to examine the relationship between AGECAT and CHATT while controlling for SEX. The result of this simple act is that now we will get two crosstabs, one showing the relationship between AGECAT and CHATT for men; and another showing the association between AGECAT and CHATT for women.

Now all you need to do before executing the command is make sure that cells are percentaged by columns execute the command [i.e. click **Cell** ... → **Columns Continue → OK**].

As we noted, this command produces more than one table. We have asked SPSS to examine the impact of AGECAT on CHATT separately for men and women. Thus, we are rewarded with the following three-variable cross-tabulation.

CHATT Recoded Church Attendance * AGECAT Recoded Age Categories * SEX RESPONDENTS SEX Crosstabulation

SEX RESPONDENTS SEX					AGECAT Recoded Age Categories				Total
					1 Under 21	2 21-39	3 40-64	4 65 and older	
1 MALE	CHATT Recoded Church Attendance	1 About weekly	Count		3	46	73	38	160
			% within AGECAT Recoded Age Categories		13.6%	18.5%	26.5%	42.2%	25.2%
		2 About monthly	Count		7	38	42	8	95
			% within AGECAT Recoded Age Categories		31.8%	15.3%	15.3%	8.9%	15.0%
		3 Seldom	Count		10	108	93	24	235
			% within AGECAT Recoded Age Categories		45.5%	43.5%	33.8%	26.7%	37.0%
		4 Never	Count		2	56	67	20	145
			% within AGECAT Recoded Age Categories		9.1%	22.6%	24.4%	22.2%	22.8%
	Total		Count		22	248	275	90	635
			% within AGECAT Recoded Age Categories		100.0%	100.0%	100.0%	100.0%	100.0%
2 FEMALE	CHATT Recoded Church Attendance	1 About weekly	Count		5	69	124	74	272
			% within AGECAT Recoded Age Categories		23.8%	21.9%	37.6%	47.4%	33.1%
		2 About monthly	Count		1	67	52	24	144
			% within AGECAT Recoded Age Categories		4.8%	21.3%	15.8%	15.4%	17.5%
		3 Seldom	Count		12	113	97	29	251
			% within AGECAT Recoded Age Categories		57.1%	35.9%	29.4%	18.6%	30.5%
		4 Never	Count		3	66	57	29	155
			% within AGECAT Recoded Age Categories		14.3%	21.0%	17.3%	18.6%	18.9%
	Total		Count		21	315	330	156	822
			% within AGECAT Recoded Age Categories		100.0%	100.0%	100.0%	100.0%	100.0%

Notice that the table is divided into two parts, male and female. For our purposes, we can create a summary table as follows that is easier to read:

Percentage Who Attend Worship Services about Weekly

	Under 21	21-39	40-64	65 and Older
Men	14	19	27	43
Women	24	22	38	47

There are three primary observations to be made regarding this table. First, women are more likely to attend worship services than are men within each age group. Second, the two causal variables (AGECAT and SEX) have a cumulative effect on religiosity in that older women are the most religious and young men are the least. As you can see, a mere 14 percent of the youngest men attend worship services weekly, contrasted to 47 percent of the oldest women.

Finally, with a minor exception, the previously observed relationship between AGECAT and CHATT is true for both men and women. In other words, the relationship between AGECAT and CHATT is nonspurious in that the introduction of a third or control variable (SEX) did not alter or diminish the strength of the relationship dramatically.

Of course, to be sure that the relationship is nonspurious we would have to continue our examination by controlling for other potential third variables that may alter the relationship between the two. What other variables besides SEX might you control for?

SPSS Command 17.1: Running Crosstabs With a Control or Third Variable

> **Analyze → Descriptive Statistics → Crosstabs . . . →**
>
> Highlight **Dependent Variable** → Click **arrow** pointing to **Row(s)**: field →
>
> Highlight **Independent Variable** → Click **arrow** pointing to **Column(s)**: field →
>
> Highlight **control/third variable** → Click **arrow** pointing toward **bottom field** →
>
> Cells . . . → **Column** in Percentages box → **Continue** → **OK**

Demonstration 17.2:
Family Status and Religiosity

If you read the excerpt by Glock et al. on the CD-ROM that accompanies this book, you will recall that, according to social deprivation theory, "family status" is also related to religiosity. Those who had "complete families" (spouse and children) were the least religious among the 1,952 Episcopal church members, suggesting that those lacking families were turning to the church for gratification.

Using **Crosstabs**, set **CHATT** as the **row** variable and **MARITAL** as the **column** variable.[2] Here's what you should get:

CHATT Recoded Church Attendance * MARITAL MARITAL STATUS Crosstabulation								
			MARITAL MARITAL STATUS					
			1 MARRIED	2 WIDOWED	3 DIVORCED	4 SEPARATED	5 NEVER MARRIED	Total
CHATT Recoded Church Attendance	1 About weekly	Count	233	67	54	8	71	433
		% within MARITAL MARITAL STATUS	35.2%	49.6%	22.5%	13.8%	19.3%	29.6%
	2 About monthly	Count	113	20	36	12	59	240
		% within MARITAL MARITAL STATUS	17.1%	14.8%	15.0%	20.7%	16.1%	16.4%
	3 Seldom	Count	206	22	91	22	149	490
		% within MARITAL MARITAL STATUS	31.1%	16.3%	37.9%	37.9%	40.6%	33.5%
	4 Never	Count	110	26	59	16	88	299
		% within MARITAL MARITAL STATUS	16.6%	19.3%	24.6%	27.6%	24.0%	20.5%
Total		Count	662	135	240	58	367	1462
		% within MARITAL MARITAL STATUS	100.0%	100.0%	100.0%	100.0%	100.0%	100.0%

---

[2] Define the value **9** as **missing** for the variable **MARITAL**.

These data certainly do not confirm the earlier finding. Although the widowed are the most religious, those currently married are next. It would not appear that those deprived of conventional family status are turning to the church for an alternative source of gratification. Perhaps the explanation for this lies in historical changes.

In the years separating these two studies, there have been many changes with regard to family life in the United States. Divorce, single-parent families, unmarried couples living together — these and other variations on the traditional family have become more acceptable and certainly more common. It would make sense, therefore, that people who lacked regular family status in 2000 would not feel as deprived as such people may have in the early 1950s.

Demonstration 17.3: Family Status and Religiosity, Controlling for Age

Before setting this issue aside, however, we should take a minute to consider whether the table we've just seen is concealing anything. In particular, can you think of any other variable that is related to both attendance at worship services and marital status? If so, that variable might be clouding the relations between marital status and religiosity.

The variable we are thinking of is age. We've already seen that age is strongly related to church attendance. It is also probably related to marital status in that young people (low in church attendance) are the most likely to be "never married." And old people (high in church attendance) are the most likely to be widowed. It is possible, therefore, that the widowed are high in church attendance only because they're mostly old, and those never married are low in church attendance only because they're young. This kind of reasoning lies near the heart of multivariate analysis, and the techniques you've mastered allow you to test this possibility.

Return to the **Crosstabs** window and add **AGECAT** as the **control** or third variable.

Once you've reviewed the resulting tables, see if you can construct the following summary table.

Percentage Who Attend Church about Weekly

	Married	*Widowed*	*Divorced*	*Separated*	*Never Married*
Under 21	—	—	—	—	—
21-39	28	—	—	—	15
40-64	37	55	28	—	27
65 & older	48	49	29	—	—

Dashes in this table indicate that there are too few cases for meaningful percentages. We required at least 10 cases, a common standard.

Once again, these findings do not seem to confirm the theory that those lacking families turn to the church for gratification, whereas those with families are the least religious. Indeed, the widowed and married appear to be among the most religious in each category. This is followed by those who are divorced. Those never married indicate comparatively low levels of church attendance in almost every age group, except for the 40-64 age category.

You can also observe in this table that the effect of age on church attendance is maintained regardless of marital status. Older respondents are more likely to attend religious services than the younger ones in each category. Social scientists often use the term *replication* for the analytic outcome we've just observed. Having discovered that church attendance increases with age overall, we've now found that this relationship holds true regardless of marital status. That's an important discovery in terms of the generalizability of what we have learned about the causes of religiosity.

Demonstration 17.4:
Social Class and Religiosity

In the earlier study, Glock and his colleagues also found that religiosity increased as social class decreased; that is, those in the lower class were more religious than those in the upper class. This fit nicely into the deprivation thesis, that those deprived of status in the secular society would turn to the church as an alternative source of gratification. The researchers indicated, however, that this finding might be limited to the Episcopalian church members under study. They suggested that the relationship might not be replicated in the general public. You have the opportunity to check it out.

Let's begin with our measure of subjective social class. Run **Crosstabs** with **column** percentages, requesting **CHATT** as the **row** variable and **CLASS** as the **column** variable.[3] Here's what you should get:

CHATT Recoded Church Attendance * CLASS SUBJECTIVE CLASS IDENTIFICATION Crosstabulation

			1 LOWER CLASS	2 WORKING CLASS	3 MIDDLE CLASS	4 UPPER CLASS	Total
CHATT Recoded Church Attendance	1 About weekly	Count	20	189	206	15	430
		% within CLASS SUBJECTIVE CLASS IDENTIFICATION	25.6%	26.9%	33.7%	23.4%	29.5%
	2 About monthly	Count	8	116	104	12	240
		% within CLASS SUBJECTIVE CLASS IDENTIFICATION	10.3%	16.5%	17.0%	18.8%	16.5%
	3 Seldom	Count	31	237	199	21	488
		% within CLASS SUBJECTIVE CLASS IDENTIFICATION	39.7%	33.7%	32.5%	32.8%	33.5%
	4 Never	Count	19	161	103	16	299
		% within CLASS SUBJECTIVE CLASS IDENTIFICATION	24.4%	22.9%	16.8%	25.0%	20.5%
Total		Count	78	703	612	64	1457
		% within CLASS SUBJECTIVE CLASS IDENTIFICATION	100.0%	100.0%	100.0%	100.0%	100.0%

(CLASS SUBJECTIVE CLASS IDENTIFICATION spans the four class columns.)

This table suggests that there is little relationship between social class and church attendance. In fact, the findings seem to run almost contrary to our expectations in some regards. To be sure of this conclusion, you might want to rerun the table, controlling for sex and for age.

At the same time, you can test the generalizability of the previously observed effects of sex and age on church attendance. Do they hold up among members of

[3] Define the values **0, 5-9** as **missing** for the variable **CLASS**.

different social classes? Once you have examined this possibility, compare your findings to those in Writing Box 17.1 below.

Writing Box 17.1

The zero-order finding that women attend church more regularly than men is replicated in each of the social class groups, although the gender difference is somewhat smaller among middle-class respondents than in the other social class groups.

By the same token, the strong relationship between age and church attendance is also replicated, with some minor variations, among the several social class groups. That is, older respondents attend church more often than younger ones regardless of their social class.

Other Variables to Explore

Notice that our analyses so far in this chapter have used CHATT as the dependent variable: the measure of religiosity. Recall our earlier comments on the shortcomings of single-item measures of variables. Perhaps our analyses have been misleading by seeking to explain church attendance. Perhaps different conclusions might be drawn if we had studied beliefs in an afterlife, or frequency of prayer. Why don't you test some of the earlier conclusions by using other measures of religiosity? If you are really ambitious, you can create a composite index of religiosity and look for causes.

Similarly, we have limited our preceding investigations in this chapter to the variables examined by Glock and his colleagues. Now that you have gotten the idea about how to create and interpret multivariate tables, you should broaden your exploration of variables that might be related to religiosity. What are some other demographic variables that might affect religiosity? Or you might want to explore the multivariate relationships between religiosity and some of the attitudinal variables we've been exploring: political philosophies, sexual attitudes, and so forth. In each instance, you should examine the bivariate relationships first, and then move on to the multivariate analyses.

Chi-Square and Measures of Association

Thus far, we've introduced the logic of multivariate analysis through the use of Crosstabs, and controlling for a third variable. You've already learned some other techniques that can be used in your examination of several variables simultaneously.

Chi-Square

First, we should remind you that you may want to use a chi-square test of statistical significance when you use Crosstabs. It's not required, but you may find it useful as an independent assessment of the relationships you discover.

Measures of Association

Second, you may also want to experiment using an appropriate measure of association such as lambda or gamma to test the strength and, in certain cases, the direction of association.

Multiple Regression

You may recall our fairly brief discussion of regression at the end of Chapter 14. At that point, we discussed a form of regression known as *simple linear regression* or just *linear regression*, which involves one independent and one dependent variable.

Regression can also be a powerful technique for exploring multivariate relationships. When you are conducting multivariate analysis involving one dependent and more than one independent variable, the technique is referred to as *multiple regression*. In both cases, regression is appropriate for two or more I/R or continuous variables.

To use either linear or multiple regression effectively, you need much more instruction than we propose to offer in this book. Still, we want to give you a brief overview of multiple regression, much in the same way we did when we introduced linear regression earlier.

In our previous use of regression (linear regression, Chapter 14), we examined the impact of EDUC on SEI, respondents' socioeconomic status scores. Now we'll open the possibility that other variables in the data set might also affect occupational prestige.

Dummy Variables

In addition to EDUC, we are also going to consider two additional independent variables: SEX and RACE. These variables were chosen because many argue that in today's workforce, men are still treated differently than women, and Whites are still treated differently than African Americans.

You will notice, however, that both SEX and RACE are nominal variables, not I/R variables. Since we told you that regression is appropriate for I/R continuous variables, you may begin to wonder how we can propose to use two nominal variables in a regression equation. That's a very good question.

The answer lies in the fact that researchers sometimes treat such items as *dummy variables* appropriate to a regression analysis. In regard to the variable SEX, for example, the logic used here transforms gender into a measure of "maleness," with male respondents being 100 percent male and female respondents 0 percent male.

Recoding SEX to Create a Dummy Variable - MALE

Let's recode SEX as described above into the new variable MALE. So take the following steps:

Transform → Recode → Into Different Variables . . .

Select **SEX** as the **Numeric Variable**. Let's call the new variable **MALE**. Using the **Old and New Values . . .** window, make these assignments.

Execute the Recode command by clicking **Continue** and then **OK**.

Before moving on to the variable RACE, make sure you set the **decimal places** for MALE to **0**. You may also want to give a brief description of MALE and define your values and labels.

Recoding RACE to Create a Dummy Variable — WHITE

We will use the same basic procedure to recode RACE as we used to recode SEX. Open the Recode dialog box by selecting **Transform → Recode → Into Different Variables . . .**

Designate **RACE** as the **Numeric Variable** and name the new variable **WHITE**. Then use the **Old and New Values** window to accomplish your recode.

You will notice that unlike the variable SEX, RACE contains three values: 1 (White), 2 (Black), and 3 (Other). Consequently, in this case we are going to recode RACE as follows:

RACE Old Values		WHITE New Values
1	→	1
2-3	→	0

With this coding scheme, the dummy code "1" designates 100 percent majority group status, "0" designates 0 percent majority group status. Once you have set the new values, click **Continue** and **OK** to execute the command.

Before we ask SPSS to run our regression analysis, make sure you set the **decimal places** for your new variable (WHITE) to **0**. In addition, you may want to provide a brief description of the variable and define the values and labels.

SPSS Command 17.2: Recoding to Create a Dummy Variable

> **Transform → Recode → Into Different Variables . . . →**
>
> Highlight name of **variable** recoding → Click **arrow** pointing toward
> "Numeric Variable . . . " field →
>
> Type **name of new variable** in rectangle under "Output Variable"
> labeled "Name:"
>
> **Change → Old and New Values . . .**
>
> **Recode Old/Add New Values . . .**
>
> **Continue → OK**

Multiple Regression[4]

Now that we have created our dummy variables, we are ready to request the multiple regression analysis.

Analyze → Regression → Linear . . . takes us to the window we want. Select **SEI** and make it the **Dependent:** variable. Then place **EDUC**, **MALE**, and **WHITE** in the **Independent(s):** field. In the window labeled **Method:**, click the **down arrow** and highlight **Stepwise**.

---

[4] In an attempt to offer a very brief and simplistic overview of multiple regression, we rely on the stepwise method. Instructors who are uncomfortable with the use of stepwise regression may, as an alternative, want to introduce students to the enter method and ask students to decide what variables to enter.

Run this command by clicking **OK**, and you will receive a mass of output. Without going into all the details, we are simply going to show you how it establishes the equation we asked for. We'll take the output a piece at a time. For our purposes, we'd like you to skip through the output on your screen until you find the following two tables (probably the second and fourth tables displayed):

Model Summary

Model	R	R Square	Adjusted R Square	Std. Error of the Estimate
1	.570[a]	.324	.324	15.5977
2	.571[b]	.327	.326	15.5774
3	.573[c]	.329	.327	15.5582

a. Predictors: (Constant), EDUC HIGHEST YEAR OF SCHOOL COMPLETED

b. Predictors: (Constant), EDUC HIGHEST YEAR OF SCHOOL COMPLETED, MALE Male dummy variable

c. Predictors: (Constant), EDUC HIGHEST YEAR OF SCHOOL COMPLETED, MALE Male dummy variable, WHITE White race

Coefficients[a]

Model		Unstandardized Coefficients		Standardized Coefficients		
		B	Std. Error	Beta	t	Sig.
1	(Constant)	-2.635	2.023		-1.303	.193
	EDUC HIGHEST YEAR OF SCHOOL COMPLETED	3.868	.148	.570	26.110	.000
2	(Constant)	-3.200	2.037		-1.571	.116
	EDUC HIGHEST YEAR OF SCHOOL COMPLETED	3.849	.148	.567	25.980	.000
	MALE Male dummy variable	1.803	.832	.047	2.167	.030
3	(Constant)	-4.688	2.152		-2.179	.029
	EDUC HIGHEST YEAR OF SCHOOL COMPLETED	3.832	.148	.564	25.857	.000
	MALE Male dummy variable	1.766	.831	.046	2.124	.034
	WHITE White race	2.178	1.026	.046	2.123	.034

We have given SPSS three variables that it might use to predict occupational prestige. In a stepwise regression, it begins by creating the most effective equation possible with only one independent variable. As you can see, it chose EDUC for that role. In other words, if you had to measure prestige on the basis of only one of the three independent variables, SPSS is telling us we'd do best with EDUC. It also reminds us of the variables not used in this first equation.

To create our equation for Model 1, we take two numbers from the Unstandardized Coefficients column: the constant (−2.635) and the B value (called the slope) for EDUC (3.868). Locate those in your output. We use these numbers to create the following equation:

$$SEI = -2.635 + (EDUC \times 3.868)$$

If someone had 10 years of education, then we would estimate his or her occupational prestige as follows:

$$SEI = -2.635 + (10 \times 3.868) = 36.045$$

Model 2 adds MALE as a predictor of occupational prestige. The meaning of this is that if we could use two variables to predict PRESTIGE, we should use EDUC and MALE. Notice that the slope for EDUC changes only slightly when we add another independent variable.

$$SEI = -3.200 + (EDUC \times 3.849) + (MALE \times 1.803)$$

Based on this, what equation would you use to predict the occupational prestige of a male with 10 years of education? Here is a hint to get you started:

$$SEI = -3.200 + (10 \times 3.849) + (\underline{\quad} \times \underline{\quad}) = \underline{\quad}$$

Model 3, the last row in the chart, uses all three variables. It's your turn to convert these data into a regression equation and experiment with it. Determine whether being White is worth any additional points of prestige when education and sex are held constant.

The column headed Standardized Coefficients gives you a guide to the relative impact of the different variables. Take a minute to consider some independent variable that has no impact on the dependent variable. What slope would it be given?

If you think about it, the only proper weight would be zero. That would mean that a person's value on that variable would never make any difference in predicting the dependent variable. By the same token, the larger the slope for any given variable, the larger its part in determining the resulting prediction.

It is possible (although it is not the case in this example) that a variable that is supposed to be a better predictor, such as EDUC, could have a smaller slope than an item such as MALE, which is not supposed to be as good a predictor of SEI. How can this happen?

The solution to this puzzle lies in the different scales used in the different variables. MALE only goes as high as 1 (Male), whereas EDUC obviously goes much higher to accommodate the different levels of educational attainment of respondents. Slopes must be standardized before they can be compared. Standardized slopes are what the slopes would be if each of the variables used the same scale. SPSS prints standardized slopes under the column Standardized Coefficients. The data presented above indicate that EDUC (.564) has the greatest impact on SEI, followed distantly by MALE (.046) and WHITE (.046). Interpreted, this means that education has the greatest impact on socioeconomic status, followed by "maleness" and "majorityness."

SPSS Command 17.3: Multiple Regression

Analyze → Regression → Linear . . . **→**

Highlight name of **dependent variable →** Click **arrow** pointing toward **Dependent:** field **→**

Highlight name of 1st **independent variable →** Click **arrow** pointing to **Independent(s):** field **→**

Repeat last step as many times as necessary until all Independent variables are listed in the Independent(s): field **→**

Click **down arrow** next to box labeled **"Method" →** Select **Stepwise → OK**

Conclusion

In this chapter, we have given you an initial peek into the logic and techniques of multivariate analysis. As you've seen, the difference between bivariate and multivariate analysis is much more than a matter of degree. Multivariate analysis does more than bring in additional variables: It represents a new logic for understanding social scientific relationships.

For this contact, we've looked at how multivariate analysis lets us explore the nature of multiple causation, seeing how two or more independent variables affect a dependent variable. In addition, we've used multivariate techniques for the purpose of testing the generalizability of relationships.

In the latter regard, we have begun using multivariate techniques for the purpose of considering hidden relationships among variables, as when we asked whether the widowed attended church frequently just because they were mostly older people. We'll pursue this kind of detective work further in the chapters to come.

Main Points

- This chapter introduced a new, more sophisticated form of statistical analysis: multivariate analysis.
- Multivariate analysis is the simultaneous analysis of three or more variables.
- The Crosstabs procedure can be used to analyze the relationship between an independent and dependent variable while controlling for a third variable.
- We examined multiple causes of religiosity in more depth by focusing on items such as: AGECAT, SEX, MARITAL, and SEI.
- Other analytic techniques may aid in the examination of several items at once, including chi-square, measures of association, and regression.
- We introduced simple linear regression in Chapter 14.
- In this chapter we introduced another regression procedure: multiple regression.
- Nominal and ordinal items can be recoded to create dummy variables that are suitable for regression analysis.

Key Terms

Multivariate analysis
Simple linear regression
Elaboration
Linear regression
Controlling for a third variable

Multiple regression
Control variable
Dummy Variables
Replication

SPSS Commands Introduced in This Chapter

17.1 Running Crosstabs With a Control or Third Variable

17.2 Recoding to Create a Dummy Variable

17.3 Multiple Regression

Review Questions

1. Describe the major differences between univariate, bivariate, and multivariate analysis.

2. If a researcher uncovers a relationship between class (independent) and prejudice (dependent variable), what technique introduced in this chapter might she use to examine the relationship further?

3. Describe the relationship between social class and church attendance. Do the findings support the "social deprivation" theory? Why or why not?

4. What does "replication" refer to?

5. Name at least two other techniques you learned (before reading Chapter 17) that you could use in your multivariate examinations.

6. Simple linear regression involves the analysis of _____ [number] independent and _____ [number] dependent variables.

7. Multiple regression involves the analysis of _____ [number] independent and _____ [number] dependent variables.

8. Regression is appropriate for variables at what level(s) of measurement?

9. What is a dummy variable?

10. Why did we recode SEX to create MALE for our multiple regression example? Why didn't we just use SEX as our measure of gender?

11. What is a better predictor of SEI, EDUC or MALE?

12. When reading your multiple regression output, which of the following rows gives a sense of the relative impact of the independent variable: Unstandardized Coefficients, Standardized Coefficients, *t*, or sig.?

NAME _____

CLASS _____

INSTRUCTOR _____

DATE _____

To complete the following exercises, you need to load the data file EXERPLUS. Answers to selected questions (1-3, 5-7, 19-21, 25) can be found in Appendix B.

1. Examine the simultaneous impact of class and race on support for national spending on crime. Before proceeding, designate the values indicated below as missing for each item. Then run Crosstabs with column percentages, and request chi-square. Use your output to complete the summary table and answer the questions below:

   Dependent variable - NATCRIME [define 0, 8, 9 as missing]
   Independent variable 1 - CLASS [define 5-9, 0 as missing]
   Independent variable 2 - RACE [define 3 as missing]

   NATCRIME: Percentage who feel the national government is spending too little fighting crime

	LOWER	WORKING	MIDDLE	UPPER	SIG. [chi-square]
WHITE	_____	_____	_____	_____	_____
BLACK	_____	_____	_____	_____	_____

2. For WHITES: The percentage who feel the national government is spending too little fighting crime _____ [increases, decreases, neither increases nor decreases] as class increases. The value of chi-square indicates that there _____ [is/is not] a statistically significant relationship.

3. For BLACKS: The percentage who feel the national government is spending too little fighting crime _____ [increases, decreases, neither increases nor decreases] as class increases. The value of chi-square indicates that there _____ [is/is not] a statistically significant relationship.

4. Summarize below the major findings from the table. Explain the primary observations that can be made regarding your findings and the table above. You may want to note, for instance, the relationship between race and support for government spending on crime, as well as the relationship between class and support for government spending on crime. Also note whether the two variables have a cumulative effect on support for national spending on crime.

That is, are lower-class Blacks more likely to feel the government is spending too little fighting crime as opposed to upper-class Whites?

5. Examine the simultaneous impact of class and gender on support for national spending on welfare. Before proceeding, designate the values indicated below as missing for each item. Then run Crosstabs and request chi-square. Use your output to complete the summary table and answer the questions below:

Dependent variable - NATFARE [define 0, 8, 9 as missing]
Independent variable 1 - CLASS
Independent variable 2 - SEX

NATFARE: Percentage who feel the national government is spending too little on welfare.

	LOWER	WORKING	MID	UPPER	Chi-square
MALE	_____	_____	_____	_____	_____
FEMALE	_____	_____	_____	_____	_____

6. For the *males*, describe the nature of the relationship between class and spending too little on welfare in terms of its strength, direction, and significance.

7. For the *females*, describe the nature of the relationship between class and spending too little on welfare in terms of its strength, direction, and significance.

NAME _____

CLASS _____

INSTRUCTOR _____

DATE _____

8. Summarize the major findings from the table. Explain the primary observations that can be made regarding the table. You may want to note, for instance, the relationship between gender and support for government spending on welfare, as well as the relationship between class and support for government spending on welfare. Also note whether the two variables have a cumulative effect on support for national spending on welfare. That is, are lower-class women more likely to feel the government is spending too little on welfare as opposed to upper-class men? In addition, be sure to discuss whether the findings are statistically significant.

Examine the simultaneous impact of two independent variables of your choice on support for the national government's spending on education [NATEDUC]. Run Crosstabs, request chi-square, and then answer the following questions and complete the summary table (use as many spaces as necessary). Don't forget to define DK as missing for NATEDUC and the other variables you choose. In addition, if you need to recode one or both of your independent variables, indicate how you did that in response to Question 9.

    9. List the two independent variables you chose.

   10. Justify your choice of the two independent variables and explain how you expect them to be related to NATEDUC.

   11. NATEDUC: Percentage who feel that the government is spending too little on education

       ____   ____   ____   ____   Chi-square

    _____

    _____

    _____

    _____

   12. Summarize your findings in detail below. Be sure to explain the primary observations that can be made regarding the table and discuss whether the findings are statistically significant.

NAME _____

CLASS _____

INSTRUCTOR _____

DATE _____

13. Choose one dependent and two independent variables and write the names of the variables you chose below.

Dependent variable _____
Independent variable 1 _____
Independent variable 2 _____

14. Write two hypotheses explaining the relationship between each independent variable and the dependent variable.

Hypothesis 1:

Hypothesis 2:

Examine the simultaneous impact of the two independent variables on the dependent variable. Run Crosstabs with chi-square and an appropriate measure of association. Then create a summary table below detailing the relationship [Question 16]. Remember to define DKs as missing and, if necessary, recode your variables and indicate how you did that in the space below Question 15.

15. Measure of association _____

16. Summary Table:

17. Summarize your findings in detail below. Be sure to explain the primary observations that can be made regarding the table. Discuss the strength and, if possible, the direction of association. Also indicate whether the findings are statistically significant and whether they support your hypotheses.

NAME _____

CLASS _____

INSTRUCTOR _____

DATE _____

18. Recode the variable RACE to create a new dummy variable WHITE.

RACE[5]   WHITE

Old Values   *New Value*

1   →   1

2-3   →   0

When you are done set the decimal places to 0.

Examine the impact of EDUC, WHITE, and AGE on the hours of television viewed each day. Designate the following values as missing before beginning your regression analysis:

EDUC - 97-99

AGE - 0, 98-99

TVHOURS - -1, 98-99

Now open the Linear regression window and designate TVHOURS as the dependent variable and EDUC, WHITE, and AGE as the independent variables. Under Options, exclude cases listwise and under Method select Enter. Then answer the following questions.

19. What is the constant for the regression equation?

Constant _____

20. What are B (beta) values for the slopes of each variable?

EDUC _____

WHITE _____

AGE _____

21. Fill in the blanks to create a prediction equation for TVHOURS.

TVHOURS = _____ + (EDUC _____) + (WHITE _____) + (AGE _____)

_____

[5] No values should be defined as missing for the variable RACE.

22. How many hours per day would we predict a 25-year-old White high school graduate would watch TV? [fill in the blanks]

_____ = _____ + (____ × _____) + (_____ × _____) + (_____ × _____)

23. How many hours per day would we predict a 48-year-old non-White college graduate would watch TV? [fill in the blanks]

_____ = _____ + (____ × _____) + (_____ × _____) + (_____ × _____)

24. Which of the three independent variables is most strongly related to TVHOURS? Explain the logic of your choice.

25. Of the three independent variables in the regression equation, which are (is) statistically significant? How do you know?

Chapter 18 **Dissecting the Political Factor**

In Chapter 12, we began exploring some of the causes of political philosophies and party identification. Now you are equipped to dig more deeply. Let's start with the relationship between political philosophy and party identification. As you'll recall, our earlier analysis showed a definite relationship, although it was not altogether consistent. Perhaps we can clarify it.

Political Philosophy and Party Identification

On the whole, Democrats in our sample were more liberal than Independents or Republicans. Also, Republicans were the most conservative, although there wasn't as large a distinction between Democrats and Independents as you might have expected. Here's the basic table from Chapter 12 examining the relationship between political philosophy (POLREC) and party identification (PARTY).[1]

			PARTY Recoded partyid			
			1 Democrat	2 Independent	3 Republican	Total
POLREC Recoded polviews	1 Liberal	Count	163	149	30	342
		% within PARTY Recoded partyid	35.1%	26.3%	8.6%	24.8%
	2 Moderate	Count	204	267	119	590
		% within PARTY Recoded partyid	44.0%	47.1%	34.1%	42.8%
	3 Conservative	Count	97	151	200	448
		% within PARTY Recoded partyid	20.9%	26.6%	57.3%	32.5%
Total		Count	464	567	349	1380
		% within PARTY Recoded partyid	100.0%	100.0%	100.0%	100.0%

POLREC Recoded polviews * PARTY Recoded partyid Crosstabulation

For purposes of this analysis, let's focus on the percentages who identify themselves as "Conservative." In the table above, the percentage difference

---

[1] In Chapter 7 we recoded the variables POLVIEWS and PARTYID to create POLREC and PARTY.

separating the Democrats and Republicans in calling themselves conservative amounts to 36 points. You'll recall, perhaps, that percentage differences are sometimes designated by the Greek letter *epsilon* or abbreviated with the letter *e*.

Demonstration 18.1: Controlling for Education

If you were to undertake a study of the political party platforms and/or the speeches of political leaders from the two major parties, you would conclude that Democrats are, in fact, somewhat more liberal than Republicans, and that Republicans are, in fact, somewhat more conservative than Democrats. If the relationship between political philosophy and party identification is not as clear as we might like, then perhaps some of the respondents simply don't know how the two parties are generally regarded.

Who do you suppose would be the least likely to know the philosophical leanings of the two parties? Perhaps those with the least education would be unaware of them. If that were the case, then we should expect a clearer relationship between political philosophy and party identification among the more educated respondents than among the less educated.

Why don't you open your DEMOPLUS file and run the SPSS command that lets you create the following three-variable summary table?[2]

	Percentage Saying They Are Conservative				
	Less Than HS	HS Grad	Some College	College Grad	Grad Studies
Democrat	31	23	22	13	10
Independent	21	25	34	30	16
Republican	46	44	57	75	76
e	25	21	35	62	66

Our suspicion seems to be confirmed. The clearest relationship between party and political philosophy appears among those with the highest level of education (post-college education), followed by those with a college education, and then those with some college. Notice, however, that Democrats and Republicans are separated by an epsilon of 25 percentage points among the least educated group, and an epsilon of 21 among high school graduates. Independents of every education level, except the lowest (less than HS), say they are more conservative than Democrats but much less so than Republicans.

This table reveals something else that relates to our earlier analysis. You may recall that we found only a weak and inconsistent relationship between education and political philosophy in our Chapter 12 analysis. There was a tendency for liberalism to increase with education (18 percentage points separated the least

---

[2] To construct this summary table, run Crosstabs with column percentages, specifying EDCAT as the column (Independent) variable, POLREC as the row (Dependent) variable, and PARTY as the control variable. In the controlled table, the number of cases in the "Other" category of POLREC is very small. With numbers so small, it is easy to compute percentages that exaggerate differences. To avoid this, we did not include the "other" category of POLREC in our summary table.

from the most educated groups in that respect). There was no relationship between conservatism and education, with the moderate point of view decreasing with education.

This new table clarifies the situation somewhat. The relationship between political philosophy and education occurs primarily among Democrats. Although the more highly educated Republicans are the most conservative, there are few differences among the other educational groups.

This table represents what social scientists call a *specification*. We have specified the relationship between education and political philosophy: It occurs primarily among Democrats. On the other hand, we could say that we have specified the relationship between political philosophy and party identification: It occurs primarily among the better educated.

Specification stands as an alternative to *replication*. You'll recall from our discussion in the last chapter that replication indicates that a relationship between two variables can be generalized to all kinds of people. Specification indicates that it cannot.

When we look at the relationship between two variables, such as political philosophy and party identification, among subgroups determined by some other variable, such as education, we often say that we are *controlling for a third variable*. Social scientists use the expression "controlling for" in the sense of creating controlled conditions: only college graduates, only those with some college, and so on. We also speak of "holding education constant" in the sense that education is no longer a variable (it is a constant) when we look at only one educational group at a time.

Why don't you experiment with this logic, testing the generalizability of the relationship between political philosophy and party identification among other subgroups, formed by holding other variables constant?

Demonstration 18.2:
The Mystery of Politics and Marital Status

In Chapter 12, we encouraged you to explore the relationship between marital status and politics. If you took us up on the invitation, you should have found an interesting relationship between marital status and political philosophy.

Recoding MARITAL

Because relatively few respondents were "Separated," we should combine them with some other group. It would seem to make sense to combine the separated with the divorced, reasoning that separation is often experienced as an interim step toward divorce.

Let's recode **MARITAL** into a new variable, **MARITAL2**, with

Transform → Recode → Into Different Variables ...

Once in the Recode window, you should enter **MARITAL** as the Input Variable and **MARITAL2** as the Output Variable. Click on **Change** to move MARITAL2 to the recode list. Then, in the **Old and New Values** window, recode as follows:

MARITAL Old Values		New Values	MARITAL2 Labels
1	→	1	Married
2	→	2	Widowed
3-4	→	3	Divorced/ separated
5	→	4	Never married

Don't forget to use **Add** to record the instructions. Then, you can **Continue** and **OK** your way to the recoded variable.

Before we move on, make sure you set the **decimal places** for your new variable to **0**, as well as **define the values and labels** for MARITAL2.

POLREC by MARITAL2

Now create a **Crosstab** with **MARITAL2** as the **column** variable and **POLREC** as the **row** variable. Ask SPSS for **column percentages** and **chi-square**. Here's what you should get:

POLREC Recoded polviews * MARITAL2 Recoded marital Crosstabulation							
			MARITAL2 Recoded marital				
			1 married	2 widowed	3 divorced/s eparated	4 never married	Total
POLREC Recoded polviews	1 Liberal	Count	135	20	84	116	355
		% within MARITAL2 Recoded marital	20.9%	15.7%	29.7%	32.9%	25.2%
	2 Moderate	Count	264	67	126	141	598
		% within MARITAL2 Recoded marital	40.9%	52.8%	44.5%	39.9%	42.5%
	3 Conservative	Count	246	40	73	96	455
		% within MARITAL2 Recoded marital	38.1%	31.5%	25.8%	27.2%	32.3%
Total		Count	645	127	283	353	1408
		% within MARITAL2 Recoded marital	100.0%	100.0%	100.0%	100.0%	100.0%

The chi-square test of statistical significance shows that this relationship is significant.

So, why is it that married and widowed respondents are more conservative than the divorced, separated, or never married? Your multivariate skills will allow you to explore this matter in more depth than was possible before.

POLREC by MARITAL2 by AGECAT

Perhaps age is the key. The widowed are likely to be older than others, and the never married are likely to be younger. As we've seen, people tend to become more conservative with age. Here is a summary table created from the results of the **Crosstab** of **POLREC** by **MARITAL2** by **AGECAT**. See if you can duplicate this yourself.

	Percentage Who Say They Are Conservative			
	Married	Divorced/ Widowed	Never Separated	Married
Under 21	—	—	—	—
21-39	37%	—	27%	28%
40-64	38%	—	27%	26%
65 and up	43%	32%	—	—

(As in other tables, the dashes here indicate that there were too few cases for meaningful percentages.)

This table helps clarify matters somewhat. The married are consistently more conservative than the divorced and never married, and the widowed tend to maintain a relatively conservative stance. Those divorced, separated, and never married seem to be slightly more liberal than those married and widowed, although the differences are not dramatic.

POLREC by MARITAL2 by SEX

How about sex? Perhaps it can shed some light on this relationship. Why don't you run the tables that would result in this summary?

	Percentage Who Say They Are Conservative			
	Married	Widowed	Divorced/ Separated	Never Married
Men	44%	32%	29%	27%
Women	33%	31%	24%	27%

As before, the married and widowed remain relatively conservative, and the divorced and never married remain slightly less conservative (except in the case of women who never married).

POLREC by MARITAL2 by EDCAT

To pursue this further, you might want to consider education. Here's the summary table you should generate if you follow this avenue.

	Percentage Who Say They Are Conservative			
	Married	Widowed	Divorced/ Separated	Never Married
Less than HS	35%	36%	—	28%
HS graduate	36%	—	26%	24%
Some college	40%	56%	33%	25%
College graduate	44%	—	—	39%
Graduate studies	38%	—	37%	—

Once more, we seem to have dug a dry well. Education does not seem to clarify the relationship we first observed between marital status and political philosophy. This is the point in an analysis where you sometimes wonder if you should ever have considered this line of inquiry.

POLREC by MARITAL2 by RACE

See what happens when we introduce race as a control.

	Percentage Who Say They Are Conservative			
	Married	Widowed	Divorced/ Separated	Never Married
White	41%	31%	27%	26%
Black	21%	—	26%	33%
Other	—	—	—	—

POLREC as Independent Variable

When we consistently fail to find a clear answer to a question—Why do people of different marital statuses differ in their political philosophies?—it is sometimes useful to reconsider the question itself. Thus far, we have been asking why marital status would affect political philosophy. Perhaps we have the question reversed. What if political philosophy affects marital status? Is that a possibility?

Perhaps those who are politically conservative are also socially conservative. Maybe it would be especially important for them to form and keep traditional families. During the last few presidential elections, the political conservatives made "traditional family values" a centerpiece of their campaign. Let's see what the table would look like if we percentaged it in the opposite direction.

MARITAL2 Recoded marital * POLREC Recoded polviews Crosstabulation

			POLREC Recoded polviews		3 Conservative	Total
			1 Liberal	2 Moderate		
MARITAL2 Recoded marital	1 married	Count	135	264	246	645
		% within POLREC Recoded polviews	38.0%	44.1%	54.1%	45.8%
	2 widowed	Count	20	67	40	127
		% within POLREC Recoded polviews	5.6%	11.2%	8.8%	9.0%
	3 divorced/separated	Count	84	126	73	283
		% within POLREC Recoded polviews	23.7%	21.1%	16.0%	20.1%
	4 never married	Count	116	141	96	353
		% within POLREC Recoded polviews	32.7%	23.6%	21.1%	25.1%
Total		Count	355	598	455	1408
		% within POLREC Recoded polviews	100.0%	100.0%	100.0%	100.0%

Look at the first row in this table. The percentage married increases steadily with increasing conservatism across the table. Divorce and singlehood, on the other hand, decrease just as steadily. Perhaps marital status is more profitably seen as a dependent variable in this context—affected to some extent by worldviews such as those that are reflected in political philosophy.

Sometimes, the direction of a relationship—which is the dependent and which is the independent variable—is clear. If we discover that voting behavior is related to gender, for instance, we can be sure that gender can affect voting, but how you vote can't change your gender. In other situations, such as the present one, the direction of a relationship is somewhat ambiguous. Ultimately, this decision must be based on theoretical reasoning. There is no way the analysis of data can determine which variable is dependent and which is independent.

If you wanted to pursue the present relationship, you might treat marital status as a dependent variable, subjecting its relationship with political philosophies to a multivariate analysis. Try, for instance, re-running the crosstab, using AGECAT, SEX, EDCAT, and RACE as control variables. After you examine your output, compare your findings to those in Writing Box 18.1 below.

Writing Box 18.1

Age does not affect the original relationship between political orientations and marital status. It is worth noting, of course, that the youngest respondents are less likely overall to be married—less likely to be separated, divorced, or widowed—than older respondents. Still, at every age level, conservatives are consistently more likely to be married than liberals.

The relationship is also true among both men and women, though stronger among men: represented by a 22 percentage point difference among men, compared to 11 percentage points among women.

Educational level does not affect the apparent impact of political orientation on marital status. While the relationship is strongest among high school graduates, education itself has no consistent impact.

Only race partially disrupts the initially observed relationship. While White conservatives are much more likely than White liberals to be married, the pattern is less clear among Blacks and other nonwhites. We see, for example, that Blacks are less likely to marry overall, and this is particularly so among Black conservatives. Among the other nonwhites, it is the high level of marriage among liberals that violates the overall relationship.

Political Issues

In Chapter 12, we began looking for the causes of opinions on two political issues:

GUNLAW   registration of firearms

CAPPUN   capital punishment

Now that you have the ability to undertake multivariate analysis, you can delve more deeply into the causes of public opinion. Let's think a little about capital punishment for the moment. Here are some variables that might logically affect how people feel about the death penalty.

POLREC and PARTY are obvious candidates. Liberals are generally more opposed to capital punishment than are conservatives. Similarly, Republicans have tended to support it more than have Democrats. You might check to see how these two variables work together on death penalty attitudes.

Given that capital punishment involves the taking of a human life, you might expect some religious effects. How do the different religious affiliations relate to support for or opposition to capital punishment?

What about beliefs in an afterlife? Do those who believe in life after death find it easier to support the taking of a life? How do religious and political factors interact in this arena?

Those opposed to capital punishment base their opposition on the view that it is wrong to take a human life. The same argument is made by those who oppose abortion. Logically, you would expect those opposed to abortion to also oppose capital punishment. Why don't you check it out? You may be surprised by what you find.

Another approach to understanding opinions about capital punishment might focus on which groups in society are most likely to be victims of it. Men are more likely to be executed than are women. Blacks are executed disproportionately often in comparison with their numbers in the population.

Conclusion

These few suggestions should launch you on an extended exploration of the nature of political orientations. Whereas people often talk pretty casually about political matters, you are now in a position to check out the facts and begin to understand why people feel as they do about political issues. Multivariate analysis techniques let you uncover some of the complexities that can make human behavior difficult to understand.

Main Points

- You can use your multivariate analysis skills to delve into the nature of political orientation.
- We began by exploring the relationship between political philosophy and party identification while controlling for education.
- Our findings indicate specification or a specified relationship between education and political philosophy.
- Unlike replication, specification indicates a relationship between two items that cannot be generalized to all kinds of people.
- You can test the generalizability of the relationship between two items by controlling for or holding a third variable constant.
- The direction of the relationship between variables (which is the dependent and which is the independent) is not always clear.
- In exploring the relationship between political philosophy and marital status we took turns examining both as the independent variable.
- We discovered that marital status is perhaps better seen as the dependent variable in this context.
- You can use your multivariate analysis skills to discover why people hold the opinions they do on volatile political issues such as gun control and capital punishment.

Key Terms

Epsilon (e)
Controlling for a third
variable

Specification
Constant
Replication

SPSS Commands Introduced in This Chapter

No new commands were introduced in this chapter.

Review Questions

1. What is specification?

2. How does specification differ from replication?

3. Give an example of specification.

4. Give an example of replication.

5. What does it mean to "control" for a third variable?

6. Is this the same or different from "holding a variable constant"?

7. If we wanted to instruct SPSS to create crosstabs examining the relationship between POLREC and PARTY while controlling for SEX, where in the Crosstabs window would we transfer SEX (i.e., to which field, the Row(s):, Column(s):, or third box near the bottom of the window)?

8. In examining the relationship between political philosophy and party identification, what other variables (besides sex and education) might you want to control for? Name at least two.

9. When conducting multivariate analysis, how do we ultimately know which variable is the dependent one and which is the independent one?

10. If we were performing multivariate analysis and found a relationship between RACE and voting behavior, could RACE be the dependent variable? Why or why not?

11. Name three variables from your data set which you think may logically affect or have an impact on how people feel about gun control (GUNLAW) and explain why.

NAME _____

CLASS _____

INSTRUCTOR _____

DATE _____

To complete the following exercises you need to load the data file EXERPLUS.SAV. You will find answers to Questions 1-2 in Appendix B.

Recode the variable RACWORK to create RACWORK2, then label the item as follows:

RACWORK		RACWORK2	
Old Values		*New Values*	*Labels*
1-2	→	1	Mostly White
3	→	2	Half White-Black
4-5	→	3	Mostly Black

Now use crosstabs to examine the relationship between RACWORK2 (recoded RACWORK) and AFFREC (recoded AFFRMACT).[3] Designate RACWORK2 as the column variable and AFFREC as the row variable, request column percentages, and chi-square. Then use your output to answer the questions below.

1. The table shows that those who work mostly with Whites are _____ [more likely/less likely/not any more or less likely] than those who work mostly with Blacks to support affirmative action.

2. The significance of chi-square is _____ [less than/more than] .05, so the relationship between AFFREC and RACWORK2 _____ [is/is not] statistically significant.

3. List three variables from the data file EXERPLUS you want to use to examine why those who work with mostly Whites are less supportive of affirmative action than those who work with mostly Blacks.

   Variable 1 _____
   Variable 2 _____
   Variable 3 _____

_____

[3] We recoded AFFRMACT to create AFFREC in SPSS Lab Exercise 15.1, Question 1. If you did not save AFFREC on your EXERPLUS file, refer back to the recode instructions before proceeding.

4. Justify your choice of variable 1 above (i.e., give theoretical reasons for choosing this variable).

5. Justify your choice of variable 2 above (i.e., give theoretical reasons for choosing this variable).

6. Justify your choice of variable 3 above (i.e., give theoretical reasons for choosing this variable).

NAME _____

CLASS _____

INSTRUCTOR _____

DATE _____

7. Examine the relationship between AFFREC and RACWORK2 while
   controlling for variable 1 above. Run Crosstabs with chi-square. If you
   had to recode variable 1, make sure you explain how you did that.
   Then create a summary table based on the results of your Crosstab and
   show it below (if you need help creating a summary table, see the
   tables in the chapter for guidance).

8. Summarize below the major findings from your table. Explain what are, in your view, the primary observations that can be made regarding the table. Be sure to note, for instance, whether the findings supported your expectations. Use chi-square as a criterion for judging whether the differences in your table are significant (if your findings are statistically significant, you may want to go back and measure the strength of the relationship and then discuss how you did that and what you found).

NAME _____

CLASS _____

INSTRUCTOR _____

DATE _____

9. Examine the relationship between AFFREC and RACWORK2 while controlling for variable 2 above. Run Crosstabs with chi-square. If you had to recode variable 2, make sure you explain how you did that. Then create a summary table based on the results of your Crosstab and show it below.

10. Summarize the major findings from your table. Explain what are, in your view, the primary observations that can be made regarding the table. Be sure to note, for instance, whether the findings supported your expectations. Use chi-square as a criterion for judging whether the differences in your table are significant (if your findings are statistically significant, you may want to go back and measure the strength of the relationship and then discuss how you did that and what you found).

NAME _____

CLASS _____

INSTRUCTOR _____

DATE _____

11. Examine the relationship between AFFREC and RACWORK2 while controlling for variable 3 above. Run Crosstabs with chi-square. If you had to recode variable 3, make sure you explain how you did that. Then create a summary table based on the results of your Crosstab and show it below.

12. Summarize the major findings from your table below. Explain what are, in your view, the primary observations that can be made regarding the table. Be sure to note, for instance, whether the findings supported your expectations. Use chi-square as a criterion for judging whether the differences in your table are significant (if your findings are statistically significant, you may want to go back and measure the strength of the relationship and then discuss how you did that and what you found).

Chapter 19 A Powerful Prediction of Attitudes Toward Abortion

In previous analyses, we've seen how complex attitudes about abortion are. As we return to our analysis of this controversial topic, you have additional tools for digging deeper. Let's begin with the religious factor. Then we'll turn to politics and other variables.

Religion and Abortion

In Chapter 13, we found that both religious affiliation and measures of religiosity were related to abortion attitudes. The clearest relationships were observed in terms of the unconditional right to abortion, because only a small minority are opposed to abortion in all circumstances.

Protestants and Catholics are generally less supportive of abortion than Jews and "Nones." And on measures of religiosity, opposition to abortion increases with increasing religiosity. The most religious are the most opposed to a woman's right to choose an abortion.

With your multivariate skills, you can examine this issue more deeply. Consider the possibility, for example, that one of these relationships is an artifact of the other.

Demonstration 19.1: Religious Affiliation and Church Attendance

To explore the possibility that one of the relationships we found in Chapter 13 is merely an artifact of another association, you need to open your DEMOPLUS.SAV file and examine the relationship between religious affiliation (RELIG) and church attendance (CHATT).[1]

---

[1] For RELIG, the values 0, 5-99 should be defined as missing.

CHATT Recoded Church Attendance * RELIG RS RELIGIOUS PREFERENCE Crosstabulation

			RELIG RS RELIGIOUS PREFERENCE				
			1 PROTES TANT	2 CATHOLIC	3 JEWISH	4 NONE	Total
CHATT Recoded Church Attendance	1 About weekly	Count	279	123	1	5	408
		% within RELIG RS RELIGIOUS PREFERENCE	35.0%	34.1%	3.2%	2.6%	29.5%
	2 About monthly	Count	162	54	4	8	228
		% within RELIG RS RELIGIOUS PREFERENCE	20.3%	15.0%	12.9%	4.1%	16.5%
	3 Seldom	Count	255	129	18	58	460
		% within RELIG RS RELIGIOUS PREFERENCE	32.0%	35.7%	58.1%	29.9%	33.2%
	4 Never	Count	102	55	8	123	288
		% within RELIG RS RELIGIOUS PREFERENCE	12.8%	15.2%	25.8%	63.4%	20.8%
Total		Count	798	361	31	194	1384
		% within RELIG RS RELIGIOUS PREFERENCE	100.0%	100.0%	100.0%	100.0%	100.0%

As you can see, there is a pretty clear relationship between these two variables. Protestants and Catholics are the most likely to attend worship services weekly or one to three times a month. Over 90% of those with no religion attend church seldom or never. If we combine the two most frequent categories, we see that 48 percent of the whole sample attends church at least one to three times a month. There are big differences among the five religious groups, however.

	Percentage Who Attend at Least 1-3 Times a Month
Protestants	55
Catholics	49
Jews	16
None	7

Demonstration 19.2: Religious Affiliation, Church Attendance, and Abortion

Because religious affiliation and church attendance are related to one another and each is related to abortion attitudes, there are two possibilities for us to explore. For example, perhaps church attendance seems to affect abortion attitudes only because Protestants and Catholics (relatively opposed to abortion) attend more often. Or, conversely, perhaps Protestants and Catholics seem more opposed to abortion simply because they attend church more often.

We can test for these possibilities by running a multivariate table, taking account of all three variables.

Recoding RELIG and ATTEND into Same Variables

To simplify our analysis, let's recode RELIG into two categories—"Christians" and "None," those respondents expressing no religious preference. While it would be interesting to compare Christians to those with other religious preferences, Christians (Protestants plus Catholics) and those responding "none" have sufficient numbers of cases for meaningful analysis. We will then recode ATTEND into two catagories as well.

Because we're going to be doing several recodes in this session, let's recode the original variables this time. In other words, rather than creating a number of new variables that we may not use again, we are going to recode the original variables RELIG and ATTEND.[2]

So, let's use **Transform → Recode → Into Same Variables . . .**

Make the recodes listed below, beginning with **RELIG** and then moving to **ATTEND**. Once you have recoded the items, access the Variable View tab and label your recoded variables. If you need to verify the process for recoding into the same variables, consult SPSS Command 19.1.

Recode RELIG			
Old Values		New Values	Labels
1-2[3]	→	1	Christian
3	→	system-missing	—
4	→	2	Other

Recode ATTEND			
Old Values		New Values	Labels
4-8	→	1	Often
0-3	→	2	Seldom

SPSS Command 19.1: Recoding into Same Variables

Transform → Recode → Into Same Variables . . . →

Highlight **variable name** → Click **right-pointing arrow** to move variable to

The Numeric Variables: field →

Click **Old and New Values . . . →**

Define **Old and New Values** in the Recode into Same Variables: Old and New . . . box →

Click **Add** to Change Old → New Values →

Click **Continue → OK**

Click **Variable View** tab → Click **right-side of rectangle** that corresponds with Recoded variable name and labels → add new labels →

---

[2] If you save your data set after this exercise, be sure to use Save As and give it a new name so that you'll still be able to get back to your original, unrecoded data.

[3] Previously we declared all cases except those coded Protestant, Catholic, Jew, and None as missing. Now we are going to collapse Protestants and Catholics into a category named Christian. Jewish respondents are being declared missing because they are too few for meaningful analysis. The code for None (4) is being changed to 2 simply to keep the code categories contiguous.

Crosstab Recoded Variables

Now run a **Crosstab** with **column percentages**. Designate **ATTEND** as the **row** variable and **RELIG** as the **column** variable.

ATTEND HOW OFTEN R ATTENDS RELIGIOUS SERVICES * RELIG RS RELIGIOUS PREFERENCE Crosstabulation

			RELIG RS RELIGIOUS PREFERENCE		
			1 Christian	2 None	Total
ATTEND HOW OFTEN R ATTENDS RELIGIOUS SERVICES	1 Often	Count	618	13	631
		% within RELIG RS RELIGIOUS PREFERENCE	53.3%	6.7%	46.6%
	2 Seldom	Count	541	181	722
		% within RELIG RS RELIGIOUS PREFERENCE	46.7%	93.3%	53.4%
Total		Count	1159	194	1353
		% within RELIG RS RELIGIOUS PREFERENCE	100.0%	100.0%	100.0%

As you can see, the relationship between religious affiliation and church attendance is still obvious after categories are collapsed on both variables.

Now let's review the relationships between each variable and abortion, again using the recoded variables.

Relationship Between ABORT and Recoded Items

ABORT Simple Abortion Index * RELIG RS RELIGIOUS PREFERENCE Crosstabulation

			RELIG RS RELIGIOUS PREFERENCE		
			1 Christian	2 None	Total
ABORT Simple Abortion Index	0 yes/approve	Count	262	67	329
		% within RELIG RS RELIGIOUS PREFERENCE	37.0%	56.3%	39.8%
	1 conditional support	Count	279	38	317
		% within RELIG RS RELIGIOUS PREFERENCE	39.4%	31.9%	38.3%
	2 no/disapprove	Count	167	14	181
		% within RELIG RS RELIGIOUS PREFERENCE	23.6%	11.8%	21.9%
Total		Count	708	119	827
		% within RELIG RS RELIGIOUS PREFERENCE	100.0%	100.0%	100.0%

ABORT Simple Abortion Index * ATTEND HOW OFTEN R ATTENDS RELIGIOUS SERVICES Crosstabulation

| | | | ATTEND HOW OFTEN R ATTENDS RELIGIOUS SERVICES | | Total |
			1 often	2 seldom	
ABORT Simple Abortion Index	0 yes/approve	Count	120	244	364
		% within ATTEND HOW OFTEN R ATTENDS RELIGIOUS SERVICES	29.9%	51.8%	41.7%
	1 conditional support	Count	166	160	326
		% within ATTEND HOW OFTEN R ATTENDS RELIGIOUS SERVICES	41.4%	34.0%	37.4%
	2 no/disapprove	Count	115	67	182
		% within ATTEND HOW OFTEN R ATTENDS RELIGIOUS SERVICES	28.7%	14.2%	20.9%
Total		Count	401	471	872
		% within ATTEND HOW OFTEN R ATTENDS RELIGIOUS SERVICES	100.0%	100.0%	100.0%

Notice that the relationship between affiliation and abortion is now represented by an epsilon of 19 percentage points. The relationship between church attendance and abortion has an epsilon of 22 percentage points.

Politics (POLREC, PARTY) and Abortion (ABORT)

As we saw in Chapter 13, political philosophies have a strong impact on attitudes toward abortion. You might want to refresh your memory by rerunning this table. (You now know how. Wow!)

ABORT Simple Abortion Index * POLREC Recoded polviews Crosstabulation

| | | | POLREC Recoded polviews | | | Total |
			1 Liberal	2 Moderate	3 Conservative	
ABORT Simple Abortion Index	0 yes/approve	Count	125	148	85	358
		% within POLREC Recoded polviews	55.3%	42.3%	31.3%	42.2%
	1 conditional support	Count	71	149	98	318
		% within POLREC Recoded polviews	31.4%	42.6%	36.0%	37.5%
	2 no/disapprove	Count	30	53	89	172
		% within POLREC Recoded polviews	13.3%	15.1%	32.7%	20.3%
Total		Count	226	350	272	848
		% within POLREC Recoded polviews	100.0%	100.0%	100.0%	100.0%

The impact of political philosophy on unconditional support for a woman's right to choose abortion equals 24 percentage points. As we saw earlier, however, political party identification—despite official party differences on the issue of abortion—does not have much of an effect.

Demonstration 19.3: The Interaction of Religion and Politics on Abortion Attitudes

In a multivariate analysis, we might next want to explore the possible interaction of religion and politics on abortion attitudes. For example, in Chapter 13, we found that Protestants and Catholics were somewhat more conservative than "Nones." Perhaps their political orientations account for the differences that the religious groups have on the issue of abortion.

With your multivariate skills, testing this new possibility is a simple matter. Take a minute to figure out the SPSS command that would provide for such a test. Then enter it and review the results. [Hint: Run Crosstabs with column percentages, specifying POLREC as the column variables, ABORT as the row variable, and RELIG as the control/third variable]

Here's a summary table of the results you should have found if you are working with the latest recode for RELIG. Be sure you can replicate this on your own.

	Percentage Who Unconditionally Support Right to Abortion		
	Liberal	Moderate	Conservative
Christian	46	39	30
None	69	51	41

This table demonstrates the independent impact of religion and politics on abortion attitudes. In addition, what would you say it tells us about the religious effect observed earlier? Does it occur among all the political groups? What, if anything, do the epsilons for each political group (23, 12, 11) tell us about the religious effect?

Overall, you can see that the joint impact of politics and religion is represented by an epsilon of 39 percentage points (69-30), a fairly powerful degree of prediction for these controversial opinions.

Demonstration 19.4: Constructing an Index of Ideological Traditionalism

To support our continued analysis, let's create an index to combine the religious and political factors. For the time being, we'll call it our "index of ideological traditionalism."

You may recall from our earlier discussion that there are several different ways to construct indexes. In Chapter 9 we introduced you to a method using COUNT. In this chapter we are going to introduce you to another method using the COMPUTE command.

As you are now aware, there are a number of steps involved in creating an index. However, all the work is worth it because in the end we will have a composite measure that captures religious and political predispositions to support abortion. In other words, we will have built an index based on our two religious items (ATTEND and RELIG) and one political item (POLREC), which allows us to predict attitudes toward abortion.

In this case, our index will range from 0 (traditional) to 4 (nontraditional). Before we begin constructing our index, it may be useful to give you a brief overview of the seven steps involved in creating our new index of ideological traditionalism, which we will call IND:

Step 1:   Create new index "IND."

Steps 2-5: Assign points on the index based on responses to the three component variables: POLREC, RELIG, and ATTEND. As noted, our index scores will run from 0 (Opposed to abortion) to 4 (Supportive of abortion). We will assign points as follows:

Step 2:   If Liberal (1) on POLREC, get 2 points on IND.

Step 3:   If Moderate (2) on POLREC, get 1 point on IND.

Step 4:   If Other (2) on RELIG, get 1 point on IND.

Step 5:   If attend religious services seldom (2) on ATTEND, get 1 point on IND.

Step 6:   Use COMPUTE to handle missing data.

Step 7:   Access Variable View tab and define IND (i.e., decimals, labels, etc . . .).

Now that you have reviewed the steps involved in creating our new index of ideological traditionalism IND, let's go through each of the steps one at a time.

Step 1: Create IND

To begin, select **Transform → Compute . . .**

In the Compute Variable: box, create a new Target Variable: called **IND** (for index).

We'll start by giving everyone a 0, so type **0** or use the calculator pad to move 0 into the Numeric Expression box. Your expression should now read "IND = 0" as shown below.

Run this instruction by selecting **OK**.

Step 2: Assign Points — If Liberal
(1) on POLREC, Get 2 Points on IND

Now we are ready to begin assigning points on our index.

Open the Compute Variable box once again by selecting **Transform →**
Compute . . .

Let's begin by giving people 2 points if they have a 1 on POLREC (Liberal). To
do this, change the Numeric Expression to **IND + 2**.

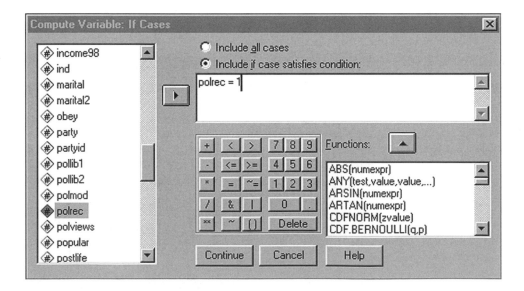

Now click **If . . .** and in the Compute Variable: If Cases box, select **Include if**
case satisfies condition:. Then, type or click **POLREC = 1** into the rectangle box,
as shown below:

Run this instruction by selecting **Continue**, **OK**, and then **OK** again to change
the existing variable IND.

At this point, we have given liberals 2 points and everyone else (including those with missing data) has 0 points.

Step 3: Assign Points—If Moderate
(2) on POLREC, Get 1 Point on IND

Now, let's give the "Moderates" 1 point on the index. Return to the Compute Variable window and make the following two changes:

- Change the Numeric Expression to **IND + 1**
- Change the If statement to **POLREC = 2**

Select **Continue, OK,** and **OK** to run this instruction.
Thus far, we have established an index as follows:

Liberals have 2 points.

Moderates have 1 point.

Conservatives have 0 points.

Those who are none of the above have 0 points on the index.
You may want to look at IND in the Data window or run Frequencies at any time in this process to see how the index is shaping up.

Step 4: Assign Points—If Other
(2) on RELIG, Get 1 Point on IND

Now we are ready to add to the index. Go back to the Compute Variable window and make the following specifications.

- Leave the Numeric Expression as IND + 1
- Change the If statement to RELIG = 2

Run this instruction by clicking **Continue → OK → OK.** Now we've added 1 point for each non-Christian.

Step 5: Assign Points—If Seldom
(2) on ATTEND, Get 1 Point on IND

Finally, return to the Compute Variable window and make these specifications:

- Leave the Numeric Expression as IND + 1
- Change the If statement to **ATTEND = 2**

Run this expression and review the logic of what we have done.
We've now created an index that presumably captures religious and political predispositions to support for a woman's right to an abortion. Scores on the index run from 0 (Opposed to abortion) to 4 (Supportive of abortion).

Step 6: Missing Data

There is one glitch in this index that we need to correct before moving on: those respondents for whom we have missing data. We don't know about the religious behavior or political orientations of those respondents for whom data were missing for ATTEND, POLREC, or RELIG. Since we can't provide an index score for respondents we don't know about, we must eliminate them from our analysis.

We can do this easily by using the NMISS function in the Compute procedure to set any cases to $SYSMIS (system missing) if they have missing information.

To do this, select **Transform → Compute . . .** , then following the instructions below:

■ With IND in the Target Variable box, type **$SYSMIS** in the Numeric Expression field, as shown below.

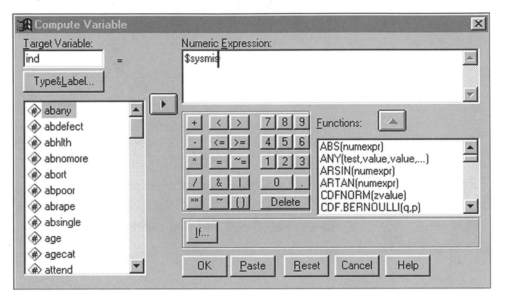

■ Now click **If . . .**
■ Click the button next to **Include if case satisfies condition:**
■ Type the following expression in the field directly below **NMISS (relig, attend, polrec) > 0**

- Click **Continue** → **OK** → **OK**

Step 7: Define IND

All that remains (thankfully!) is to define our new index. You can do that by accessing the **Variable View tab**, and setting the **Decimals, Width,** and **Values**.

SPSS Command 19.2: Creating an Index Using Compute

Step 1: Create New Index

Transform → **Compute . . .** → **Type name of new index** in Target Variable:
Field → Type/Paste **0** in Numeric Expression: field → **OK** →

Step 2: Add points to Index

Transform → **Compute . . .** → Keep new index name in Target Variable: field → **Begin assigning points** by adding appropriate points to new variable [i.e., IND + #] → **If . . .** → **Include if case satisfies condition:** → Type/paste **condition under which points should be added** to new index [i.e. if respondent was liberal: POLREC = 1] → **Continue** → **OK** → **OK**

Repeat this step as many times as necessary until complete adding points to index

Step 3: Handle Missing Data

Transform → **Compute . . .** Keep new index name in Target Variable: field →
Type **$SYSMIS** in Numeric Expression: field → **If . . .** → **Include if case satisfies condition** → Type "**NMISS** (variable names which compose index) **> 0**" → **Continue** → **OK** → **OK**

Step 4: Define New Index

Click **Variable View** tab → set Decimals, Width, Labels, etc . . .

Run Frequencies to Check IND

Having created such an index, it is always a good practice to check the frequencies. Run **Frequencies** on **IND** and you should get this:

IND Ideological Traditionalism					
		Frequency	Percent	Valid Percent	Cumulative Percent
Valid	0 Traditional	242	16.1	19.0	19.0
	1	385	25.7	30.2	49.2
	2	391	26.1	30.7	79.9
	3	183	12.2	14.4	94.3
	4 Nontraditional	73	4.9	5.7	100.0
	Total	1274	84.9	100.0	
Missing	System	226	15.1		
Total		1500	100.0		

Does IND Predict Attitudes Toward Abortion?

After all that work, let's finally see how well our index predicts abortion attitudes. To do this, run the following table.

ABORT Simple Abortion Index * IND Ideological Traditionalism Crosstabulation			IND Ideological Traditionalism					
			0 Traditional	1	2	3	4 Nontraditional	Total
ABORT Simple Abortion Index	0 yes/approve	Count	29	84	103	60	28	304
		% within IND Ideological Traditionalism	19.3%	38.5%	42.2%	51.7%	68.3%	39.5%
	1 conditional support	Count	62	80	107	42	9	300
		% within IND Ideological Traditionalism	41.3%	36.7%	43.9%	36.2%	22.0%	39.0%
	2 no/disapprove	Count	59	54	34	14	4	165
		% within IND Ideological Traditionalism	39.3%	24.8%	13.9%	12.1%	9.8%	21.5%
Total		Count	150	218	244	116	41	769
		% within IND Ideological Traditionalism	100.0%	100.0%	100.0%	100.0%	100.0%	100.0%

As you can see, the index provides a very strong prediction of support for the unconditional right to an abortion: from 19 percent to 68 percent, for an epsilon of 49 percentage points. Let's see if we can improve on our ability to predict.

Sexual Attitudes and Abortion

Earlier, we discovered that attitudes about various forms of sexual behavior were also related to abortion attitudes. As you'll recall, people were asked whether they felt premarital sex and homosexuality were "Always wrong," "Almost always wrong," "Sometimes wrong," or "Not wrong at all." In addition, respondents were asked whether they had attended an X-rated movie during the past year. Each of these items was related to abortion attitudes, with those most permissive in sexual matters also being more permissive about abortion.

Demonstration 19.5: Recode PREMARSX and HOMOSEX

Because we want to pursue this phenomenon, why don't you recode HOMOSEX and PREMARSX into dichotomies (only two values) of "Always or almost always Wrong" versus "Only sometimes or never wrong"? That will make it easier to conduct the following analysis.

Just as when we recoded ATTEND and RELIG, we want to recode HOMOSEX and PREMARSX "into same variables."[4] If you need to review the steps involved in doing this, see SPSS Command 19.1. In addition, the following hints may be useful to get you started.

Keep in mind that because both HOMOSEX and PREMARSX have the same values and labels, you can create the dichotomies for these two sexual attitude variables with a single command plus another to create new value labels.

Transform → Recode → Into Same Variables . . .

---

[4] For HOMOSEX and PREMARSX, the values 0, 5-9 should be defined as missing.

Old Values for BOTH HOMOSEX and PREMARSX		New Values	Labels
1-2	→	1	Wrong
3-4	→	2	Okay

As we noted earlier, if you save your data set after this session, be sure to use **Save As** and give it a new name, so that you will still be able to get back to your original, unrecoded data.

Demonstration 19.6: The Relationship Between Sexual Permissiveness and IND

Now, let's see whether the sexual behavior attitudes are related to our political-religious index that predicts abortion attitudes so powerfully. Why don't you run each of those tables now? Here's a summary of what you should find.

Percentage Who Are Permissive About	Index of Ideological Traditionalism				
	0	1	2	3	4
Premarital sex	34	54	71	87	88
Homosexuality	17	29	40	52	76

Even though there is a great difference in the overall level of permissiveness on these issues, we can see that the political-religious index is clearly related to each one.

Why don't you also go ahead and check to see if the index predicts whether people have taken in an X-rated movie during the past year? Once you have completed your analysis, compare your findings to those in Writing Box 19.1.

Writing Box 19.1

We see by inspection that the Index of Ideological Traditionalism strongly predicts whether people have attended an X-rated movie: progressing steadily from 9 percent of those scored 0 (traditional) on the index to 46 percent among those scored 4 (nontraditional). The nontraditional respondents are four times more likely to have seen an X-rated movie. This conclusion is confirmed by the chi-square value of 41.6, significant at less than the .001 level.

Demonstration 19.7: Exploring the Relationship Further

Now, let's see if the previously observed relationship between attitudes about sexual behavior and attitudes about abortion is really just a product of religious and political factors. Here's a summary of one of the tables you might look at.

Percentage Who Support Unconditional Abortion	Index of Ideological Traditionalism				
	0	1	2	3	4
Premarital sex wrong	–	25	25	–	–
Premarital sex okay	24	47	50	49	65

Obviously, our index combining religious affiliation, church attendance, and political philosophy does not explain away the relationship between attitudes on premarital sex and attitudes on abortion. Regardless of their scores on the index, those who find premarital sex somewhat acceptable are more supportive of abortion than are those who disapprove of premarital sex.

Why don't you continue this analysis by focusing on the other sexual attitudes?

You could also consider expanding the index by including the items on sexual attitudes.

The suggestions above are just two of the many avenues you could take if you are interested in pursuing this line of inquiry further. Clearly, we have gone a long way toward accounting for people's opinions on the issue of abortion. At the same time, we've moved quickly to give you a broad view. If attitudes toward abortion interest you, there are any number of directions you could follow up on in a more focused and deliberate analysis.

Conclusion

You've had an opportunity now to see how social scientists might set out to understand people's attitudes toward abortion. We know this is a topic about which you hear a great deal in the popular media, and it may be an issue that concerns you and about which you have strong opinions. The analyses above should give you some insight into the sources of opinions on this topic.

We hope this chapter has also expanded your understanding of the possibilities for multivariate analysis. Whereas bivariate analysis allows for some simple explanations of human thoughts and behaviors, multivariate analysis permits more sophisticated investigations and discoveries.

Main Points

- You can use your multivariate analysis skills to delve more deeply into the sources of opinion on controversial issues such as abortion.
- The primary goal in this chapter was to try to predict attitudes toward abortion.
- To that end, we went through a number of items which were earlier found to have an impact on abortion attitudes: religious affiliation, measures of religiosity, political philosophy, and sexual attitudes.
- A composite measure or index, called IND, was constructed to predict support for a woman's right to have an abortion.
- IND was made up of the following component variables: ATTEND, POLREC, and RELIG.
- After working through the demonstrations in this chapter, you should have a better understanding of how a social scientist might try to begin to account for opinion on an issue such as abortion.

- With the univariate, bivariate, and multivariate analysis skills you have learned, you should now be able to design a more careful and deliberate study dealing with this or another issue/topic which interests and excites you.

Key Term

Dichotomies

SPSS Commands Introduced in This Chapter

19.1 Recoding into Same Variables

19.2 Creating an Index Using Compute

Review Questions

Answer True or False for Questions 1-5.

1. In the 2000 GSS, church attendance was related to abortion attitudes, but religious affiliation was not.

2. According to the 2000 GSS, opposition to abortion tends to decrease with decreasing measures of religiosity.

3. According to the 2000 GSS, religious affiliation and church attendance are related to one another, but both are not related to abortion attitudes.

4. In the 2000 GSS, political philosophy was related to abortion attitudes, but party identification was not.

5. In the 2000 GSS, those who are somewhat permissive about premarital and homosexual sex also tend to oppose abortion.

6. List the commands for instructing SPSS to recode an original variable (Into same variable).

7. If you save your data set after recoding an original variable, what should you remember to do?

8. List two findings from our multivariate analysis of the relationship between abortion, religious affiliation, and church attendance.

9. Name the three items we used to construct our index of ideological traditionalism IND.

10. Scores on IND ranged from _____ to _____.

11. Does a score of 4 on IND indicate support for or opposition to abortion?

12. How well did IND predict abortion attitudes?

13. How might you expand the index IND to include one (or more) of the variables dealing with sexual attitudes?

NAME _____

CLASS _____

INSTRUCTOR _____

DATE _____

To complete the following exercises, you need to load the data file EXERPLUS.SAV. Answers to Questions 4-5 can be found in Appendix B.

In this exercise we are going to create a simple index combining attitudes toward teen sex (PILLOK, SEXEDUC, and TEENSEX). The goal is to construct an index/composite measure called IND1 that can be used to predict attitudes toward sex and family roles. To create IND1, simply follow the steps listed below. After we set up the index initially, you will be given a chance to expand it and explore its capabilities on your own.

1. Define the following values for each item listed below as missing:

   A) PILLOK -   0, 8, 9
   B) SEXEDUC -   0, 3-9
   [Hint: Use Range plus one discrete missing value.]
   C) TEENSEX -   0, 5-9
   [Hint: Use Range plus one discrete missing value.]
   D) FEPRESC -   0, 8, 9
   E) FECHLD -   0, 8, 9

2. Recode PILLOK, TEENSEX, FEPRESCH, and FECHLD into dichotomies as shown below. Use Transform → Recode → Into Same Variables to recode the original variables. As noted earlier, if you save your data set after this exercise, be sure to use Save As and give the data set a new name, so that you are able to get back to the original, unrecoded data.

   A) PILLOK

Old Values		New Values	Labels
1-2	→	1	Okay/Agree
3-4	→	2	Wrong/Disagree

   B) TEENSEX

Old Values		New Values	Labels
1-2	→	2	Wrong
3-4	→	1	Okay

   C) FEPRESCH

Old Values		New Values	Labels
1-2	→	1	Agree
3-4	→	2	Disagree

   D) FECHLD

Old Values		New Values	Labels
1-2	→	1	Agree
3-4	→	2	Disagree

3. Create a simple index called IND1 built on the items PILLOK, SEXEDUC, and TEENSEX (which we just recoded). There are a number of ways to create IND1. Feel free to design your own method or follow the general steps below. You may also want to refer to our discussion in the chapter if you need to refresh your memory.

Step 1: Create IND1

Step 2: Assign Points for IND1 based on scores for three component items (PILLOK, SEXEDUC, TEENSEX) as follows:
   * If Wrong/Disagree (2) on PILLOK, give 1 point on IND1.
   * If Oppose (2) on SEXEDUC, give 1 point on IND1.
   * If Wrong (2) on TEENSEX, give 1 point on IND1.

Our goal is to create an index (IND1) with scores ranging from 0 (least traditional attitudes toward sex and family roles—or, if you like, least conservative/most liberal views) to 3 (most traditional attitudes toward sex and family roles—most conservative/least liberal views).

Step 3: Missing data

Step 4: Define IND1

When you are done, you will have created an index (IND1) that captures predisposition's to hold traditional attitudes toward sex and family roles. Again, scores on the index range from 0 (least traditional) to 3 (most traditional).

4. Run Frequencies for IND1, then use your output to fill in the blanks below.

Frequencies: IND1

	<u>Frequency</u>	<u>Valid Percent</u>
0 least traditional	_____	_____
1	_____	_____
2	_____	_____
3 most traditional	_____	_____

5. See how well IND1 predicts attitudes toward sex and family roles. Run Crosstabs with column percentages and chi-square, specifying FEPRESCH and FECHLD as Row variables, and IND1 as column variable. Then use your output to fill in the blanks below:

		IND1			
		0	*1*	*2*	*3*
		Least tradit.			*Most Tradit.*
FEPRESCH					
1	*Agree*	_____	_____	_____	_____
FECHLD					
2	*Disagree*	_____	_____	_____	_____

NAME _____

CLASS _____

INSTRUCTOR _____

DATE _____

6. Does the index (IND1) provide a strong prediction of support for attitudes toward sex and family roles as measured by FEPRESCH and FECHLD? Discuss the findings of your analysis in detail below (keep in mind that FEPRESCH and FECHLD ask different questions).

7. You are now on your own! Expand IND1 to include another item of your choosing from your data file EXER.SAV (keep in mind that you may need to recode your item(s) before adding them to IND1). When you have expanded the index, run Frequencies, and then see how well your new expanded index predicts attitudes toward sex and family roles. Print both your frequencies and table(s), and then discuss your findings in detail below.

8. Continue your analysis by checking to see if your new expanded index predicts FEFAM and FEHIRE. Print your table(s) and discuss your findings in detail below (keep in mind that you may need to recode FEFAM and FEHIRE).

Chapter 20 Suggestions for Further Multivariate Analyses

In each of the previous analytic chapters, we have tried to leave a large number of "loose ends" for you to pursue on your own. If you are using this book in connection with a college class, you may want to follow up on some of those leads in the form of a term paper or a class project.

This chapter will build on some of those suggestions and offer some additional possibilities for your analyses. We begin with some suggestions regarding "ideal family size." We will then move to discuss other possibilities involving issues such as child training, the Protestant ethic, and prejudice. You should realize, however, that even within these fairly limited data sets, there are a number of analytic possibilities we have not considered.

Ideal Family Size and Abortion

Before leaving the topic of abortion altogether, we'd like to suggest another explanatory variable you might consider: ideal family size. We've seen previously that those who favor small families are more supportive of abortion than are those who favor large families. Now you are able to pursue this matter further using the data on your DEMOPLUS file. Here's the basic relationship with which you might start. Notice that you'll have to recode CHLDIDEL if you haven't already done that.

ABORT Simple Abortion Index * CHLDIDEL RECODED IDEAL NUMBER OF CHILDREN Crosstabulation						
			CHLDIDEL RECODED IDEAL NUMBER OF CHILDREN			
			1 0 to 2	2 3 to 4	3 5 or more	Total
ABORT Simple Abortion Index	0 yes/approve	Count	116	37	16	169
		% within CHLDIDEL RECODED IDEAL NUMBER OF CHILDREN	46.4%	25.0%	41.0%	38.7%
	1 conditional support	Count	99	68	12	179
		% within CHLDIDEL RECODED IDEAL NUMBER OF CHILDREN	39.6%	45.9%	30.8%	41.0%
	2 no/disapprove	Count	35	43	11	89
		% within CHLDIDEL RECODED IDEAL NUMBER OF CHILDREN	14.0%	29.1%	28.2%	20.4%
Total		Count	250	148	39	437
		% within CHLDIDEL RECODED IDEAL NUMBER OF CHILDREN	100.0%	100.0%	100.0%	100.0%

Why don't you see whether the index of ideological traditionalism (IND) is related to the ideal family sizes people reported? If it is, you should see whether relationship of ideal family size to abortion attitude is merely a matter of politics and religion or if it has an independent effect. You could substitute CHLDIDEL for the sexual attitudes in the preceding chapter. (Hint: Use gamma to measure relationship strength.)

Writing Box 20.1

There is an overall relationship between scores on IND and family-size preferences: those scored high on the index are more likely to prefer small families. The gamma calculation indicates it is a statistically significant relationship.

However, controlling for attitudes on abortion *specifies* the relationship: it only holds up among those who disapprove of abortion, reflected in the gamma of $-.480$ ($p = .001$). Among those supporting abortion, even partially, the index of traditional values has no significant impact on preferred family size.

As a somewhat more focused approach, you might review two articles that appear on the CD-ROM: Renzi's "Ideal Family Size as an Intervening Variable between Religion and Attitudes towards Abortion" (1975) and D'Antonio and Stack's "Religion, Ideal Family Size, and Abortion: Extending Renzi's Hypothesis" (1980). See if you can replicate portions of the published analyses. Perhaps you can see additional variables that should be taken into account.

Child Training

In Chapter 16, we began to look into some of the factors that might affect people's views of the qualities most important to develop in children. As a reminder, the qualities were as follows:

OBEY	to obey
POPULAR	to be well-liked or popular
THNKSELF	to think for himself or herself
WORKHARD	to work hard
HELPOTH	to help others when they need help

We suggested that you start your analysis with some basic demographic variables, such as age, sex, and race. We encouraged you to consider relationships you might logically expect, such as that more educated respondents might place higher value on children's thinking for themselves.

Now you are able to explore all the possibilities in greater depth. To stay with the example of education and independence of thought in children, you could see if there are variables that shed more light on that relationship.

You might check POLVIEWS, for example. Before you do, ask yourself what you would expect to find. You might also check the effect of gender while you're at it.

Earlier, we suggested you look at the impact of the sexual attitude items. Those who are permissive regarding violations of the established norms for sexual conduct often feel that they are thinking for themselves in those regards. How do such people feel about encouraging that trait in young people? With your multivariate skills, you can examine that matter with some sophistication.

Perhaps you will find it useful to combine some of the "quality" items into an index. On the face of it, OBEY and THNKSELF appear to value opposite traits. Are they negatively related to one another? Would they fit into an index of "conformity-independence," perhaps? If that seems a fruitful index to create, to which other variables does it relate?

The Protestant Ethic

One of the most famous of all books in the social sciences is Max Weber's *The Protestant Ethic and the Spirit of Capitalism* (1905/1958). In it, Weber traces the religious roots (in Calvinism) of the ethic of hard work and thrift that he found to forge the beginnings of capitalism. This ethic is something you might like to explore.

A central notion of the "Protestant ethic" is the idea of "hard work," the belief that individuals are responsible for their own economic well-being. People's wealth is taken as a sign of how hardworking and diligent they are. In its most extreme form, the Protestant ethic sees poverty as the result of slothfulness and laziness, and wealth as the product of persistence and hard work.

The GETAHEAD item in your GSS data set provides a measure of at least one dimension of the Protestant ethic that you might like to explore. To measure the degree to which people took responsibility for their own economic well-being, respondents were read this statement: "Some people say that people get ahead by their own hard work; others say that lucky breaks or help from other people are more important." Following the statement, they were asked, "Which do you think is most important?"

Why don't you begin by examining how GETAHEAD is related to other variables? It would seem logical that GETAHEAD would be related to WORKHARD. Are people who are in disadvantaged groups or have low incomes more apt to believe their fates are governed by luck rather than hard work? Or, does the belief in luck for success provide a rationalization for people who have little power to control the events that affect their lives? Because these variables are not the ratio measures that Pearson's *r* assumes, you can't take the results literally, but perhaps they can give you a first glimpse. Do not use this technique as a substitution for other, statistically appropriate, examinations.

If you follow these suggestions, you'll need to be prepared for some surprises - even disappointments—so it may take some hard work (not inappropriate) for you to create a measure of commitment to the Protestant ethic that you like. Then you can begin the multivariate search for the causes of this point of view. Be sure to check out the Protestants, but don't expect an easy answer.

Prejudice

In your analysis of the Protestant ethic, you may have looked at the place of the two prejudice items: RACMAR and RACPUSH. If not, you may want to do so now. Logically, the belief that people get ahead by hard work alone would seem to rule out the limits imposed by prejudice and discrimination. You can explore the relationship between some of the work ethic and prejudice items to see if this is the case.

Some beliefs about African Americans seem to be part and parcel of a racist point of view. Prejudiced images can lead to beliefs that, when turned into action, become discrimination. As part of the 2000 GSS, respondents were read the statement, "On the average, African Americans have worse jobs, income, and housing than white people." Then, they were asked if they thought the "differences" were because "most African-Americans just don't have the motivation or will power to pull themselves out of poverty?" Their responses are recorded in the item RACDIF4.

Demonstration 20.1: The Relationship Between RACDIF4, RACMAR, and RACPUSH

See the extent to which prejudicial beliefs are associated with the belief that African Americans should not push themselves where they are not wanted, the belief that interracial marriage should be made illegal, and the belief that African Americans don't have the willpower to pull themselves out of poverty. Be sure to define the values **0**, **8**, and **9** as **missing** for **RACDIF4**, **RACMAR**, and **RACPUSH** before creating the following tables.

RACPUSH BLACKS SHOULDNT PUSH * RACDIF4 DIFFERENCES DUE TO LACK OF WILL Crosstabulation

| | | | RACDIF4 DIFFERENCES DUE TO LACK OF WILL | | |
			1 YES	2 NO	Total
RACPUSH BLACKS SHOULDNT PUSH	1 AGREE STRONGLY	Count	54	11	65
		% within RACDIF4 DIFFERENCES DUE TO LACK OF WILL	28.0%	6.0%	17.2%
	2 AGREE SLIGHTLY	Count	66	31	97
		% within RACDIF4 DIFFERENCES DUE TO LACK OF WILL	34.2%	16.8%	25.7%
	3 DISAGREE SLIGHTLY	Count	40	46	86
		% within RACDIF4 DIFFERENCES DUE TO LACK OF WILL	20.7%	25.0%	22.8%
	4 DISAGREE STRONGLY	Count	33	96	129
		% within RACDIF4 DIFFERENCES DUE TO LACK OF WILL	17.1%	52.2%	34.2%
Total		Count	193	184	377
		% within RACDIF4 DIFFERENCES DUE TO LACK OF WILL	100.0%	100.0%	100.0%

RACMAR FAVOR LAW AGAINST RACIAL INTERMARRIAGE * RACDIF4 DIFFERENCES DUE TO LACK OF WILL Crosstabulation					
			RACDIF4 DIFFERENCES DUE TO LACK OF WILL		
			1 YES	2 NO	Total
RACMAR FAVOR LAW AGAINST RACIAL INTERMARRIAGE	1 YES	Count	34	8	42
		% within RACDIF4 DIFFERENCES DUE TO LACK OF WILL	17.8%	4.2%	11.0%
	2 NO	Count	157	184	341
		% within RACDIF4 DIFFERENCES DUE TO LACK OF WILL	82.2%	95.8%	89.0%
Total		Count	191	192	383
		% within RACDIF4 DIFFERENCES DUE TO LACK OF WILL	100.0%	100.0%	100.0%

What do the tables show? Is the opinion that poverty is a result of a "lack of motivation and will" related to the view that African-Americans shouldn't push? Similarly, is RACDIF4 related to attitudes toward the legalization of interracial marriage? Examine you output and then compare your findings to those in Writing Box 20.2.

Writing Box 20.2

Clearly, the view that racial differences in success are due to a lack of will among Blacks represents a broader range of racial prejudice. For example, among those who feel Blacks lack will, 62 percent say Blacks shouldn't push in where they are not wanted (agree strongly or slightly) as compared to only 23 percent of those who disagree with the statement about Blacks lacking will.

And while only one respondent in nine would support a law prohibiting interracial marriages, 18 percent would do so among those who say Blacks lack will, contrasted with only 4 percent of those who disagree that the status of Black Americans is due to a lack of will.

Demonstration 20.2:
Controlling for RACE

To test the racist quality in the first item further, let's control for RACE. If there is a racist element, we should expect to find the correlation only among whites.

Before beginning our analysis, let's **recode RACPUSH Into Same Variables** as follows:

Old Values		New Values	Labels
1-2	→	1	**Agree**
3-4	→	2	**Disagree**

Now go ahead and run your analysis:

RACPUSH BLACKS SHOULDNT PUSH * RACDIF4 DIFFERENCES DUE TO LACK OF WILL * RACE RACE OF RESPONDENT Crosstabulation					RACDIF4 DIFFERENCES DUE TO LACK OF WILL		
RACE RACE OF RESPONDENT					1 YES	2 NO	Total
1 WHITE	RACPUSH BLACKS SHOULDNT PUSH	1 agree	Count		101	35	136
			% Due to lack of will		63.1%	26.1%	46.3%
		2 disagree	Count		59	99	158
			% Due to lack of will		36.9%	73.9%	53.7%
	Total		Count		160	134	294
			% Due to lack of will		100.0%	100.0%	100.0%
2 BLACK	RACPUSH BLACKS SHOULDNT PUSH	1 agree	Count		17	6	23
			% Due to lack of will		65.4%	14.6%	34.3%
		2 disagree	Count		9	35	44
			% Due to lack of will		34.6%	85.4%	65.7%
	Total		Count		26	41	67
			% Due to lack of will		100.0%	100.0%	100.0%
3 OTHER	RACPUSH BLACKS SHOULDNT PUSH	1 agree	Count		2	1	3
			% Due to lack of will		28.6%	11.1%	18.8%
		2 disagree	Count		5	8	13
			% Due to lack of will		71.4%	88.9%	81.3%
	Total		Count		7	9	16
			% Due to lack of will		100.0%	100.0%	100.0%

Looking at the table, would you say that the racist element we were looking for is evident? Is there a correlation between the opinion that poverty is a result of a "lack of motivation and will" and the belief that African-Americans shouldn't push only among whites?

Here's how you might summarize these tables in a term paper or journal article:

Percentage Who Say African Americans Shouldn't Push	Agree	Disagree
Whites	63%	37%
Blacks	65%	35%

You may also want to look at the relationship between RACDIF4 and RACMAR while controlling for RACE. Is there a racist element evident here?

Writing Box 20.3

White respondents are twice as likely (13 percent) to favor a law prohibiting interracial marriage as are Blacks (6 percent). However, the belief that Blacks' relatively lower status is due to a lack of will increases opposition to interracial marriages within both groups: 20 vs 5 percent among whites and 12 vs 2 percent among Blacks. None of the relatively few "Others" favored the racist law.

We've taken you through this complex multivariate analysis to demonstrate the importance of ascertaining the sometimes-hidden meanings that lie behind the responses that people give to survey questions. That's a big part of the *adventure* of social research. (We wanted to call this book *Earl, Fred, and Jeanne's Excellent Adventure*, but you know publishers.)

If you would like to continue this line of analysis, why don't you substitute POLREC for RACMAR in the above analysis? We leave that possibility in your able, multivariate hands.

Conclusion

The National Rifle Association and other proponents of extensive gun distribution (see GUNLAW) are fond of saying, "Guns don't kill people; people kill people." Well, in a more pacific spirit, we'd like to suggest that SPSS doesn't analyze data; analysts analyze data. And the good news is that you are now a bona fide, certifiable data analyst.

We've given you about all the guidance and assistance that we planned when we started this adventure. Remember, we said, "Just add you" in Chapter 1; well, it's show time. You're on your own now, although you should have a support network behind you. If you read this book in connection with a college course, you have your instructor.

The final section of this book expands the horizons of social research even further. It suggests a number of ways that you might reach out beyond the GSS data set we have provided for your introductory experience with the adventure of social research.

Main Points

- This chapter offers suggestions for further multivariate analyses.
- If you are using this book in connection with a college course, these suggestions may be useful in helping you design a term paper or class project.
- Even within the limited data sets that accompany this text, there are numerous analytic possibilities that we have not explored or considered.
- The suggestions offered here are built on the questions and issues addressed in your data file DEMOPLUS.SAV.
- The suggestions cover issues such as ideal family size, child training, the Protestant ethic, and prejudice.
- These suggestions are just a small portion of the analytic possibilities stemming from the data contained in your DEMOPLUS file.

Key Terms

No new terms were introduced in this chapter.

SPSS Commands Introduced in This Chapter

No new commands were introduced in this chapter.

Review Question

1. Discuss how you might apply the techniques and procedures we covered in Part V (Chapters 17-20) on multivariate analyses to examine the following topics/issues:

   1. Ideal Family Size
   2. Child Training
   3. Protestant Work Ethic
   4. Prejudice

NAME _____

CLASS _____

INSTRUCTOR _____

DATE _____

In Lab Exercise 16.1 we asked you to use bivariate techniques to examine one of the topics from the EXERPLUS file: sex roles, law enforcement, environment, mass media (use and confidence), national government spending priorities, teen sex, affirmative action, or equalization.

In this exercise you will be given an opportunity to expand your analysis of this issue by applying some of the multivariate techniques discussed in Chapters 17-19.

1. List the general topic/issue you examined in Lab Exercise 16.1.

2. List the variables (including any recoded variables or indexes) in your EXERPLUS file that pertain to this issue.

3. In Lab Exercise 16.1 you developed two hypotheses. List Hypotheses 1 and 2 below, identifying the dependent and independent variables in each.

A: Hypothesis 1:

Independent Variable: _____

Dependent Variable: _____

B: Hypothesis 2:

Independent Variable: _____

Dependent Variable: _____

4. Describe the strength and significance of the relationship between the variables in Hypothesis 1. In particular, you should note whether the relationship is worth exploring further.

NAME _____

CLASS _____

INSTRUCTOR _____

DATE _____

5. Describe the strength and significance of the relationship between the variables in Hypothesis 2. In particular, you should note whether the relationship is worth exploring further.

6. Based on your responses to Questions 4 and 5, choose one hypothesis you would like to explore further [list abbreviated variable names]. If neither hypothesis is worth exploring further, develop a new hypothesis, and run through the exercises in SPSS Lab Exercise 16.1 (Questions 4-10) again, before continuing with this exercise. Once you have identified a hypothesis that is worth exploring further, fill in the blanks below.
Independent Variable: _____
Dependent Variable: _____

7. List a variable from your EXERPLUS file that you think may be related to the independent and dependent variables listed in response to Question 6 and explain your reasoning.

Third variable A: _____

8. List another variable from your EXERPLUS file that you think may be related to the independent and dependent variables listed in response to Question 6 and explain your reasoning.

Third variable B: _____

9. From the list of techniques reviewed in previous Chapters, circle the procedures that are appropriate to examine the relationship between your independent, dependent, and third variable A (Question 7). [Hint: You should circle at least one technique in each "Group"]

A. Group 1:
   * Running Crosstabs with a control variable

B. Group 2:
   * Recoding to create a dummy variable
   * Multiple Regression
   * Recoding into Same Variable
   * Creating an Index Using Compute

C. Group 3
   * Measure of association (lambda, gamma, correlation matrix with Pearson's *r*, regression, scatterplot with regression line)
   * Tests of significance (chi-square, *t*-test, ANOVA)

10. From the list of techniques reviewed in previous Chapters, circle the procedures that are appropriate to examine the relationship between your independent, dependent, and third variable B (Question 8). [Hint: You should circle at least one technique in each "Group"]

A. Group 1:
   * Running Crosstabs with a control variable

B. Group 2:
   * Recoding to create a dummy variable
   * Multiple Regression
   * Recoding into Same Variable
   * Creating an Index Using Compute

B. Group 3
   * Measure of association (lambda, gamma, correlation matrix with Pearson's r, regression, scatterplot with regression line)
   * Tests of significance (chi-square, t-test, ANOVA)

NAME   _____

CLASS   _____

INSTRUCTOR   _____

DATE   _____

11. Use the techniques you identified as appropriate in response to Question 9 to examine the relationship between your independent, dependent, and third variable A. Once you have conducted your analysis:

- print and attach your output to this sheet
- summarize your findings in prose

12. Use the techniques you identified as appropriate in response to Question 10 to examine the relationship between your independent, dependent, and third variable B. Once you have conducted your analysis:
   - print and attach your output to this sheet
   - summarize your findings in prose

Part VI **The Adventure Continues**

In the concluding chapters, we want to explore several different ideas that may support your continued investigations into the nature of human beings and the societies they create.

It struck us that you might be interested in conducting your own survey—perhaps as a class project. Consequently, in Chapter 21, Appendix C, and CD-Appendixes D, E, and F, we begin by taking a step back to look at the process of social research and the research proposal. We then focus specifically on survey research. In particular, we delve into designing and administering a survey, defining and entering data in SPSS, and writing a research report.

In Chapter 22, we suggest other avenues for pursuing your social investigations. Among other things, we talk about the unabridged GSS, other data sources you might explore, and other computer programs you might find useful.

We hope that by the time you finish these chapters, you will have fully realized the two purposes that lay behind our writing this book: to help you learn (a) the logic of social research and (b) how to pursue that logic through the use of SPSS. In addition, we hope you will have experienced some of the excitement and challenge that makes social research such a marvelous adventure.

Chapter 21 **Designing and Executing Your Own Survey**

The GSS data sets provided with this book are of special interest to researchers because they offer a window on American public opinion. We thought you might be interested in learning about the thoughts and actions of people across the country.

At the same time, it occurred to us that many of you may be interested in conducting your own survey, investigating topics, issues, and populations not addressed by the GSS or other data sets. Conducting your own survey is a good idea because data analysis in a classroom setting is sometimes more meaningful if the data are more personal. Perhaps you would like to analyze the opinions and behaviors of your own class (if it's a large one), the opinions of students elsewhere in your school, or even the attitudes of members of your community.

If you are interested in conducting a survey, this chapter, Appendix C, and CD-Appendixes D, E, and F are designed to help you get started developing and administering the survey, defining and entering the data in SPSS, and writing a research report (you already know how to analyze the data!). This chapter and the supporting appendixes are our (albeit brief) answer to those students and readers who ask, "How can I do this myself?"

While we cannot hope to provide you with an in-depth understanding of the intricacies of survey research in such a short time, we do give you a brief overview of the steps involved in designing and implementing your own survey. When possible, we will also point you toward other resources that you may find useful as you launch your own original study.

The Social Research Process and Proposal

Before we focus on designing and executing your own survey, we want to take a step back and place survey research and data analysis, which have been the central focus of this book, in the context of the social research process as a whole.

Our primary focus in this book has been a secondary analysis of a small portion of a nationwide survey, the 2000 GSS. As you are aware, survey research is just one of many methods of data collection used by social researchers. Other methods include, but are not limited to, experimentation, participant observation, focus groups, intensive interviews, and content analysis.

Not only has our focus been limited to just one method of data collection, but it has also been limited to one (albeit crucial) step in the social research process—data analysis. We have focused on the use of one of the most popular computer software programs, SPSS, to analyze survey data. As we will discuss in the next chapter, there are other software packages that you might want to consider using as well.

Because our focus has been on the statistical analysis of survey data using SPSS, our discussions of the practice and process of social research have been necessarily limited to data analysis. Before conducting your own study, you may find it helpful to review the entire social research process and to get some tips on writing a research proposal (which is often the first step in the research process) and, most importantly, to locate texts that will give you more detailed descriptions of parts of the research process not covered here.

CD-Appendix E includes an excerpt from Russell K. Schutt's comprehensive research methods text, *Investigating the Social World* (2001). The excerpt focuses on the major steps involved in designing a research project and gives some guidelines for writing a research proposal. As Schutt notes, the research proposal is a crucial step in the social research process because it goes "a long way toward shaping the final research report and will make it easier to progress at later research stages" (p. 429).

Schutt's text is just one of many research methods texts that you may find useful. Others include Babbie, *The Practice of Social Research* (2001); Bailey, *Methods of Social Research* (1994); Judd, Smith, and Kidder, *Research Methods in the Social Sciences* (1991); and Neuman, *Social Research Methods: Qualitative and Quantitative* (1996). While this list is by no means exhaustive, it should be useful in helping to locate a text that will provide you with a comprehensive overview of social research.

Designing and Executing Your Own Survey

Like all methods of data collection, survey research has its own peculiar advantages and disadvantages, benefits and liabilities. Nevertheless, a carefully constructed and executed survey can yield results that are considered valid, reliable, and generalizable. The 2000 GSS is a good example of a carefully designed and implemented survey, yielding data from which findings can be generalized to all English-speaking, noninstitutionalized American adults, eighteen years of age and older.

To design and conduct a survey that meets scientific standards, you need to pay particular attention to the steps required for survey research: research design, sampling, questionnaire construction, data collection, data processing, data analysis, and report writing.

To help you design and implement your own survey, we have included an excerpt from a guide called "SPSS Survey Tips" in CD-Appendix F; this appendix discusses some of the key considerations in planning, developing, and executing a survey. You should think of these tips as a general guide to designing and executing your own survey rather than as hard and fast rules. Keep in mind that it is unlikely that all social scientists or pollsters would agree with every recommendation. Moreover, in the "real world" the process of developing and implementing a survey is seldom as "neat" as the sequential ordering of the "tips" may suggest.

Despite these caveats, we think you will find "SPSS Survey Tips" a useful and concise overview of the steps involved in developing and implementing your own survey. In addition, you may also want to consult one of the many texts devoted to the principles and techniques of survey research. In particular, we draw your attention to Alreck and Settle, *The Survey Research Handbook* (1985); Babbie, *Survey Research Methods* (1990); and Czaja and Blair, *Designing Surveys: A Guide to Decisions and Procedures* (1996).

Sample Questionnaire

To help you collect your own data, we have included a Sample Questionnaire in Appendix C that asks some of the same questions found in the subset of GSS items included in your DEMO file. We've also provided the tools you may need to make any modifications that you might like in the interest of local relevance. If you wish, you can make copies of the questionnaire and use it to collect your own data.[1]

If you are more ambitious, you might choose to design a totally different questionnaire that deals with whatever variables interest you. There is no need for you to be limited to the GSS variables that we've analyzed in this book or that we've suggested in the sample questionnaire. You have learned a technology that is much more broadly usable than that. To get ideas about the kinds of things sociologists and other social scientists study, you might go to the library and thumb through the research categories in Sociological Abstracts.

Whatever survey you choose to conduct, the following section tells you how to get your data into a form that SPSS will accept for analysis.

Getting Ready for Data Analysis Using SPSS

Once you have designed and administered your questionnaire (or collected your data) you are ready to begin analyzing your data. Getting data ready for analysis with SPSS is really a three-step process:

Step 1: Defining Your Data

Step 2: Editing and Coding Data

Step 3: Entering Raw Data

Step 1 – Defining Your Data

The first step, often called *data definition*, involves giving each item from your questionnaire a variable name, setting the data type, describing the variable, indicating values and labels, designating missing values, setting the item's level of measurement, and designating a place to store this information.

This process can begin even before you have completed collecting the data if you are certain that the questionnaire itself is not going to be altered or revised.

---

[1] We have also included an empty data file LOCAL.SAV on the CD that came with this book. As we will discuss later in the chapter, this file is already defined and can be used to enter data from a sample population.

Demonstration 21.1: Example 1—Defining ID

To walk you through this process, we are going to use the Sample Questionnaire provided in Appendix C. You may want to take a moment to review the Questionnaire before we begin defining the first variable, ID.

Go ahead and launch SPSS. If you get the "What would you like to do now?" dialog box, simply click **Cancel**. Now you should now be looking at the Data View portion of the Data Editor.

Since we will define our data in the Variable View screen, go ahead and click on the **Variable View** tab.

As you know from previous chapters, Variable View contains descriptions of the variables contained in a data file. In Variable View, each row describes a variable while the variable attributes (Name, Type, Width, Decimals, etc . . .) are contained the columns. Unlike your earlier experience with Variable View, now you are creating a variable definition rather than simply modifying one that has been supplied by someone else.

We will define the first variable ID (the case identification number) from our Sample Questionnaire. Since each row in Variable View represents a variable, looking at our Sample Questionnaire, you can see that the variables we'll be putting in the numbered rows start with ID, then move to CHLDIDEL, OBEY, POPULAR, and so on until we come to the last variable, SEX. For each variable, we will start by typing its name in the first column and then working our way across the columns from left to right (Name to Measure).

Variable Names

To begin, double click on the first cell in the upper-left corner (the one that corresponds with Row #1 and Column "Name). Now type the abbreviated variable name, **ID**.[2]

Untitled - SPSS Data Editor

File Edit View Data Transform Analyze Graphs Utilities Window Help

	Name	Type	Width	Decimals	Label	Values	Missing	Columns	Align	Measure
1	id									
2										
3										

Now go ahead and hit **Enter**. Once you do that, you will notice that the cell which corresponds with Row #1 and the second column (Type) becomes the active cell. Moreover, SPSS automatically gives you the default variable attributes for ID.

Type

There are several types of data, including "Comma," "Dot," "Scientific Notation," and others. To get a sense of the various types of data, **double click on**

---

[2] If you are designing your own survey and planning to use SPSS to analyze the data, there are several "rules" to keep in mind when constructing abbreviated variable names. Among the most important "rules" to keep in mind: Each name must begin with a letter (letters, digits, periods, or the symbols @, #, _, or $ can follow); variable names should not exceed 8 characters in length; variable names cannot end with a period; and each variable name on a file must be unique.

the small gray box with the three dots (ellipses), in the right side of the Row #1-Type cell.

SPSS has probably chosen "Numeric" by default. If not, click the **Numeric** button and then select **Enter**. If the "Numeric" type has already been selected, simply click **Cancel** or the **X** (Close button) to exit. All of the data we have used in this text and certainly in the Sample Questionnaire are "Numeric."

Decimal

For a moment, skip over the Width column, and click on the **right side of the cell** corresponding with Row #1 and the Decimal column. When you do, you will notice that a set of up and down arrows appears, allowing you to either increase or decrease the decimal places. Since our variable, ID, does not require any decimal places, click the **down arrow** until it reaches **0**.

Width

Now go ahead and click on the right side of the cell corresponding with Row #1 and the Width column. Once again, you will see up and down arrows allowing you to specify the width or the number of characters for the column.

While this column is not crucial for our purposes, you can go ahead and decrease the width to 3 or more if you wish.

Label

Now go ahead and **double click** in the **cell corresponding with Row #1 and the column Label**. This cell allows you to insert the variable label or a brief description of your variable. Variable labels can be approximately 255 characters long if necessary.

In this case, once you have double clicked on the cell, go ahead and insert a Variable Label for ID, such as "**Respondent's Identification Number**." When you do that, you will see the width of the column expands somewhat.

Once you are done, simply select Enter or use your cursor to click on the next cell, Values.

Values

Once again, double-click on the gray box with the ellipse on the right side of the cell to open the Value Labels box. The Value labels box allows you to assign values and labels for your variable. For instance, if we were defining the variable SEX, we would want to enter the values 1 and 2 for male and female respectively. 1 would be placed in the Value: box, male in the Value Label: box and then simply click enter.

In the case of ID, however, we do not need to assign values and labels because each respondent has a unique identification number. When we go through the next variable, CHLDIDEL, we will give you an opportunity to practice filling in the values and labels.

Click on the Cancel or X button to close the Value Labels box.

Missing

There are obviously no missing values for ID, so we do not have to open the Missing Values dialog box in this case.

However, if we wanted to define missing values (as we will in the case of CHLDIDEL), all we have to do is double-click on the gray box with ellipses in the right side of the cell.

Then in the Missing Values box we would define the missing values as we have done previously, by choosing No missing values (in the case of ID and SPSS's default setting), Discrete missing values, Range of missing values, or Range plus one discrete missing value.

If you opened the Missing Value box, you can click **Cancel** or **X** to exit.

Columns and Align

The following two columns (Columns and Align) allow us to define the width of the columns in the Data Editor and to specify the alignment of data values. By default, SPSS sets the column width to 8 and aligns the data on the right. If you wish to change either of these settings, you can double click on the right hand side of the cell and use the arrows. Since we don't need to change either the column width or alignment, we can skip to the last column "Measure."

Measure

The last step in the process of defining your variable is indicating the level of measurement. When you click on the right side of the cell which corresponds with Row #1 and the Measure column, you will see a down arrow. By clicking on the down arrow you can specify the level of measurement as either Scale (I/R), Ordinal, or Nominal.

In the case of ID, the level of measurement is nominal, each case having its own category.

After you change the level of measurement to nominal, you are done defining the first variable. If you like, click on the Data View tab at the bottom left side of the screen. You will now see that ID is magically placed in the first column at the top left-hand corner of your Data Editor.

To return to the Variable View screen, either **double-click** on the variable name (**ID**) at the top of the column or click the **Variable View tab**.

Demonstration 21.2:
Example 2 - Defining CHLDIDEL

Now that you have successfully defined the first variable from our Sample Questionnaire, why don't we go ahead and practice by defining the second item CHLDIDEL together as well. This time we will list the commands in an easy to read format. You should already be in the Variable View screen. We will place CHLDIDELin Row #2. Each of the following commands refers to variable attribute in Row #2.

- **Double-click** on the **cell** corresponding with Row #2 and the column Name
- Type **CHLDIDEL**
- Click **Enter**
- By default, SPSS will set the Type to Numeric, so there is no need to change that setting.
- Click on the **right side** of the **cell** corresponding with Row #2 and the column Decimal
- Use **down-arrow** to set decimal to **0**
- Click on the **right side** of the **cell** corresponding with Row #2 and the column Width
- Use **down-arrow** to change width to **2**
- Double click cell corresponding with Row #2 and the column Label
- Type a descriptive variable label, such as "**Respondent's ideal number of children**"
- Click **enter** or use **cursor** to move to next column, **Values**
- **Double-click** in **gray box** to open Value Labels dialog box
- Type **–1** in Value: box → type **NAP** in Value Labels: box → click **Add**
- You will notice that "-1=NAP" is now specified in the box below. If you wanted to change or revise the statement for any reason, simply highlight "-1=NAP." Once you do that, you will notice that you are able to select Remove to delete the statement.
- Now go ahead and enter the other values and labels for CHLDIDEL: seven +, DK, NA.

Keep in mind that the Sample Questionnaire contains questions taken from your DEMO.SAV file. Consequently, you can refer to that file or the Code Book in Appendix A to verify the values and labels for the variables in the Sample Questionnaire.

- Click **Enter** or use your **cursor** to move to the next column
- Click in the **gray box on the right-side** of the **Missing column** to open the Missing Values dialog box
- Select **Discrete missing values** and type the values **–1, 9** → Click **OK**
- By default, SPSS has probably already selected "Scale" as the level of measurement. If not, use the down-arrows to set the level of measurement to "Scale"
- Click on the **Data View** tab and you will see CHLDIDEL in the second column in your Data Editor window.

You have now successfully defined the first two items in our Sample Questionnaire, ID and CHLDIDEL. As you can probably see, while it is not a difficult process, it can be fairly time-consuming to define all the variables from a questionnaire, even one as small as our Sample Questionnaire.

SPSS Command 21.1: Defining a Variable

Make sure the **Variable View** screen is the **active window** →

Double-click on the **cell** corresponding with the appropriate Row and the column Name → **Type abbreviated variable name** → **Enter** →

Move through the cells corresponding with that Row and each applicable column from Left (Name) to Right (Measure) → Click or double-click on the right side of the cell to access either the arrows or the appropriate dialog box → For our purposes, the most important columns are: Name, Decimals, Labels, Values Missing, and Measure →

Once you are done, click on the Data View tab → Your new variable will be situated in a column at the top of the screen

Copying Variables
With Shared Attributes: Abortion Variables

One way to cut down on the time consuming process of defining variables is to copy and paste variables that share similar attributes or characteristics.

The seven abortion variables in our Sample Questionnaire, for instance, all use the numeric codes 1 and 2 to represent "Yes" and "No," 0 to represent "NAP," 8 to represent "DK," and 9 to represent "NA." Moreover in each case, 0, 8, and 9 are defined as "missing values."

In cases like these, it is not necessary to define each variable individually; instead, you can simply copy a variable. We will use the abortion variables to illustrate how this works.

Demonstration 21.3: Copying a Variable

Now that you are comfortable defining variables in SPSS, go ahead and define ABDEFECT, the first abortion variable in our Sample Questionnaire. Place

ABDEFECT in Row #3 directly below CHLDIDEL.[3] If you need to review the steps for defining a variable, refer to SPSS Command 21.1.

Once you have defined ABDEFECT, you can easily define the other six abortion variables (ABNOMORE, ABHLTH, ABPOOR, ABRAPE, ABSINGLE, and ABANY) by copying and pasting.

To do this, click on the **Row #** (3) to the left of the cell containing "ABDEFECT." When you do that, you will notice that the row is highlighted.

Now choose **Edit → Copy** from the drop-down menu.[4]

Then go ahead and **select the row** (most likely Row #4) where you would like to place the next variable (ABNOMORE). Now all you have to do is select **Edit → Paste**[5].

Since we need to define five more abortion variables, we can follow the same basic procedure again. This time, however, just click on the appropriate **row**, and select **Copy → Paste**. If you do that five times, you will have successfully defined all seven abortion variables. The only thing you need to do after that is to insert a unique variable name and label for each.

---

[3] We are placing ABDEFECT in Row #3 for illustrative purposes only. If you were actually to set up this data file, Row #3 would be occupied by OBEY, Row #4 by POPULAR, Row #5 by THNKSELF, and so on. The proper order is displayed on the LOCAL.SAV file on your CD-Rom.

[4] Alternatively, you can click on the **right-button** on your **mouse** and choose **Copy**.

[5] You can also click on the **right-button** on your **mouse** and select **Paste**.

SPSS Command 21.2: Copying a Variable

> In **Variable View** → Click **on left side of row** to be copied → **Edit** → **Copy** →
>
> *OR* **right-click on mouse** → **Copy**
>
> Click on **left side of row** copying to → **Edit** → **Copy** *OR* **right-click**
> **on mouse** →   **Paste** →

Demonstration 21.4: Saving Your New File

Before you end this (or any other) data definition session, remember to save the new file with a name that will remind you of its contents.

To save a new data file, make the **Data Editor** the active window. Then from the menu choose **File** → **Save As . . .** to open the: Save Data As dialog box. Now click on the **down-arrow** to the right of the **Save in:** field to choose the appropriate drive (usually 3½ floppy **A:** if you are saving to a floppy disk).

Then in the **File name:** field type in a descriptive file name and click **Save.**

SPSS Command 21.3: Saving a New Data File

> **Data Editor** active → **File Save As . . .** →
>
> Use **down-arrow** to right of Save in: field to select appropriate **drive** →
>
> **Type file name** in File name: field → **Save**

LOCAL.SAV

Now that you have mastered the commands for defining a variable and saving your new data file, we are going to let you in on a little secret. To save you the time and trouble of having to define all the variables in the Sample Questionnaire, we have included a file named **LOCAL.SAV** on the CD-ROM that came with this book. It contains the data definition for this particular questionnaire. In short, because we know you are getting toward the end of the book and are probably anxious to begin your own adventure, we wanted to save you the time and work of having to define all the variables included in the Sample Questionnaire so we did it for you (think of it as a gift of sorts)!

For now, however, just keep the existence of LOCAL.SAV in the back of your mind. We'll show you how to use it after we discuss the next step (Step 2) in the process of getting your data ready for analysis with SPSS—editing and coding your data.

Step 2—Editing and Coding Your Data

The second step in the process of getting your data ready for analysis with SPSS is editing and *coding* your data. People do not always follow instructions when filling out a questionnaire. Verbal or written responses have to be transformed into a numeric code for processing with SPSS. For ease of entry, questionnaires should be edited for proper completion and coding before you attempt to key or enter them into an SPSS file.

To the extent we could, we designed the Sample Questionnaire to be self-coding. By having a number next to each response for the *closed-ended* questions, the interviewer assigns a code as the respondent answers the question. Some questions we have had to leave *open-ended*, either because there would be too many responses to print on the questionnaire or because we couldn't anticipate all of the possible responses.

There are essentially four steps involved in editing and coding your data: making sure each questionnaire has a unique ID number, coding open-ended questions, making sure the codes are easy to read, and editing each questionnaire.

Unique ID Number

Each questionnaire should have a unique number in the ID field. We do this not because we want to identify individuals but because errors that show up later are frequently made in the coding process. For instance, we coded SEX as 1 for male and 2 for female, but in our analysis, we find a respondent with SEX coded 7. What we need to do is find the record with the erroneous code 7. To do this, we look up the ID number, go back to the original questionnaire, find out what code SEX should have been, and fix it.

Coding Open-ended Questions

Next in the editing process, we have to code the open-ended questions. All the people coding questions should be following the same written instructions for coding. For instance, at the end of Appendix C, we included a list of occupations and their socioeconomic statuses for coding SEI, the socioeconomic index. Other coding schemes might not be as elaborate. For instance, in a medical study, patients might be asked about the illnesses that brought them to the hospital. Coding might be as simple as classifying the illnesses as acute or chronic.

Insuring That Codes Are Easy to Read

Finally, the codes need to be written so that they are easy to read. We have designed our questionnaire to be *edge-coded*. If you look in the right margin, you will see that we put a space for each variable's code. We included these numbers because some statistics require that variables be placed in specific "columns" across each "record." Happily, that is not a requirement of SPSS for Windows. We'll use just the numbered blanks as a convenient place to write our codes.

Editing Questionnaires

Whether you are going to edit the Sample Questionnaire that we have been using as an example throughout this section or another questionnaire you designed on your own, you should get a copy of the codes used to define the file you are working with (i.e., a copy of the work you did in Step 1 when you defined your data). For this example we will access the codes used to define our LOCAL.SAV file.

Demonstration 21.5:
Accessing File Information for Coding and Editing

When you **open** the **LOCAL.SAV** data file that is contained on the CD-ROM, you will notice that the data cells are empty. Don't panic; they are supposed to be empty. This is the empty, but defined, data file LOCAL.SAV we mentioned earlier.

To display the codes for your use in coding your data, click **Utilities** followed by **File Info**. You should see the information for ID and the other variables in your Output window. To have the codes printed, simply click **File** and then **Print**.

Here is an example of the coding information you will find for the variable MARITAL, responses to Question number 4 on the questionnaire: "Are you - married, widowed, divorced, separated, or have you never been married?"

MARITAL		MARITAL STATUS
Measurement Level:		Ordinal
Column Width:		Unknown
Alignment:		Right
Print Format:		F
Write Format:		F1
Missing Values:		9
Value		Label
1		MARRIED
2		WIDOWED
3		DIVORCED
4		SEPARATED
5		NEVER MARRIED
9	M	NA

For people who are married, code 1 is used. For people who are widowed, code 2 is used; divorced, code 3, and so on. Notice that code 9, no answer, has an M next to it. This means that code 9 has been designated a missing code. All missing codes are thrown out of the analysis. If respondents fail to answer a question or give two responses for one question, they should be assigned the missing value code for that variable.

After printing the coding information for each variable, you should go through each questionnaire, one at a time, to make sure the coding is correct, that there is only one code per question, and so on.

SPSS Command 21:4: Accessing File Information for Coding and Editing

> **Utilities → File Information →**

Step 3—Entering Your Data

Once you have edited and coded each of your questionnaires, you can move to the final step in the process, entering your raw data. Once again, we are going to use our Sample Questionnaire as an example.

Because the LOCAL.SAV file is on CD-ROM, in order to enter data on it, you need to **save** the **file** to a floppy disk (or if you are working on your own PC, to the hard drive). Go ahead and do that now.

Once you are done, you can open the file and we will run through the process of entering data.

After opening your file, you should be looking at an empty data matrix in the Data View portion of the Data Editor. This is where we will enter our raw data. At this point the matrix should be empty, except for the variable names across the top and record numbers down the left side. You will notice that the order of the variables across the record is the same as the order of the variables on the questionnaire. We placed them in that order to make data entry easier and less error-prone.

Demonstration 21.6:
Moving Through Data View

You can easily move from cell to cell in the data matrix. Pressing just the **Tab** key moves the *active cell* to the right, and pressing the **Shift and Tab** keys moves the active cell to the left. You can tell the active cell by its thick black border.

Pressing the **Enter** key moves the active cell down to the next row (record or respondent). The **directional arrows** on your keyboard will also move the active cell, one cell at a time. The **mouse** can be used to make a cell active just by pointing and clicking. Long-distance moves can be made by pressing **Ctrl and Home** to move to the left-most cell on the first case and **Ctrl and End** to move to the rightmost cell on the last case.

SPSS Command 21.5: Some Tips for Moving Through Data View

> **Tab** – move active cell to right
>
> **Shift & Tab** – move active cell to left
>
> **Enter** – move active cell down to next row
>
> **Directional arrows** – move active cell, one cell at a time
>
> **Ctrl & Home** – move active cell to left-most cell, first case
>
> **Ctrl & End** – move active cell to right-most cell, last case

Demonstration 21.7: Entering Data

To enter data, simply **select the appropriate cell** in the Data Editor, making it the active cell. When you do that, you will notice that the record number and the variable name appear in the rectangle at the top left-hand corner of the Data Editor, directly below the tool bar. You can now enter the appropriate **value**.

When you enter your data you will notice that they first appear in the *Cell Editor* at the top of the Data Editor window, just below the toolbar.

Simply press **Enter, Tab** or **move to another cell** to record your data.

SPSS Command 21.6: Entering Numeric Data[6]

> In **Data View** → **Click** appropriate **cell** → Type **value** → **Enter** *OR* **move to another cell** to record data

---

[6] We specify "Numeric" because the data we work with in the text are numeric. More importantly, to enter anything other than numeric data in SPSS you must first specify the variable type. Consequently, the commands for entering nonnumeric data are somewhat different than those discussed here.

Demonstration 21.8: Revising or Deleting Data

Data may be changed at any time just by moving to the appropriate cell, **keying in new values**, and pressing **Enter** or **moving** to **another cell**.

If a particular case turns into a disaster, you can get rid of the entire case by **clicking on the record number** at the extreme left of a record and pressing the **Delete** key.

SPSS Command 21.7: Deleting an Entire Case

Click **Record Number** at far left side → **Delete** →

Demonstration 21.9: Saving Your Data File

After you are done entering data, or if you want to stop entering data and continue at a later time, make sure you save your data. By clicking **File** and **Save**, you will save your data under the name that was used at the beginning of the session (for instance, **LOCAL.SAV** or whatever other name you used when you saved the LOCAL.SAV file on disk or hard-drive).

If you wish to save it under another name, click on **File** and **Save As**. Be careful of which disk drive you save to.

Writing a Research Report

After you design and execute your survey and enter and analyze the data, it is finally time to report your results. To help you through this crucial aspect of the research process, we have included an excerpt in CD Appendix D which, among other things, presents guidelines for reporting analyses that you may find useful.

In addition, many research methods texts (including some of those we referenced earlier, such as Schutt, 2001) devote sections to writing research reports. Alreck and Settle (1985) and Babbie (1990) each devote a chapter specifically to reporting survey research results. You may also want to reference one of the many books devoted to writing, particularly those designed with social scientists in mind, such as Howard Becker, *Writing for Social Scientists* (1986) or Lee Cuba, *A Short Guide to Writing About Social Science* (1997).

Conclusion

Although there is a fair amount of work involved in doing your own survey, entering and analyzing your own data, and then reporting your results, there can also be a special reward or excitement about coming to an understanding of the opinions and behaviors of a group of people with whom you are directly familiar. The benefits of conducting your own study are even more evident if your survey focuses on topics and issues that are meaningful, relevant, or otherwise important to you or those in your community. In fact, the main advantage of designing and executing your own original or *primary research* is that you can focus specifically on those issues, topics, populations, and variables that interest you. Since you are in charge of the design, implementation, analysis, and reporting of your study, you do not have to depend on the work of other social scientists who may have approached the issue, topic, or problem differently. The downside, of course, is the fact that the time and resources involved in conducting your own study can often be tremendous. Nevertheless, we think you will find that whereas there are various advantages and disadvantages to both primary and secondary research, the rewards and excitement that come from both types of research make the time, energy, and commitment involved worth it.

Main Points

- This chapter, Appendix C, and CD-Appendixes D, E, and F are designed to help you construct and administer your own survey, enter the data in SPSS, and write a research report.
- CD-Appendix E includes an excerpt designed to give you a sense of the steps involved in the social research process and some hints on writing a research proposal (often the first step in the research process).
- There are various considerations involved in constructing and implementing a survey that is reliable, valid, and generalizable.
- SPSS Survey Tips, which is reprinted in CD-Appendix F, is included to give you an overview of how to design and execute your own survey.
- Appendix C contains a Sample Questionnaire with questions drawn from the 2000 GSS.
- There are three main steps involved in getting ready for data analysis using SPSS.
- Defining your data is the first step in the process.
- The LOCAL.SAV file includes the data definition for the Sample Questionnaire.
- The second step in the process is editing and coding your data.
- The third step in the process is entering your data.
- The excerpt in CD-Appendix D discusses one of the most important and difficult aspects of the social research process—writing a research report.

Key Terms

Data definition	Active cell
Open-ended	Close-ended
LOCAL.SAV	Cell editor
Edge-coded	Primary research
Coding	

SPSS Commands Introduced in This Chapter

21.1 Defining a Variable

21.2 Copying a Variable

21.3 Saving a New Data File

21.4 Accessing File Information for Coding and Editing

Review Questions

1. Name two methods social scientists use to collect data (besides survey research).

2. Name three decisions involved in designing a social research project.

3. Why is it important to write a research proposal?

4. Briefly describe at least four of the "tips" included in SPSS's Survey Tips.

5. List the primary three steps involved in getting ready for data analysis using SPSS.

6. What does "data definition" refer to?

7. Name two guidelines or rules for choosing a variable name that SPSS will accept.

8. What is a shortcut that can be used to define variables that share similar attributes?

9. What does the LOCAL.SAV file on your disk contain?

10. List two things you need to do when editing and coding your data.

11. List two ways you can move through the data matrix.

12. When you key in data, where does it appear before it is recorded (i.e., before you press Enter or move to another cell)?

13. Name two considerations involved in writing a research report.

14. Name two guidelines for reporting analyses.

NAME _____

CLASS _____

INSTRUCTOR _____

DATE _____

Our goal in this exercise is to allow you to practice defining, editing, coding, and entering data you collect from a small number of respondents.

1. Make 10 copies of the Sample Questionnaire contained in Appendix C (as an alternative, make 10 copies of a questionnaire you designed on your own). Then administer the questionnaire to 10 respondents (it can be friends, family, colleagues, etc . . .).

2. After collecting the data, go through the three steps involved in getting data ready for analysis using SPSS:

   A) Define Your Data

   B) Edit and Code Your Data

   C) Enter Your Data

3. After you have gone through these three steps, use the **Utilities → File Information** command to print coding information about your new data file. Then attach your output to this sheet.

4. Access the SPSS Tutorial [**Help → Tutorial**]. Click on the **Table of Contents** [the icon that looks like a house in the lower-right side of the screen] Work through the portion of the Tutorial labeled "**Using the Data Editor.**"

Chapter 22 **Further Opportunities for Social Research**

Well, we've come to the end of our introduction to SPSS. In this final chapter, we want to suggest ways in which you can expand beyond the scope of this book. In particular, we are going to focus briefly on the unabridged GSS, other data sets, and other computer programs that you may find useful as you continue your social research adventure.

The Unabridged GSS

The GSS data sets that accompany this book are limited to 41 (DEMO.SAV) and 47 (EXER.SAV) variables in order to accommodate all versions of SPSS. At the same time, you should realize that the data available through the GSS program are vastly more extensive. For instance, the 2000 data contain 1,063 variables and 2,817 cases. The cumulative data file that merges all the General Social Surveys conducted between 1972 and 2000 contains 3,500 variables and 40,933 cases.

Since the first General Social Survey was conducted in 1972, data have been collected on thousands of variables of interest to researchers around the country and, indeed, around the world. As we noted earlier, the National Opinion Research Center maintains an Internet site called GSSDIRS (General Social Survey Data and Information Retrieval System). You can access the GSSDIRS on the internet at http://www.icpsr.umich.edu/GSS.

The GSSDIRS site houses an interactive cumulative index to the GSS, indexing variables by subject, as well as abbreviated variable name. In addition, it contains a search engine that locates abstracts of research reports produced from GSS data, an electronic edition of the complete GSS codebook, an extensive GSS bibliography, and a data extraction system that permits downloading GSS data in a format that can be used with any version of SPSS.

Now that you are familiar with the use of GSS data through SPSS, you may be able to locate other GSS data sets through your school. You can also get information about purchasing GSS data from one of the following sources:

The Roper Center for Public Opinion Research
341 Mansfield Road, Unit 1164
University of Connecticut
Storrs, CT 06269-1164

Phone: (860) 486-4440
Fax: (860) 486-6308
Home page: http://www.ropercenter.uconn.edu/
E-mail: gssdata@ropercenter.uconn.edu

The Interuniversity Consortium for Political and Social Research (ICPSR)
P.O. Box 1248
University of Michigan
Ann Arbor, MI 48106-1248
Phone: (734) 998-9900
Fax: (734) 998-9889
Home page: http://www.icprs.umich.edu/
E-mail: netmail@icpsr.umich.edu

An important reference book for your use with GSS data is the *Cumulative Codebook* published by the National Opinion Research Center at the University of Chicago (e.g., see Davis, Smith, and Marsden, 2000).

Available both in book and computer forms, it may be purchased from the Roper Center. Or, if you wish, use the electronic version mentioned above.

The 2000 edition of the *Codebook* (Davis, Smith, and Marsden) contains information on all aspects of the GSS from 1972 to 2000, including exact questions, response codes, frequency counts, and so on. The table of contents for the latest edition, which is shown below, will give you an overview of the type of information included in this valuable resource:

Codebook TABLE OF CONTENTS

Here is a sample of some of the information available to you in the main body of the *Codebook*. This selection shows how coding has been accomplished for two of the abortion items that are included in your DEMO.SAV file.

206. Please tell me whether or not *you* think it should be possible for a pregnant woman to obtain a *legal* abortion

if . . . READ EACH STATEMENT, AND CIRCLE ONE CODE FOR EACH.

A. If there is a strong chance of serious defect in the baby?

[VAR: ABDEFECT]

RESPONSE	PUNCH	YEAR										COL. 780
		1972-82	1982B	1983-87	1987B	1988-91	1993	1994	1996	1998	2000	ALL
Yes	1	10980	236	4625	236	3056	840	1585	1514	1415	1397	25884
No	2	2195	92	1210	94	707	193	341	336	385	377	5930
Don't know	8	419	25	187	21	141	37	68	66	79	83	1126
No answer	9	32	1	50	2	16	5	2	7	3	4	122
Not applicable ..BK		0	0	1470	0	1987	531	996	981	950	956	7871

B. If she is married and does not want any more children?

[VAR: ABNOMORE]

RESPONSE	PUNCH	YEAR										COL. 781
		1972-82	1982B	1983-87	1987B	1988-91	1993	1994	1996	1998	2000	ALL
Yes	1	5920	111	2387	125	1640	480	930	853	758	720	13924
No	2	7133	216	3452	206	2129	539	995	972	1033	1050	17725
Don't know	8	542	26	181	20	132	51	65	91	86	85	1279
No answer	9	31	1	52	2	19	5	6	7	5	6	134
Not applicable ..BK		0	0	1470	0	1987	531	996	981	950	956	7871

In addition to the advantage of working with many more variables than we've included in the present file, the larger GSS data set permits you to conduct longitudinal research—to analyze changes in opinions and behaviors over the years.

The initial experience of the GSS data set in connection with this book has put you in touch with a powerful research resource that we hope you'll be able to use more extensively in the future.

Other Data Sets

As if the full GSS weren't enough, there are thousands of other data sets in existence that are appropriate for analysis with SPSS.

To begin, there is a global network of data archives, or data libraries, that operate somewhat like book libraries. Instead of lending books, these archives lend or sell sets of data that have been collected previously. The National Opinion Research Center, which administers the GSS, is one such archive. Another major archive is the Roper Center for Public Opinion Research.

Other data archives are maintained in the survey research centers of major universities, such as the University of California, Berkeley and Los Angeles campuses; the University of Michigan; and the University of Wisconsin.

Most of these data libraries, and in many cases the data they house, are accessible via the world wide web (www). We have already given you the web site addresses for the NORC and Roper Center. However, bear in mind that you can also access other data archives such as the Princeton University Survey Research Center at http://www.wws.princeton.edu/~psrc or the University of Michigan Documents Center at http://www.lib.umich.edu/govdocs/stats.html, just to name a few.

The data sets available for *secondary analysis* at these and other archives include, for example, studies conducted by university faculty researchers that may have been financed by federal research grants. Thus, the results of studies that may have cost hundreds of thousands of dollars to conduct can be yours now for the nominal cost of copying and shipping the data.

The Roper Center, for instance, is a repository for all the data collected by the Gallup Organization, including not only American "Gallup Polls" but those conducted by Gallup in other countries. Survey research is an active enterprise in many countries. In Japan, for example, the major newspapers, such as the *Mainichi Shimbun* and *Yomiuri Shimbun*, conduct countless surveys, and it is possible for you to obtain and analyze some of those survey data through data archives in the United States.

You should realize that the U.S. government also conducts a great many surveys that produce data suitable for analysis with SPSS. The U.S. Census (http://www.census.gov/) is a chief example, and it is possible for researchers to obtain and analyze data collected in the decennial censuses. Two other examples include the Bureau of Justice Statistics and the Bureau of Labor Statistics, which can be accessed at http://www.ojp.usdoj.gov/bjs and http://stats.bls.gov/datahome.htm, respectively. For access to an almost full range of statistics produced by more than 100 U.S. federal agencies, you may want to log on to "FedStats: One Stop Shopping For Federal Statistics" at http://www.fedstats.gov/.

It is worth recalling that when Emile Durkheim set about his major analysis of suicide in Europe, he was forced to work with printed government reports of suicide rates in various countries and regions. Moreover, his analysis needed to be done by hand.

With the advent of computers for mass data storage and analytic programs such as SPSS, the possibilities for secondary analysis have been revolutionized. You live at an enviable time in that regard.

To get a sense of the types of data sets available for secondary analysis that cover issues and topics in your discipline, you may want to search the world wide web. One site that may help you get started is "Dr. B's Wide World of Web Data," a statistical tool created at Arizona State University. You can access the site at http://research.ed.asu.edu and then click on "Multimedia" and search under "Other Resources." Once you do that, you will be able to link to data sets by choosing among topics that range from crime and law enforcement, demographics, and drug use and abuse to education, environment, medicine and health, and social sciences. You can also get some help locating statistical data online by searching RobertNiles.com at http://nilesonline.com/data.

This is, of course, just the tip of the iceberg. These limited recommendations don't even begin to scratch the surface of the numerous sites available to help you locate and access statistical data on the world wide web. While you should make use of the www to locate and, in some cases, access data, please bear in mind that you also have to be cautious and wary when conducting online searches. This is particularly true in light of the fact that anyone can post information online, so the accuracy of the data or other information you locate may not necessarily be conducive to sound social research. Also bear in mind that different search engines are likely to identify different sites, even when provided with the same search terms.[1]

Other Computer Programs

We have organized this book around the use of SPSS because this program is so widely used by social scientists. Quite frankly, we spent a fair amount of time considering other programs as the focus for the book, but ultimately decided it would be most useful to the greatest number of students if we used SPSS. And by the way, SPSS's popularity is due largely to its excellence as a tool for social research.

At the same time, we want you to know that there are several other excellent analytic programs available. We'll mention some of these here in the event that you may have access to them. You should realize that the commands and procedures used in other programs will differ from those of SPSS, but the logic of data analysis that we've presented in this book applies across the various programs available.

Probably the program package next most commonly used by social scientists is *SAS*. Like SPSS, it is an omnibus package of techniques that goes far beyond those we've introduced you to in this book. Should it be useful to you, SAS functions within a broader set of programs for accounting, management, and other activities. You can learn more about SAS by accessing the SAS homepage at http://www.sas.com/.

SYSTAT is another widely used package of programs designed for social science research. Like SAS and SPSS, SYSTAT is also an omnibus package with graphing, statistical, and other analytical capabilities that are much more advanced than those we have discussed here. For a complete overview of this software, its general features, and system requirements see the SYSTAT Software, Inc. homepage at http://www.systat.com.

A few other programs that you may find useful for social science data analysis include: Minitab, P-STAT, STATA.

---

[1] For a brief overview on searching the web and an annotated list of web sites, see Schutt, 2000, Appendix B (B6-B12), Appendix H (H1-H6).

Conclusion

We hope you've had some fun as you've worked through this book and that you've learned some important research techniques and some facts about the American public. We hope you have discovered that social research, although very important, especially considering the range of social problems we confront today, is also a fascinating enterprise.

Like the investigative detective, the social researcher must possess large amounts of curiosity and ingenuity. Sit beside a social researcher at work, and you'll hear him or her muttering things like, "Wait a minute. If that's the case, then I'd expect to find . . . "; "Hey, that probably explains why . . . "; "Omigod! That means . . . " Maybe you've overheard yourself practicing these social scientific incantations. If so, congratulations and welcome. If not, you have a delightful adventure waiting for you just around the corner. We'll see you there.

Main Points

- To accommodate the student version of SPSS, the data sets that accompany this text are just a small portion of the 2000 GSS.
- The unabridged 2000 GSS contains 2,817 cases and 1,063 variables, only a small portion of which are reflected in your DEMO.SAV and EXER.SAV files.
- Since the first GSS in 1972, over 40,933 respondents have been asked more than 3,500 questions.
- There are many ways to access the unabridged GSS.
- The NORC web site, the GSSDIRS, is a very useful resource.
- The *Cumulative Codebook* is a valuable resource for researchers using the GSS.
- The GSS is just one of many data sets available to social researchers.
- Data sets of interest to social scientists (of which there are many) are often housed at one of the data archives, and in some cases, accessible via the world wide web.
- The federal government is an important source of statistical data of interest to social scientists.
- We focused this text on SPSS because it is so widely used by social researchers. However, it is not the only statistical package available.
- Other excellent software programs often used by social researchers include (but are not limited to): SAS, SYSTAT, and STATA, just to name a few.

Key Terms

Secondary analysis
SYSTAT
SAS

SPSS Commands Introduced in This Chapter

No new commands were introduced in this chapter.

Review Questions

1. How many variables and cases are contained on your DEMO.SAV file?

2. How many variables and cases are contained on your EXER.SAV file?

3. How many cases are contained in the entire 2000 GSS?

4. From 1972 to 2000, how many different questions were asked as part of the GSS?

5. How many respondents took part in the GSS from 1972 to 2000?

6. What is the GSSDIRS and what type of information does it contain?

7. How can you access the GSS data?

8. What type of information does the *Codebook* contain?

9. What are data archives?

10. Name two data archives.

11. Name two specific data sets relevant to your particular discipline.

12. Besides SPSS, what statistical package is most commonly used by social scientists?

APPENDIXES

APPENDIX A: THE CODEBOOK

This codebook contains the following information for each of the items contained on your DEMO.SAV and EXER.SAV files: abbreviated variable name, the full wording used in the interview (item wording), values, labels, and level of measurement.

Please note, that we have excluded those values and labels normally designated as "missing" (NA – No Answer, DK – Don't Know, and NAP – Not Applicable). You can use SPSS to identify these values/labels in a number of different ways. For instance, you can access the **Variable View** tab and then locate the information in the **"Values"** column. Alternatively, you can click on **Utilities → Variables** or **Utilities → File Information**.

Subsample 1: DEMO.SAV

As noted in Chapter 4, DEMO.SAV is used in the demonstrations in the body of the chapters. This sub-sample contains 1,500 cases and 41 variables drawn from the 2000 GSS. The items are arranged according to the following subject categories: Abortion, Children, Family, Politics, Religion, Social-Political Opinions, and Sexual Attitudes.

The following list contains only 32 variables because it does NOT include either the identification variable or demographic variables (nine in all, including the ID variable). Since these variables are contained on both your DEMO.SAV and EXER.SAV files, they are listed separately at the end of Appendix A.

Abortion

Please tell me whether or not *you* think it should be possible for a pregnant woman to obtain a *legal* abortion if . . .

1) ABANY   . . . The woman wants it for any reason?
    [Nominal]
    1   Yes
    2   No

2) ABDEFECT   . . . There is a strong chance of serious defect in the baby?
    [Nominal]
    1   Yes
    2   No

3) ABHLTH   . . . The woman's own health is seriously endangered by the pregnancy?
    [Nominal]
    1   Yes
    2   No

4) ABNOMORE   . . . She is married and does not want any more children?
    [Nominal]
    1   Yes
    2   No

5) ABPOOR   . . . The family has a very low income and cannot afford any more children?
    [Nominal]
    1   Yes
    2   No

6) ABRAPE   . . . She became pregnant as a result of rape?
    [Nominal]
    1   Yes
    2   No

7) ABSINGLE   . . . She is not married and does not want to marry the man?
    [Nominal]
    1   Yes
    2   No

Children

8) CHLDIDEL

What do you think is the ideal number of children for a family to have?
[Interval/Ratio [I/R]][1]

0   None
1   One
2   Two
3   Three
4   Four
5   Five
6   Six
7   7 or more
8   As many as you want

If you had to choose, which thing on this list would you pick as the most important for a child to learn to prepare him or her for life? To obey, to be well-liked or popular, to think for himself or herself, to work hard, to help others when they need help. Which comes next in importance? Which comes third? Which comes fourth?

9) OBEY

To obey.
[Ordinal]
1   Most important
2   Second important
3   Third important
4   Fourth important
5   Least important

10) POPULAR

To be well-liked or popular.
[Ordinal]
1   Most important
2   Second important
3   Third important
4   Fourth important
5   Least important

11) THNKSELF

To think for himself or herself.
[Ordinal]
1   Most important
2   Second important
3   Third important
4   Fourth important
5   Least important

12) WORKHARD

To work hard.
[Ordinal]
1   Most important
2   Second important
3   Third important
4   Fourth important
5   Least important

13) HELPOTH

To help others when they need help.
[Ordinal]
1   Most important
2   Second important
3   Third important
4   Fourth important
5   Least important

Family

14) MARITAL

Are you currently—married, widowed, divorced, separated, or have you never been married?
[Nominal]
1   Married

[1] SPSS refers to "interval" and "ratio" data as "scale," as opposed to distinguishing between the two. In order to simplify reference, we will use "I/R" to refer to both interval and ratio data.

Politics

18) PARTYID

Generally speaking, do you usually think of yourself as a Republican, Democrat, Independent, or what?
[Ordinal]
0 Strong Democrat
1 Not strong Democrat
2 Independent, near Democrat
3 Independent
4 Independent, near Republican
5 Not strong Republican
6 Strong Republican
7 Other party

19) POLVIEWS

We hear a lot of talk these days about liberals and conservatives. I'm going to show you a seven-point scale on which the political views that people might hold are arranged from extremely liberal—point 1—to extremely conservative—point 7. Where would you place yourself on this scale?
[Ordinal]
1 Extremely liberal
2 Liberal
3 Slightly liberal
4 Moderate
5 Slightly conservative
6 Conservative
7 Extremely conservative

Religion

20) ATTEND

How often do you attend religious services?
[Ordinal]
0 Never

15) DIVORCE

2 Widowed
3 Divorced
4 Separated
5 Never married

[If currently married or widowed] Have you ever been divorced or legally separated?
[Nominal]
1 Yes
2 No

16) CHILDS

How many children have you ever had? Please count all that were born alive at any time (including any you had from a previous marriage).
[I/R]
0 None
1 One
2 Two
3 Three
4 Four
5 Five
6 Six
7 Seven
8 Eight or more

17) SIBS

How many brothers and sisters did you have? Please count those born alive, but no longer living, as well as those alive now. Also include stepbrothers and stepsisters, and children adopted by your parents.
[I/R]
Responses in actual number (i.e. 00, 01, 02, etc . . .)

1 Less than once a year
2 Once a year
3 Several times a year
4 Once a month
5 2-3 times a month
6 Nearly every week
7 Every week
8 More than once a week

21) POSTLIFE   Do you believe there is a life after death?
[Nominal]
1 Yes
2 No
8 Undecided

22) PRAY   About how often do you pray?
(cont)
[Ordinal]
1 Several times a day
2 Once a day
3 Several times a week
4 Once a week
5 Less than once a week
6 Never

23) RELIG   What is your religious preference? Is it Protestant, Catholic, Jewish, some other religion, or no religion?
[Nominal]
1 Protestant
2 Catholic
3 Jewish
4 None
5 Other (specify)
6 Buddhism
7 Hinduism
8 Other Eastern
9 Moslem/Islam
10 Orthodox-Christian
11 Christian
12 Native American
13 Inter-nondenominational

Social-Political Opinions

24) CAPPUN   Do you favor or oppose the death penalty for persons convicted of murder?
[Nominal]
1 Favor
2 Oppose

25) GETAHEAD   Some people say that people get ahead by their own hard work; others say that lucky breaks or help from other people are more important. Which do you think is most important?
[Ordinal]
1 Hard work
2 Both equally
3 Luck or help
4 Other

26) GUNLAW   Would you favor or oppose a law which would require a person to obtain a police permit before he or she could buy a gun?
[Nominal]
1 Favor
2 Oppose

Note: For the following three questions, interviewers were instructed to use the term Black or African-American, depending on the customary usage in their area.

27) RACDIF4   On the average (Blacks / African-Americans) have worse jobs, income, and housing than

white people. Do you think this difference is because most (Blacks / African- Americans) just don't have the motivation or will power to pull themselves out of poverty?
[Nominal]
1   Yes
2   No

28) RACMAR

Do you think there should be laws against marriages between (Blacks / African-Americans) and Whites?
[Nominal]
1   Yes
2   No

29) RACPUSH

Here are some opinions other people have expressed in connection with (Black / African-American)-White relations. Which statement on the card comes closest to how you, yourself feel? (Blacks / African-Americans) shouldn't push themselves where they're not wanted.
[Ordinal]
1   Agree strongly
2   Agree slightly
3   Disagree slightly
4   Disagree strongly

Sexual Attitudes

30) HOMOSEX

What about sexual relations between two adults of the same sex—do you think it is always wrong, almost always wrong, wrong only sometimes, or not wrong at all?
[Ordinal]
1   Always wrong
2   Almost always wrong
3   Sometimes wrong
4   Not wrong at all
5   Other

31) XMOVIE

Have you seen an X-rated movie in the last year?
[Nominal]
1   Yes
2   No

32) PREMARSX

DV

There's been a lot of discussion about the way morals and attitudes about sex are changing in this country. If a man and woman have sex relations before marriage, do you think it is always wrong, almost always wrong, wrong only sometimes, or not wrong at all?
[Ordinal]
1   Always wrong
2   Almost always wrong
3   Sometimes wrong
4   Not wrong at all
5   Other

Subsample 2: EXER.SAV

EXER.SAV is used primarily in the exercises at the end of the chapters. This file contains 1,500 cases and 47 variables drawn from the 2000 GSS. The 38 items below are arranged according to the following subject categories: Sex Roles, Police, Health, Mass Media, National Government Spending Priorities, Teen Sex, Affirmative Action, Equalization, and Environment.

This list does not include the nine variables that are contained in both the DEMO.SAV and EXER.SAV files. These variables are listed in a separate section at the end of the Appendix.

Sex Roles

Now I'm going to read several statements. As I read each one, please tell me whether you strongly agree, agree, disagree, or strongly disagree with it. For example, here is the statement.

1) FECHLD

A working mother can establish just as warm and secure a relationship with her children as a mother who doesn't work.

[Ordinal]
1 Strongly agree
2 Agree
3 Disagree
4 Strongly disagree

2) FEPRESCH

A preschool child is likely to suffer if his or her mother works.

[Ordinal]
1 Strongly agree
2 Agree
3 Disagree
4 Strongly disagree

3) FEFAM

It is much better for everyone involved if the man is the achiever outside the home and the woman takes care of the home and family.

[Ordinal]
1 Strongly agree
2 Agree
3 Disagree
4 Strongly disagree

Now I'm going to read several statements. As I read each one, please tell me whether you strongly agree, agree, neither agree nor disagree, disagree, or strongly disagree.

4) FEHIRE

Because of past discrimination, employers should make special efforts to hire and promote qualified women.

[Ordinal]
Strongly agree
Agree
Neither agree nor disagree
Disagree
Strongly disagree

Health

5) HEALTH

Would you say your own health, in general, is excellent, good, fair, or poor.

[Ordinal]
Excellent
Good
Fair
Poor

Police

6) POLHITOK

Are there any situations you can imagine in which you would approve of a policeman striking an adult male citizen?

[Nominal]
1 Yes
2 No
8 Not sure

If YES or Not Sure: Would you approve of a policeman striking a citizen who . . .

7) POLABUSE

. . . Had said vulgar and obscene things to the policeman?

[Nominal]
1 Yes
2 No

8) POLMURDR   . . . Was being questioned as a suspect in a
                  murder case?
                  [Nominal]
                  1   Yes
                  2   No

9) POLESCAP   . . . Was attempting to escape from custody?
                  [Nominal]
                  1   Yes
                  2   No

10) POLATTAK   . . . Was attacking the policeman with his fists?
                  [Nominal]
                  1   Yes
                  2   No

Mass Media

11) NEWS   How often do you read the newspaper—
                  every day, a few times a week, once a week, less
                  than once a week, or never?
                  [Ordinal]
                  1   Every day
                  2   Few times a week
                  3   Once a week
                  4   Less than once a week
                  5   Never

12) TVHOURS   On the average day, about how many hours do
                  you personally watch television?
                  [I/R]
                  Responses in actual hours

I am going to name some institutions in this country. As far as the
people running these institutions are concerned, would you say you
have a great deal of confidence, only some confidence, or hardly any
confidence at all in them? . . . .

13) CONPRESS   . . . Press?
                  [Ordinal]
                  1   A great deal
                  2   Only some
                  3   Hardly any

14) CONTV   . . . TV?
                  [Ordinal]
                  1   A great deal
                  2   Only some
                  3   Hardly any

National Government Spending Priorities

We are faced with many problems in this country, none of which can be
solved easily or inexpensively. I'm going to name some of these
problems, and for each one I'd like you to tell me whether you think
we're spending too much money on it, too little money, or about the
right amount. Are we spending too much money, too little money, or
about the right amount.

15) NATHEAL   . . . Improving and protecting the nation's health.
                  [Ordinal]
                  1   Too little
                  2   About right
                  3   Too much

16) NATCITY   . . . Solving the problems of the big cities.
                  [Ordinal]
                  1   Too little
                  2   About right
                  3   Too much

17) NATCRIME   . . . Halting the rising crime rate.
                  [Ordinal]
                  1   Too little
                  2   About right
                  3   Too much

457

18) NATDRUG ... Dealing with drug addiction.
[Ordinal]
1 Too little
2 About right
3 Too much

19) NATEDUC ... Improving the nation's education system.
[Ordinal]
1 Too little
2 About right
3 Too much

20) NATRACE ... Improving the conditions of Blacks.
[Ordinal]
1 Too little
2 About right
3 Too much

21) NATFARE ... Welfare.
[Ordinal]
1 Too little
2 About right
3 Too much

Teen Sex

22) PILLOK Do you strongly agree, agree, disagree, or strongly disagree that methods of birth control should be available to teenagers between the ages of 14 and 16 if their parents do not approve?
[Ordinal]
1 Strongly agree
2 Agree
3 Disagree
4 Strongly disagree

23) SEXEDUC Would you be for or against sex education in the public schools?
[Nominal]
1 For
2 Against
3 Depends

24) TEENSEX What if they are in their early teens, say 14 to 16 years old? In that case, do you think sex relations before marriage are always wrong, almost always wrong, wrong only sometimes, or not wrong at all?
[Ordinal]
1 Always wrong
2 Almost always wrong
3 Wrong only sometimes
4 Not wrong at all

Affirmative Action

25) AFFRMACT Some people say that because of past discrimination, Blacks should be given preference in hiring and promotion. Others say that such preference in hiring and promotion of Blacks is wrong because it discriminates against Whites. What about your opinion — are you for or against preferential hiring and promotion of Blacks? IF FAVOR: Do you favor preference in hiring and promotion strongly or not strongly? IF OPPOSE: Do you oppose preference in hiring and promotion strongly or not strongly?
[Ordinal]
1 Strongly support preference
2 Support preference
3 Oppose preference
4 Strongly oppose preference

26) WRKWAYUP

Do you agree strongly, agree somewhat, neither agree nor disagree, disagree somewhat, or disagree strongly with the following statement: Irish, Italians, Jewish and many other minorities overcame prejudice and worked their way up. Blacks should do the same without special favors.

[Ordinal]

1   Agree strongly
2   Agree somewhat
3   Neither agree nor disagree
4   Disagree somewhat
5   Disagree strongly

27) RACWORK

Are the people who work where you work all white, mostly white, about half and half, mostly black, or all black?

[Ordinal]

1   All white
2   Mostly white
3   Half white-black
4   Mostly black
5   All black
6   Works alone

28) DISCAFF

What do you think the chances are these days that a white person won't get a job or promotion while an equally or less qualified Black person gets one instead? Is this very likely, somewhat likely, or not very likely to happen these days?

[Ordinal]

1   Very likely
2   Somewhat likely
3   Not very likely

Equalization

29) EQWLTH

Some people think that the government in Washington ought to reduce the income differences between the rich and the poor, perhaps by raising the taxes of wealthy families or by giving income assistance to the poor. Others think that the government should not concern itself with reducing the income difference between the rich and the poor. Here is a card with a scale from 1 to 7. Think of a score of 1 as meaning that the government ought to reduce the income differences between rich and poor, and a score of 7 as meaning that the government should not concern itself with reducing income differences. What score between one and seven comes closest to the way you feel?

[Ordinal]

1   Government reduce differences
2
3
4
5
6
7   No government action

Environment

30) GRWTHARM

How much do you agree or disagree with each of the following statements. Economic growth always harms the environment.

[Ordinal]

1   Strongly agree
2   Agree

459

3 Neither agree nor disagree
4 Disagree
5 Strongly disagree

31) NATURGOD

Please check one box to show which statement is closest to your views.

[Nominal]
1 Nature created by God
2 Nature sacred in itself
3 Nature important, but not sacred

32) GRNPRICE

How willing would you be to pay much higher prices in order to protect the environment?

[Ordinal]
Very willing
Fairly willing
Neither willing nor unwilling
Not very willing
Not at all willing

33) GRNTAXES

And how willing would you be to pay much higher taxes in order to protect the environment?

[Ordinal]
Very willing
Fairly willing
Neither willing nor unwilling
Not very willing
Not at all willing

34) GRNSOL

And how willing would you be to accept cuts in your standard of living in order to protect the environment?

[Ordinal]
Very willing
Fairly willing
Neither willing nor unwilling
Not very willing
Not at all willing

35) IHLPGRN

How much do you agree or disagree with each of the following statements. I do what is right for the environment, even when it costs more money and takes up more time.

[Ordinal]
Strongly agree
Agree
Neither agree nor disagree
Disagree
Strongly disagree

36) GRNEXAGG

How much do you agree or disagree with each of these statements. Many of the claims about the environment are exaggerated.

[Ordinal]
Strongly agree
Agree
Neither agree nor disagree
Disagree
Strongly disagree

37) HARMSGRN

Please check one box for each of these statements to show how much you agree or disagree with it. Almost everything we do in modern life harms the environment.

[Ordinal]
Strongly agree
Agree
Neither agree nor disagree
Disagree
Strongly disagree

38) AMPROGRN

Some countries are doing more to protect the world environment than other countries are.

years of college for credit—not including schooling such as business college, technical, or vocational school? [If yes] How many years did you complete? Do you have any college degrees? [If yes] What degree or degrees?
[I/R]
Responses coded in actual years (i.e. 2,3,4,...)

In general, do you think that America is doing....
[Ordinal]
More than enough
About the right amount
Or, too little
ID and Demographic Variables

Demographic and ID Varible

Both of the files on your CD-ROM (DEMO.SAV and EXER.SAV) contain the following nine identification and demographic variables.

1) ID

Respondent Identification Number [assigned by the interviewer]
[Nominal]

2) AGE

Date of birth?
[I/R]
Recoded into actual age in years.

3) CLASS

If you were asked to use one of the four names for your social class, which would you say you belong to: the lower class, the working class, the middle class, or the upper class?
[Ordinal]
1   Lower class
2   Working class
3   Middle class
4   Upper class
5   No class

4) EDUC

What is the highest grade in elementary school or high school that you finished and got credit for? [If finished 9th-12th grade or DK] Did you ever get a high school diploma or a GED certificate? Did you complete one or more

5) INCOME98

In which of these groups did your total family income, from all sources, fall last year, before taxes, that is?
[Ordinal]
1   Under $1,000
2   $1,000 to 2,999
3   $3,000 to 3,999
4   $4,000 to 4,999
5   $5,000 to 5,999
6   $6,000 to 6,999
7   $7,000 to 7,999
8   $8,000 to 9,999
9   $10,000 to 12,499
10 $12,500 to 14,999
11 $15,000 to 17,499
12 $17,500 to 19,999
13 $20,000 to 22,499
14 $22,500 to 24,999
15 $25,000 to 29,999
16 $30,000 to 34,999
17 $35,000 to 39,999
18 $40,000 to 49,999
19 $50,000 to 59,999
20 $60,000 to 74,999
21 $75,000 to 89,999
22 $90,000 to 109,999
23 $110,000 or over
24 Refused

6) SEI   Hodge-Siegel-Rossi socioeconomic ratings for
                respondents' occupations.[2]
                [I/R]

7) RACE   What race do you consider yourself?
                [Nominal]
                1 White
                2 Black
                3 Other

8) RINCOM98   In which of these groups did your earnings
                from[occupation from a previous question] fall
                for last year? That is, before taxes or other
                deductions?
                [Ordinal]
                Coded the same as INCOME98

9) SEX   Coded by the interviewers, based on
                observation.
                [Nominal]
                1 Male
                2 Female

462

[2] Information about the Hodge-Siegel-Rossi occupational prestige score, is available online at **http://www.icpsr. umich.edu/GSS/**. Once you access the GSSDIRS, click on **Appendix - G.** See also Davis, Smith, and Marsden (1998) and Nakao and Treas (1994) for an in-depth discussion of the updated occupational prestige and socioeconomic scores.

APPENDIX B: ANSWERS TO SELECTED SPSS LAB EXERCISES

Chapter 5   SPSS Lab Exercise 5.1 (Questions 1-8)

1.   ECONomic GRoWTH ALWAYS HARMS ENVIRonment

2.   Case #89   0   NAP
     Case #837   1   Strongly Agree
     Case #1243   4   Disagree

3.   PAY HIGHER PRICES TO HELP ENVIRonment

4.   Case #1   2   Fairly [willing]
     Case #500   0   NAP
     Case #1500   1   Very [willing]

5.   PAY HIGHER TAXES TO HELP ENVIRonment

6.   Case #11   5   Not at all [willing]
     Case #902   1   Very [willing]
     Case #1236   2   Fairly [willing]

7.   ACCEPT CUT IN LIVING StaNDarDS TO HELP ENVIRonment

8.   Case #7   2   Fairly willing
     Case #389   4   Not very willing
     Case #495   3   Neither willing nor unwilling

Chapter 6   SPSS Lab Exercise 6.1 (Questions 1-9, 13, 17-18, 21-22)

1.   White   79%[1]   Black   16%

2.   Mode   Nominal   White (1)

3.   46%   31%   23%

4.   Median   Ordinal   Good (2)

5.   88%   4%   8%

6.   Median   Ordinal   Always Wrong (1)

7.   13 (13.29) 10 (10.49) 16 (16.01)

8.   3 (2.96)   .358   5.562

9.   The majority of respondents to the 2000 GSS are dissatisfied with the amount of money being spent to deal with the rising crime rate and drug addiction. Nearly two-thirds (61%) of respondents say that we are spending "too little" to deal with these problems. While

---

[1] All percentages have been rounded

approximately one-third of respondents feel we are spending the "right amount" and less than 10% feel we are spending "too much."

13. Pay higher taxes to help environment.

15. 1 Willing   33%
    2 Neither   29%
    3 Unwilling   39%

17. How often does R (respondent) read the newspaper

18. 1 Once a Week or More   76%
    2 Less than Once a Week   15%
    3 Never   9%

21. Highest year of school completed

22. 1 Less than high school education   16%
    2 High school graduate   31%
    3 Some college   29%
    4 College graduate   13%
    5 Graduate studies and beyond   11%

Chapter 7   SPSS Lab Exercise 7.1 (Questions 1-5a, 5d)

1a. How often does respondent [R] read the newspaper?

1b. Ordinal

1c. Bar or Pie

1d. three-quarters (76-77%)[2]   15%   9%

2a. Hours per day respondent [R] watches television.

2b. continuous

2c. Histogram or Line

2d. .4 and 5.6

3a. Bar or Pie

3b. The vast majority of respondents to the 2000 GSS do not exhibit a great deal of confidence in the press. Only one in ten (10%) of respondents said they have "a great deal of confidence" in the press, compared to nine out of ten (90%) who reported having only "some" (49%) or "hardly any" (41%) confidence in the press.

4a. Bar or Pie

4b. Almost half of respondents (48%) said they have only "some" confidence in television, followed closely by 43% of the sample who said they have "hardly any" confidence in television. Less than 10% of respondents reported having "a great deal" of confidence in television.

5a. Histogram or Line

5d. Bar or Pie

---

[2] Percentages may be different by 1% due to rounding: bar chart – 77%, pie chart – 76%.

Chapter 8   SPSS Lab Exercise 8.1 (Questions 1-14)

1a. POLHITOK   Citizen ever approve of police striking a citizen

1b. POLABUSE   Citizen said vulgar or obscene things

1c. POLATTAK   Citizen attacking policeman with fists

1d. POLESCAP   Citizen attempting to escape custody

1e. POLMURDR Citizen questioned as murder suspect

2.   67%

3.   33%

4a. POLATTAK   92%

4b. POLESCAP   71%

5a. POLMURDR   6%

5b. POLABUSE   6%

6a. POLATTAK   92%

6b. POLESCAP   71%

6c. POLMURDR   6%

6d. POLABUSE   6%

7.   [Example] The table indicates that there is a great deal of agreement among respondents in terms of situations in which they would and would not support a police officer striking a citizen. Moreover, the table shows the complexity of opinion on this issue and respondents' ability or willingness to strike a balance between two competing "rights": the general public's right to safety and security and an individual's civil rights. For instance, 92% of respondents said they would support a police officer striking a citizen if the officer was being attacked. Likewise, more than 70% said they would support an officer striking a citizen if the citizen was attempting to escape custody. At the same time, a clear majority made a distinction between those situations and other cases in which the officer and public were not in serious, immediate or potential physical danger. In these instances, the vast majority of respondents said they would not approve a police officer striking a citizen. These include, for instance, cases in which the citizen said vulgar or obscene things or if the citizen was being questioned as a murder suspect.

8.   55

9.   841

10. 81

11.   0

12. 896   81

13.   55   922

14. Your analysis should include some or all of the following information:
     ■ 267 disapprove in either situation
     ■ 46 approve in both situations
     ■ 625 approve in one case, but not the other
     ■ Of those, 618 approve if a citizen is attempting to escape, but not a murder suspect

■ This suggests respondents make fine distinctions. They approve of an officer striking when the public's safety is at risk. The fact that 7 approve striking a murder suspect, but not an escapee shows that not all respondents are capable of making such fine distinctions (or perhaps misunderstood the question).

Chapter 9   SPSS Lab Exercise 9.1 (Questions 1-3, 5-6, 8, 10, 12-15)

1-2.   Would you support a police officer striking an adult male citizen if . . .

1.   POLABUSE – Citizen said vulgar or obscene things

2.   POLATTAK – Citizen attacking police officer with fists.

3.   0   NAP

     1   Yes

     2   No

     8   DK

     9   NAP

5.   Lower

6.   Higher

8.

	Value POLABUSE	Value POLATTAK	Expected Score	Actual POLIN Score
Case #1	0	0	MISSING	MISSING
Case #2	2	1	1	1
Case #3	2	1	1	1
Case #4	2	1	1	1
Case #5	0	0	MISSING	MISSING
Case #6	2	1	1	1

Based on a comparison of the Expected and Actual POLIN scores for Respondents (Case) #1-6, the Index appears to have been constructed correctly.

10.   6%
     86%
     8%

12.   94%
     75%
     16%

13.   31%
     4%
     8%

14.   77%
     71%
     29%

15.   Example: The index (POLIN) was validated because it accurately predicts differences in responses to the other "Police striking" variables. In each case, those with a lower score on the index are more likely to support a police officer striking a citizen under the conditions specified than those with a higher score on the index.

Chapter 11   SPSS Lab Exercise 11.1 (Questions 1-10)

1.   Example: Whites are more likely than Blacks to believe that women who work have a detrimental impact on their children.

2.   Independent Variable – Respondents' race [RACE]
     Dependent Variable – attitudes toward working mothers [FECHLD]

3.   FECHLD

4.   RACE

5.   Nominal

6.   Ordinal

7.   FECHLD by RACE

	White	Black	Other
Line A	White	Black	Other
Line B	60%	67%	68%[5]

8.   A slightly higher percentage of Blacks (67%) are more likely than Whites (60%) to agree with the statement that a working mother does *not* have a detrimental impact on her children. While the association between FECHLD and RACE may be worth investigating further, the percentage point difference (7%) is fairly small.

9.   7 [67-60]

10. Example: While there appears to be a weak association between FECHLD and RACE that may warrant further investigation, we have not proven our hypothesis. Consequently, the table is best looked at as some evidence of, although certainly not proof of, a causal relationship.

Chapter 12   SPSS Lab Exercise 12.1 (Questions 1-2, 12-13)

1.   NATHEAL by HEALTH

	Excellent	Good	Fair	Poor
Line A	Excellent	Good	Fair	Poor
Line B	73%	74%	71%	77%

2.   Example: There does not appear to be a relationship between respondents' health and attitudes towards government spending on health care. Although respondents in poor health are slightly more likely to believe that the government is spending too little on health care, the percentage point difference is relatively small. Interestingly, those in excellent and good health are slightly more likely to believe the government is spending too little on health care than those in poor health. Nevertheless, the percentage point difference is small (2-3%).
     As shown in both the output and the table re-constructed above, the dependent variable (NATHEAL) changes only slightly with changes in the independent variable (HEALTH).

12. Are environmental threats exaggerated?

13. RECGRNT is the recoded form of GRNTAXES (created in Lab Exercise 6.1, Question 15). GRNTAXES examines whether respondents are willing to pay higher taxes to help the environment.

---

[5] Percentages have been rounded.

Chapter 13 SPSS Lab Exercise 13.1 (Questions 1-2, 5-10)

1a. PILLOK – Agree/disagree that birth control should be available to teens ages 14-16 even if their parents do not approve.

1b. SEXEDUC – Favor/oppose sex education in public schools.

1c. TEENSEX – Whether or not premarital sex is okay for 14-16 year olds.

2a. PILLOK   0 – NAP
                       1 – Strongly agree
                       2 – Agree
                       3 – Disagree
                       4 – Strongly disagree
                       8 – DK
                       9 – NA

2b. SEXEDUC 0 – NAP
                       1 – Favor
                       2 – Oppose
                       3 – Depends
                       8 – DK
                       9 – NA

2c. TEENSEX 0 – NAP
                       1 – Always wrong
                       2 – Almost always wrong
                       3 – Sometimes wrong
                       4 – Not wrong at all
                       5 – Other
                       8 – DK
                       9 – NA

5.

	Men	Women
PILLREC	57%	61%
SEXEDUC	89%	87%
TEENREC	14%	10%

6. Example: The table shows that there is little difference between men and women on these three items. Men are slightly more permissive than women on SEXEDUC and TEENREC, however the percentage point difference is relatively small (2-4%). Women, on the other hand, are a little more permissive than men on PILLREC, although once again the percentage point difference is fairly small (4%). Regardless of gender, respondents tend to support sex education in the public schools. While just over half of men and 6 out of 10 women favor making birth control available to teens and very few agree with the statement that premarital sex for teens 14-16 is okay.

7.

	Strng A.	Agr	Disagr	Strng. D.
PILLREC	43%	53%	64%	68%
SEXEDUC	71%	83%	92%	96%
TEENREC	2%	8%	16%	17%

8. Example: The table shows that people who agree with traditional domestic sex roles are less likely than those who disagree to be permissive in their attitudes toward teen sex.

9.

	Strng. A	Agr	Disagr	Strng. D.
PILLREC	44%	61%	62%	60%
SEXEDUC	74%	85%	92%	94%
TEENREC	3%	11%	15%	14%

10. Example: The table shows that respondents who strongly agree with the statement that children tend to suffer when their mother works outside the home are also less likely to be permissive on teen sex. It is interesting to note, however that those who agree with the statement are only somewhat less permissive on teen sex than those who disagree and strongly disagree that a working mother has a detrimental impact on her children.

Chapter 14   SPSS Lab Exercise 14.1 (Questions 1-7, 13-20, 27-36)

1. Nominal

2. Nominal

3. Lambda

4.

	White	Black	Other
Yes	75%	38%	37%

5. Example: Whites are more than about twice as likely as Blacks and those of "other" races to say that there are situations in which they would approve of a police officer striking a citizen.

6. .151

7. Example: The value of lambda for RACE and POLHITOK is .151, this indicates that there is a moderate relationship between the variables that may be worth noting and perhaps examining further.

13. Ordinal

14. Ordinal

15. Gamma

16.

	All Wt.	Mstly. Wt.	Half-Half	Mstly. Blk.	All Blk.
Very Likely	21%	16%	20%	18%	25%
Somewhat Likely	51%	47%	35%	24%	50%

17. Example: Interestingly, those respondents who work with all Blacks are somewhat more likely than others to say it is very likely that whites are hurt by affirmative action. Among those who say it is somewhat likely that whites are hurt by affirmative action, there is not a difference between those who work with all Whites and all Blacks. However, those who work with all Blacks are almost two times as likely as those who work with mostly Blacks to agree it is somewhat likely that whites are hurt by affirmative action.

18. .166

19. Example: The relationship between the variables as indicated by the value of gamma (.166) is moderate, worth noting, and perhaps exploring further.

20. The direction of association is positive.

27. I/R

28. I/R

29. −.001

30. Example: Pearson's r for AGE and SEI is -.001. This indicates that there is no association between the variables that is worth noting or exploring further.

31. I/R

32. I/R

33. Negative

34. Decrease somewhat

35. Example: The direction of the association between the variables is negative. As years of education increase, the number of hours of television watched per day decreases somewhat. Judging from the spread of the "dots" (cases) around the regression line, the relationship seems to be moderate.

36. Pearson's r for EDUC and TVHOURS is -.234. This indicates a moderate to somewhat strong relationship that is fairly interesting, worth noting, and exploring further.

Chapter 15   SPSS Lab Exercise 15.1 (Questions 2-15, 17-18)

2.

	White	Black	Other	Chi-Square Asymp. Sig.
Percentage Support	13%	41%	27%	.000

	Male	Female		Chi-Square Asymp. Sig.
Percentage Support	19%	18%		.823

3. Example: The table shows that Whites are much less likely than Blacks or those of other races to support affirmative action.

4. .000 Less than .05

5. Example: Yes. The significance of chi-square is .000, so the relationship between RACE and AFFREC is statistically significant.

6. Example: There is no difference between men and women in terms of their support for affirmative action.

7. .823 More than .05

8. Example: No. The significance of chi-square is .832, more than .05, so the relationship between SEX and AFFREC is not statistically significant.

9.

		White	Black
AGE			
	Mean	47.25	42.66
	Sig	.000	
EDUC			
	Mean	13.38	12.69
	Sig.	.000	
SEI			
	Mean	49.801	45.325
	Sig.	.001	

10.   Higher $47.25 - 42.66 = 4.59$

11.   Example: The mean age of Whites is higher than that of Blacks, and the difference is significant.

12.   Higher $13.38 - 12.69 = .69$

13.   Example: The mean education level of Whites is slightly higher than that of Blacks, and the difference is significant.

14.   Higher $49.801 - 45.325 = 4.476$

15.   Example: The mean SEI of Whites is higher than that of Blacks, and the difference is significant.

17.   .000 No because if the significance level is .05 or less, the variances are considered significantly different.

18.   No because ANOVA should not be used when the variances are considered significantly different.

Chapter 17   SPSS Lab Exercise 17.1 (Questions 1-3, 5-7, 19-21, 25)

1.   NATCRIME: Percentage who feel the national government is spending too little fighting crime

	LOWER	WORKING	MIDDLE	UPPER	SIG.
WHITE	70%	64%	55%	40%	.046
BLACK	50%	75%	69%	86%	.613

2.   decreases; is not

3.   increases (although not steadily); is not

5.   NATFARE: Percentage who feel the national government is spending too little on welfare

	LOWER	WORKING	MIDDLE	UPPER	SIG.
MALE	20%	22%	14%	25%	.021
FEMALE	25%	23%	21%	29%	.878

6.   Middle class men are less likely to feel the national government is spending too little time on welfare than men in the lower, working or upper classes.

7.   The relationship between class and feelings of the national government's spending on welfare for women is not significant.

19.   5.681

20.   EDUC $= -.190$, WHITE $= -1.198$, AGE $= -.016$

21.   TVHOURS $= 5.681 + (EDUC \times -.190) + (WHITE \times -1.198) + (AGE \times .016)$

25.   All three are significant. Each has a significance level below .05.

Chapter 18   SPSS Lab Exercise 18.1 (Questions 1-2)

1.   less likely

2.   more; is not

Chapter 19   SPSS Lab Exercise 19.1 (Questions 4-5)

4.   IND1

	Frequency	Valid Percent
0 least traditional	90	10%
1	463	49%
2	310	33%
3 most traditional	85	9%

5.   IND1

	0 least tradit.	1	2	3 most tradit.
FEPRESCH 1 Agree	32%	46%	43%	72%
FECHLD 2 Disagree	29%	36%	40%	67%

ID____ ____ ____ (CODE LEADING ZEROS)

____ ____ ____
1   2   3

CHLDIDEL   1.   What do you think is the ideal number of children for a family to have?
____ ____ (CODE LEADING ZERO IF < 10)

____ ____
4   5

2. If you had to choose, which thing on this list would you say is the most important for a child to learn to prepare him or her for life? (CODE 1)

[INTERVIEWER: READ CHOICES BELOW]

OBEY   ____   A.   to obey

____
6

POPULAR   ____   B.   to be well liked or popular

____
7

THNKSELF   ____   C.   to think for himself or herself

____
8

WORKHARD   ____   D.   to work hard

____
9

HELPOTH   ____   E.   to help others

____
10

a. Which comes next in importance? (Code 2)
b. Which comes third? (Code 3)
c. Which comes forth? (Code 4)
d. Which comes fifth? (Code 5)
(no response: Code 9)

SIBS   3.   How many brothers and sisters did you have?
Please count those born alive, but no longer living,
as well as those alive now. Also include stepbrothers and
stepsisters, and children adopted by your parents.

____ ____
11 12

____ ____ (CODE NUMBER WITH LEADING ZERO)

MARITAL   4.   Are you married, widowed, divorced, separated,
or have you never been married?

____
13

____ 1. married
____ 2. widowed
____ 3. divorced
____ 4. separated
____ 5. never married
____ 9. no answer

[INTERVIEWER: ASK QUESTION 5 ONLY IF MARRIED OR WIDOWED]

DIVORCE   5. Have you ever been divorced or legally separated?   ____
                  _____ 1. yes   14
                  _____ 2. no
                  _____ 3. no answer or not applicable

PARTYID   6. Generally speaking, do you usually think of yourself   ____
                  as a Republican, Democrat, Independent, or what?   15
                  _____ 0. strong Democrat
                  _____ 1. not very strong Democrat
                  _____ 2. Independent, close to Democrat
                  _____ 3. Independent, neither, or no response
                  _____ 4. Independent, close to Republican
                  _____ 5. not very strong Republican
                  _____ 6. strong Republican
                  _____ 7. other party, refused to say
                  _____ 9. no answer

POLVIEWS   7. We hear a lot of talk these days about liberals and conservatives.   ____
                  I'm going to read you a set of seven categories of political   16
                  views that people might hold, arranged from extremely liberal
                  to extremely conservative. Which best describes you,
                  or haven't you thought much about this?
                  _____ 1. extremely liberal
                  _____ 2. liberal
                  _____ 3. slightly liberal
                  _____ 4. moderate, middle-of-the-road
                  _____ 5. slightly conservative
                  _____ 6. conservative
                  _____ 7. extremely conservative
                  _____ 9. no answer or not applicable

CAPPUN   8. Do you favor or oppose the death penalty for murder?   ____
                  _____ 1. favor   17
                  _____ 2. oppose
                  _____ 9. don't know, no answer

GUNLAW   9. Would you favor or oppose a law that would require a   ____
                  person to obtain a police permit before he or she could   18
                  buy a gun?
                  _____ 1. favor
                  _____ 2. oppose
                  _____ 9. don't know, no answer

GETAHEAD   10. Some people say that people get ahead by their   ____
                  own hard work; others say that lucky breaks or help   19
                  from other people is more important. Which do you
                  think is most important?
                  _____ 1. hard work most important
                  _____ 2. hard work, luck equally important
                  _____ 3. luck most important
                  _____ 9. other, don't know, no answer

RACDIF4   11. On the average, African Americans have worse jobs,   ____
               income and housing than white people. Do you think this   20
               is because African Americans just don't have the
               motivation or will to pull themselves up out of poverty?
               _____ 1. yes
               _____ 2. no

RACMAR   12. Do you think there should be laws against   ____
               marriages between (Negroes/Blacks/African   21
               Americans) and whites?
               _____ 1. yes
               _____ 2. no
               _____ 8. don't know
               _____ 9. no answer, not applicable

RACPUSH   13. Some people have expressed the opinion   ____
               that (Negroes/Blacks/African-Americans) shouldn't push   22
               themselves where they're not wanted. Which of these responses
               comes closest to how you, yourself, feel?
               _____ 1. agree strongly
               _____ 2. agree slightly
               _____ 3. disagree slightly
               _____ 4. disagree strongly
               _____ 8. no opinion
               _____ 9. no answer, not applicable

           14. Please tell me whether or not you think it should be possible for a
               pregnant woman to obtain a legal abortion if . . .

ABDEFECT   A. If there is a strong chance of serious defect in   ____
              the baby?   23
               _____ 1. yes
               _____ 2. no
               _____ 3. don't know, no answer

ABNOMORE   B. If she is married and does not want any more   ____
              children?   24
               _____ 1. yes
               _____ 2. no
               _____ 3. don't know, no answer

ABHLTH   C. If the woman's own health is seriously endangered   ____
              by the pregnancy?   25
               _____ 1. yes
               _____ 2. no
               _____ 3. don't know, no answer

ABPOOR   D. If the family has a very low income and cannot afford   ____
              any more children?   26
               _____ 1. yes
               _____ 2. no
               _____ 3. don't know, no answer

ABRAPE   E.   If she became pregnant as a result of rape?

      _____ 1. yes   27

      _____ 2. no

      _____ 3. don't know, no answer

ABSINGLE   F.   If she is not married and does not want to marry the man?

      _____ 1. yes   28

      _____ 2. no

      _____ 3. don't know, no answer

ABANY   G.   If the woman wants it for any reason?

      _____ 1. yes   29

      _____ 2. no

      _____ 3. don't know, no answer

RELIG   15.   What is your religious preference? Is it Protestant, Catholic, Jewish, some other religion, or no religion?

      _____ 1. Protestant   30

      _____ 2. Catholic

      _____ 3. Jewish

      _____ 4. none

      _____ 5. other

      _____ 9. no answer, no response

ATTEND   16.   How often do you attend religious services?

      _____ 0. never   31

      _____ 1. less than once a year

      _____ 2. about once or twice a year

      _____ 3. several times a year

      _____ 4. about once a month

      _____ 5. 2 or 3 times a month

      _____ 6. nearly every week

      _____ 7. every week

      _____ 8. several times a week

      _____ 9. don't know, no answer

POSTLIFE   17.   Do you believe there is a life after death?

      _____ 1. yes   32

      _____ 2. no

      _____ 9. undecided, no answer, not applicable

PRAY   18.   About how often do you pray?

      _____ 1. several times a day   33

      _____ 2. once a day

      _____ 3. several times a week

      _____ 4. once a week

_____ 5. less than once a week

_____ 6. never

_____ 9. don't know, no answer, not applicable

PREMARSX   19. There has been a lot of discussion about the way   _____
morals and attitudes about sex are changing in this   34
country. If a man and woman have sex relations before
marriage, do you think it is always wrong, almost
always wrong, wrong only sometimes, or not wrong at all?

_____ 1. always wrong

_____ 2. almost always wrong

_____ 3. wrong only sometimes

_____ 4. not wrong at all

_____ 9. don't know, no answer

HOMOSEX   20. What about sexual relations between two adults   _____
of the same sex do you think it is always wrong, almost   35
always wrong, wrong only sometimes, or not wrong at all?

_____ 1. always wrong

_____ 2. almost always wrong

_____ 3. wrong only sometimes

_____ 4. not wrong at all

_____ 9. don't know, no answer

XMOVIE   21. Have you seen an X-rated movie in the last year?   _____
_____ 1. yes   36

_____ 2. no

_____ 3. don't know, no answer

EDUC   22. What is the highest grade in elementary   _____ _____
school or high school that you finished and   37   38
got credit for?

_____

[INTERVIEWER: IF RESPONDENT COMPLETED 12 GRADES, ASK QUESTION 23.]

23. Did you complete one or more years of college for credit
not including schooling such as business college or technical
or vocational school?

_____ 1. yes

_____ 2. no

[INTERVIEWER: IF YES TO QUESTION 23, GO TO QUESTION 24; ELSE GO TO QUESTION 25.]

24. How many years did you complete?

_____

CODING INSTRUCTION: ADD YEARS FROM QUESTION 22 TO YEARS
FROM QUESTION 24 AND CODE WITH LEADING ZERO IF NECESSARY IN
COLUMNS 37 AND 38. USE CODE 99 FOR NO RESPONSE.

SEI   25. What is your occupation?   _____ _____
39   40

_____ (write in)

[INTERVIEWER: IF RESPONDENT HAS NOT BEEN EMPLOYED FULL-TIME, RECORD HIS OR HER FATHER'S OCCUPATION.]

CODING INSTRUCTION: LOOK UP OCCUPATION ON HODGE, SIEGEL, AND ROSSI PRESTIGE SCALE AND RECORD SCORE IN COLUMNS 39 AND 40. USE CODE 99 FOR NO RESPONSE.

CLASS   26. If you were asked to use one of four names for   ____
                 your social class, which would you say you belong   41
                 in: the lower class, the working class, the middle
                 class, or the upper class?
                 _____ 1. lower class
                 _____ 2. working class
                 _____ 3. middle class
                 _____ 4. upper class
                 _____ 9. don't know, no answer

AGE   27. In what year were you born?   ____ ____
                                                                      42   43

                 _____

                 CODING INSTRUCTION: SUBTRACT BIRTH YEAR FROM THIS
                 YEAR TO GET AGE IN YEARS. CODE IN COLUMNS 42 AND 43.
                 CODE 99 FOR NO RESPONSE.

INCOME98   28. In which of these groups did your total family   ____ ____
                 income, from all sources, fall last year, before   44   45
                 taxes, that is? Just tell me to stop when I say the
                 category that describes your family.
                 _____ 1 under $1,000
                 _____ 2 $1 000 to 2 999
                 _____ 3 $3 000 to 3 999
                 _____ 4 $4 000 to 4 999
                 _____ 5 $5 000 to 5 999
                 _____ 6 $6 000 to 6 999
                 _____ 7 $7 000 to 7 999
                 _____ 8 $8 000 to 9 999
                 _____ 9 $10000 to 12499
                 _____ 10 $12500 to 14999
                 _____ 11 $15000 to 17499
                 _____ 12 $17500 to 19999
                 _____ 13 $20000 to 22499
                 _____ 14 $22500 to 24999
                 _____ 15 $25000 to 29999
                 _____ 16 $30000 to 34999
                 _____ 17 $35000 to 39999
                 _____ 18 $40000 to 49999
                 _____ 19 $50000 to 59999
                 _____ 20 $60000 to 74999
                 _____ 21 $75000 to $89999
                 _____ 22 $90000 - $109999
                 _____ 23 $110000 or over
                 _____ 99 refused, don't know, not applicable

RACE   30. CODING INSTRUCTION: CODE WITHOUT ASKING   ____
                ONLY IF THERE IS NO DOUBT IN YOUR MIND.   46
                _____ 1. white
                _____ 2. black
                _____ 3. other

SEX   31. CODING INSTRUCTION: CODE RESPONDENT'S SEX.   ____
                                                                 47
                _____ 1. male
                _____ 2. female

OCCUPATIONAL TITLE AND SOCIOECONOMIC PRESTIGE SCORES

Below are occupational titles and socioeconomic prestige scores for use in coding Question 25, SEI, on the above questionnaire. To find a respondent's prestige score, look through the occupational titles until you find one that matches or is similar to the respondent's occupation. Write the number that appears to the right of the occupation in the space provided for it in the right margin of Question 25 on the questionnaire.

The occupational prestige scores were developed by Hodge, Siegel, and Rossi at the University of Chicago. You can learn more about how the prestige scores were obtained by reading Appendixes F and G in *General Social Surveys, 1972-1998: Cumulative Codebook* (Davis, Smith, and Marsden, 1998).

Occupational Title	SEI Score	Occupational Title	SEI Score
Professional, Technical, and Kindred Workers		Librarians, archivists, and curators	
Accountants	57	Librarians	55
Architects	71	Archivists and curators	66
Computer specialists		Mathematical specialists	
Computer programmers	51	Actuaries	55
Computer systems analysts	51	Mathematicians	65
Computer specialists, n.e.c.	51	Statisticians	55
Engineers		Life and Physical scientists	
Aeronautical astronautical engineers	71	Agricultural scientists	56
Chemical engineers	67	Atmospheric and space scientists	68
Civil engineers	68	Biological scientists	68
Electrical and electronic engineers	69	Chemists	69
Industrial engineers	54	Geologists	67
Mechanical engineers	62	Marine scientists	68
Metallurgical and materials engineers	56	Physicists and astronomers	74
		Life and Physical scientists, n.e.c.	68
Mining engineers	62	Operations and systems	
Petroleum engineers	67	researchers and analysts	51
Sales engineers	51	Personnel and labor relation workers	56
Engineers, n.e.c.	67		
Farm management advisers	54	Physicians, dentists, and	
Foresters and conservationists	54	related practitioners	
Home management advisers	54	Chiropractors	60
		Dentists	74
Lawyers and judges		Optometrists	62
Judges	76	Pharmacists	61
Lawyers	76	Physicians, including osteopaths	82

Occupational Title	SEI Score	Occupational Title	SEI Score
Podiatrists	37	Psychology teachers	78
Veterinarians	60	Business and commerce teachers	78
Health practitioners, n.e.c.	51	Economics teachers	78
		History teachers	78
Nurses, dieticians, and therapists		Sociology teachers	78
Dieticians	52	Social science teachers, n.e.c.	78
Registered nurses	62	Art, drama, and music teachers	78
Therapists	37	Coaches and physical education teachers	78
		Education teachers	78
Health technologists and technicians		English teachers	78
Clinical laboratory technologists and technicians	61	Foreign language teachers	78
Dental hygienists	61	Home economics teachers	78
Health record technologists and technicians	61	Law teachers	78
Radiologic technologists and technicians	61	Theology teachers	78
Therapy assistants	37	Trade, industrial, and technical teachers	78
Health technologists and technicians, n.e.c.	47	Miscellaneous teachers, college and university	78
		Teachers, college and university, subject not specified	78
Religious workers			
Clergymen	69	Teachers, except college and university	
Religious workers, n.e.c.	56	Adult education teachers	43
		Elementary school teachers	60
Social scientists		Pre-kindergarten and kindergarten teachers	60
Economists	57	Secondary school teachers	63
Political scientists	66	Teachers, except college and university, n.e.c.	43
Psychologists	71		
Sociologists	66		
Urban and regional planners	66	Engineering and science technicians	
Social scientists, n.e.c.	66	Agriculture and biological technicians, except health	47
		Chemical technicians	47
Social and recreation workers		Draftsmen	56
Social workers	52	Electrical and electronic engineering technicians	47
Recreation workers	49	Industrial engineering technicians	47
		Mechanical engineering technicians	47
Teachers, college and university		Mathematical technicians	47
Agriculture teachers	78	Surveyors	53
Atmospheric, earth, marine, and space teachers	78	Engineering and science technicians, n.e.c.	47
Biology teachers	78		
Chemistry teachers	78		
Physics teachers	78		
Engineering teachers	78		
Mathematics teachers	78		
Health specialists teachers	78		

Occupational Title	SEI Score
Technicians, except health, engineering, and science	
Airplane pilots	70
Air traffic controllers	43
Embalmers	52
Flight engineers	47
Radio operators	43
Tool programmers, numerical control	47
Technicians, n.e.c.	47
Vocational and educational counselors	51
Writers, artists, and entertainers	
Actors	55
Athletes and kindred workers	51
Authors	60
Dancers	38
Designers	58
Editors and reporters	51
Musicians and composers	46
Painters and sculptors	56
Photographers	41
Public relations men and publicity writers	57
Radio and television announcers	51
Writers, artists, and entertainers, n.e.c.	51
Research workers, not specified	51
Professional, technical, and kindred workers—allocated	51
Managers and Administrators Except Farm	
Assessors, controllers, and treasurers, local public administration	61
Bank officers and financial managers	72
Buyers and shippers, farm products	41
Buyers, wholesale and retail trade	50
Credit Men	49
Funeral directors	52
Health administrators	61
Construction inspectors, public administration	41
Inspectors, except construction, public administration	41
Managers and superintendents, building	38
Office managers, n.e.c.	50
Officers, pilots, and pursers; ship	60

Occupational Title	SEI Score
Officials and administrators; public administration, n.e.c.	61
Officials of lodges, societies, and unions	58
Postmasters and mail superintendents	58
Purchasing agents and buyers, n.e.c	48
Railroad conductors	41
Restaurant, cafeteria and bar managers	39
Sales managers and department heads, retail	50
Sales managers, except retail trade	50
School administrators, college	61
School administrators, elementary and secondary	60
Managers and administrators, n.e.c.	50
Managers and administrators, except farm—allocated	50
Sales Workers	
Advertising agents and salesmen	42
Auctioneers	32
Demonstrators	28
Hucksters and peddlers	18
Insurance agents, brokers, and underwriters	47
Newsboys	15
Real estate agents and brokers	44
Stocks and bonds salesmen	51
Salesmen and sales clerks, n.e.c.	34
Sales representatives, manufacturing industries	49
Sales representatives, wholesale trade	40
Sales clerks, retail trade	29
Salesmen, retail trade	29
Salesmen of services and construction	34
Sales workers—allocated	34
Clerical And Kindred Workers	
Bank tellers	50
Billings clerks	45
Bookkeepers	48
Cashiers	31
Clerical assistants, social welfare	36
Clerical supervisors, n.e.c	36
Collectors, bill and account	26
Counter clerks, except food	36
Dispatchers and starters, vehicle	34

Occupational Title	SEI Score
Enumerators and interviewers	36
Estimators and investigators, n.e.c.	36
Expediters and production controllers	36
File clerks	30
Insurance adjusters, examiners, and investigators	48
Library attendants and assistants	41
Mail carriers, post office	42
Mailhandlers, except post office	36
Messengers and office boys	19
Meter readers, utilities	36
Office machine operators	
Bookkeeping and billing machine operators	45
Calculating machine operator	45
Computer and peripheral equipment operators	45
Duplicating machine operators	45
Keypunch operators	45
Tabulating machine operators	45
Office machine operators, n.e.c.	45
Payroll and timekeeping clerks	41
Postal clerks	43
Proofreaders	36
Real estate appraisers	43
Receptionists	39
Secretaries	
Secretaries, legal	46
Secretaries, medical	46
Secretaries, n.e.c.	46
Shipping and receiving clerks	29
Statistical clerks	36
Stenographers	43
Stock clerks and storekeepers	23
Teacher aides, except school monitors	36
Telegraph messengers	30
Telegraph operators	44
Telephone operators	40
Ticket, station, and express agents	35
Typists	41
Weighers	36
Miscellaneous clerical workers	36
Not specified clerical workers	36
Clerical and kindred workers—allocated	36

Occupational Title	SEI Score
Craftsmen and Kindred Workers	
Automobile accessories installers	47
Bakers	34
Blacksmiths	36
Boilermakers	31
Bookbinders	31
Brickmasons and stonemasons	36
Brickmasons and stonemasons, apprentice	36
Bulldozer operators	33
Cabinetmakers	39
Carpenters	40
Carpenter apprentices	40
Carpet installers	47
Cement and concrete finishers	32
Compositors and typesetters	38
Printing trades apprentices, except pressmen	40
Cranemen, derrickmen, and hoistmen	39
Decorators and window dressers	37
Dental laboratory technicians	47
Electricians	49
Electrician apprentices	41
Electric power linemen and cablemen	39
Electrotypers and stereotypers	38
Engravers, except photoengravers	41
Excavating, grading and road machine operators, except bulldozer	33
Floor layers, except tile setters	40
Foremen, n.e.c.	45
Forgemen and hammermen	36
Furniture and wood finishers	29
Furriers	35
Glaziers	26
Heat treaters, annealers, and temperers	36
Inspectors, scalers, and graders: log and lumber	31
Inspectors, n.e.c.	31
Jewelers and watchmakers	37
Job and die setters, metal	48
Locomotive engineers	51
Locomotive firemen	36
Machinists	48
Machinist apprentices	41

Occupational Title	SEI Score	Occupational Title	SEI Score
Mechanics and repairmen		Shoe repairmen	3
Air conditioning, heating, and		Sign painters and letterers	0
refrigeration	37	Stationary engineers	35
Aircraft	48	Stone cutters and stone carvers	33
Automobile body repairmen	37	Structural metal craftsmen	36
Automobile mechanics	37	Tailors	41
Automobile mechanic apprentices	37	Telephone installers and repairmen	39
Data processing machine repairmen	34	Telephone linemen and splicers	39
Farm implements	33	Tile setters	36
Heavy equipment mechanics,		Tool and die makers	42
including diesel	33	Tool and die maker apprentices	41
Household appliance and accessory		Upholsterers	30
installers and mechanics	33	Specified craft apprentices, n.e.c.	41
Loom fixers	30	Not specified apprentices	41
Office machines	34	Craftsmen and kindred workers, n.e.c.	47
Radio and television	35	Former members of the Armed Forces	47
Railroad and car shop	37	Craftsmen and kindred	
Mechanic, except auto, apprentices	41	workers—allocated	47
Miscellaneous mechanics and		Current members of the Armed Forces	47
repairmen	35		
Millers; grain, flour, and feed	25	*Operatives, Except Transport*	
Millwrights	40	Asbestos and insulation workers	28
Molders, metal	39	Assemblers	27
Molder, apprentices	39	Blasters and powdermen	32
Motion picture projectionists	34	Bottling and canning operatives	23
Opticians, and lens grinders		Chainmen, rodmen, and axmen;	
and polishers	51	surveying	39
Painters, construction and		Checkers, examiners, and inspectors;	
maintenance	30	manufacturing	36
Painter apprentices	30	Clothing ironers and pressers	18
Paperhangers	24	Cutting operatives, n.e.c.	26
Pattern and model makers,		Dressmakers and seamstresses,	
except paper	39	except factory	32
Photoengravers and lithographers	40	Drillers, earth	27
Piano and organ tuners and repairmen	32	Dry wall installers and lathers	27
Plasterers	33	Dyers	25
Plasterer apprentices	33	Filers, polishers, sanders, and buffers	19
Plumber and pipe fitters	41	Furnacemen, smeltermen,	
Plumber and pipe fitter apprentices	41	and pourers	33
Power station operators	39	Garage workers and gas station	
Pressmen and plate printers, printing	0	attendants	22
Pressmen apprentices	0	Graders and sorters, manufacturing	33
Rollers and finishers, metal	6	Produce graders and packers,	
Roofers and slaters	1	except factory and farm	19
Sheetmetal workers and tinsmiths	7	Heaters, metal	33
Sheetmetal apprentices	7	Laundry and dry cleaning	
Shipfitters	6	operatives, n.e.c.	18

Occupational Title	SEI Score	Occupational Title	SEI Score
Meat cutters and butchers, except manufacturing	32	Conductors and motormen, urban rail transit	28
Meat cutters and butchers manufacturing	28	Deliverymen and routemen	28
Meat wrappers, retail trade	19	Fork lift and tow motor operatives	29
Metal platers	29	Motormen; mine, factory, logging camp, etc.	27
Milliners	33	Parking attendants	22
Mine operatives, n.e.c.	26	Railroad brakemen	35
Mixing operatives	29	Railroad switchmen	33
Oilers and greasers, except auto	24	Taxicab drivers and chauffeurs	22
Packers and wrappers, n.e.c	19	Truck drivers	32
Painters, manufactured articles	29	Transport equipment operatives—allocated	29
Photographic process workers	36		
		Laborers, Except Farm	
Precision machine operatives		Animal caretakers, except farm	29
Drill press operatives	29	Carpenters' helpers	23
Grinding machine operatives	29	Construction laborers, except carpenters' helpers	17
Lathe and milling machine operatives	29	Fishermen and oystermen	30
Precision machine operatives, n.e.c	29	Freight and material handlers	17
Punch and stamping press operatives	29	Garbage collectors	17
Riveters and fasteners	29	Gardeners and groundkeepers, except farm	23
Sailors and deckhands	34	Longshoremen and stevedores	24
Sawyers	28	Lumbermen, raftsmen, and woodchoppers	26
Sewers and stitchers	25	Stockhandlers	17
Shoemaking machine operatives	32	Teamsters	12
Solderers	29	Vehicle washers and equipment cleaners	17
Stationary firemen	33	Warehousemen, n.e.c.	20
		Miscellaneous laborers	17
Textile operatives		Not specified laborers	17
Carding, lapping, and combing operatives	29	Laborers, except farm—allocated	17
Knitters, loopers, and toppers	29		
Spinners, twisters, and winders	25	*Farmers and Farm Managers*	
Weavers	25	Farmers (owners and tenants)	41
Textile operatives, n.e.c.	29	Farm managers	44
Welders and flame-cutters	40	Farmers and farm managers—allocated	41
Winding operatives, n.e.c.	29		
Machine operatives, miscellaneous specified	32	*Farmers, Laborers and Farm Foremen*	
Machine operatives, not specified	32	Farm foremen	35
Miscellaneous operatives	32	Farm laborers, wage workers	18
Not specified operatives	32	Farm laborers, unpaid family workers	18
Operatives, except transport—allocated	32		
Transport Equipment Operatives			
Boatmen and canalmen	37		
Bus drivers	32		

Occupational Title	SEI Score
Farm service laborers, self-employed	27
Farm laborers, farm foremen, and kindred workers—allocated	19
Service Workers, Except Private Household	
Cleaning service workers	
Chambermaids and maids, except private household	14
Cleaners and charwomen	12
Janitors and sextons	16
Food service workers	
Bartenders	20
Busboys	22
Cooks, except private household	26
Dishwashers	22
Food counters and fountain workers	15
Waiters	20
Food service workers, n.e.c., except private household	22
Health service workers	
Dental assistants	48
Health aides, except nursing	48
Health trainees	36
Midwives	23

Occupational Title	SEI Score
Nursing aides, orderlies, and attendants	36
Practical nurses	42
Personal service workers	
Airline stewardesses	36
Attendants, recreation and amusement	15
Attendants, personal service, n.e.c.	14
Baggage porters and bell hops	14
Barbers	38
Boarding and lodging housekeepers	22
Bootblacks	9
Child care workers, except private households	25
Elevator operators	21
Hairdressers and cosmetologists	33
Personal service apprentices	14
Housekeepers, except private households	36
School monitors	22
Ushers, recreation and amusement	15
Welfare service aides	14
Protective service workers	
Crossing guards and bridge tenders	24
Firemen, fire protection	44

Note: n.e.c = not elsewhere classified

CD-APPENDIX D: THE RESEARCH REPORT

Contents

CD-APPENDIX E: THE RESEARCH PROPOSAL

Contents

CD-APPENDIX F: SPSS SURVEY TIPS

Contents

APPENDIX G: SPSS COMMANDS

SPSS Commands (listed by Chapter and SPSS Command Number)

Chapter 5

5.1 **Starting an SPSS Session**
Once you are in Windows you have two major options:

Option 1:
Double-click **SPSS icon**

Option 2:
Click **Start → Programs → SPSS for Windows**

5.2 **Accessing the Help Menu**

Click **Help →** select the Help option you wish to access (i.e., Topics, Tutorial, etc . . .)

5.3 **Getting Help in a Dialog Box**

Option 1:
Right click on any control/command

Option 2:
Click on **Help** push button

Option 3:
Click on **question mark (?)** in upper right hand corner -> click on **command/control need help with**

5.4 **Moving Through the Data Screen**

Option 1:
Use horizontal and/or vertical scroll bars

Option 2:
Use cursor **→** click

Option 3:
Use arrow keys on key pad

5.5 **Opening a Data File**

Option 1: Menu Bar
Click on **File → Open → Data →**

Option 2: Tool Bar
Click on **Open File tool →**

Once the Open File dialog box is displayed:
Click on the **Look in field: →** Select the **drive** that contains your CD **→** Click **down arrow** to choose **SPSS (*.sav)** from Files of type: drop down list **→** highlight the **name of the data file →** **double click** OR click **Open**

5.6   Finding Information on Variables

Option 1: Variables Box
Click **Utilities** → **Variables** → OR click on the **Variable icon** on the tool bar → **highlight variable name** in list on left side

Option 2: Toggling
Click **View** → **Value Labels**

Option 3: Value Labels Tool
Click **Value Labels** tool

Option 4: Variable View
In the Variable View portion of the Data Editor . . .

Click on cell corresponding with the variable at question (row) and Value (column)

5.7   Ending Your SPSS Session

Option 1: Close Button
Click on "**X**" (Close button)

Option 2: File Menu
Click **File** → **Exit**

Chapter 6

6.1   Shortcut for Opening a Frequently Used Data File

Click **File** → Select **Recently Used Data** → Click on **File name**

6.2   Setting Options - Displaying Abbreviated Variable Names Alphabetically

Click **Edit** → **Options** → **General** tab → **Display names** → **Alphabetical** → **OK** → **OK**

6.3   Setting Options - Output Labels

Click **Edit** → **Options** → **Output Labels** tab → Click **down arrow** next to "Variables in labels shown as:" → **Names and Labels** → Click **down arrow** next to "Variable values in labels shown as:" → **Values and Labels** → **OK**

6.4   Running Frequency Distributions

Click **Analyze** → **Descriptive Statistics** → **Frequencies** . . . → Highlight the abbreviated variable name → Click on arrow pointing right (toward Variable field) OR **double-click variable name** → **OK**

6.5   Navigating Through the SPSS Viewer

Option 1:
Use the **vertical** or **horizontal scroll bars**

Option 2:
Use the **arrow** or **page up** and **page down keys** on your keyboard

Option 3:
Click on **item** in the **Outline pane**

6.6   Changing the Width of the Outline Pane

Click and **drag border** to right of outline pane

6.7   Hiding and Displaying Results in the Viewer

Option 1:
Double-click on **book icon** in Outline pane

To display again – **Double-click** on **book icon**

Option 2:
Highlight item in Outline pane → Click **View** → **Hide**

To display again - **Highlight item** in Outline pane → Click **View** → **Show**

Option 3:
Highlight item → Click **closed book (Hide) icon**

To display again – **Highlight item** in Outline pane → Click **open book (Show) icon**

6.8   Hiding and Displaying All Results From a Procedure

Click on **box** to left of procedure name in Outline with **minus sign (−)**

To display again – click on **box** with **plus (+) sign**

6.9   Running Frequency Distributions with Two or More Variables

Analyze → **Descriptive Statistics** → **Frequencies . . .** → **Double-click** on **variable name** OR
Highlight variable name → click on right pointing **arrow** → **Repeat this step** until all variables
have been transferred to the Variable(s): field → **OK**

6.10   The Frequencies Procedure - Descriptive Statistics (Discrete Variables)

Click **Analyze** → **Descriptive Statistics** → **Frequencies . . .** → Highlight the **variable name** and
click on the **right pointing arrow** OR **double-click** on the **variable name** → Select **Statistics . . .**
→ Choose statistics by clicking on the **button(s)** next to the appropriate measures → click →
Continue → **OK**

6.11   The Descriptives Procedure - Descriptive Statistics (Continuous Variables)

Click **Analyze** → **Descriptive Statistics** → **Descriptives . . .**
Highlight variable name and **double click** OR **click** on the **right pointing arrow** →
Click **Options . . .** → Choose **statistic(s)** by clicking on the button next to the appropriate
measure(s) → Click **Continue** → **OK**

6.12   Setting Values and Labels as Missing

Access **Variable View** tab → Click on **cell** that corresponds with column **Missing**
and row containing appropriate **Variable** → In "Missing Values" box use one of
several options available (i.e., **Discrete missing values . . .**) to insert appropriate missing values
→ **OK**

6.13   Recoding a Variable

Click **Transform** → **Compute** → **Into Different Variables . . .** →
Highlight name of variable to be recoded → Click on **right pointing
arrow** OR **double-click on variable name** →

In Output Variable field **name** and **label new variable** → Click **Change** →
Click **Old and New Values . . .** →
Choose option for specifying old values you want to recode (i.e.
Range, etc . . .) → Enter **old value codes** → enter **new value recodes** →
click **Add** →
[Repeat this step until all old values are recoded] →
Click **Continue** → **OK** →

To Define New, Recoded Variable:

Select **Variable View tab** → identify new, **recoded variable** in last row →
Click on **cells** corresponding with new, recoded variable and the following
columns to change **Width**, **Decimals**, **Values**, and **Measure**

6.14   Printing Your Output (Viewer)

Make sure **SPSS Viewer** is **active window**
To select only certain items to print:
Highlight item in Contents or Outline pane → Click **File** →
Print → **Selection** → **OK**

To print all visible output:

File → **Print** → **All visible Output** → **OK**

6.15   Print Preview

File → **Print Preview** →

6.16   Adding Headers and Footers

Click **File** → **Page Setup** → **Options . . .** → Add information in Header and/or Footer
fields → **OK** → **OK**

6.17   Adding Title/Text

Click on area in Contents or Outline pane where wish to add Title or Text → Click on
Insert Title OR **Insert Text** tools on the tool bar → Add text or titles

6.18   Saving Your Output (Viewer)

Make sure the SPSS Viewer/Output is the active window → Click **File** → **Save As** Or click on
Save File tool → choose appropriate **drive** → **name your file** → click **Save**

6.19   Saving Changes Made to an Existing Data Set

Make sure the Data Editor is the active window → Click **File** → **Save As** →
Select **appropriate drive** → **name** your **file** → **Save**

Chapter 7

7.1   Simple Bar Chart

Click **Graphs** → **Bar . . .** → **Simple** → **Define** →
Highlight the **variable name** → Click **arrow** pointing to the "Category Axis:" box →
Select option for **vertical ("y") axis** in "Bars Represent" box →
Click **Options . . .** → Make sure there is **NOT** a **check mark** next to the

"Display groups defined by missing values" option → Click
Continue → OK

7.2   SPSS Chart Editor

Double-click on chart you wish to edit → click on appropriate
icon in SPSS Chart Editor to make necessary changes . . .→

7.3   Pie Chart

Click **Graphs → Pie . . . → Define →**
Highlight **variable name →** Click **arrow** pointing to Define Slices
by: → Select desired **option** in Slices Represent box →
Click **Options . . . →** Click on **check mark** next to Display Groups
Defined by Missing Values to remove it → Click **Continue → OK**

7.4   Accessing Pie Options (SPSS Chart Editor)

Double-click on **pie chart** in SPSS Viewer → select **Chart Options
icon →**

Click **Percents → OK →** Click X *OR* **File → Close**

7.5   Histogram

Click **Graphs → Histogram . . . → double-click** on **variable name** *OR*
highlight **variable** and click on **arrow** pointing toward the variable field → Click **OK**

7.6   Setting Values/Labels as Missing Using Range Plus One Option

Access **Variable View tab → double-click** on **right side of cell**
that corresponds with appropriate variable and column "Missing" → Click on **circle** next to
Range plus one optional discrete missing value → Insert appropriate Low: High: and Discrete:
values → Click **OK**

7.7   Simple Line Chart

Click **Graphs → Line . . . → Simple → Define →**
Highlight the **variable name →** Click **arrow** pointing toward the
"Category Axis:" box
Click **Options . . . →** Click on the **check mark** next to the Display
groups defined by missing values option to make sure it is NOT showing → Click
Continue → OK

Chapter 8

8.1   Identifying Variables – File Info

Click **Utilities → File Info** . . .

8.2   Running Frequencies for Several Variables (Not Clustered)

Click **Analyze → Descriptive Statistics → Frequencies . . . →**
Press and hold down Ctrl (Control key) on your keyboard **as you** click on the
names of the variables →

Click on the **right pointing arrow** to transfer selected variables to **"Variable(s):"**
field → **OK**

8.3   Producing Crosstabs

Click **Analyze** → **Descriptive Statistics** → **Crosstabs . . .** →
Highlight **variable name** → click on **arrow** pointing toward **Row(s):** box →
Highlight **variable name** → click on **arrow** pointing toward **Column(s):**
Box → Click **OK**

Chapter 9

9.1   Creating a Simple Index using COUNT

Creating Index
Click **Transform** → **Count . . .** →
Type new **variable name** in **Target Variable:** field →
Type new **variable label** in **Target Label:** field →
Transfer variables for which specified values will be counted to **Numeric Variables:** field →
Click **Define Values . . .** → Intert **Value(s)** to be counted → click **Add** → **Continue** →
Click **If . . .** → click **Include if case satisfies condition:** → **Type or paste Expression** (ex.
missing(abdefect,absingle) = 0) → click **Continue** → **OK**

Defining New Variable
Access **Variable View** tab → scroll to **new variable** in last row → set **Type, Width, Values,**
Measure →

Checking New Variable
Compare Expected and Actual Index scores →
Run **Frequencies** for new variable →

9.2   Producing Crosstabs with Column Percentages

Click **Analyze** → **Descriptive Statistics** → **Crosstabs . . .** →
Highlight **variable name** → click **arrow** pointing to the **Row(s):** box →
Highlight **variable name** → click **arrow** pointing to the **Column(s):** box →
Click **Cells . . .** → choose **Column** in Percentages box → **Continue** → **OK**

Chapter 11

11.1   Running Crosstabs – Specifying the Dependent and Independent Variables

Click **Analyze** → **Descriptive Statistics** → **Crosstabs . . .** →
Highlight the **dependent variable** → Click **arrow** pointing to the **Row(s):** box →
Highlight the **independent variable** → Click **arrow** pointing to the **Column(s):** box →
Click **Cells . . .** → Select **Column** in the Percentages box → Click **Continue** → **OK**

Chapter 14

14.1   Running Crosstabs and Lambda

Click **Analyze** → **Descriptive Statistics** → **Crosstabs . . .** →
Specify **dependent variable** as the **Row(s):** variable →
Specify **independent variable** as the **Column(s):** variable →

Click **Cells . . . →**
[Make sure "Column" under "Percentages" is not selected (there should not be a check mark next to "Column")][1]
Click **Continue →**
Click **Statistics . . . → Lambda → Continue → OK**

14.2 Running Crosstabs and Gamma

Click **Analyze → Descriptive Statistics → Crosstabs . . . →**
Specify **dependent variable** as the **Row(s):** variable **→**
Specify **independent variable** as the **Column(s):** variable **→**
Click **Cells . . . →**
[Make sure "Column" under "Percentages" is not selected (there should not be a check mark next to "Column")][2]
Click **Continue →**
Click **Statistics . . . → Gamma → Continue → OK**

14.3 Producing a Correlation Matrix and Pearson's *r*

Click **Analyze → Correlate → Bivariate . . . →**
Highlight **variable name →** Click **right-pointing arrow** to transfer variable to "Variables:" field **→**
Repeat previous step until all variables have been transferred **→**
Click **Pearson →**
Click **Options . . . → Exclude cases** either **listwise** OR pairwise **→**
Continue → OK

14.4 Regression

Click **Analyze → Regression → Linear . . . →**
Highlight **dependent variable** and click **right-pointing arrow** to transfer it to Dependent: field **→**
Highlight **independent variable** and click **right-pointing arrow** to transfer it to Independent(s): field **→**
Click **OK**

14.5 Producing a Scatterplot with Regression Line

Click **Graphs → Scatter . . . → Simple → Define →**
Highlight **independent variable →** click **right-pointing arrow** to transfer to X Axis: **→**
Highlight **dependent variable →** click **right-pointing arrow** to transfer to Y Axis: **→**
Click **OK →**

To Add Regression Line:
Double click on **Scatteplot** to open the SPSS Chart Editor **→**
Click **Chart Options** icon **→ Total → OK →**
Click **Close** button (**X**) *OR* **File → Close** to close the SPSS Chart Editor

---

[1] Usually percentages are requested in order to see how the column percentages change or move. We purposefully omitted the percentages in Demonstration 14.1 in order to make the table easier to read.

[2] Usually percentages are requested in order to see how the column percentages change or move. We purposefully omitted the percentages in Demonstrations 14.2 and 14.3 in order to make the table easier to read.

Chapter 15

15.1 Producing Crosstabs with Chi-Square

Click **Analyze → Descriptive Statistics → Crosstabs . . . →**
Highlight **dependent** variable → Click **arrow** to transfer to **Row(s):**
field →
Highlight **independent** variable → Click **arrow** to transfer to **Column(s):**
field →
Click **Cells . . . →** Click **Column** in Percentages box → **Continue →**
Statistics . . . → Chi-Square → Continue → OK

15.2 Running *t* Test (Independent Samples *t* Test)

Click **Analyze → Compare Means → Independent-Samples T Test . . . →**
Highlight **test variable** in variable list →
Click **arrow** pointing to the **Test Variable(s):** box →
Highlight name of **grouping variable** in variable list →
Click **arrow** pointing to the **Grouping Variable:** box →
Click **Define Groups . . . →** Define **Group 1:** and **Group 2:** →
Continue → OK

15.3 ANOVA (GLM Univariate)

Click **Analyze → General Linear Model → Univariate . . . →**
Highlight **dependent variable** → Click **arrow** pointing to **Dependent**
Variable: field →
Highlight **factor variable** → Click **arrow** pointing to **Fixed Factor(s):**
field →
Click **Options →** check **box** next to **Homogeneity tests → Continue → OK**

CD-APPENDIX H: READINGS

Contents

INDEX/GLOSSARY

active cell In the SPSS data editor, the cell with heavy black lines around it that can be moved in numerous ways.
algorithm A detailed sequence of actions or steps to perform in order to accomplish a task.
analysis of variance (ANOVA) An analytical technique aimed at determining whether variables are related to each other. It is based on a comparison of the differences (income, for example) between three or more subgroups and the variance on the same variable within each of the subgroups. For example, how does the difference in average income compare with income differences among Whites, Blacks, and Asians?

B

bar chart A chart that displays the frequency or percentage of various categories of a variable. Categories of the variable are displayed along the horizontal axis, while frequencies or percentages are displayed along the vertical axis. The height of the bar indicates the frequency or percentage of cases in each category. Bar charts are particularly useful in displaying variables with a relatively small number of categories, such as discrete/categorical data and data at the nominal or ordinal levels of measurement.
bivariate analysis A mode of data analysis in which two variables are examined simultaneously to discover whether they are related to each other or independent of one another. An example would be the analysis of gender and attitudes toward abortion. It is the beginning foundation for causal analysis.

C

categorical variables Categorical or discrete variables are those who attributes or values are completely separate from one another: such as gender, with the attributes male and female. Distinguished from continuous variables.
category/categories The specific attributes that make up a variable. For example, the categories or attributes of the variable SEX (gender) are "male" and "female," while the categories or attributes of the variable MARITAL (marital status) are "married," "widowed," "divorced," "separated," and "never married." It is sometimes easy to confuse the categories or attributes of a variable with the variable itself.
ceiling effect A term used to refer to a situation in which, for example, the overall percentage of respondents agreeing to something approaches 100%, making it impossible for there to be much variation among subgroups.
cell editor The small window just below the Tool bar in the SPSS Data Editor. When entering data in SPSS, you will notice that it appears in the Cell Editor before being recorded in the Data Matrix.

dummy variables, recoding for, 354
ending SPSS session, 53
frequency distributions, running of, 66, 76, 78, 133
gamma, crosstabs and, 269
header/footer addition, 91
help menu access, 41
hiding/displaying results, 68
histograms, 119
index creation, COUNT, 156
lambda, crosstabs and, 259
line charts, 123
multiple regression, 357
numeric data entry, 435
opening data file, 46, 62
options setting, alphabetical display, 63
outline pane, width change, 67
output labels, options setting, 64
overview of, 495–502
Pearson's *r*, correlation matrix and, 279
pie charts, 114, 115
printing output, SPSS viewer, 90
print preview, 91
recoding into same variables, 386–387
recoding variables, 90
regression, 286
saving new data file, 431
saving output, SPSS viewer, 92, 93
scatterplot with regression line, 290
setting values/labels as missing, 87, 121
SPSS viewer, navigations through, 67
starting SPSS session, 39
title/text addition, 91
toggling, 49
t tests, independent samples, 314
value labels tool, 50
variable identification, file info, 132
variable information location, 48–51

SPSS Mainframe   The largest and most powerful version of SPSS available for use with all major mainframe computers, it can be used to analyze millions of cases and thousands of variables.

SPSS Student Version   A scaled-down version of SPSS which, unlike the Mainframe version, is limited to 50 variables and 1,500 cases.

SPSSwin icon   The picture symbol or icon on your desktop that activates SPSS.

standard deviation   A measure of dispersion appropriate to ratio variables.

statistical significance   A measure of the likelihood that an observed relationship between variables in a probability sample represents something that exists in the population rather than being due to sampling error.

Statistical significance: 303–304, 319 (table)
analysis of variance-ANOVA, 316–319
chi-square, calculation of, 308–309
chi-square, logic of, 305–308
goodness-of-fit and, 307
inferential statistics and, 304
measures of association and, 304–305, 309–310, 310 (table)
null hypothesis, 320
sampling errors and, 304

substantive significance, 309
t tests, 311–315

strength of association   Statistical measures of association such as lambda, gamma, and Pearson's r indicate the strength of the relationship or association between two variables. For example, values of lambda can vary from 0–1. The closer the value of lambda to 1, the stronger the relationship between the two variables, while the closer the value of lambda to 0, the weaker the association between the two variables.

substantive significance   A term used to refer to the importance of an association between variables that cannot be determined by empirical analysis alone but depends, instead, on practical and theoretical considerations.

Survey design, 421–423, 493
accessing file information, 433–434
alternative data sets, 444–445
copying a variable, 429–431
data definition process, 423–429
editing/coding data, 432–434
entering data, 435
LOCAL.SAV and, 432, 433–434, 436
moving through data view, 434–435
occupational title/socioeconomic prestige score list, 481–487
questionnaire sample, 423, 473–479
research reports, 436
revising/deleting data, 436
saving data file, 436
saving new file, 431–432
See also General Social Survey (GSS)

SYSTAT software, 445

T

Tau, 291
Term papers, 3–4
Textual additions, 91

theory   An interrelated set of general principles that describes the relationships among a number of variables.

Theory: 9–10, 11 (table)
Title additions, 91

toggling   The process of switching back and forth between numeric values and labels in the SPSS data editor.

toolbar   A row of icons that allows easy activation of program features with mouse clicks. Each SPSS window has one or more toolbars for each access to common tasks.

***t* test**   A class of significance tests used to test for significant differences between different kinds of means. In this book, the independent samples *t* test is used to test whether the observed difference between two means could have easily happened by chance, or if it is so unlikely, we believe the difference we see in our sample also exists in the population from which the sample was taken.

t test: 311–315
Tutorial-SPSS, xxv–xxvi

U

univariate analysis   The analysis of a single variable for
    the purpose of description. Contrasted with
    bivariate and multivariate analysis. 59, 187

V

valid percentage   In SPSS, usually the third column in a
    frequency distribution that contains the relative
    percentage of times each value of a variable
    occurred in a given sample, excluding any
    missing data.

validity   The extent to which an empirical measure
    actually taps the quality intended.

value   Each category or attribute of a variable is
    assigned a specific value or code. In this text, we
    have seen many examples of numeric values or
    codes to represent nonnumeric data, such as 1
    for "male" and 2 for "female" or 1 for "yes" and
    2 for "no." In these examples, 1 and 2 are the
    values, also called *numeric values* or *codes*.

value label   The descriptive value label assigned to each
    value of a variable. For example, the value labels
    for the variable CAPPUN are "favor" and
    "oppose," while the values are "1" and "2"
    respectively.

variable   Logical set of attributes. For example, gender
    is a variable comprised of the attributes: male
    and female.

variable name   Unique name given to each variable in
    a data set for each: ABANY, SEX, CHLDIDEL,
    and MARITAL.

variable templates   Templates created in SPSS that help
    simplify the task of data definition by allowing
    the analyst, when appropriate, to assign the
    same variable definition information to more
    than one item on a questionnaire. Variable
    templates are used when entering data to
    assign the same variable definition information
    (type, values and labels, missing values, etc.) to
    multiple items.

variance   A statistic that measures the variability of a
    distribution and is determined by dividing the
    sum of the squared deviations by 1 less than the
    number of cases ($N-1$). Often close the mean of
    the sum of squared deviations.

vertical (y) axis   In a graph, such as a line or bar chart,
    the axis that runs up and down on the far left
    side and usually represents the dependent
    variable.

Viewer (SPSS)   A window in SPSS that contains the
    results of procedures or output. The SPSS Viewer
    is divided into two panes: the left pane (Outline
    or Output Navigator) and the right pane (Viewer
    Document).

W

z scores. Useful for comparing variables that come from
    distributions with different means and standard
    deviations.